Bridge Engineering
Fundamentals and Practices

桥梁工程
基本原理与实践

Shouxin WU　　Song XIA　　Zhanhui LIU
武守信　　　　夏　嵩　　　刘占辉

西南交通大学出版社
·成　都·

图书在版编目（CIP）数据

桥梁工程：基本原理与实践 = Bridge Engineering – Fundamentals and Practices：英文 / 武守信，夏嵩，刘占辉著. —成都：西南交通大学出版社，2021.5
ISBN 978-7-5643-8027-4

Ⅰ.①桥… Ⅱ.①武… ②夏… ③刘… Ⅲ.①铁路桥 – 桥梁工程 – 英文 Ⅳ.①U448.13

中国版本图书馆 CIP 数据核字（2021）第 084782 号

Bridge Engineering
Fundamentals and Practices

桥梁工程
基本原理与实践

武守信　夏嵩　刘占辉　著

责 任 编 辑	王同晓
封 面 设 计	曹天擎
出 版 发 行	西南交通大学出版社 （四川省成都市金牛区二环路北一段 111 号 西南交通大学创新大厦 21 楼）
发行部电话	028-87600564　028-87600533
邮 政 编 码	610031
网　　　址	http://www.xnjdcbs.com
印　　　刷	四川森林印务有限责任公司
成 品 尺 寸	185 mm×260 mm
印　　　张	22.5
字　　　数	524 千
版　　　次	2021 年 5 月第 1 版
印　　　次	2021 年 5 月第 1 次
书　　　号	ISBN 978-7-5643-8027-4
定　　　价	65.00 元

课件咨询电话：028-81435775
图书如有印装质量问题　本社负责退换
版权所有　盗版必究　举报电话：028-87600562

CONTENTS

Preface ·· vii

Chapter 1 Introduction ··· 001

    1.1 Definition, constituent parts, and functionalities ··············· 001
    1.2 Role and significance ·· 003
    1.3 Structural types and aesthetics ·· 005
    1.4 Historic development ·· 015
    1.5 Advancement of bridges in China ··· 023
    References ··· 030

Chapter 2 Loads ·· 033

    2.1 Introduction ··· 033
    2.2 Dead loads ··· 035
    2.3 Chinese railway live loads ·· 036
    2.4 Braking and traction forces ·· 042
    2.5 Wind loads ··· 043
    2.6 Seismic loads ··· 046
    2.7 Pedestrian loads ·· 049
    2.8 Chinese highway live loads ·· 050
    2.9 Other loads ·· 053
    2.10 Load combinations ·· 054
    References ··· 059

Chapter 3 Design Philosophies and Specifications ··························· 060

    3.1 Introduction ··· 060
    3.2 Allowable stress design (ASD) ·· 062
    3.3 Load factor design (LFD) ·· 064

  3.4 Load and resistance factor design (LRFD) ······················ 066
  References ·· 074

Chapter 4 Concrete Girder Bridge Deck and Load Distributions ·········· 076

  4.1 Introduction ·· 076
  4.2 Configurations of bridge deck ·· 076
  4.3 Design calculation of deck slabs ·· 081
  4.4 Transverse load distribution·· 091
  References ·· 120

Chapter 5 Reinforced Concrete Girder Bridges ···································· 122

  5.1 Introduction ·· 122
  5.2 Design methods ·· 123
  5.3 Detailing of reinforcement ·· 128
  5.4 Bridge examples ·· 136
  References ·· 146

Chapter 6 Prestressed Concrete Girder Bridges ································ 148

  6.1 Introduction ·· 148
  6.2 Principles of prestressing ·· 150
  6.3 Prestressing systems ·· 162
  6.4 Loss of prestress ·· 169
  6.5 Design methods ·· 171
  6.6 Example bridges ·· 192
  References ·· 199

Chapter 7 Concrete Continuous and Rigid Continuous Bridges ·········· 201

  7.1 Introduction ·· 201
  7.2 Overview of prestressed concrete continuous bridges ·········· 202
  7.3 Layout of span lengths with girder depths ···························· 204
  7.4 Cross-sections··· 206
  7.5 Layouts and detailing of prestressing tendons ······················ 208
  7.6 Design issues ·· 212
  References ·· 217

Chapter 8 Construction of Concrete Girder Bridges ········· 219
    8.1 Introduction ········ 219
    8.2 Construction of concrete elements ········ 219
    8.3 Temporary works ········ 222
    8.4 Erection methods ········ 226
    References ········ 237

Chapter 9 Steel bridges ········ 239
    9.1 Introduction ········ 239
    9.2 Types of steel bridges ········ 245
    9.3 Plate girder bridges ········ 248
    9.4 Truss girder bridges ········ 264
    9.5 Design calculations and analysis of steel components ········ 276
    9.6 Construction of steel bridges ········ 288
    References ········ 296

Chapter 10 Arch Bridges ········ 298
    10.1 Introduction ········ 298
    10.2 Terminology of arch bridges ········ 299
    10.3 Materials for arch bridges ········ 299
    10.4 Structural classification of the arch ········ 302
    10.5 Structural characteristics of arch bridges ········ 304
    10.6 Construction methods for arch bridges ········ 313
    References ········ 317

Chapter 11 Cable-Stayed Bridges ········ 318
    11.1 Introduction ········ 318
    11.2 Structural characteristics of cable-stayed bridges ········ 319
    11.3 Configuration of cable-stayed bridges ········ 320
    11.4 Construction method of cable-stayed bridges ········ 336
    References ········ 339

Appendix A Distribution Factors for the Guyon-Massonnet Method ···· 340

PREFACE

There have been a great amount of railway and highway bridges built in China over the last 40 decades, which has been driven by the development of modern transportation networks, especially the high-speed railways. The advances in design approaches and construction technology of bridges have been reflected in the up-to-date design and construction codes and specifications. In China's universities and colleges, courses in bridge engineering are offered in the civil engineering program to prepare students for design, construction, and maintenance of modern railway and highway bridges. Thus, there have always been needs for textbooks providing the students with the knowledge of modern bridge engineering based on current codes and specifications. Although there are many Chinese textbooks on bridge engineering available, there is a growing need for textbooks in English for international students studying in China and the Chinese students who want the course to be taught in English. The purpose of this textbook is to meet this need.

This is an introductory textbook on modern bridge engineering. The objectives of the text are to provide students and practicing engineers an introduction to bridge engineering and to present the fundamentals of design and construction of bridge superstructures. Since bridge engineering is a broad subject which includes many aspects, such as design, construction, inspection, maintenance, rehabilitation, it is impossible to cover all topics of bridge engineering in one volume. Thus, the emphasis of the text is on the overview and basic fundamentals of design and construction of common bridge types. The text is intended to be used in classroom teaching for a one-semester course in the senior year of undergraduate studies, and not to be used as a manual.

The text is organized into 11 chapters. Chapter 1 introduces the basic components of a typical bridge, structural types and aesthetics, historical development of bridge engineering, and advances of bridges in China. Chapter 2 describes the nature, magnitude, and placement of the various loads that act on railway and highway bridges. Chapter 3 reviews the design philosophies and methods. The principles of the allowable stress design and the probability-based design load and resistance factor design (LRFD) are briefly discussed in this chapter. Chapter 4 presents the methods for determining the maximum force effects in bridge deck slab due to moving vehicles and the transverse distribution of live loadings on bridge girders.

Chapters 5 and 6 deal with reinforced and prestressed concrete girder bridges, respectively, with emphases on the dimensioning of the cross-section, detailing of reinforcement, and layouts of prestressing tendons. Since the students are assumed to have the background of design principles of concrete structures, detailed analysis of stresses and deformations and design checks are not addressed in these chapters. Chapter 7 gives a brief review of continuous prestressed concrete bridges with discussion on the secondary forces and the transformation of structural system during construction. Chapter 8 provides overview of the construction methods for concrete girder bridges. Steel bridges are covered in Chapter 9, which includes the configurations, design principles, and construction methods for steel girder and truss bridges. Chapters 10 and 11 discuss the arch bridges and cable-stayed bridges, respectively, giving an overview of the structural forms and construction method of these two bridge types suitable for long-spans.

At the end of each chapter, a reference list is provided for those who what to increase their knowledge and to dig for more details by further reading. The reference lists are far from exhaustive but give major source of materials for independent study. In addition to the references provided in the text, valuable sources of material for this textbook have been the journal articles, reports, books, and manuals published online of in print by universities and technological institutes in China and other countries, such as the FHWA, AASHTO, ICE, AREMA, ASCE, AISC, ACI, PCI, and ASTM. Contributions from these institutes are greatly acknowledged. Some standard drawings on railway bridges were provided by Mr. Pengxiang Wang, the senior engineer at China Railway Engineering Consulting Group Co., Ltd. This help is gratefully appreciated.

The authors of the chapters in this textbook are as follows: Chapters 1 through 8 were written by Dr. Shouxin Wu; Chapter 9 were written by Dr. Wu with the help of Dr. Zhanhui Liu, who provided some Chinese reference materials and wrote some parts in Chinese; Chapters 10 and 11 were written by Dr. Song Xia and amended by Dr. Wu. The entire text was gone through and proofread by Dr. Wu.

This textbook was planned in November, 2017, on the suggestion of Ms. Xue Zhang, the former editor-in-chief of the Southwest Jiaotong University

Press. Later on, the proposal was accepted and the project was supported by the Academic Affairs Office of the Southwest Jiaotong University (SWJTU). I wish to acknowledge those who have contributed directly to the publication of the book: Mr. Bo Zhang, the vice president of the company, Mr. Tongxiao Wang, the project editor, and Ms. Wenyue Zhang, the copy editor. Special thanks go to Ms. Xue Zhang for her kind help and understanding. Finally, I wish to thank Ms. Man Ding, the section chief of the academic affairs office at SWJTU for her encouragement and assistance.

The financial support from the School of Civil Engineering and the academic affairs office of the Southwest Jiaotong University is gratefully acknowledged.

Shouxin Wu
Southwest Jiaotong University, Chengdu
October, 2020

Chapter 1 *Introduction*

1.1 Definition, constituent parts, and functionalities

A bridge is a structure carrying a pathway or roadway across a physical obstacle such as a river, a valley, or a road underneath to provide a passage over the obstacle (Figure 1.1). Although main purpose of bridges is to carry traffic and people, some pipeline bridges are built to convey water (also called aqueducts) [Figure 1.2(a)], other liquids such as petroleum [Figure 1.2(b)], or even gases.

Figure 1.1 (a) A railway bridge crossing a river; (b) A highway bridge crossing a valley; (c) A pedestrian bridge crossing a road.

(a)

(b)

Figure 1.2 (a) A bridge conveying water; (b) A pipeline bridge conveying petroleum.

A typical bridge comprises roughly three main structural parts: the superstructure, the substructure, and the bearing between them, as indicated in Figure 1.3. Each of these parts has other components within them. These main parts are defined and have the functionalities as follows:

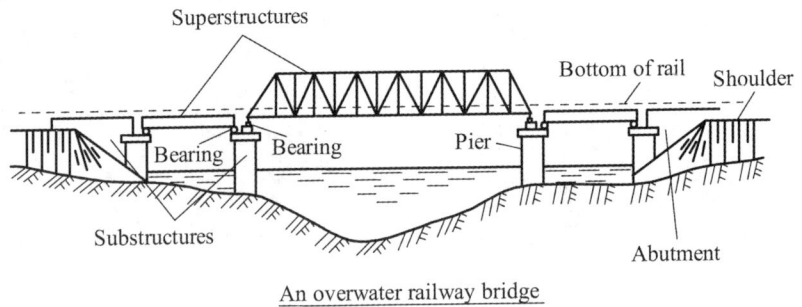

Figure 1.3 Main components of a typical railway bridge.

1. The superstructure

The superstructure of a bridge is the portion of the bridge above the bearings. It consists of deck slab, girder, truss, arch, or cables, etc., which vary depending on the structural type of the bridge and the materials used. The function of the superstructure is to support the load passing over it and to transmit the forces generated by the load to the bearings and in turn, to the substructures.

2. The bearing

A bearing of a bridge is an element which provides an interface between the superstructure and the substructure. The primary function of a bridge bearing is to transmit all loads from the superstructure to the substructure. The bearing accommodates longitudinal and rotational movements of the superstructure relative to the substructure. These relative movements may be caused by axial or/and bending deformation of the girder subjected to dead and live loads, or by elongation and shortening of the girder due to thermal actions.

3. The substructure

The substructure of a bridge is the portion of the bridge below the bearings. It includes piers, abutments, earth-retaining structures, and foundations. The functions of the substructure are to support the superstructure stably and transfer the load to the bearing strata below the ground.

In addition to the above main structural components, there are also some accessories, such as parapets, drainage, waterproofing, and expansion joints, which are provided on a bridge. These accessories serve some purposes in the overall functionality of the structure, and are not of structural importance.

It should be noted that, for some types of bridges, the boundaries between the above three parts are not always distinct. For example, for cable-stayed or suspension bridges, the upper part of a tower seems to be a superstructure, while the lower part seems to be a substructure. However, a tower is actually a continuous structural member, so it cannot be treated as two separate parts. For concrete fixed arch bridges and rigid-frame bridges, no bearings are provided between the superstructure and the substructure. Instead, the connections of the superstructure and substructure are rigid. In these cases, division of a bridge structure into superstructures and substructures is generally based on the functions, but not on the spatial positions, of the bridge's components.

1.2 Role and significance

A bridge controls the load-carrying capacity and traffic volume of a transportation network. If a bridge collapses, the whole transportation system will fail to work. If the strength of a bridge is not sufficient to support the maximum loads on the roadway, overloaded vehicles have to be rerouted and, as a result, the capacity of the road is reduced.

Bridges do more than simply carry loads and cross obstacles: bridges representing the creativity of mankind. Some great bridges have become symbolic elements of the place they are located. With soaring towers and graceful spans, the Golden Gate Bridge, one of the best-known bridges in the world, is frequently viewed as the symbol of San Francisco (Figure 1.4), while the Brooklyn Bridge is symbol of New York City (Figure 1.5). The Zhaozhou Bridge, a famous ancient stone arch bridge in China, which was built about 1 400 years ago, has becomes the symbolic building of the Zhao county in Hebei, China (Figure 1.6).

Figure 1.4　The Golden Gate Bridge, San Francisco, USA.

Figure 1.5　The Brooklyn Bridge, New York, USA.

Figure 1.6　The Anji Bridge, an ancient arch bridge, Zhao county, China.

Building bridges is a great challenge to all the engineers and workers involved. Ever increasing span lengths, widths, and loads generate the need for new design, new materials, and new construction method which are used for the first time to build the bridge as specified. Failure may happen during construction period or even when it is in service (Figure 1.7 and Figure 1.8).

Figure 1.7 Failure of a Bridge during construction.

Figure 1.8 Failure of a Bridge in service.

The causes of bridge failure may be structural overload, deterioration of structural members due to corrosion or fatigue, scour of the foundation soils, and many others. Therefore, bridge engineers involved in design, construction, and maintenance of a bridge should always carry out their duties properly to assure the structural integrity and safety of the bridge for the intended lifetime.

1.3 Structural types and aesthetics

Bridges can be classified in different ways. They can be categorized as concrete bridges, steel bridges, aluminum bridges, wooden bridges, and composite bridges according the materials used in construction; or they can be divided into railway bridges, highway bridges, pedestrian bridges, and pipeline bridges by their usage and functions. However, from an engineering standpoint, the most meaningful classification of bridges is usually based on their structural types, i.e. the load-resisting mechanism of a bridge by which gravitational and lateral loads is transferred from the deck to the foundation. This is because, in different types of bridges, transfer of the loads from the deck to the foundations follows different paths. Therefore, the method employed in the structural analysis of a bridge is mainly dependent on its structural type. For certain range of span lengths, only certain structural types of bridges are suitable and economically viable. From this perspective, bridges can be classified as girder bridges, arch bridges, truss bridges, cable-stayed bridges and suspension bridges, irrespective of their materials and usage. This classification is not strict and absolute, for each type of these bridges may have more than one subtype or variant. In practice, some bridge combines the features of more than one bridge type, thus it does not fall into any category of the bridge types mentioned above.

1.3.1 Girder bridges

The girder bridge is also called the slab-on-stringer bridge or the beam bridge. A girder bridge consists mainly of a deck, a set of girders that support the deck slab, and several diaphragms that connect the girders together (Figure 1.9a). All the girders are supported on abutments (for single-span bridges) or piers (for multi-span bridges). In a girder bridge, loads are transferred from deck to girders, and then to abutments or piers. The girder is the main load-resisting component which carries the vertical loads by its bending and shearing resistance, while the deck slab is designed to bend in the direction perpendicular to the plane of bending of the girders. Generally, the deck is built from reinforced concrete, while the girder can be made of steel, reinforced concrete, prestressed concrete, or combination of concrete and steel.

The girder bridge is the most common bridge type, which includes simply-supported girder bridges, continuous girder bridges, rigid-frame girder bridges, and continuous rigid-frame girder bridges[Figure 1.9(a)(b)(c)(d)], among which the simply-supported girder bridge is the simplest type of bridge. The principal advantages of the girder bridges are in the following. First, the structural form is simple and straightforward. Second, the girder bridge is suitable for a uniform design which can be standardized easily. Standardization and uniformity minimize the need for designing and manufacturing structural members of different sizes for different bridge projects, thus reduce the construction cost and period in repairing or replacing deteriorated structures. Third, construction of girder bridges is relatively straightforward. Prefabricated primary members, like steel girders or prestressed concrete girders, allow for quick erection and provide for economical use of materials.

Girder bridges are primarily for short- to medium-span lengths, say, for the span length less than 75 m. The simply supported girder bridges are most suitable for short-span lengths, whereas continuous and continuous rigid-frame girder bridges are the better choices for medium- and longer-span bridges. Currently, the span-length of the continuous rigid-frame girder bridge in China has reached more than 200 m. When the span length becomes excessive, other type of bridges become viable alternatives.

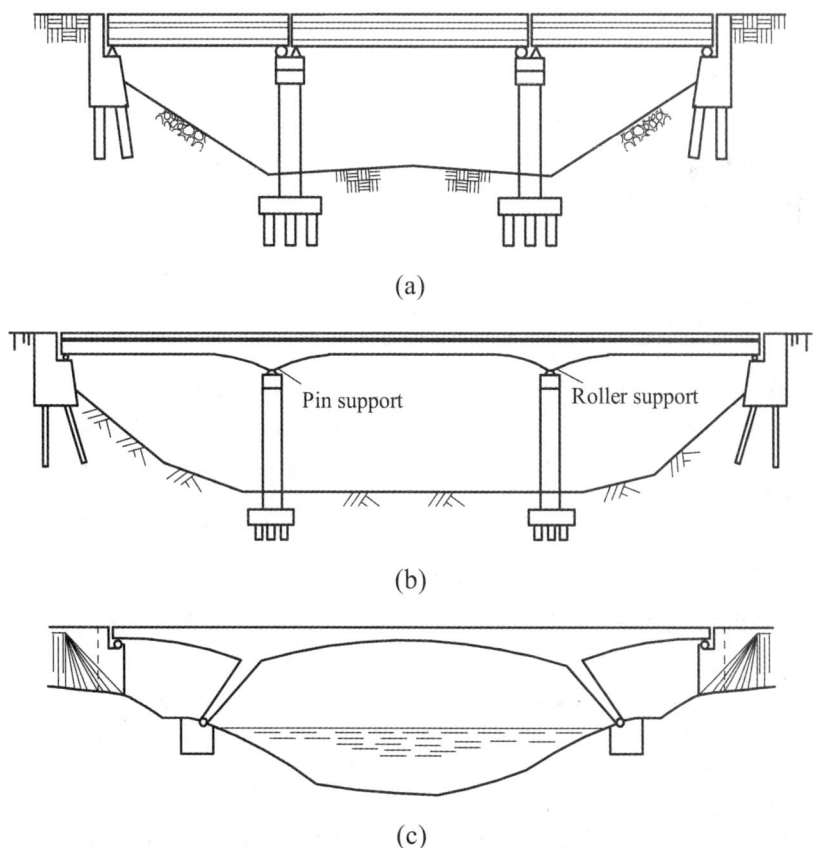

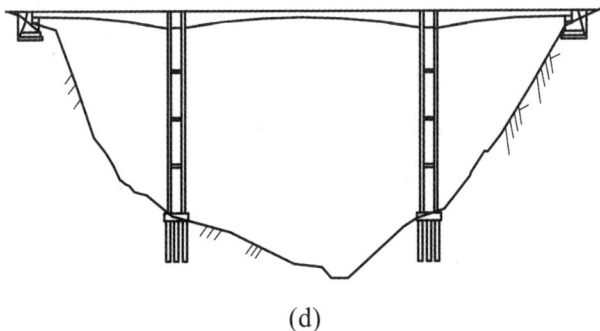

(d)

Figure 1.9 Girder bridges: (a) simply-supported; (b) continuous; (c) rigid-frame; (d) continuous rigid-frame.

1.3.2 Arch bridges

An arch bridge is a bridge whose main load-resisting structures or members are curved arches (Figure 1.10). The common feature of all the arch bridges is that the gravitational loads are transmitted to the supports primarily by axial compressive forces in the arch. This makes such brittle materials as rock, brick, or concrete, which are strong in compression but weak in tension, suitable for construction of the arch. In modern arch bridges, the arch can be made up of a truss of various forms. At each end of the arch, horizontal thrust as well as the vertical force is exerted on the support. Arch bridges are usually divided into three types according to the relative position of the deck with respect to the arch: deck arch bridges, through arch bridges, and tied-arch bridges.

The deck arch bridge is a typical arch bridge whose main structure—arch— is below the deck line. This type of bridge consists of an arch, a deck, which is completely above the arch, and columns or solid fill in the spandrel to transfer the roads from the deck to the arch. If the spandrel is filled with solids, as in a masonry or stone arch bridge, the bridge is called a closed-spandrel arch bridge [Figure 1.10(a)]; if the deck is supported by columns rising from the arch, the bridge is termed as an open-spandrel arch bridge [Figure 1.10(b)].

The half-through arch bridge is a type of arch bridge whose deck passes through the arch, i.e., the top of the arch is above the deck, while the springings of the arch are below the deck. As a result, the central part of the deck is supported by the arch via cables or tie bars, whereas the side part of the deck, which is close to the springings, is supported below by the columns resting on the arch [Figure 1.10(c)].

The tied-arch bridge is also known as the bowstring arch bridge. In this type of arch bridge, the thrust at the ends of an arch is resisted by tie-rods connecting the two ends of the arch. The deck is suspended from the arch and the loads are thus transferred from the deck to the arch through tension hangers. Because the tie-rods are at the deck level and the traffic loads pass through completely between and the arch and deck slab, a tied-arch bridge is also a through arch bridge [Figure 1.10(d)].

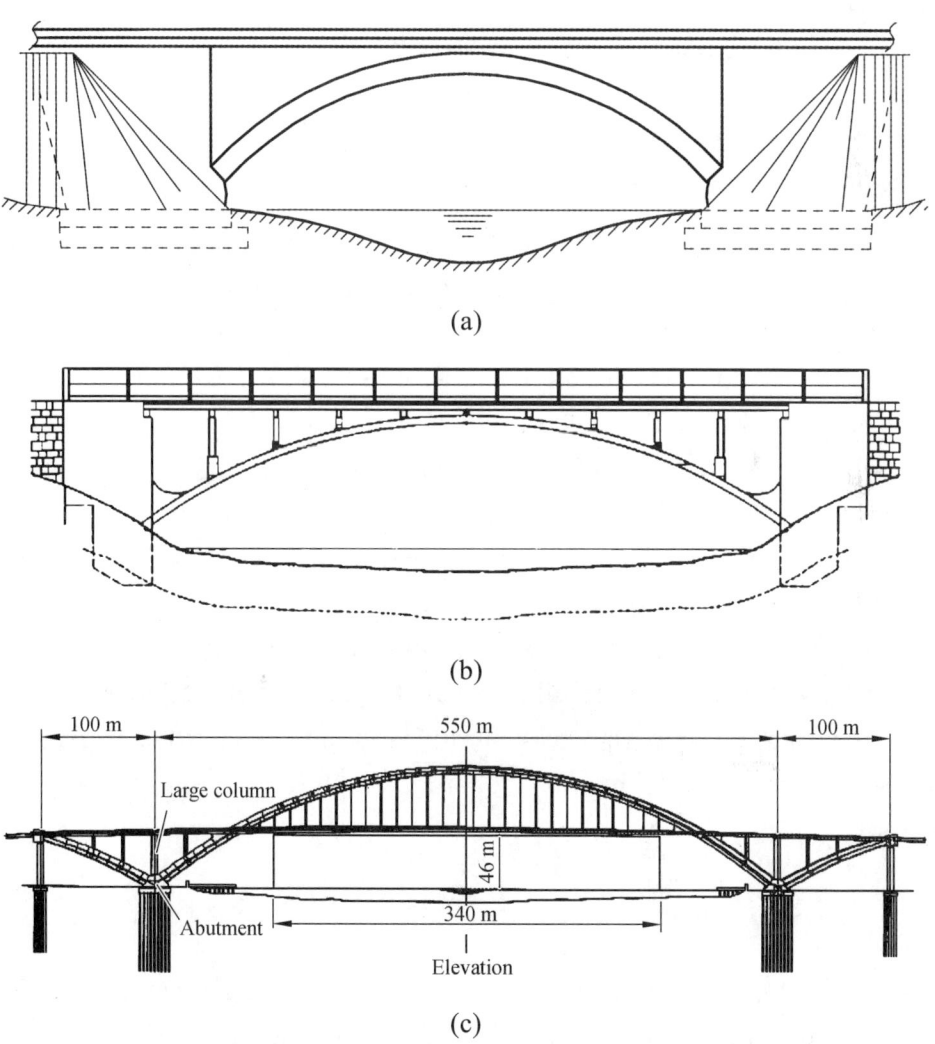

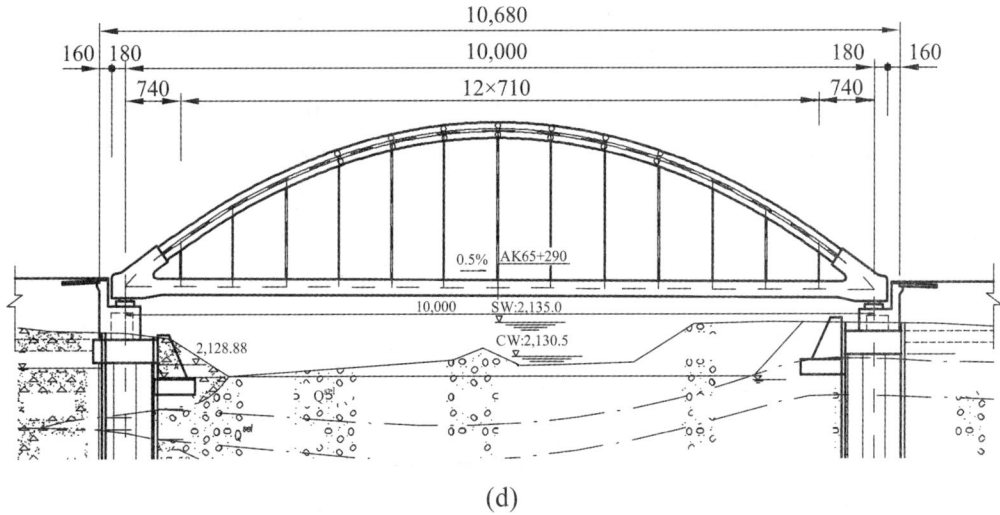

(d)

Figure 1.10 Various types of arch bridges: (a) closed spandrel arch; (b) open spandrel arch; (c) half-through arch; (d) tied-arch.

The distinctive features of the arch bridge are: (i) the arch is predominantly a compression structure and thus favors concrete or rock as construction materials; as a result, a masonry arch bridges can be designed such that the arch is always under compression as it carries all the vertical loads above; (ii) this type of bridge is most suitable for crossing a deep valley with the arch foundations located on the dry rock slopes, so that the vertical settling and horizontal sliding of the arch ends can be restrained by the foundations. In modern practices, the arch is usually built from plain concrete, reinforced concrete, and steel trusses, with cross-sections being of I-shape, T-shape, or box-shape.

Arch bridges are economical for medium and long spans. Aesthetically, the arch is the most successful of all types of bridge: the curved shape is almost always pleasing. By experience or familiarity, not only bridge engineers but also the average people regard the arch structures as understandable and expressive.

1.3.3 Truss bridges

A truss bridge is a bridge whose main load-resisting structure consists of twomain planar trusses each of which is an assemblage of triangular units that comprises "two-force" members connected at joints (Figure 1.11). The two main planar trusses are tied together with cross girders and lateral bracing to form a three-dimensional truss that can resist vertical and lateral loads. Provided the loads are applied at the nodes of a truss, the members in the truss will carry primarily axial tension or compression forces. Thus, a truss bridge can support large amounts of loads with a comparatively small amount of construction materials.

Modern truss bridges are built mostly from steel. However, the first truss bridges were built from wood, and several of these are still in existence and preserved as historic civil engineering landmarks [Figure 1.12(a)]. Some of early truss bridges were also built from wrought iron. There are also a few modern truss bridges that are made up from reinforced or prestressed concrete members, in which precompression is introduced to counterbalance a portion of the tensile stresses caused by the loads [Figure 1.12(b)].

The major structural advantages of the truss bridges are: (i) the primary forces in the members of the truss are axial tension or compression; (ii) the open web system permits the use of a larger overall height of the truss than an equivalent solid web girder does. These factors lead to economy in material and a reduced self-weight of the bridge. The increased height of the truss also leads to reduced deflections of the bridge under traffic loads

Truss bridges can be classified as deck, through, and half-through truss bridges, according to the relative position of the deck to the upper or lower chord of the truss. In a deck truss, the deck is supported at the joints of the upper chords of the trusses by floor beams with stringers [Figure 1.11(a)]. Thus the main load-carrying structure is completely below the deck. In a through-type truss, the deck is supported at the joints of the lower chords, as a result, the whole trusses located above the deck and the vehicular or pedestrian traffic passes through the trusses [Figure 1.11(b)]. The half-through truss bridge is similar to the through truss bridge except that the upper chords are not braced laterally because the vertical clearance requirements for the live load prevent the incorporation of a lateral bracing system for the upper chords [Figure 1.11(c)].

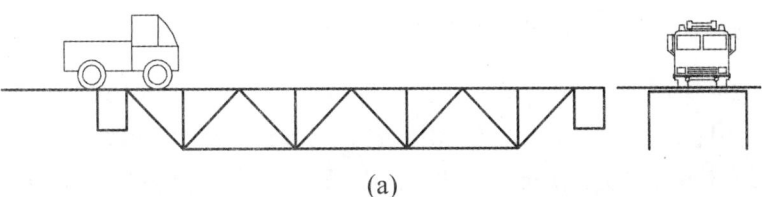

(a)

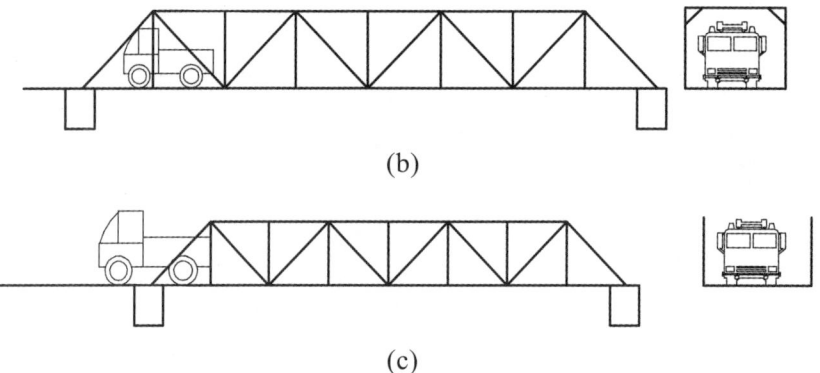

(b)

(c)

Figure 1.11 Truss bridges: (a) deck truss; (b) through truss; (c) half-through truss.

(a)

(b)

Figure 1.12 (a) timber truss bridge; (b) prestressed truss bridge.

The truss bridge may be simple spans or continuous spans, and is a favorable structural type for medium to long span railway bridges. The applied span lengths of truss bridges are generally 50 to 110 m. For spans smaller than 100 m, trusses are hardly economical for highway bridges. For long span lengths, other types of bridges, e.g., prestressed concrete box girder, steel box girder, or cable-stayed bridges, become more competitive with truss bridges.

1.3.4 Cable-stayed bridges

A cable-stayed bridge consists of one or two towers or pylons, a stiffening girder, and multiple stay cables that radiate from the towers and are anchored at several intermediate points on the stiffening girder (Figure 1.13). The traffic loads on the deck are transferred by the stiffening girder to the stay cables, and subsequently to the towers by the cables through tension. This structural system results in compressive axial forces in the stiffening girder and in the pylons which are in equilibrium with tensile forces in the cables. In other words, the traffic loads are mainly transferred by axial forces rather than by bending, which can substantially reduce the depth of the stiffening girder, and in turn reduce the self-weight of the girder. Thus, the cable-stayed bridges are suitable for crossing long distance.

The cable-stayed bridges can be built with steel, concrete, or both. The stay cables are usually made from high strength steel, while the stiffening girders are made up of either prestressed concrete or steel or both. Some cable-stayed bridges have been arranged with a steel stiffening girder in the main span and concrete girder in the side spans so that the weight of the longer main span is balanced by the heavier section in the side spans. The towers are normally constructed of cellular sections and are fabricated of structural steel or reinforced concrete or prestressed concrete.

The cable-stayed bridges have proven more economic, for mediate span lengths, i.e., 100 ~ 350 m, than either the suspension or arch bridges. However, the cable-stayed bridges with span lengths of more than 1,000 m have been successfully built and in service. Today, the cable-stayed bridge has become a competitive choice for major crossings within a wide range of span lengths.

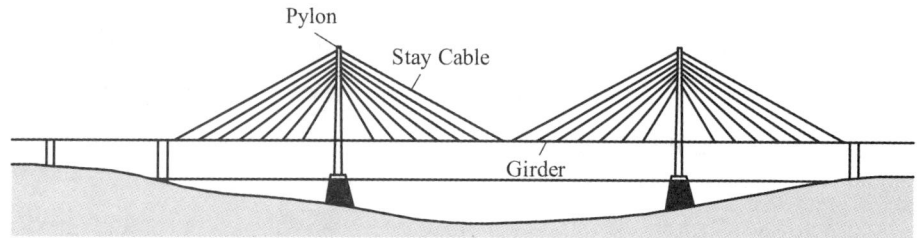

Figure 1.13 A typical cable-stayed bridge.

1.3.5 Suspension bridges

A suspension bridge is a type of bridge in which the traffic-carrying deck is hung below suspension cables by vertical suspenders. A classical three-span suspension bridge consists of two main cables, a deck structure together with a longitudinal stiffening system, two towers to support the main cables, and two anchorages to secure the ends of the main cables against movement (Figure 1.14). In a suspension bridge, the traffic loads are transferred to the main cables through vertical hangers, and then the main cables transfer the loads, by direct tension, to the supporting towers and anchorages. In modern suspension bridges, the main cables and suspenders are made of high-strength steel wire, and the deck and the stiffening system are made up of a separate orthotropic steel deck stiffened with steel truss, or a steel box girder combining the traffic deck and stiffening functions. The tower can be constructed with steel or concrete, but the anchorages are usually built of masonry or concrete and are embedded deeply below the ground.

Suspension bridges are recognized for spanning the longest distances and for their superior aesthetics. With cables constructed from very high-strength steel and loaded in direct tension, suspension bridges are ideally suitable for longer spans, and is often the most favorable structural type among the long-span bridges. Although cable-stayed bridges are competitive for the span range previously considered to be the domain of suspension bridges, the suspension bridges remain the unchallenged choice for spans over 1200 m. When well designed and proportioned, suspension bridges are the most beautiful among all types of bridges.

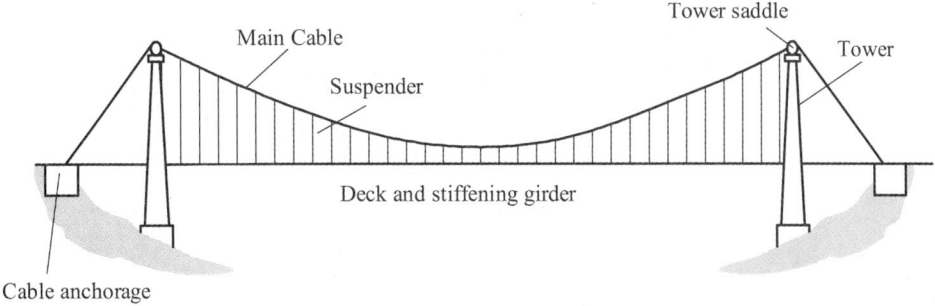

Figure 1.14 A typical suspension bridge.

1.4 Historic development

Bridges appeared in ancient times. The first bridges were believed to be made by nature – a log could fall across a stream and form a natural bridge (Figure 1.15). The first man-made bridges were probably spans of wooden logs or planks or slabs of stone, supported on stepping stones or river banks, which came to be known as clapper bridges (Figure 1.16). For longer spans, a group of hanging ropes, made from twisted natural fibre, such as vine or bamboo, tied on tree trunks or rocks in opposite banks of a river or on either side of a gorge (Figure 1.17), provide a passage over the obstacle and therefore became the primitive suspension bridge. These simple rope and bamboo suspension

Figure 1.16 A clapper bridge.

Figure 1.17 A primitive suspension bridge made of natural fibre.

bridges are still in regular use today in the mountainous reaches of China, India, Columbia, Nepal, and Peru. It was not until 4000 B. C. that humans discovered the secrets of arch construction. By the end of the Third Dynasty around 2 475 B. C., the Egyptians had also mastered the arch and used it frequently in constructing relieving arches and passageways for their temples and pyramids.

In China, records of bridges exist from the time of Emperor Yao in around 2300 B. C. on the traditions of bridge building. It is believed that ancient China was the birthplace of the floating bridge, which is a collection of boats about 9 m long, connected together to cross a river, with a walkway or deck attached on top (Figure 1.18). The other bridge forms in ancient China were the timber beam bridges, cantilever bridges, and rope suspension bridges. Timber beam bridges were often supported on rows of timber piles driven into the riverbed. The cantilever bridges were built by extending beams out from the piers on both sides of a stream. A primitive cantilever bridge with interdigitating timber members in China's southwestern provinces is shown in Figure 1.19. In later centuries development of bridges in China was dominated by stone arch bridges.

Stone arch bridges are the earliest bridges built that represent the bridge-building skill in ancient times. Many stone arch bridges were built by engineers of the Roman empire, some of which are still in service after more than 2000 years. In China, the oldest stone arch bridge, the Anji Bridge (also called Zhaozhou Bridge)(Figure 1.6), located in Hebei Province, was built in Sui Dynasty (A.D. 595-605) . It has a single span length of 37.02 m with two small arches in each of its spandrels. Another stone arch bridge , Baodai Bridge

Figure 1.18　A floating bridge.

Figure 1.19　A primitive cantilever bridge made of wood.

(Figure 1.20), located in Suzhou City, was built in the Tang Dynasty (A.D. 618-907) and has thin arch rib and light piers to adapt to the low load-bearing capacity of the soft foundation soil. With a length of 316.8 m, the Baodai Bridge was the longest old stone arch bridge in China.

Although the ancient people built bridges, and even built great bridges, such as the cantilever bridges and the arch bridges, they lacked understanding of structural mechanics of bridges. The curves of their arches were always semicircular in form, and the sizes of the cross-section of arches and beams were determined by only empirical rules, without the use of any theory. The only building materials for bridges in ancient times were stone and timber, which are available in nature.

Figure 1.20 The Baodai Bridge, China.

The Renaissance period from the 14th through the 16th centuries brought advances in both the art and science, and gave birth to the modern science. Several renowned scientists lived in this period, such as Leonardo da Vinci (1452-1519) and Galileo Galilei (1564-1642). Although many new scientific theories were developed during this period, relatively little advancement was made in construction. Leonardo da Vinci developed new ideas on the mechanics of military bridges, introduced the concept of the moment of a force, and considered the strength of beams. Galileo, regarded as the founder of structural mechanics, proposed the theory of structural mechanics which formed the basis of structural engineering and material strength. Galileo discussed fundamental principles of stress analysis for beams and framed structures, and examined how the properties, shape, and size of a member would affect its breaking strength.

The post-renaissance period saw the birth of many great scientists such as Robert Hooke (1635-1703), Isaac Newton (1642-1727), Daniel Bernoulli (1700-1782), and Leonard Euler (1707-1783). Robert Hooke (1635-1703) proposed the arch theory in 1670 and the famous Hooke's law. Later, the arch theory was expounded upon by Thomas Young (1773-1829), who, 130 years later, defined the modulus of elasticity. It was Hooke who first obtained the correct linear distribution of both compressive and tensile stresses across the cross section of a beam, and found that that planar cross-sections before bending remained plane after bending, a fundamental assumption of beam theory. The most significant contribution of the Renaissance to bridge technology was the development of the truss structures. With trusses, wooden members of shorter lengths could be used to build longer bridges. Andrea Palladio (1518-1580), an Italian architect, first proposed the principle of truss, and built a 108-ft-span truss bridge over the Cismone between Trent and Bassano, Italy. After that, a lot of wooden truss bridges were built in many countries in Europe and in the United States.

The industrial revolution in the 19th century brought about a revolutionary change in the technology of bridge building. The arrival of the railways demanded longer and stronger bridges. With the advent of iron as a structural material, development of the railway promoted greatly the construction of bridges. Early in the eighteenth century, the iron appeared and was later used in the construction of compression members of arch or truss bridges. The world's first cast-iron bridge (Figure 1.21) was built in 1777-1779 by Abraham Darby III (1750-1791), in Coalbrookdale, England, over the Severn River. This 30-m-span semicircular arch bridge is made up of five arch ribs, each cast in two 21-ft halves. However, cast iron is brittle, so it is used only in compression members. Many years later, wrought iron, a ductile material, was produced and used in the members carrying tension. In truss bridge, compression members were made from cast iron, whereas the tensile members were made from wrought iron. However, iron was used in bridges only for a short time, because iron bridges suffered some of the worst failures and disasters in the history of bridge building. In 1879, an iron bridge, called the Tay Rail Bridge, which is located in Scotland and made up of iron truss girders, collapsed during a

Figure 1.21 The first cast-iron bridge in Coalbrookdale, England.

violent storm. This catastrophic failure marked the end of the iron bridge. By the end of the nineteenth century, the use of wrought iron in bridges was discarded and replaced by that of steel.

The advent of steel heralded a new era of bridge construction and greatly advanced the technology for construction of long-span bridges. Starting from the late 19th century, the steel arch, the steel truss, and the steel suspension bridges were pioneered in USA. Later on, UK led the field of the cantilever truss bridge and the steel box girder bridges. Some of the world's greatest bridges were built at that time.

The triple-arch bridge over the Mississippi river in St Louis, Mississippi (Figure 1.22), completed in 1874, was the first to use steel in truss construction, and marked extensive use of steel in bridge building. In the UK, another steel truss arch bridge, the Tyne Bridge, was built in the 1920s.

Figure 1.22 The Eads Bridge in St Louis Bridge, Mississippi, USA.

The evolution of modern suspension bridges occurred in the United States and in Europe. Two major suspension bridges that bear all the hallmarks of modem suspension bridges were built in the United States in the nineteenth century. The Wheeling Suspension Bridge, with 310-m-long main span length, crossing the main channel of the Ohio River at Wheeling, Virginia, USA, was built by Charles Ellet, Jr. (1810-1862). The bridge was the longest suspension bridge at the time. However, this great bridge was destroyed by wind six years later. The other major suspension bridge, Brooklyn Bridge (Figure 1.5), having a main span length of 486 m, crossing the east river in the New York City, was completed in 1883. It was designed by John Augustus Roebling (1806-1869), the inventor of modem suspension bridges, and completed by his son Washington Roebling. It was the first suspension bridge to use the cables made up of steel wire.

The advent of cement and concrete in the late 19th century brought about the birth of reinforced and prestressed concrete bridges. Francois Hennebique, a French engineer, developed the T-shaped cross-section for reinforced concrete members. His disciple, the Swiss engineer Robert Maillart (1872-1940) built several famous reinforced concrete arch bridges. Eugene Freysinnet, another French engineer, proposed the prestressing technology for construction of bridges and provided to bridge industry one of the most efficient methods for constructing bridge deck. The Walnut Lane Memorial Bridge (Figure 1.23) located in Philadelphia, Pennsylvania, USA, completed in 1951, was the first major prestressed concrete bridges built in the USA. This three-span prestressed girder bridge, each spanning 49 m, revolutionized the prestressed concrete in the world. Since then, the prestressed concrete has gradually used in construction of bridges of short to medium or even long spans. With advances of prestressing technology and high-strength steel and concrete, Prestressed concrete bridges have becomes popular around the world. The lower cost of concrete relative to steel and invention of the cantilever or the segmental method of construction has made the prestressed concrete the preferred type for short and medium spans, and competitive with steel bridges in long-spans.

Figure 1.23 The first major prestressed concrete bridge in USA – the Walnut Lane Memorial Bridge, USA.

Concurrent with the advances of prestressed concrete bridges were the evolution of the cable-stayed bridges. The modern cable-stay bridges were pioneered by German engineers Fritz Leonhardt, Rene Walter, and Jörge Schlaich, after the World War Ⅱ. A cable-stayed bridge can use steel girders or prestressed concrete girder to stiffen the deck. In many modern cable-stay bridges, prestressed concrete box girders are usually used as decks. The first modern cable-stayed bridge was built in 1955 at Strömsund, Sweden, with steel deck and span length of 74 m+183 m + 74 m (Figure 1.24). Later, several other cable-stayed bridges were built in Europe and USA, with steel or prestressed concrete girders supporting the decks. The cable-stayed bridges fill the void between continuous girder bridges and suspension bridges. In the late 19th century and early 21st century, many long-span cable-stayed bridges have been built throughout the world, and significant advances have been achieved in the construction technology and spanning capabilities of this type of bridges. The Sutong Yangtze River Bridge, a cable-stayed bridge with prestressed concrete deck, located in Jiangsu Province of China, has a main span of 1 088 m which was the longest among the main span lengths of all the cable-stayed bridges in the world until 2012 (Figure 1.25).

Figure 1.24　The first modern cable-stayed bridge – Strömsund Bridge, Sweden.

Figure 1.25   The Sutong Yangtze River Bridge, China.

In summary, the historic development of bridges accompanied the evolution of structural theory and development of new materials and advances of construction technology. In modern times, rapid improvement of computer hardware and development of computer aided design technology makes design and analysis of long-span and complex bridges easier and more efficient than before. Many great girder, arch, cable-stayed, and suspension bridges of record-breaking span lengths have been built worldwide, especially in Asia. They are standing as symbols of structure engineering achievements. Nevertheless, construction of a bridge, especially a long-span bridge, is still a formidable task. Bridge engineers are still faced with the challenge of building longer, stronger, and reliable bridges crossing ocean or arduous mountainous terrains in the future.

1.5   Advancement of bridges in China

China has a long history of bridge construction. From 1100 B. C. to A. D. 220, the period from Zhou Dynasty to the Han Dynasties, the Chinese built lots of girder bridges and arch bridges with timber and stone. The girder bridge usually consists of one or several timber beams supported on the stone piers or abutments, but there were some short span bridges made up of stone beams. The arch bridges are always made from stone. Although there were thousands of bridges built in ancient times of China according to historic records, very few of them have survived until today.

The oldest bridge that survives today in China is the Anji Bridge (or Zhaozhou Bridge) built in A. D. 605. It is a single-span stone arch bridge (Figure 1.6) comprising 28 arch ribs bonded together transversely and having a span length of 37.02 m and a rise of 7.23 m above the springing line.

The longest ancient stone beam bridge is the Anping Bridge (Figure 1.26) across a sea bay in Jinjiang, Fujian Province. Completed in A. D. 1151, the Anping Bridge consists of 362 spans with the longest span length of 8.6 m. Each span has 5 to 8 stone beams, each beam being 5 m to 11 m long with rectangular cross-section 0.6 m to 1 m wide and 0.5 m to 1 m deep. The total length of the Anping Bridge is 2255 m.

Figure 1.26 The Anping Bridge - the longest ancient stone beam bridge, China.

Another famous ancient Chinese bridge is the Lugou Bridge (Figure 1.27), located in Beijing. It is a multi-span stone arch bridge consisting of 11 semicircular stone arches, each spanning 11.4 m to 13.45 m. The whole bridge is 212.2 m long, 9.3 m wide.

Figure 1.27　The Lugou Bridge - an ancient multi-span stone arch bridge, China.

Although some railway bridges appeared in China in 19th century, most of those early bridges were designed and constructed by foreign engineers until 1950s. During that time, most of the construction material—steel was imported from foreign countries, such as Britain and Belgium. However, a few steel bridges were independently constructed by Chinese engineers. One of those bridges was the Qiantang River Bridge, a truss bridge with a double-deck for highway and railway traffic (Figure 1.28). Built in 1937, the Qiantang River Bridge consists of 16 simply supported truss bridges each with a span length of 66 m. Its total length is 1 453 m, and it is the first modern bridge designed by a Chinese engineer. The bridge was destroyed in the World War Ⅱ and a new bridge has been built to replace old one.

Figure 1.28　The Qiantang River Bridge built 1937, China.

After the 1950s, the China's booming economy and rapid development of highways and railways created the need for a great amount of new bridges to be constructed. The first prestressed concrete highway bridge, with a span length of 20 m, was completed in China in 1956. One year later, the Wuhan

Yangtze River Bridge (Figure 1.29), the first bridge across the Yangtze River, was built. It is a double-deck steel truss bridge, carrying two railroad tracks on the lower deck and highway traffic on the upper deck. The bridge has nine main spans, each of 128 m, and the total length of the bridge is 1 155 m. The steel used in the trusses are produced in China and the structural components are manufactured in China's bridge factories. The Wuhan Yangtze River Bridge is a mile stone in the history of modern bridges in China. Following the success of this bridge, another steel truss bridge, the Nanjing Yangtze River Bridge (Figure 1.30), which have longer span lengths, was completed in 1968. Since then, hundreds of bridges have been built crossing the Yangtze River.

Figure 1.29   The Wuhan Yangtze River Bridge, China.

Figure 1.30   The Nanjing Yangtze River Bridge, China.

Beginning from 1960s, cantilever construction technology was adopted to erect T-shape rigid frame prestressed concrete bridges. During the 1970s, more prestressed concrete continuous bridges were constructed. In this period, Chinese engineer developed new erection techniques such as the lift-push launching method, the traveling formwork method, the span-by-span erecting method, and other novel construction method for various types of bridges. By using these methods, two reinforced concrete cable-stayed bridges were constructed in 1975, which marked the beginning of the construction of modern cable-stayed bridges in China.

Construction of long-span bridges started from 1980s. Since then, many great long-span bridges have completed in China.

The Luzhou Yangtze River Bridge (Figure 1.31), located in Sichuan Province, is 1 252.5 m in total length with main span of 170 m (105 m+3×170 m+105 m). The prestressed T-shape rigid-frame bridge was completed in 1982, and the design loads are Truck-20 and Trailer-100.

Figure 1.31　The Luzhou Yangtze River Bridge.

The Luoxi Bridge (Figure 1.32), located in Guangdong Province, is 1916 m in total length with main span of 180 m (65 m+125 m+180 m+110 m). The prestressed T-shape rigid-frame bridge was completed in 1988, and the design loads are Truck-20 and Trailer-100.

The Wanxian Yangtze River Bridge (Figure 1.33), located in Wanzhou, Chongqing City, is 856.12 m in total length with main span of 420 m. The reinforced concrete steel-pipe-frame box-rib arch bridge was completed in 1997, and it ranks the first among the similar bridges in the world. The design loads are Truck-super 20 and Trailer-120.

Figure 1.32　The Luoxi　Bridge, China.

Figure 1.33　The Wanxian Yangtze River Bridge, China.

The Wuhu Yangtzi River Bridge (Figure 1.34), located in Wuhu City, Anhui Province, is 6 078.4 m in total length and 312 m in main span length (180 m+312 m+180 m). The double-pylon double plane cable-stayed bridge with steel truss and reinforced concrete composite girder was completed in 2000. The design loads are Truck-super-20 and Trailer-120.

The Sutong Yangtze River Bridge (Figure 1.30), located in Jiangsu Province, connecting Nantong and Changshu. With a main span of 1 088 m (3 570 ft), it held the longest main span in the world between 2008 and 2012. Its two side spans are 300 metres each.The bridge received the 2010 Outstanding Civil Engineering Achievement award (OCEA) from ASCE. Two towers of the bridge are 306 metres (1 004 ft) high and thus the second tallest in the world. The bridge was opened to traffic on 25 May 2008.

Figure 1.34　The Wuhu Yangtzi River Bridge, China.

The Ma'anshan Yangtze River Bridge (Figure 1.35), located in Man'anshan City, Anhui Province, is a two-main-span suspension bridge with three towers. The total length of the suspension bridge is 2 880 m with the layout of the span length 360 m+1080 m+1080 m+360 m. The height of the pylon is 178.8 m. The design load is Highway Class-I. It was completed and open to traffic in 2014.

Figure 1.35　The Ma'anshan Yangtzi River Bridge, China.

Up to 2014, 590 000 highway bridges with a total length of 250 000 km have been built in China, among which 165 long-span bridges are across the Yangtze River with structural types of rigid frame, arch, cable-stayed, and suspension. Since the 1990s, 72 long-span bridges with main span lengths of more than 400 m each have been completed in China, among which three sea-crossing bridges more than 20 000 m long each, were built after 2005.

Driven by urbanization, increasing traffic, and demand for infrastructure, China is in great need of new bridges. Large progress was made in the construction of extra longe-span bridges crossing ocean over the last two decades. The world's longest sea bridge, the Hong Kong-Zhuhai-Macau Bridge (Figure 1.36), was completed in 2017 and open to traffic in 2018, after seven years of construction. Spanning 55 km, the bridge-tunnel project consists of several steel box girder bridges in non-navigable spans and three cable-stayed bridges with maximum span length of 1 150 m in the navigable spans, one undersea tunnel, and three artificial islands. The grand bridge links the two special administrative regions of Hong Kong and Macau with the mainland of China, cutting travel time from Hong Kong to Zhuhai down to 30 minutes from 3 hours and linking up to 60 million people into a metropolis-style economy.

Chinese bridge builders have come a long way since they built the first modern prestressed concrete bridge and the steel truss bridge. The progress in the construction of bridges represents the advances of civil engineering in China. In the next decade, China's investment in the construction of infrastructure continues to increase. Chinese bridge engineers have more opportunities than before to design and construct longer, record-breaking bridges, crossing wider and deeper rivers, gorges, and sea channels.

Figure 1.36 The Hong Kong-Zhuhai-Macau Bridge, China.

References

[1.1] Barker R. M., Puckett J. A., Design of Highway Bridges: An LRFD Approach, 3rd ed., John Wiley & Sons, Hoboken, New Jersey, 2013.

[1.2] Taly, N., Design of Modern Highway Bridges, McGraw-Hill, New York, 1998.

[1.3] Sukhen C., The Design of Modern Steel Bridges, 2nd ed., Blackwell Science Ltd., Malden, MA, 2003.

[1.4] Unsworth J. F., Design and Construction of Modern Steel Railway Bridges, 2nd ed., CRC Press, London, 2018.

[1.5] Tonias D. E. and Zhao J. J., Bridge Engineering, 2nd ed., McGraw-Hill, New York, 2007.

[1.6] Chen W.-F. and Duan L., eds., Bridge Engineering Handbook-Superstructure Design, CRC Press, Boca Raton, FL, 2000.

[1.7] Parke G. and Hewson N., eds., ICE Manual of Bridge Engineering, 2nd ed., Thomas Telford Ltd, London, 2008.

[1.8] Troyano L. F., Bridge Engineering – A Global Perspective, Thomas Telford Ltd, London, 2003.

[1.9] Li, Y.-D., ed., *Introduction to Bridge Engineering* (in Chinese), 3rd ed., Southwest Jiaotong University Press, Chengdu, China, 2005.
李亚东. 桥梁工程概论. 3版. 成都：西南交通大学出版社，2014.

[1.10] Yao L.-S, ed., (Xiang, H.-F., Gu, A.-B., reviewers), *Bridge Engineering*, 2nd ed., China Communications Press, Beijing, China, 2008.
姚玲森. 桥梁工程. 2版. 项海帆，顾安邦，主审. 北京：人民交通出版社，2008.

[1.11] Fan, L.-C., ed., Bridge *Engineering*, 2nd ed., China Communications Press, Beijing, China, 1988.
范立础. 桥梁工程. 2版. 北京：人民交通出版社，1988.

[1.12] Shao, X.-D., ed., (Gu, A.-B., reviewer), *Bridge Engineering*, 4th ed., China Communications Press Co., Ltd., Beijing, China, 2018.
邵旭东. 桥梁工程. 4版. 北京：人民交通出版社，2018.

[1.13] Qiang S.-Z., ed., Shao X.-D., assoc. ed., *Bridge Engineering*, 2nd ed., Higher Education Press, Beijing, 2011.
强士中. 桥梁工程. 2版. 北京：高等教育出版社，2011.

[1.14] He G.-H., Che H.-M., and Xie Y.-F., *Railway Reinforced Concrete Bridges*, China Railway Press, Beijing, 1986.
何广汉，车惠民，谢幼藩. 铁路钢筋混凝土桥. 北京：中国铁道出版社，1986.

[1.15] Tang, J.-S., ed., (Yang, J. reviewer), *Railway Bridges*, China Railway Press, Beijing, 2015.

唐继舜. 铁路桥梁. 杨进，主审. 北京：中国铁道出版社，2015.

[1.16] Zhao, R.-D., ed., (Gao, Z.-Y., reviewer), Long-Span Railway Bridges, China Railway Press, Beijing, 2012.

赵人达. 大跨度铁路桥梁. 高宗余，主审. 北京：中国铁道出版社，2012.

[1.17] Fan, L.-C., ed., Prestressed Concrete Continuous Bridges, China Communications Press, Beijing, 1988.

范立础. 预应力混凝土连续梁桥. 北京，1988.

Chapter 2 *Loads*

2.1　Introduction

The purpose of a road bridge is to carry traffic across a given span length, although the purpose of a pipeline bridge is to support the pipes containing liquids or gases for transportation over an opening. Thus, traffic loads or the weights of liquids or gases that the bridge is designed to support are the primary loads. In addition, various other kinds of loads may act on the bridge once it has been constructed. For example, the wind-induced load can act on bridge superstructures in the transverse directions; earthquake- induced loads can act on bridge superstructures and substructures in the form of inertial forces. For bridges crossing waterways, the substructures of a bridge may be subjected to earth pressure, water pressure, or even ice pressure. Since the traffic loads are moving, road bridges are also subjected to the impact force caused by the dynamics of moving loads.

Since the primary loads for a road bridge are determined by the types of traffic passing over it, highway bridges, railway bridges, and pedestrian bridges have different primary loads on them. In this text, focus is on the loads acting on railway bridges in accordance with Chinese railway standards. The loads on highway bridges are only reviewed briefly.

Classification of the loads on bridges can be based on different criteria. Usually, the loads applied to a bridge across its service life are roughly divided into two categories: dead loads and live loads. This classification is according to if the position and the magnitude of a load are varying with time or not. Dead loads are those that are constant in magnitude and fixed in spatial position throughout the lifetime of the bridge. Obviously, the self-weights of the structural members are dead loads. Live loads are those that their magnitudes and distributions are changing with time, and are random at a given time. For example, the vehicular loads are live loads for the obvious reason, and the moving pedestrians are also live loads. In addition to the dead and live loads, a bridge may be subjected to other loads caused by environment. These loads are sometimes called environmental loads. Wind pressure, snow loads, inertial forces caused by earthquake motions, and soil pressures on bridge substructures are examples of environmental loads. Like live loads, some of environmental loads are uncertain in both magnitude and distribution.

Different countries specify different design loads which are representative of the worst loadings to which a bridge may be subjected. For designing railway bridges in China. various kinds of design loads are specified in the Table 4.1.1 of the Code for *Design of Railway Bridges and Culverts* (TB 10002). These are listed Table 2.1 and are discussed in the following sections.

Table 2.1 Design loads for railway bridges (TB 10002 / J460)

Type of load		Load
Primary load	Dead load	Self-weights of structural members and accessories; Prestressing forces; Effect of shrinkage and creep of concrete; Earth pressure; hydrostatic pressure and upward buoyant forces; Effect of displacement of foundations
Primary load	Live load	Static gravity loads of trains; Vehicular gravity loads (for city roads); Dynamic effect of moving trains; Centrifugal forces; Nosing force; Earth pressure generated by live loads Pedestrian loads Aerodynamic Forces
Additional force		Braking forces or/and traction forces; Friction force at bearings; Wind force; Stream flow pressure; Ice pressure; Effect of temperature change; Frost heaving forces; Wave forces.
Special load		Derailment loads; Vessel or raft collision loads; Vehicular collision loads; Temporary construction loads; Earthquake loads; Longitudinal force from long rails (expansion-contraction force; deflection-induced force; broken-rail force)

2.2 Dead loads

The dead load on a bridge superstructure consists of the self-weights of all the structural members, such as truss members, girders, floor beams, deck slab, and those of nonstructural accessories, such as track (rails and fastenings), ballast, sidewalks, guard railings, signing posts, and other utilities. For a highway bridge, the wearing surface, curbs, parapets and lighting fixtures are also included as dead loads. All of these dead loads can be calculated with good precision from the design configurations, dimensions of the members, and unit weights of the materials used. The unit weights of common materials used in Chinese railway bridges are recommended in Article 4.2.1 of the railway code TB 10002, which are listed in Table 2.2.

When the reinforcement ratio of a reinforced concrete member is greater than 3%, the unit weight of the member should be the weight of the concrete in the unit volume of the member excluding the volume taken up by reinforcement steel, plus the weight of the reinforcement steel in the volumetric space. If sidewalks are placed on two sides of the bridges, the dead load of the two sidewalks is suggested to be 8 kN/m for wooden deck slabs, and 10 kN/m for reinforced concrete or steel deck slabs. The weight of the welds in an all-welded steel structure or in the bolted-welded steel structure is stipulated as 1.5% of the self-weight of the steel plates.

The dead load on bridge substructures, such as abutments, piers, and foundations, also includes lateral earth pressure, hydrostatic pressure, stream flow pressure, and buoyant force. Calculations of those dead loads for the design of bridge substructures are stipulated in Articles 4.2.2 and 4.2.3 of Chinese railway code TB 10002.

Table 2.2 Unit weights of materials (Article 4.2.1 of TB 10002)

Material	Unit Weight (kN/m^3)
Steel or cast steel	78.5
Cast iron	72.5
Lead	114.0
Reinforce concrete or prestressed concrete (reinforcement ratio ⩽3%)	25.0 ~ 26.0

Continued

Material	Unit Weight (kN/m^3)
Plain concrete or rubble concrete	24.0
Mortared ashler masonry	24.0 ~ 25.0
Mortared rubble masonry	23.0
Dry ashler or rubble masonry	21.0
Crushed-stone or gravel	21.0
Graded crushed-stone	22.0
Earth fills	17.0 ~ 18.0
Filler stones (rock debris)	19.0 ~ 20.0
Crushed stone ballast	21.0
Poured asphalt	15.0
Compacted asphalt	20.0
Oil-treated wood	7.5
Non-oil-treated wood	9.0

2.3 Chinese railway live loads

The live load on a bridge comprises the weights of vehicles and pedestrians for a highway bridge, and of locomotives and rolling stock for a railway bridge. These loads represent the principal effects of the traffic loads that a bridge is required to resist. But other effects may be significant and must be considered in the design. Such effects include impact or dynamic effect of moving vehicles, hauling or braking forces, and centrifugal forces when the bridge is located in a curve. Different countries have different design standards and codes in which the live load patterns and axle weights that reflect the worst loading configurations of the traffic on the bridge are specified. In China, the design live loads for railway and highway bridges are specified in the *Code for Train Load Diagram* (TB/T 3466) and *General Design Specifications for Highway Bridges and Culverts* (JTG D60), respectively. The design live loads for railway bridges in UK, Europe, and USA are specified in BS 5400-2: 2006, EN 1991-2: 2003, and AREMA (American Railway Engineering and Maintenance-of-way Association) *Manual for Railway Engineering*, respectively.

2.3.1 Static live loads (TB/T 3466)

China's railway live loadings consist of four types of loading: Type-ZK loading, Type-ZC loading Type-ZKH loading and Type-ZH loading (as shown in Figure 2.1). These types of loading apply to the following four classes of railways:
- The Type-ZK loading applies to high-speed railways;
- The Type-ZC loading applies to inter-city railways;
- The Type-ZKH loading applies to shared passenger-freight railways;
- The Type-ZH loading applies to heavy haul railways.

Each type of live loading includes two loading models: normal live loading model and special live loading model. The normal loading model consists of four concentrated loadings, which represent the locomotive axle loads, preceded, and followed, by a uniformly distributed load which represent the loadings applied by passenger or freight cars. The special loading model consists of only four concentrated axle loads, reflecting the effect of concentrated axle loads on short loaded lengths. The normal loading model represents the worst loading pattern caused by normal railway traffic and can be used for any span lengths, while the special load model is used for design of short-span bridges and for checking the safety of some local structural members.

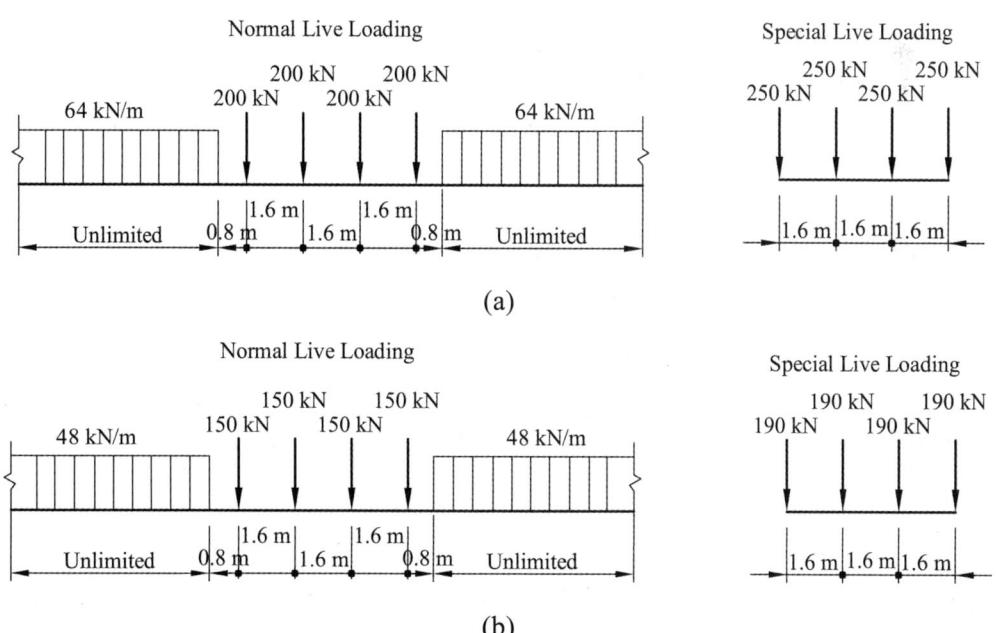

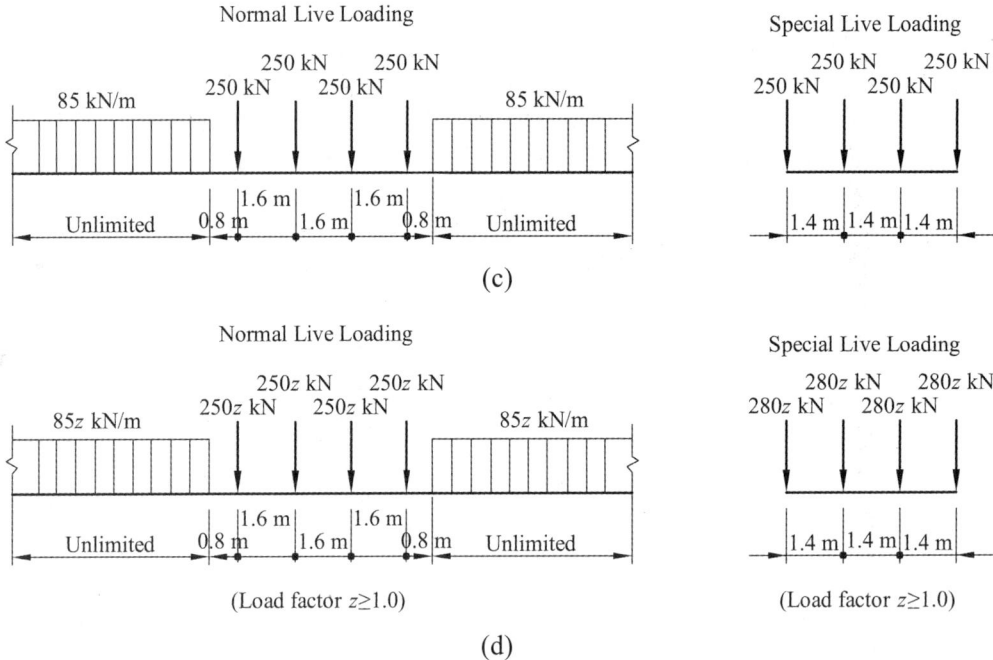

Figure 2.1 Chinese railway standard live loadings (TB/T 3466): (a) Type-ZK; (b) Type-ZC; (c) Type-ZKH; (d) Type-ZH.

2.3.2 Dynamic effects

For railway bridges, the interaction between the moving vehicles, track, and the bridge superstructure results in dynamic amplification of the moving loads, resulting in vibrations and increased stresses in structural members. For highway bridges, since the roadway surface is not perfectly smooth, the vehicle suspension must react to roadway roughness by compression and extension of the suspension system, and therefore creates axle loadings that exceed the static weight of the vehicle.

In traditional design codes and practices, the dynamic effects are taken into consideration by an impact factor μ, defined as the ratio of the additional load due to dynamic effect to the equivalent static load:

$$\mu = \frac{\text{Dynamic Load} - \text{Static Load}}{\text{Static Load}} \tag{2.1}$$

Then, the total load, termed the dynamic load which includes the static load and the dynamic effects, is calculated as

$$\text{Dynamic Load} = (1+\mu) \cdot \text{Static Load} \tag{2.2}$$

where, the coefficient $(1+\mu)$ is termed dynamic factor.

In some design codes, the term "impact factor" has been given up and replaced by other terms that emphasize the dynamic effects on the bridges caused by moving vehicles. In AASHTO (2014), this term is replaced by the term "dynamic load allowance", which is defined as an increase in the applied static force effects to account for the dynamic interaction between the bridge and moving vehicles. The dynamic load allowance is denoted by IM which is abbreviated from "impact", and is percentage of increase in the static load. In British and European railway standards, dynamic factor $\varPhi$, which is equivalent to $(1+\mu)$, is used. Chinese railway design code adopts the dynamic factor $(1+\mu)$ to consider the impact forces due to moving locomotives and trains. Different dynamic factors are specified for use in the design of different types of railway bridge structures.

(1) For the bridges on heavy haul or shared passenger-freight railways:

(i) For simply-supported or continuous steel bridge superstructures or steel piers:

$$1+\mu = 1+\frac{28}{40+L} \tag{2.3}$$

(ii) For steel-reinforced concrete composite beams:

$$1+\mu = 1+\frac{22}{40+L} \tag{2.4}$$

(iii) For bridge superstructures or culverts made up of reinforced concrete, plain concrete, and masonry, if the thickness of the fill soil, h, at the top of the bridges, is less than 3 m:

$$1+\mu = 1+\alpha\left(\frac{6}{30+L}\right) \tag{2.5}$$

where, $\alpha = 0.32(3-h)^2$, $h = 0.3$ m if $h < 0.5$ m; If $h \geqslant 3$ m, the dynamic effects are not considered.

(iv) For the arch ribs of the open-spandrel reinforced concrete arch bridges:

$$1+\mu = 1+\frac{15}{100+\lambda}\left(1+\frac{0.4L}{f}\right) \tag{2.6}$$

where, λ is the calculation span length of the arch bridge, if the members concerned are the main structural members. For the members subjected to local live loadings, λ is the length of one or several spacings of columns, f is the rise of the arch.

The symbol L in Eq.(2.3) through Eq. (2.6) denotes the span length of the bridge.

(2) For high-speed railways and inter-city railways:

$$1+\mu =1+\left(\frac{1.44}{\sqrt{L_\varphi-0.2}}-0.18\right)\geqslant 1.0 \qquad (2.7)$$

where L_φ is the loading length. Take $L_\varphi=3.61$ when $L_\varphi<3.61$. For simple-supported bridges, L_φ is the span length of the bridge; for continuous bridges, L_φ is taken as the averaged span length multiplied by the span adjustment coefficient in Table 2.3, and cannot be less than the maximum span length.

Table 2.3 Span adjustment coefficients for continuous bridges

Number of spans	2	3	4	$\geqslant 5$
Span adjustment coefficient	1.2	1.3	1.4	1.5

2.3.3 Centrifugal forces

The centrifugal force is generated by moving vehicles along a curved path and is transmitted to the path itself. This force is inversely proportional to the radius of curvature, and thus the sharper the curve, the larger the centrifugal force. Where the track on a railway bridge is curved over the whole or part of the length of the bridge, the centrifugal force should be taken into account.

The centrifugal force acts horizontally at the vehicle center of gravity, and is transferred to the bridge deck by the track. For each axle load or distributed load shown in Figure 2.1, the corresponding centrifugal force can be calculated by

$$F = f \cdot C \cdot W = f \cdot \frac{V^2}{127R} \cdot W \qquad (2.8)$$

where, C is the centrifugal ratio, and $C=\dfrac{V^2}{127R}$; V is the velocity (in km/h) and is taken as $V = 250$ if $V > 250$ km/h; W represents the concentrated (in kN) or distributed loading (in kN/m); R is the radius of curvature (in m); f is the reduction factor for the live loading given by

$$f = 1.00 - \frac{V-120}{1\,000}\left(\frac{814}{V}+1.75\right)\left(1-\sqrt{\frac{2.88}{L}}\right) \tag{2.9}$$

where, L is the influence length of the loaded part of curved track on the bridge. The value of f should satisfy the following conditions:

$$f = 1.0 \quad \text{for either } L \leqslant 2.88 \text{ m or} \quad V \leqslant 120 \text{ km/h}; \tag{2.10a}$$

$$f = 1.0 \quad \text{for } f > 1.0; \tag{2.10b}$$

$$f_{(L>150)} = f_{(L=150)}; \tag{2.10c}$$

$$f = 1.0 \quad \text{for inter-city or heavy haul railways.} \tag{2.10d}$$

The centrifugal forces should be taken to act outwards in a horizontal direction at a height of 2.0 m above the running surface (top of the rails) for shared passenger-freight railways. For high-speed railways and inter-city railways, the centrifugal forces should act at the height of 1.8 m above the top of the rails. For heavy haul railways, this height should be taken as 2.4 m.

When the design speed $V > 120$ km/h, the following combinations of vertical live loadings with centrifugal forces should be considered:

(i) Undeducted vertical live loadings with the centrifugal forces at $V = 120$ km/h ($f = 1.0$);

(ii) Deducted vertical live loadings with the centrifugal forces at the design speed ($f < 1.0$);

(iii) Vertical live loadings without centrifugal forces.

2.3.4 The lateral force (nosing force)

The nosing force represents the maximum contact force applied to the rails by the wheel flanges of railway vehicles, due to lateral track alignment irregularities. The nosing force should be taken as a concentrated force acting horizontally, at the top of the rails, perpendicular to the centre-line of track. It shall be applied on both straight track and curved track. Table 2.4 lists the nosing forces for different classes of railways.

Table 2.4 Values of the nosing force

Class of railway	Heavy haul railways	Shared passenger-freight railways	High-speed railways	Inter-city railways
Nosing force/kN	$100z^*$	100	80	60

* z is equal to the load factor for the heavy haul railways

For a bridge carrying multiple tracks, it is allowed to consider the nosing force acting only on one track. The nosing force shall always be combined with a vertical traffic load. For a bridge on a heavy haul railway or shared passenger- freight railway, the nosing force shall be considered if the bridge is loaded with an empty train.

2.4 Braking and traction forces

Longitudinal forces resulting from train braking and traction of locomotive are considerable for railway freight vehicles. The traction or braking force of a vehicle shall be taken as 10% of the sum of axle loads, and when both the centrifugal force and the static live loading are considered simultaneously, the traction or braking force should be taken as 3% of the static live loads within the loaded length.

For heavy haul railways, the traction and braking forces act at the height of 2.4 above the top of the rails; for other railways, the traction and braking forces act at the height of 2 m above the top of the rails. For design of piers or abutments, the traction and braking forces can be treated as acting on the center of bearings, and when considering the actions on the top of abutments, on the rigid frame bridges, and on the arch bridges, the traction or braking forces can be regarded as acting on the bottom of the rails.

In the case of a bridge carrying two tracks, only the braking or traction forces on one track are considered; if the bridge carries three or more than three tracks, only the braking or traction forces on two tracks are considered.

For the bridges located within railway stations, consideration should be given to the possibility of concurrence of braking and traction forces, dependent on the bridges' structural forms.

The traction or braking forces loaded within the range of the failure wedge of the backfill behind abutments may be neglected. When the special live loadings are used, the corresponding traction or braking forces are not considered.

2.5 Wind loads

Wind loads constitute a major component of lateral loads acting on all civil structures including bridges. Wind actions vary with time and act directly as pressures on the external surfaces of structures and, due to porosity of the external surface, also act indirectly on the internal surfaces. Fluctuating wind may also cause severe vibrations of slender structures.

Bridges are frequently built on exposed sites and thus may be subject to severe wind actions. Wind effects on a bridge structures include static effects and dynamic effects, depending on the type of the bridge, the terrain, and the properties of the wind, such as the wind velocity, angle of attack, and the gust characteristics. For many bridges, the wind-induced vibrations are negligible, and the deflection or deformation of bridges under wind loads can be calculated using procedures applicable for static load. Thus wind loads can be treated as static pressures on structures. Dynamic effects are usually obvious and important for long-span slender bridge structures, such as cable-stayed bridges and suspension bridges. These bridges are very prone to vibration under wind forces in a number of different modes, at low frequencies, which may be catastrophic under some critical conditions. The typical railway bridges, such as those comprising beam, girder, truss, and arch spans need not consider aerodynamic effects of the wind in design. However, the static effects of the wind on the bridge and moving train must be considered.

In accordance with Article 4.4.1 of the Chinese railway code TB 10002, the wind pressure should be calculated by

$$W = K_1 K_2 K_3 W_0 \tag{2.11}$$

where, W is the wind pressure (in Pa); W_0 is the basic wind pressure defined by

$$W_0 = \frac{1}{1.6} v^2 \tag{2.12}$$

in which, v is the basic wind velocity (in m/s), which is the mean value of the maximum wind velocity in 10 minutes with frequency of occurrence of 1/100, at 20 m above ground level in open country. Usually, W_0 can be determined from the national wind pressure map (in Appendix C of the code) and checked with field investigations. K_1 is Shape coefficient of structural elements. For bridge piers, K_1 takes the values listed in Table 2.5 according to shapes of cross-sections of piers. For other structural elements, $K_1 = 1.3$. K_2 is Height coefficient of wind loads, which is given in Table 2.6. The wind pressure varies with height of the structure above ground or water level. To simplify calculation, the wind pressure at the top of rails can be treated as that acting on all the structural members except special tall piers. K_3 is Orography coefficient, which is listed in Table 2.7

Table 2.5 Shape coefficients of structural elements for wind loads

Number	Shape of cross-section		Width/Depth ratio	Shape coefficient K_1
1		Circular	—	0.8
2		Square	$l/b \leqslant 1.5$	1.4
3		Rectangular, with narrow face upwind	$l/b \leqslant 1.5$	1.2
			$l/b > 1.5$	0.9
4		Rectangular with wide face upwind	$l/b \leqslant 1.5$	1.4
			$l/b > 1.5$	1.3
5		Round ended rectangular with narrow face upwind	$l/b \geqslant 1.5$	0.3
6		Round ended rectangular with wide face upwind	$l/b \leqslant 1.5$	0.8
			$l/b > 1.5$	1.1

Table 2.6 Height coefficients of wind loads

Height above ground or normal water lever/m	$\leqslant 20$	30	40	50	60	70	80	90	100
K_2	1.0	1.13	1.22	1.3	1.37	1.42	1.47	1.52	1.56

Table 2.7 Orography coefficients for wind loads

Orographic condition	≤20
Flat, open terrain	1.0
Urban area, basin in forest regions, and when there exist obstructions blocking winds	0.85 ~ 0.9
Mountain, gorge, mountain passes, wind gaps	1.15 ~ 1.30
Special wind gaps	Determined by surveys or measurements

Wind loads acting on a bridge consist of two parts: (i) the wind load on the structure including superstructure and substructure, and (ii) wind load on the moving vehicles on the bridge.

The loaded area of a bridge superstructure by winds in the lateral direction is taken as the projected area of the structure in elevation multiplied by a deduction factor α which takes the following values:

(i) $\alpha = 0.4$ for the area of a steel truss girder or column;

(ii) $\alpha = 0.5$ for the area between chords in a steel arch;

(iii) $\alpha = 0.2$ for the area between the central line of the lower chords and the tie for the truss tied-arch bridge or the area between the central line of upper chords and the roadway (for the deck truss arch bridge);

(iv) $\alpha = 1$ for integrated solid superstructure.

The lateral wind load on the moving train is treated as acting at a distance 2 m above the top of the rails, and the loaded area is regarded as rectangular, with a height of 3 m and a length of the train.

If the wind loads on the bridge and the train are considered at the same time, the wind pressure used in design can be reduced to 80% of W calculated by Eq.(2.11) and not exceed 1,250 MPa. If only the wind loads on the bridge are considered, W does not need to be reduced.

Calculation of longitudinal wind loads is the same as that for the lateral wind load. The longitudinal wind loads on the train, decks, and other girder bridges may be neglected. The longitudinal wind pressure on the through-type truss bridges and truss columns can be taken as 40% of the lateral wind pressure on these structures.

For higher piers or towers which have long periods of free vibrations, wind-induced vibrations should be considered.

2.6 Seismic loads

The seismic loadings on bridge structures during an earthquake result from inertial forces which were generated by ground accelerations. The magnitude of these loadings is determined by the mass of the bridge components, dynamic properties of the bridge structures, the properties of the ground motion, and soil-structure interaction. Since bridges are one of the most important connections between the lifelines of the modem world, it is of extreme importance that bridges can resist earthquake-induced loads and can maintain their essential functions in case of catastrophic earthquakes.

In spite of earthquake-induced damages to buildings and highway bridges worldwide, railway bridges historically have performed better than highway bridges and other types of bridges. This is due to several factors which are unique to railway bridges: (i) railway bridges are traversed by a track structure which functions as a restraint against longitudinal and lateral movement during earthquakes; (ii) configurations, structural details, and material strengths of railway bridges are typically different from the bridges of other types; (iii) conservative design criteria are used in the design of railway bridges, and therefore railway bridges have more margin of safety than highway bridges.

Observations and investigations on the damaged and collapsed bridges indicate that failures of bridges due to earthquake are not caused by failure of any single element of the superstructure but rather by superstructure's being shaken off the bearings and falling to the ground or by the loss of strength of the foundation soil under the substructure as a result of the vibrations of the ground.

Modern codes such as Eurocode 1998-2, AASHTO (2014), AREMA (2015), and China's *code for seismic design of railway engineering* (GB 50111) recommend three different methods of analysis to consider the seismic action:

(1) The equivalent static force method. This method is based on elastic analysis of the structure. The seismic action is treated as an equivalent static force applied to the structure for calculating forces and displacements on bridge elements. In this method, the structural responses to the first or fundamental vibration mode are primarily considered, higher vibration modes

are usually neglected. This method is applicable to simply-supported two or multi-span regular bridges.

(2) Response spectrum modal analysis. This method takes contributions of the second and higher vibration modes to the forces and deformations of structural elements into consideration. A response spectrum is a plot of the peak response (acceleration, velocity, displacement) of a single-degree-of-freedom elastic system of varying frequencies to earthquake ground motions versus the periods or frequencies of the system for a given level of damping. The response spectrum is actually a summary of a whole series of time-history analysis. This method is used in design and analyses of irregular, long-span, or slender bridges.

(3) Time history method. The step-by-step time history analysis is a rigorous method of analysis that gives the response of a structure to the ground motions over time. This analysis involves a step-by-step integration of the equations of motion for a bridge structure when it is subjected to ground accelerations that vary with time. The method can address not only the linear vibrations but also nonlinear vibrations including geometrical and material nonlinearity, and is mostly used in the design and analyses of critical bridges.

China's *code for seismic design of railway structures* (GB 50111) classifies the railway structures into four importance classes, depending on the consequences of collapse for human life, on their importance for public safety and civil protection, and on the difficulty of post-earthquake retrofit. For a seismic intensity, each importance class corresponds to a resisted seismic intensity. Table 2.8 defines the importance classes of railway structures and Table 2.9 lists the resisted seismic intensities corresponding to seismic intensities defined in the Chinese seismic intensity scale for each importance class. The seismic peak ground accelerations corresponding to the seismic intensities are listed in Table 2.10. The seismic design code GB 50111 also defines three post-earthquake performance criteria for railway structures to meet under earthquakes, which is summarized in Table 2.11. The seismic design methods for bridges of different importance classes to meet different performance levels are given in Table 2.12. The response spectrum modal analysis and time-history analysis are advanced analysis methods for seismic design and will not be discussed in depth in this textbook.

Table 2.8 Importance classes for railway bridges (GB 50111)

Importance class	Bridges
A	Sea-crossing, river-crossing, complex or special bridges that are difficult to retrofit after earthquakes.
B	(i) Shared passenger-freight bridges: simply-supported concrete bridges with spans equal or larger than 48 m; simply-supported steel bridges with spans equal or larger than 64 m; concrete continuous bridges with main spans equal or larger than 80 m; continuous steel bridges with main spans equal or larger than 96 m; (ii) High-speed railways and passenger railways (including intercity railways): bridges with main spans equal or larger than 40 m; (iii) Bridges with heights of piers equal or larger than 40 m; (iv) Bridges with the normal depth of water larger than 8 m. (v) Complex or special bridges that are difficult to retrofit
C	(i) Normal bridges on high-speed railways and passenger railways (including intercity railways); (ii) Bridges with heights of piers between 30 and 40 m; (iii) Bridges with the normal depth of water between 5 and 8
D	Other bridges

Table 2.9 Resisted seismic intensities corresponding to various importance classes (GB 50111)

Importance class	Seismic intensity according to the Chinese seismic intensity scale			
	6	7	8	9
A	7	8	9	By investigation
B	7	7	8	9
C	7	7	8	9
D	—	7	8	9

Table 2.10 Correspondence between resisted seismic intensities and seismic peak ground accelerations A_g (GB 50111)

Seismic intensity	6	7		8		9
seismic peak ground acceleration	0.05g	0.10g	0.15g	0.20g	0.30g	0.40g

Table 2.11 post-earthquake performance criteria for railway structures

Performance level I	Structures are not damaged or slightly damaged, normal functions can be maintained and structural behavior is still elastic.
Performance level II	Structures may be damaged, but their normal functions can be restored in a short period of time after retrofit; the whole structure' behavior is inelastic.
Performance level III	Structures are seriously damaged but do not collapse. Bridges' basic functions can be restored after emergency repair and traffic can pass over the retrofitted bridges with restricted speeds. Structural behavior is elastoplastic.

Table 2.12 Seismic design methods for railway bridges according to the performance levels

Earthquake level	Low-level earthquake	Design earthquake	High-level earthquake
Performance level	Performance level I	Performance level II	Performance level III
Bridge	Typical bridges	Abutments, connections between structural elements	Bridges with reinforced concrete piers
Seismic design method	Response spectrum method used for bridges of importance class D; response spectrum or time-history method used for bridges of class B and C	Equivalent static force method is generally used. Response spectrum method can be used for design of supports of continuous bridges	Simplified ductility design method is used for design of reinforced concrete piers; nonlinear time-history analysis is used for design of bridges of class B and bridges of new structural form.

Note: (i) the connections in the superstructure and substructure of a bridge include the anti-seismic stopper and the constructions for preventing beam falling;
(ii) The method in this table is not applicable to the bridge with seismic isolators or absorbers installed;
(iii) The high-level earthquake should be employed to check the safety of the bearings on the reinforced concrete piers designed to ductility requirements.

2.7 Pedestrian loads

Pedestrian walkways on railway bridges are used for maintenance and inspection by only railway employees and not by the general public. In Chinese code TB 10002, the static live load of pedestrians on the walkway is specified as a uniformly distributed live load of 4.0 kPa for ballasted deck bridges and opendeck bridges. When the bridge deck is maintained manually, the weight of ballast should be considered as an additional load. When inspection cars are used in maintenance, the weights of inspection cars should be treated as live loadings. In addition, the strength of the walkway slab should be checked by applying a concentrated load of 1.5 kN. The design loads for guardrails and posts are also specified in TB 10002.

2.8 Chinese highway live loads

The design live loads for Chinese highway bridges are specified in China's General Specifications for Design of Highway Bridges and Culverts (JTG D60). The live loading consists of lane loading and truck loading. The lane loading is used for loading the whole span of a bridge, while the truck loading is used to generate critical internal forces in a local member of the bridge. The magnitudes of the lane loadings and the truck loadings depend on the class of the highway on which the bridge is located.

2.8.1 The lane loading

The lane loading comprises a uniformly distributed load of q_k in the longitudinal direction and a concentrated load of P_k (Figure 2.2). For Highway Class-I, the standard value for q_k is 10.5 kN/m; the value of P_k, depending on the calculational span length L_0, is specified in Table 2.13. When the lane loading is used for calculating the shear forces, these values should be multiplied by a coefficient of 1.2. For Highway Class-II, q_k and P_k are reduced to 75% of their respective values for the Highway Class-I.

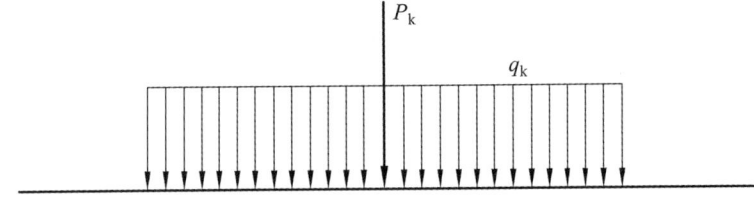

Figure 2.2 Lane loading.

Table 2.13 The concentrated load of P_k for lane loading.

Calculational span length L_0/m	$L_0 \leqslant 5$	$5 < L_0 < 50$	$L_0 \geqslant 50$
P_k/kN	270	$2(L_0+130)$	360

* Calculational span length L_0 is defined as the horizontal distance between centers of adjacent bearings. For the bridges without bearings, L_0 is the horizontal distance between adjacent centers of interfaces between superstructure and substructure.

2.8.2 The truck loading

The design truck for highway bridges consists of five axial loads in the longitudinal direction, as shown in Figure 2.3, each axle load being twice the wheel load. The plane view of the typical arrangement of truck wheels is shown in Figure 2.3(b). If more than one design truck is laid out in the transverse direction, the clear distance between the design trucks shall meet the requirement shown in Figure 2.3(c).

The tire contact area of a wheel consisting of one or two tires is assumed to be a single rectangle, whose dimensions are 0.3 m (width) ×0.2 m (length) for a front wheel and 0.6 m (width) ×0.2 m (length) for an intermediate or a rear wheel. The tire pressure could be assumed to be uniformly distributed over the contact area.

When multiple lanes are loaded with design trucks, the live load effect shall be multiplied by a multiple presence factor to account for the probability of simultaneous occupation of the lanes by the design trucks. The multiple presence factors, *m* are specified in Table 14. In principle, when two lanes are loaded, the truck loads are fully applied. When only one lane is loaded, the truck load shall be increased by 20%; when more than two lanes are loaded, the truck loads shall be reduced by a factor less than 1.

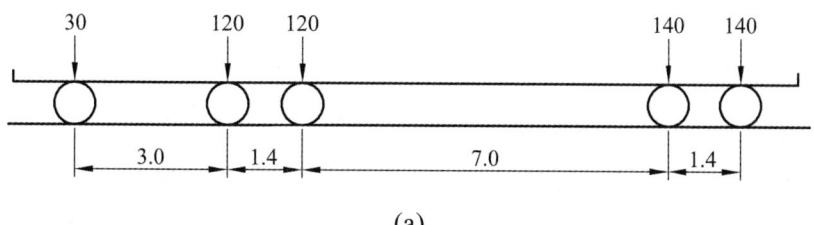

(a)

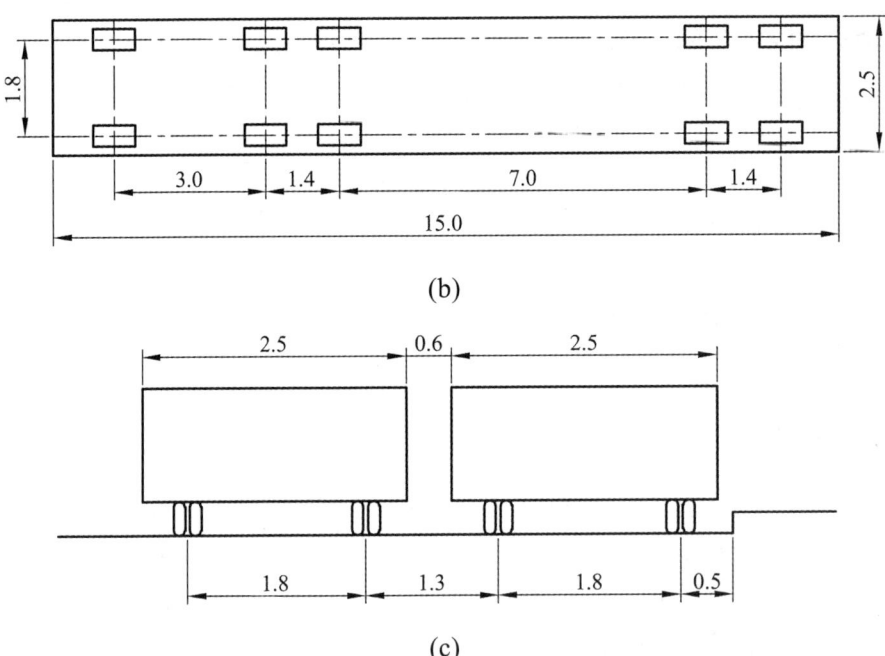

Figure 2.3 The design truck loading: (a) Elevation view; (b) Plane view; (c) The layout in the transverse direction.

For long-span bridges, the truck load effect is reducing with increased span length. For the span length larger than 150 m, the truck load shall be multiplied by a long-span reduction factor specified in Table 2.15 to take into account the reduction of the load effect with increased span length. When applied to a multi-span continuous bridges, the long-span reduction factor shall be calculated in terms of the maximum span length.

Table 2.14 Multiple presence factors

Number of loaded lanes	1	2	3	4	5	6	7	8
Multiple presence factors/m	1.20	1.00	0.78	0.67	0.60	0.55	0.52	0.50

Table 2.15

Calculational span length L_0 /m	$150 < L_0 < 400$	$400 \leqslant L_0 < 600$	$600 \leqslant L_0 < 800$	$800 \leqslant L_0 < 1000$	$L_0 \geqslant 1000$
Long-span reduction factor α	0.97	0.96	0.95	0.94	0.93

2.8.3 The impact factor

The Chinese highway design code JTG D60 specifies the impact forces of the truck loads to bridges as the static live loads multiplied by an impact factor μ, which is a function of the fundamental frequency of the bridge:

$$\mu = \begin{cases} 0.05, & \text{for } f < 1.5 \text{ Hz} \\ 0.1767 \ \ln(f) - 0.0157, & \text{for } 1.5 \text{ Hz} \leqslant f \leqslant 14 \text{ Hz} \\ 0.45, & \text{for } f > 14 \text{ Hz} \end{cases} \quad (2.13)$$

where, f is the fundamental frequency of the bridge. For the arch bridges with the thickness of the fill material at the top of the bridge larger than 0.5 m, culverts, and gravity abutments and piers, the impact forces are not considered. If the truck load is applied locally on the overhanging flanges of T-girders or the box girders, the impact factor of the truck load shall be taken as 0.3.

2.8.4 Centrifugal forces

For design of bridges on curved highways, the centrifugal effect on the truck loads shall be considered. The centrifugal force on the truck load shall be taken as the product of the static truck load and the centrifugal ratio C, defined by

$$C = \frac{v^2}{127R} \quad (2.14)$$

where, v is highway design speed (km/h); R is radius of curvature of traffic lane.

When multiple traffic lanes are loaded simultaneously, the multiple presence factors specified in Table 2.14 shall apply.

Centrifugal forces shall be applied horizontally at a distance 1.2 m above the roadway surface. For convenience of design calculation, the acting positions can be translated to the roadway surface without considering the additional effects caused by such translation.

2.9 Other loads

Determination of other loads, such as the earth pressure, stream flow pressure, effect of temperature change, and vehicular collision loads, can be found in the railway and highway design specifications. For some loads which are specific to some type of bridge structures some construction sites, the design specifications may not provide specific methods of calculation. In this case, the designers need consult design manuals or conduct theoretical or experimental research to determine the appropriate loads on the structures for the design purposes.

2.10 Load combinations

2.10.1 Load combinations for design of railway bridges

For design of railway bridges, the loads listed in Table 2.1 have different frequencies of occurrence. The primary loads are those acting on a bridge most frequently or even permanently, such as vehicular loads and the self-weights of bridge components; while the additional loads, such as braking forces, occurs less frequently. The special loads, such as earthquake loads, appear with very low frequency. However, there are possibilities that some loads can occur simultaneously during the service life of a bridge. For example, the vehicular live loads and earthquake loads can act on a bridge at the same time. But, for other loads, actions cannot occur simultaneously. For instance, there is little chance that a train passing through a bridge is braked when ice pressure is loading on the piers. Thus, the braking force or the traction force could not occur simultaneously with ice pressure.

Chinese design code for railway bridges specifies that the primary loads listed in Table 2.1 shall be combined with one additional load that is acting either in longitudinal or transverse direction. For some structural members, if the purpose of the member is to resist some additional loads, the additional loads shall be treated as primary loads. When special loads are considered in design of a bridge, their combinations with primary and additional loads shall meet the following requirements:

(1) The stream flow pressure shall not be combined with ice pressure, and the two pressure shall not be combined with braking forces and traction forces.

(2) Derailment loads shall be combined only with dead loads, and not with live loads and any other special loads.

(3) Among the vessel or raft collision loads and vehicular collision loads, only one is combined with primary loads. These special loads shall not be combined with additional loads.

(4) Earthquake loads shall be combined with the loads listed in Table 2.16. When the live loads are combined with earthquake loads, the earthquake loads in the longitudinal direction caused by live load mass shall not be considered. The arthquake loads in the transverse direction shall be determined according to 50% of the live load on the bridge superstructure. The earthquake loads act at a distance of 2 m above the rail top. For double track railway bridges, only the live loads on one track need to be considered.

Table 2.16 The loads that can be combined with earthquake loads

Type of load	Load
Dead load	Self-weight of structures
	Earth pressure
	Hydrostatic pressure and upward buoyant forces
Live load	Static gravity loads of trains
	Centrifugal forces
	Earth pressure due to live loads surcharge

For different load combinations, the allowable stresses of bridge components and bearing capacity of foundation soil shall be different, and in general, shall be increased by a factor. For design of prestressed concrete structures, different safety factors shall be used in checking the strength and cracking resistance under different load combinations.

For design of combined road-rail bridges, the railway live loading used in design shall meet the requirements specified in the design code for railway bridges TB/T 3466, but only 75% of highway live loading specified in the design code for highway bridges need to be considered in the design. For some structural members subjected to only highway live loads, full highway live loading shall be applied.

2.10.2 Load combinations for design of highway bridges

Unlike the design of railway bridges, design of highway bridges in China is based on limit-state design method which is probability-based to provide a relatively uniform component reliability by explicitly considering uncertainties in load and resistance. The Chinese design code for highway bridges specifies different load combinations for different design limit-states. For each load combination, specific load factors are used. In the following, the basics of load combination in two design limit-states are introduced briefly.

1. Strength limit state

(1) Fundamental combination of actions.

Fundamental combination of actions refers to the combination of design values of permanent actions with design values of variable actions. The design value of the effect of combination can be expressed as

$$S_{ud} = \gamma_0 S\left(\sum_{i=1}^{m} \gamma_{G_i} G_{ik}, \gamma_{Q_1} \gamma_L Q_{1k}, \psi_c \sum_{j=2}^{n} \gamma_{L_j} \gamma_{Q_j} Q_{jk}\right) \quad (2.15)$$

or

$$S_{ud} = \gamma_0 S\left(\sum_{i=1}^{m} G_{id}, Q_{1d}, \sum_{j=2}^{n} Q_{jd}\right) \quad (2.16)$$

where, S_{ud} is the design value of the effect of the fundamental combination of actions;

$S(\cdot)$ is the effect function of the combined actions;

γ_0 is importance factor taken from Table 4.1.5-1 of the Chinese highway design specifications JTG D60 for different safety classes;

γ_{G_i} is the safety factor for the ith permanent action taken from Table 4.1.5-2;

G_{ik}, G_{id} are the standard value and design value of the ith permanent action, respectively;

γ_{Q_1} is the safety factor of the truck load (including impact and centrifugal forces). For the lane load and the truck load, γ_{Q_1} is taken as 1.4 and 1.8, respectively. If the effect of some other load is greater than the truck load, this load can replace the truck load and γ_{Q_1} is taken as 1.4.

Q_{1k}, Q_{1d} are the standard and design values of the truck load (including impact and centrifugal forces), respectively;

γ_{Q_j} is the safety factor of the *j*th variable action (excluding the truck load)=1.4. For the wind load, γ_{Q_j} is taken as 1.1. Q_{jk}, Q_{jd} is the standard and design values of the *j*th variable action, excluding the truck load;

ψ_c is the combination factor of the variable action excluding the truck load = 0.75.

$\psi_c Q_{jk}$ is the combining value of the *j*th variable action;

γ_{L_j} is the adjustment factor for the working life of the *j*th variable action. If the design service life of the bridge meets the requirements set up by the *technical standards of highway structures* (JTG B01), γ_{L_j} can be taken as 1.0; otherwise, specific investigation should be carried out.

It is should be pointed out that when the actions and the effects of actions are linearly related, the design value of the effect of the combined actions can be obtained by superposition of the effect of the individual actions. For design of curved bridges, when the centrifugal force are combined with the braking force, only 70% of the standard or design value of the braking force is used.

(2) Accidental combination of actions.

The accidental combination refers to the combination of design values of permanent actions with a representative value of variable actions and the design value of one accidental action. The representative value of variable actions can be the frequent value of a variable action or quasi-permanent value of a variable action, both of which can be determined by observation data and engineering experience. The design value of the effect of the accidental combination can be expressed as

$$S_{ad} = S\left(\sum_{i=1}^{m} G_{ik}, A_d, (\psi_{f1} \text{ or } \psi_{q1})Q_{1k}, \sum_{j=2}^{n} \psi_{qj}Q_{jk} \right) \quad (2.17)$$

where, S_{ad} is the design value of the effect of the accidental combination of actions. A_d is the design value of the accidental action. ψ_{f1} is the frequency factor of the truck load (including impact and centrifugal forces) =0.7. Some other variable action can replace the truck load if its effect is greater than that of the truck load. If so, ψ_{f1} can be taken as 1.0, 0.75 and 0.8 for the pedestrian load, the wind load, and the temperature gradient action, respectively. For other type of loads, ψ_{f1} is taken as 1.0. $\psi_{f1}Q_{1k}$ is the frequent value of the truck load.

ψ_{q1} and ψ_{qj} are the factors of the quasi-permanent value of the first and the jth variable action, respectively. For the truck load, the pedestrian load, the wind load, and the temperature gradient action, ψ_q can be taken as 0.4, 0.4, 0.75, and 0.8, respectively. For other type of loads, ψ_q is taken as 1.0. $\psi_{q1}Q_{1k}$ and $\psi_{qj}Q_{jk}$ are the quasi-permanent values of the first and the jth variable action, respectively.

2. <u>Service limit state</u>

The load combinations in the service limit state consists of frequent combinations and the quasi-permanent combinations

(1) Frequent combinations.

The frequent load combinations are the combinations of the standard values of the permanent actions, frequent values of truck loads, and the quasi-permanent values of other variable actions. The design value of the effect of a frequent combination can be expressed as

$$S_{fd} = S\left(\sum_{i=1}^{m} G_{ik}, \psi_{f1}Q_{1k}, \sum_{j=2}^{n}\psi_{qj}Q_{jk}\right) \tag{2.18}$$

where, S_{fd} is the design value of effect of the frequent combination; ψ_{f1} is frequency factor of the truck load (not including impact) = 0.7.

(2) Quasi-permanent combinations.

The quasi-permanent combinations are the combinations of the standard values of the permanent actions and the quasi-permanent values of variable actions. The design value of the effect of a quasi-permanent combination can be expressed as

$$S_{qd} = S\left(\sum_{i=1}^{m} G_{ik}, \sum_{j=1}^{n}\psi_{qj}Q_{jk}\right) \tag{2.19}$$

where, S_{qd} is the design value of effect of the quasi-permanent combination; ψ_{qj} is the factor of quasi-permanent value of the truck load = 0.4.

For the above two load combinations in the service limit-state, if the effects of actions depend linearly on the corresponding actions, the design value of the effect of a combination can be obtained by linear superposition of effects of individual actions.

References

[2.1] TB 10002-2017, *Code for Design on Railway Bridges and Culverts*, China National Railway Bureau, 2017.

[2.2] TB/T 3466-2016, *Code For Train Load Diagrams*, China National Railway Bureau, 2016.

[2.3] JTG D60-2015, *General Specifications for Design of Highway Bridges and Culverts*, China's Transportation Ministry, 2015.

[2.4] BS 5400-2:2006, *Specification for loads*, British Standard Institution, 2006

[2.5] O'Connor C. and Shaw P. A., *Bridge Loads - An International Perspective*, Spon Press, London, 2000.

[2.6] AASHTO, LRFD Bridge Design Specifications, 5th ed., American Association for State Highway and Transportation Officials, Washington, DC., 2014.

[2.7] American Railway Engineering and Maintenance-of-Way Association (AREMA), *Manual for Railway Engineering*, Lanham, MD. 2015,

[2.8] EN 1998-2:2005+A2, *Design of structures for earthquake resistance - Part 2: Bridges*, European Committee For Standardization, 2011.

[2.9] GB 50111-2006, *Code for Seismic Design of Railway Engineering*, China's Housing and Building Construction Ministry, 2006.

Chapter 3 Design Philosophies and Specifications

3.1 Introduction

A bridge design should fulfill the objectives of safety, serviceability, constructability and economy. Any acceptable bridge structures should first satisfy the requirements of safety and performance. Simply put, a bridge design should permit the bridge structure to perform its intended function safely and normally under service loads, during its design life. A design philosophy is a set of assumptions and procedures which are used to achieve the objectives of the structural design. The design philosophies for bridge structures have developed for more than half a century. Advances in the understanding of structural and material behavior, in structural analysis techniques, and in construction experience resulted in advancement of the design theory of bridge structures. In particular, the development of applied mechanics and advent of electronic computers in the 20th century has greatly influenced the design methodologies; more advanced mathematical models and even numerical methods have been introduced into design procedure.

Regardless of the design methodologies, a general statement for assuring safety of a bridge structure is that the resistance of the components shall be greater than the effects of the applied loads, that is,

$$M = R - S \geqslant 0 \qquad (3.1)$$

where, M is called the safety margin, R and S represent the resistance and the corresponding load effect, respectively. Note that R and S shall be evaluated for the same conditions. For example, if the effect of applied loads is to produce bending moments in a component, S represents the bending moment generated by the loads and R is the bending moment that the component can resist. In the allowable stress design procedure, R and S often represent the stress induced by the applied loads and that the material can resist, respectively.

Over the past years, design methods have been developed by bridge engineers to provide satisfactory safety margin. These methods were based on the bridge engineer's confidence in the theory of structural analysis for the determination of the load effects and the failure theory of the materials making up the structural members. As analysis techniques improved and quality control on materials became better, the design philosophies changed accordingly.

Allowable stress design (ASD), Load Factor Design (LFD), and Load and Resistance factor design (LRFD) are three distinct design philosophies. The LRFD is also known as Limit State Design (LSD) in European countries. Prior to 1970, the only design philosophy was ASD. Beginning in early 1970, a new design philosophy LFD was introduced. The LSD was developed early in the USSR (Union of Soviet Socialist Republics) and was based on the research led by Professor N.S. Streletski. It was introduced in building regulations of USSR in 1955 and has been adopted in European codes since 1980's. General use of the LSD method in North America has been somewhat slower. In the United States, design codes and standards are issued by diverse organizations, some of which have adopted LSD, and others have not. The probability-based LRFD (or LSD) design philosophy was first adopted in "AASHTO LRFD Bridge Design Specifications" (AASHTO 1994) and continues in the 7th Edition (AASHTO 2014). The LRFD Specifications had not been widely used until AASHTO discontinued updating of its Standard Specifications in 2003. By the US Federal Highway Administration (FHWA) policy, all bridges designed after 2007 were required to be designed based on the LRFD method. For design of railway bridges, AREMA sets forth guidelines for both ASD and LSD, but the LRFD method is currently not used. In China, the current code for the design of railway bridges is still based on ASD method, while the code for the design of highway bridges is based on LSD method. The main reasons for using different design philosophies for highway and railway bridges are as follows: ① the railway bridges are subjected to heavier live loadings than the highway bridges, and thus need more safety reserve; ② LSD target reliability indices and load factors are usually calibrated to the statistical parameters of existing ASD designs, consequently, the LSD based designs are not expected to be substantially different from the ASD based designs.

3.2 Allowable stress design (ASD)

This design method, also known as Working Stress Design (WSD) method or service load design method, is based on the assumption that the structural component will safely carry the applied loads if the maximum stress generated in a structural component by the applied loads do not exceed a predefined allowable stress of the material. The general ASD design equation can be expressed as:

$$\sigma_{app} \leqslant \sigma_{allow} \tag{3.2}$$

where, σ_{app} and σ_{allow} represent applied stress and the allowable stress, respectively.

The allowable stress σ_{allow} is defined as a limiting stress of the material, f, divided by a factor of safety F_S:

$$\sigma_{allow} = \frac{f}{F_S} \tag{3.3}$$

For steel, f is typically the yield strength or the ultimate strength, denoted by f_y or f_u, respectively. For concrete, f is generally the 28-day compressive strength, denoted by f_c'. The allowable stress could also be defined by some other controlling criterion such as the buckling stress.

The magnitude of a factor of safety is primarily based on past experience and engineering judgment. In Chinese railway design codes, the F_S for axial tension and axial compression in structural concretes are 3.0 and 2.5, respectively; the F_S for structural steels is 1.7 if $f = f_y$ or 2.5 if $f = f_u$.

In this method it is assumed that the material behaves elastically, i.e., it obeys Hooke's law under service. Thus the applied stress σ_{app} is obtained by an elastic structural analysis for the applied loads. The structural performance beyond the elastic limit is not considered. For a beam in bending, the working stress is defined by

$$\sigma_{app} = \frac{Mc}{I} \tag{3.4}$$

where, M is maximum bending moment;

c is the distance from the extreme fiber to the neutral axis;

I is second moment of area of the beam cross section.

The ASD method assumes that all the loads in a given load combination have the same statistical variability. The dead, live, wind and other loads are all treated equally in ASD. It does not recognize that different loads have different levels of uncertainty, and it does not consider the probability of a higher-than-expected load and a lower-than-expected strength occurring simultaneously. The factor of safety is applied to the resistance side of design inequality (3.1) and the load side is not factored. Because the factor of safety chosen is based on experience and judgment, quantitative measures of risk cannot be determined by ASD method.

A more general ASD design equation can be expressed as

$$\sum S_i \leqslant \frac{R}{F_S} \tag{3.5}$$

where, S_i denotes the effect of an applied load, R represent the limit resistance. Then, a graphical representation of the ASD philosophy can be shown in Figure 3.1. As seen in the figure, the loads and resistances in the ASD method have the same probability of occurrence of 1.0.

The primary advantage of ASD is that it has an inherent simplicity. Because it does not involve the use of load factors or resistance factors, the calculations in the design process are relatively simple

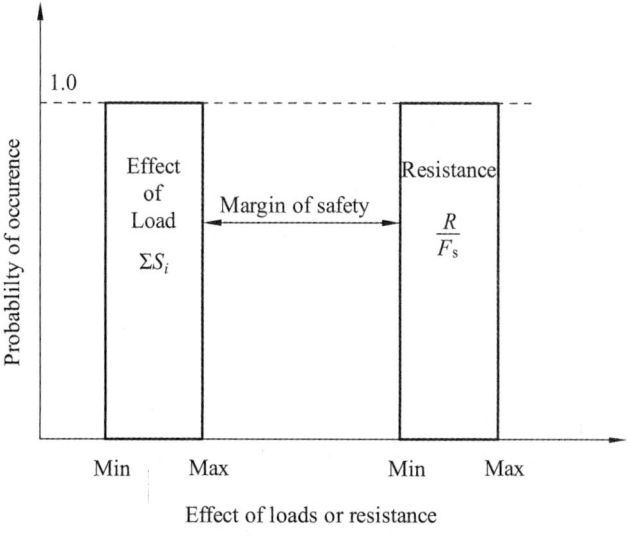

Figure 3.1 The graphical representation of the ASD philosophy.

The primary drawbacks of ASD are:

(i) The safely factor is applied only to resistance, and no consideration is given to the fact that various types of loads have different levels of uncertainty.

(ii) The resistance concepts are based on elastic behavior of materials.

(iii) The allowable stress is not a reasonable measure of strength.

(iv) Selection of a safety factor is subjective, and it is not a measure of reliability in terms of probability of material failure.

3.3 Load factor design (LFD)

The load factor design (LFD) is the first limit-states design method, which was developed in the 1960s in an effort to refine the ASD philosophy. LFD was developed as a method for proportioning structural members for the design loads multiplied by load factors and load combination coefficients to satisfy specified structural performance requirements. The factored loads are combined to produce a maximum effect in a member. Load factors vary by type of load and reflect the uncertainty in estimating magnitudes of different types of loads. With properly selected load factors and load combination factors, the bridge designed by LFD method is ensured to permit:

(i) the expected number of passages of ordinary vehicles during the service life of the bridge;

(ii) occasional passages of overload vehicles without permanent damage, and

(iii) in an extreme emergency, very few passages of exceptionally heavy vehicles.

The underlying philosophy of the LFD is to ensure both safety and serviceablity, while at the same time providing a consistent live-load carrying capacity for all bridges on the system.

Uncertainty is also considered in the strength of the structural components. The nominal resistance of the a structural component is multiplied by a reduction factor, which is generally less than unity to account for variability of material properties, structural dimensions, and workmanship. The combination of the factored loads cannot exceed the reduced resistance of the component. Thus, the LFD design philosophy can be expressed as

$$\gamma(\sum \beta_D S_D + \sum \beta_L S_L) \leq \phi R \qquad (3.6)$$

where, S_D is dead loads applied to the component under consideration;
S_L is live loads applied to the component under consideration;
R is ultimate capacity of the component under consideration
γ is load factor applied to the load combination;
β_D is load combination coefficient for dead loads;
β_L is load combination coefficient for live loads;
ϕ is strength reduction factor.

In LFD method, three distinct load levels are recognized — Service Load, Overload, and Maximum Load. Service Load represents normal vehicles operating on the highways without special permit. In AASHTO, Service Load is represented as the sum of the dead loads S_D and the standard live loads plus impact, i.e., $S_L(1+\mu)$. The primary structural performance requirements at Service Load are to provide adequate fatigue life and to control live-load deflections of the structure under live-loads and cracking of concrete. Overload is defined as the maximum live load that can be allowed on the bridge on infrequent occasions. Infrequency means that the stresses caused by these loads do not cause fatigue problems. The single structural performance requirement at Overload is the control of permanent deformations caused by localized yielding and connection slip to ensure good ride quality.

It is evident that Service Load and Overload addresses only serviceability requirements. To ensure adequate safety, the Maximum Load level is introduced. The single structural performance requirement at Maximum Load is that the bridge be able to safely resist the load. For flexure and shear design in LFD, ϕ is shifted to the left-hand side of the Eq. (3.6). The resulting γ/ϕ term, together with the load factors β_D and β_L, establishes the margin of safety in LFD for flexural members. The value of the γ/ϕ term was established based on past experience using ASD practice as a guide. The minimum margin of safety in ASD is associated with short spans. In order to provide both safe and economical designs in LFD, a value of γ/ϕ would be selected that yields the same steel section by LFD as that by ASD for a short simple-span bridge. It was found that a value of γ/ϕ equal to 1.3 would yield about the same minimum level of safety by ASD and LFD for an approximately 45-foot long non-composite simple-span bridge. As the span length increases, the live-load margin of safety increases slightly in LFD since different load factors are applied to the dead and live loads, while the margin of safety remains nearly constant in ASD.

The primary advantages of LFD are the following:

(i) In LFD, a load factor is applied to each load combination to account for the possibility that a specific combination of loads would occur simultaneously;

(ii) In LFD, consideration is given to the fact that various types of loads have different levels of uncertainty. For example, the dead load of a bridge can be estimated with a higher degree of accuracy than the live loads. Therefore, the load combination coefficient for live load is greater than that for dead load.

The primary disadvantages of LFD are:

(i) It does not give relatively uniform levels of safety for various bridges and their components on a system.

(ii) In the LFD specifications, the load and resistance factors are not calibrated in a manner that takes into account the statistical variability of design parameters in nature; instead, they are determined only by a simple calibration process based on judgment and experience to achieve a more uniform live-load carrying capacity than is possible using ASD.

3.4　Load and resistance factor design (LRFD)

A bridge is designed to carry certain loads functionally and safely. "functionally" means a structure performs its intended function. "safely" implies that the structure operates in a way that structural failure is avoided. In a popular sense, failure is associated with structural collapse. However, from an engineer's standpoint, failure can be defined strictly as a phenomenon related to a specific structural response or material behavior. For example, failure may be said to have occurred if the stress induced by loads exceeds yield stress; or one can define failure as a condition in which the load-induced stress exceeds the ultimate stress of the material. Failure can also be defined in terms of the serviceability criteria: we can say that failure has occurred when excessive deflection of beams occurs. Cracking and fracture of members due to fatigue can be other instances of failure. All of these definitions of failure refer to some limit conditions of the structure's state. Not all these limits cause structural collapse. A limit state is thus defined as a condition of a structure beyond which it would be considered to have failed to fulfill some purposes of the structure.

In LRFD method, the term "limit state" is preferred over "failure". Structural safety is thus reflected in different limit states. The LRFD philosophy is similar to that of LFD. On the load side of the Eq. (3.6), LRFD utilizes load factors but not load combination coefficients. Each specific load combination corresponds to a specific limit state. To meet the design criteria in each limit state, the combination of the factored loads cannot exceed the resistance of the material multiplied by a resistance factor less than or equal to unity. The philosophy can be formulated as

$$\sum \gamma_i S_i \leqslant \phi R \tag{3.7}$$

where, S_i is the ith load effect;

γ_i is the load factor for S_i.

Unlike in the LFD method, the load and resistance factors in the LRFD method are determined through statistical studies of the variability of loads and resistances, which is considered to be a more realistic approach than the judgment-based deterministic approach. LRFD predicts how often the loads will be greater than the resistance of a structure. The LRFD design criteria ensure that a limit state is violated only with an acceptably small probability, by selecting the load factors, resistance factors, nominal loads, and resistance values that will never be exceeded under the design assumptions. In the calibration process, load and resistance factors are calculated to provide a target level of reliability for a wide variety of structural types and configurations.

3.4.1 Principle of probability-based design

Probability-based bridge design is to ensure that probability of the failure of a bridge structure is less than an acceptable level. It directly takes into consideration the statistical mean value of resistance, the statistical mean value of loads, the nominal value of the loads, the nominal value of resistance, and the variation of the resistance and loads. There are several levels of probabilistic design. The level-III probabilistic design is the fully probabilistic method, which is the most complex and requires the probability distribution of each random variable, such as resistance and load, and correlation between these variables. Because this information is seldom available, it is very difficult to implement the fully probabilistic design in practice. Level II probabilistic methods assume that the load and resistance are statistically independent with each other and use simpler statistical characteristics of the load and resistance variables. The load and resistance factors employed in the AASHTO LRFD Bridge Specifications were determined by level II procedures and other simpler methods when information was insufficient to use the level II methods. However, in Eurocodes, the partial factors in the limit state design equations are calibrated primarily to previous experience, Level II and Lever-III probabilistic approach have not been employed for the calibration.

3.4.2 Probabilistic foundation of LRFD specifications

The probability-based LRFD Specifications are centered around the load effects S and the resistances R which are treated as statistically independent random variables. Figure 3.2 illustrate the probability density functions of S and R as separate curves. The mean value of the load effects (S) and the mean value of the resistance (R) are denoted by $\overline{S}$ and $\overline{R}$, respectively. S_n and R_n are the nominal values of the load effect and the resistance, respectively.

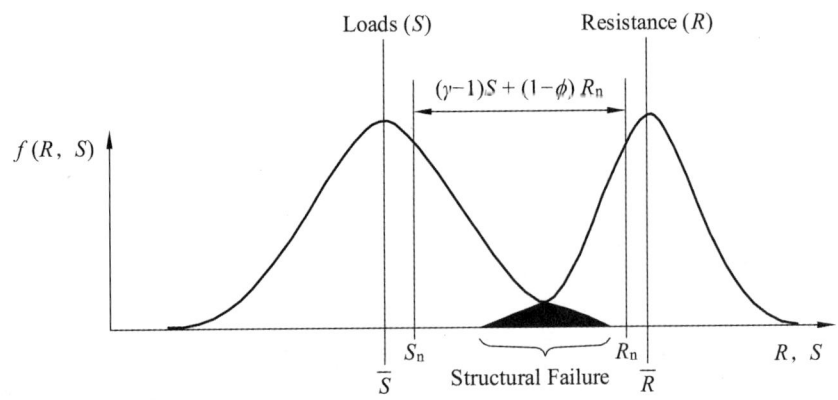

Figure 3.2 Probability density functions of load Effect *S* and resistance *R*.

As long as the resistance R is greater than the load effects S, a margin of safety for a specific limit state exists. However, since S and R are random variables, there exists a small probability that R may be less than S. In Figure 3.2, the overlap shadow area shows the probability of $R < Q$. For both the load effect and the resistance, the value somewhat offset from the mean value is the "nominal" value which is used by designers The objective of the probability-based design philosophy is to separate the distribution of resistance from the distribution of load effect, such that the area of overlap, i.e., the area where load effect is greater than resistance, is acceptably small.

A quantitative measure of safety is the probability of survival of a structure given by:

$$P_s = P(R > S) \tag{3.8}$$

where, $P(R > S)$ represents the probability that R is greater than S. The complement of the probability of survival is the probability of failure, which can be expressed as:

$$P_f = 1 - P_s = P(R < S) \tag{3.9}$$

The shaded area in Figure 3.2 indicates the region of failure, but the area is not equal to the probability of failure because it is a mixture of areas coming from distributions with different ratios of standard deviation to mean value. For quantitative evaluation of probability of failure, it is convenient to use the probability of the margin of safety, i.e., $P(M) = P(R - S)$ to represents the probability of failure. With its own unique statistics, the safety index can be determined in a straightforward manner. If resistance R and load S are both normally distributed random variables, and are statistically independent, the mean value of M is given by

$$\bar{M} = \bar{R} - \bar{S} \tag{3.10}$$

and its standard deviation is

$$\sigma_M = \sqrt{\sigma_R^2 + \sigma_S^2} \tag{3.11}$$

where, $\bar{R}$ and $\bar{S}$ are mean values and σ_R and σ_S are standard deviations of R and S.

Probability of "failure" or "achievement of a limit state" can be examined by comparing R and S as shown in Figure 3.3. Potential structural failure is represented by region to the left of "$R - S = 0$" line. The distance between the "$R\text{-}S=0$" line and the mean value of the function of $R\text{-}S$ is defined as $\beta\sigma_M$, where σ_M is the standard deviation of the function of $R - S$ and β is called the "reliability index" or "safety index". The larger β is, the greater the margin of safety.

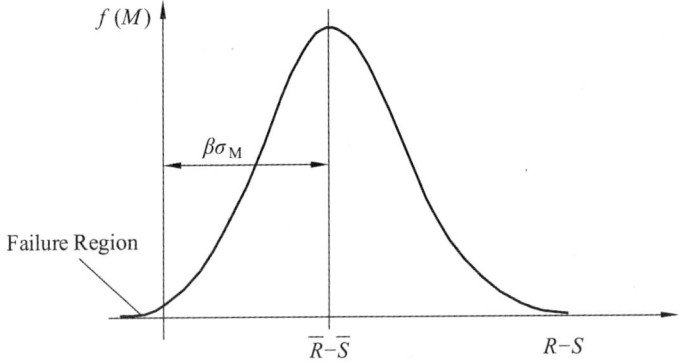

Figure 3.3 Definition of reliability index.

The probability of $R < S$ depends on the distribution shapes of each of many design variables, such as material, loads, dimensions of structural members. Usually, the mean values and the standard deviations or the coefficients of variation of many variables involved in R and S can be estimated. By applying the simple advanced first-order second-moment method and assuming that both the resistance and load effect are normal random variables, the reliability index β can be obtained as:

$$\beta = \frac{\overline{R} - \overline{S}}{\sqrt{\sigma_R^2 + \sigma_S^2}} \tag{3.12}$$

Considering variations of both the load effect and the resistance, the generic design equation can be written as:

$$\phi R_n = \sum \gamma_i S_{n,i} \tag{3.13}$$

where, $S_{n,i}$ is the ith nominal load component and γ_i is the corresponding load factor; R_n is the nominal resistance. Let's define λ as the ratio of the mean value of R to the nominal value R_n, i.e.,

$$\lambda = \frac{\overline{R}}{R_n} \tag{3.14}$$

where, λ is also called "bias". Then Eq.(3.13) can be rewritten as

$$\lambda R_n = \frac{1}{\phi}\sum \gamma_i S_i \tag{3.15}$$

From Eq. (3.13) and Eq. (3.15), one can arrive at

$$\phi = \frac{\lambda \sum \gamma_i S_i}{\overline{Q}+\beta\sqrt{\sigma_R^2+\sigma_S^2}} \tag{3.16}$$

in which, the resistance factor ϕ can be obtained if the reliability index β and the load factors γ_i are known.

The reliability index gives an indication of the consistency of safety for a bridge designed by traditional methods. It can be used to establish new methods which will have consistent margins of safety. One group of bridges having a reliability index which is greater than a second group of bridges has more inherent safety. Thus existing bridges designed by traditional ASD or LFD methods can be used to obtain the target, or code specified reliability index and the load and resistance factors in the LRFD Specifications.

3.4.3 Calibration of load and resistance factors

A target value of the reliability index β, usually denoted by β_T, is chosen by a code-writing body. Eq.(3.16) still indicates that both the load and resistance factors must be found. One way to solve this problem is to select the load factors and then calculate the resistance factors. This process has been used by several code-writing authorities. The basic steps of calibration of the load and resistance factors for the LRFD Specifications include:

(i) Select sample bridges from current bridge inventory.

(ii) Compile the statistical database for load and resistance parameters. The statistical data for loads are obtained by truck survey and weigh-in-motion measurement; statistical data for resistance are obtained by material tests, component tests, and field measurements.

(iii) Examine the variability of loads and materials by calculating the coefficients of variation and estimate the reliability indices inherent in current design methods.

(iv) Select a target reliability index based on the margin of safety implied in current designs.

(v) Calculate load and resistance factors consistent with the selected target reliability index.

In the Unite State of America, about 200 representative bridges (Nowak, 1993) were selected from various regions of the country. The selection was based on structural-type, material, and geographic location to represent a full-range of materials and design loads and practices all over the country. Statistically- projected live load and the notional values of live load effects were calculated. Resistance was calculated in terms of the moment and the shear capacity for each structure according to the the AASHTO Standard Specifications (AASHTO, 1989) for load factor design. Based on the relative amounts of the loads identified for each of the combinations of span and spacing and type of construction in the database, a simulated set of 175 bridges was developed. The simulated group was comprised of non-composite steel girder bridges, composite steel girder bridges, reinforced concrete T-beam bridges, and prestressed concrete I-beam bridges.

The reliability indices were calculated for each simulated and each actual bridge for both the shear and the moment. The range of reliability indices which resulted from this calibration process is presented in Figure 3.4. It can be seen that a wide-range of values were obtained using the Standard

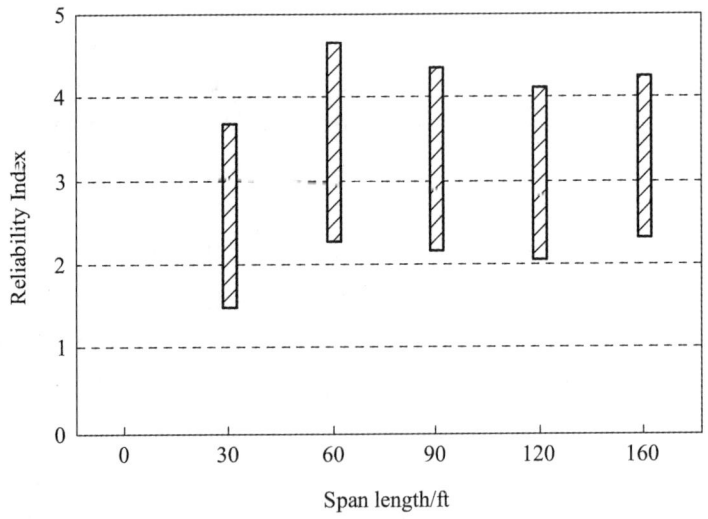

Figure 3.4 Reliability Indices Inherent in the 1989 AASHTO Standard Specifications.

Specifications. These calculated reliability indices, as well as past calibration of other specifications, served as a basis for the selection of the target reliability index, β_T. A target reliability index $\beta_T = 3.5$ is representative of past LFD practice. Hence, this value was selected as a target for the calibration of the LRFD Specifications.

The proposed values of load factors are simplified to be practical for bridge design. One factor is specified for weight of both shop-built and field-built components: $\gamma = 1.25$. For weight of asphalt and utilities, a higher value $\gamma = 1.50$ is used. For live load, a conservative value of $\gamma = 1.75$ is utilized in the LRFD Specifications. The resistance factors are then calculated by Eq.(3.16) using the load components for each of the 175 simulated bridges. The acceptance criterion for the selection of resistance factors is how close the calculated reliability indices are to the target value of the reliability index, β_T. Consequently, the proposed resistance factors are as follows: $\phi = 0.95$ for steel girders (moment and shear); $\phi = 1.00$ for prestressed- concrete girders (moment); $\phi = 0.90$ for reinforced-concrete T-beams (moment); and $\phi = 0.85$ for reinforced and prestressed concrete (shear). For all nonstrength limit states, $\phi = 1.0$.

3.4.4 Limit states

LRFD limit states are generally classified into four major categories – service, fatigue and fracture, strength, and extreme event. Each limit state contains several load combinations of different load types with different load factors, based on the intended loading condition and the probability of simultaneous occurrence of loadings, to analyze a structure for certain responses, such as deflections, permanent deformations, ultimate capacity, and inelastic responses without failure.

(1) Service Limit State: Refers to restrictions on stresses, deflections, and crack widths of bridge components that occur under regular service conditions. These provisions are intended to ensure the bridge functions normally acceptably during its design life. For the service limit state, the resistance factors $\phi = 1.0$, and nearly all of the load factors $\gamma_i's$ are equal to 1.0.

(2) Fatigue and Fracture Limit State: Refers to a set of restrictions on stress range under specified truck loading reflecting the number of expected

stress range excursions. They are intended to limit crack growth under repetitive loads and to prevent fracture due to cumulative stress effects in steel elements, components, and connections. For the fatigue and fracture limit state, $\phi = 1.0$.

(3) Strength Limit State: Refer to providing sufficient strength and stability, both local and global, are provided to resist the statistically-significant load combinations during the life of a bridge. The overall structural integrity is expected to be maintained. The statistically determined resistance factor ϕ will usually be less than 1.0 and will have different values for different materials and strength limit states.

(4) Extreme Event Limit State: Ensures the structural survival of a bridge during a major earthquake, collision by a vessel, vehicle or ice flow, possibly under scoured conditions. The probability of these events occurring simultaneously is extremely low; therefore, they are specified to be applied separately. The recurrence interval of extreme events may be significantly greater than the design life of the bridge. Under these extreme conditions, the structure is expected to undergo considerable inelastic deformation. For the extreme event limit state, $\phi = 1.0$.

It should be noted that not all these limit states need to be checked for all structures. The bridge designers should determine the applicable limit states for a specific bridge. When all applicable limit states and combinations are satisfied, the bridge design is acceptable under the LRFD design philosophy.

References

[3.1] Kulicki J. M., "Design Philosophies for Highway Bridges," in Chen, W.-F. and Duan, L., eds., *Bridge Engineering Handbook-Superstructure Design*, CRC Press, Boca Raton, FL, 2000.

[3.2] Duan L., "Chapter 1 Bridge Design Specifications," in *Bridge Design Practice (BDP)*, 4th edition, State of California Department of Transportation, 2015.

[3.3] Barker R. M. and Puckett J. A., *Design of Highway Bridges: An LRFD Approach*, 3rd ed., John Wiley & Sons, Hoboken, New Jersey, 2013.

[3.4] Grubb M. A., Wilson, K. E., White, C. D., William N. Nickas, W. N., *Load and Resistance Factor Design (LRFD) For Highway Bridge*

[ ] *Superstructures - Reference Manual*, FHWA-NHI-15-047, Federal Highway Administration, National Highway Institute (HNHI-10), Arlington, VA, 2015.

[3.5] Borges J. F., "Probability Based Structural Codes: Past And Future," in C. Guedes Soares (ed.), *Probabilistic Methods for Structural Design*, Kluwer Academic Publishers, 1997.

[3.6] Mohaghegh M., "Evolution of Structures Design Philosophy and Criteria," *Journal of Aircraft*, Vol. 42, No. 4, July–August 2005.

[3.7] Salgado R., San Inn Woo, S. I., Kim, D., *Development of Load and Resistance Factor Design for Ultimate and Serviceability Limit States of Transportation Structure Foundations*, Joint Transportation Research Program, Purdue University, West Lafayette, IN, 2011.

[3.8] AASHTO, LRFD Bridge Design Specifications, 5th ed., American Association for State Highway and Transportation Officials, Washington, DC., 2014.

Chapter 4 Concrete Girder Bridge Deck and Load Distributions

4.1 Introduction

The bridge deck is the surface of a bridge. The principal function of the bridge deck is to support the vehicle loads from highway or railway traffic, or the load from pedestrians, and to transmit these loads to the primary superstructure of the bridge. Thus, the bridge deck must be continuous along a bridge span and across multiple spans. A bridge deck can be constructed of concrete or steel or composite materials. Only the deck built from reinforced concrete is discussed in this chapter, and the steel deck will be discussed in Chapter 9.

A concrete deck is usually an integral part of the bridge superstructure. It may consist of the top flange of the T-girder and the asphalt concrete pavement over it. For the slab-and-girder bridges, the deck is supported by concrete or steel I-girders. For railway bridges, the deck is covered with railroad bed and tracks.

In this chapter, configurations of the concrete girder bridge deck are introduced and design calculation for concrete deck slab and the transverse load distribution are discussed. All design specifications referenced in this chapter are those for Chinese railway or highway bridges.

4.2 Configurations of bridge deck

4.2.1 Railway bridges

A typical railway reinforced concrete girder bridge is shown in Figure 4.1. A conventional reinforced concrete girder bridge on a single-track railway comprises two girders for supporting the live loads which are transferred from the two rails. The common cross-sections are slab-shape, π-shape, and T-shape, as shown in Figure 4.2(a) ~ (c), respectively.

Figure 4.1 A typical railway reinforced concrete girder bridge.

The slab bridge is the simplest form of reinforced concrete bridge deck [Figure 4.2(a)]. It is suitable for the railway bridges whose span lengths are less than or equal to 6 m, and is the most economic type for short span bridges. When the span length is in the range of 6 to 16 m, thicker slabs are needed. As a result, the slab becomes substantially heavy and the structure becomes uneconomical. In this case, a reinforced concrete deck slab supported over a reinforced concrete girder is in order, resulting in a cast-in-place π-girder [Figure 4.2(b)] or T-girder bridge [Figure 4.2(c)]. Since each π-girder in a bridge needs four bearings which are difficult to lie in the same plane, and also casting of π-girders needs much formwork, the π-girders had not been used any more since 1980's. Instead, the T-girder bridge becomes the standard form of

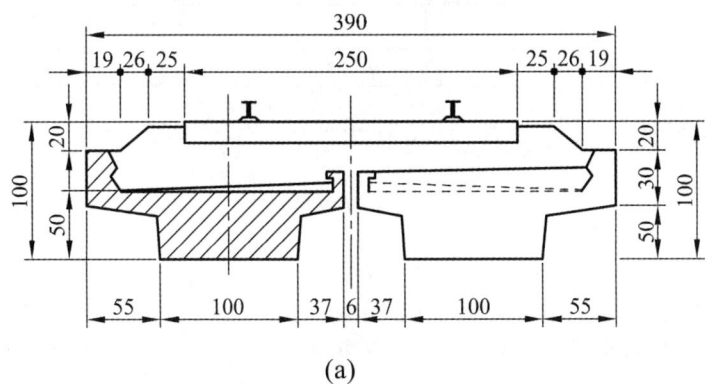

(a)

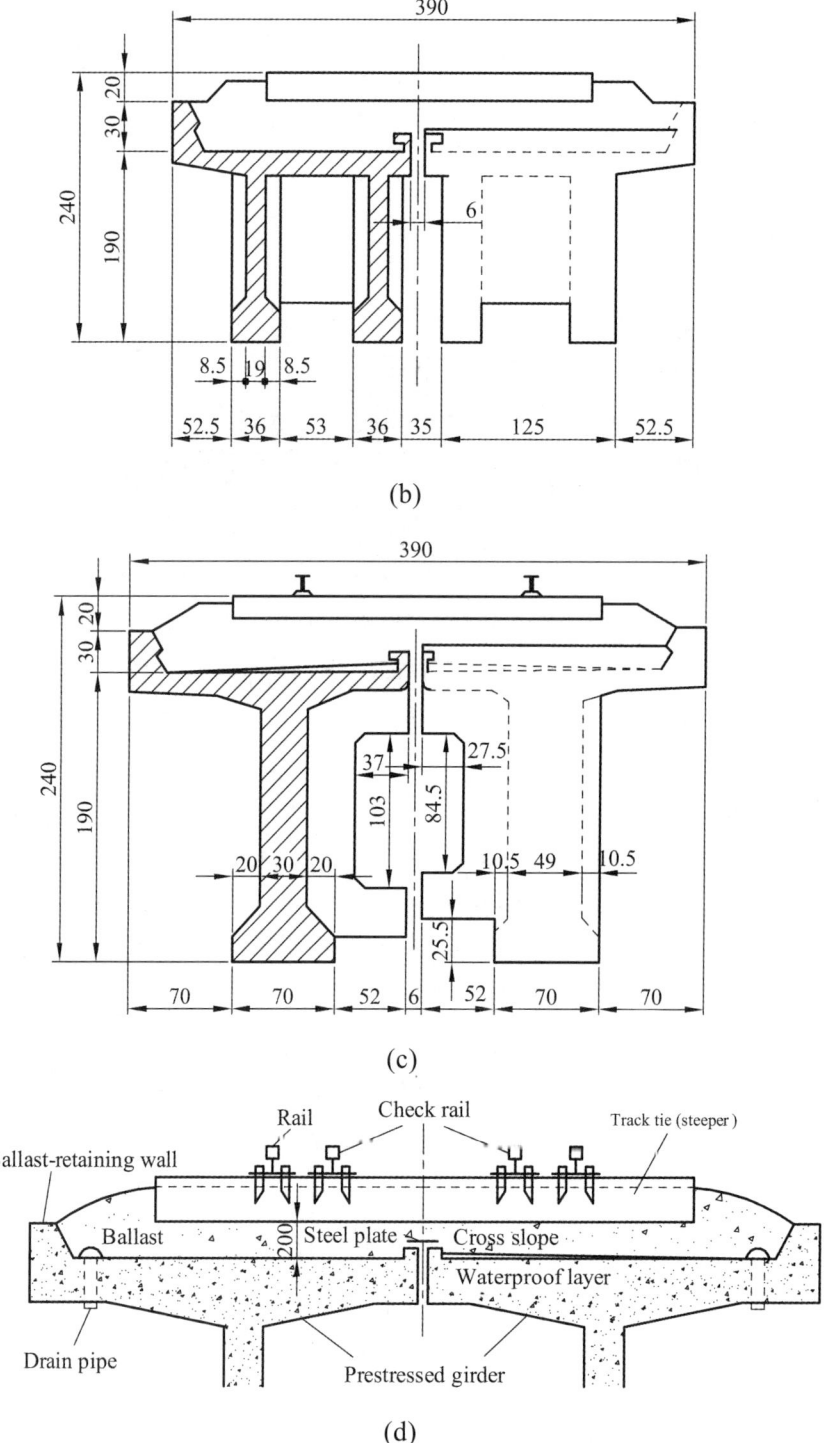

Figure 4.2 Common cross-sections of railway reinforced concrete girder bridges (units in cm): (a) slab-shape; (b) Π-shape; (c) T-shape; (d) details of the bridge deck.

the railway reinforced concrete girder bridges for span longer than 6 m. To improve the transverse load distribution properties and maintain the lateral stability of the two T-girders, several diaphragms are provided within the span and in the two ends of the girders.

4.2.2 Highway bridges

A typical highway reinforced concrete girder bridge is illustrated in Figure 4.3. Unlike a railway bridge, which typically consists of two girders, a highway girder bridge usually consists of more than two girders, most often four or five girders, to support the deck slab. This is because the width of the roadway of a highway bridge is generally wider than that of a railway bridge. As a result, the transverse beams or diaphragms are provided to connect the girders to increase the transverse stiffness and to help distribute live loads in the transverse direction.

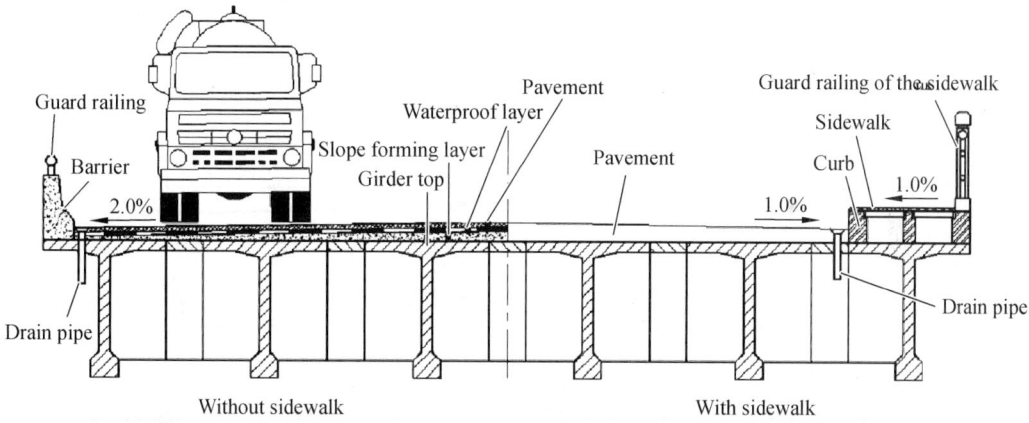

Figure 4.3 Overview of a typical highway reinforced concrete girder bridge.

The girder can be cast-in-place or precast, depending on many factors, such as span length, construction cost and speed required by the owner. The usual cross-sections for the highway reinforced concrete girder bridges are solid-slab, voided-slab, I-shape, T-shape, and box-shape, as shown in Figure 4.4 ~ Figure 4.6.

Highway slab bridges have the simplest superstructure configuration and the neatest appearance (Figure 4.4). They normally require more concrete and reinforcing steel than girder bridges of the same span, but the formwork is simpler and less expensive; hence, they are the most economical for the span lengths less or equal to 9 m. The T-girder bridges are used for the spans between 7 m and 20 m long (Figure 4.5), since the slab bridges in this span range are not economical and efficient. When the span length is larger than 20 m, the box-girder becomes a competitive choice. The box girder, which can be viewed as a voided slab girder for small spans, is usually economical for spans in excess of 16 m. A box-shape cross-section can also be seen as a strengthened T-shape cross-section in which the webs of a T-shape cross-section are all connected by a common bottom flange, resulting in a cellular superstructure (Figure 4.6). Depending on the number of interior webs, box girders can be single-cell or multi-cell structures. Compared with the T-girders, the box-girders have excellent transverse stiffness and torsional resistance. But box girders are often made of prestressed concrete to increase the cracking resistance and the longitudinal stiffness of the girder. This will be discussed in the following chapter.

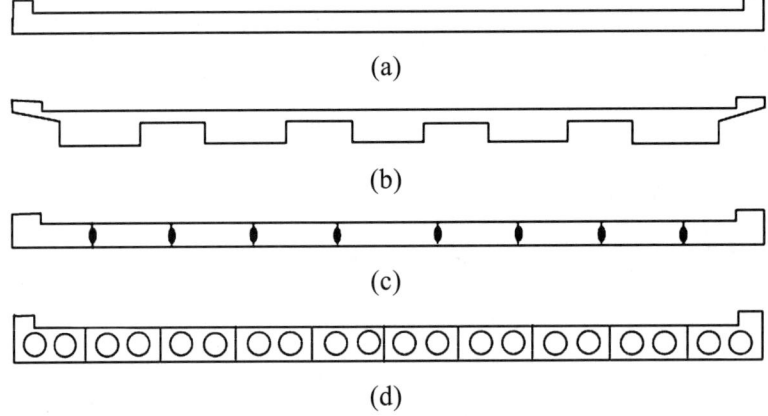

Figure 4.4 Slab cross-sections of highway reinforced concrete girder bridge: (a) solid slab; (b) low-stem slab; (c) precast solid slab; (d) voided slab.

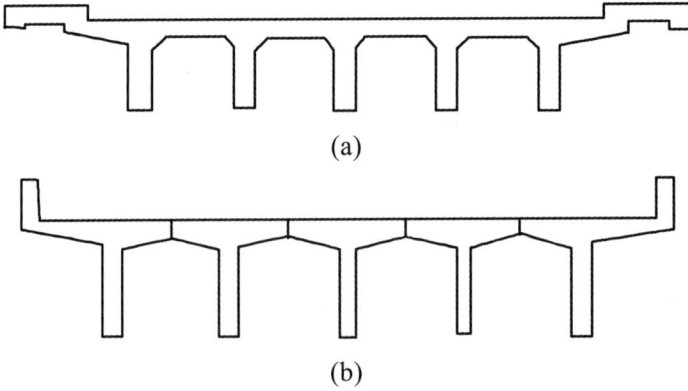

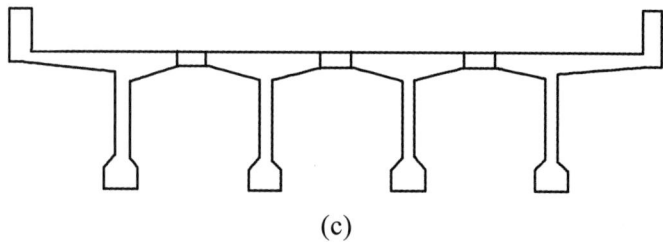

(c)

Figure 4.5 T-shape cross-sections of highway reinforced concrete girder bridge: (a) monolithic T-girder; (b) fabricated T-girder; (c) fabricated T-girder with bottom flanges.

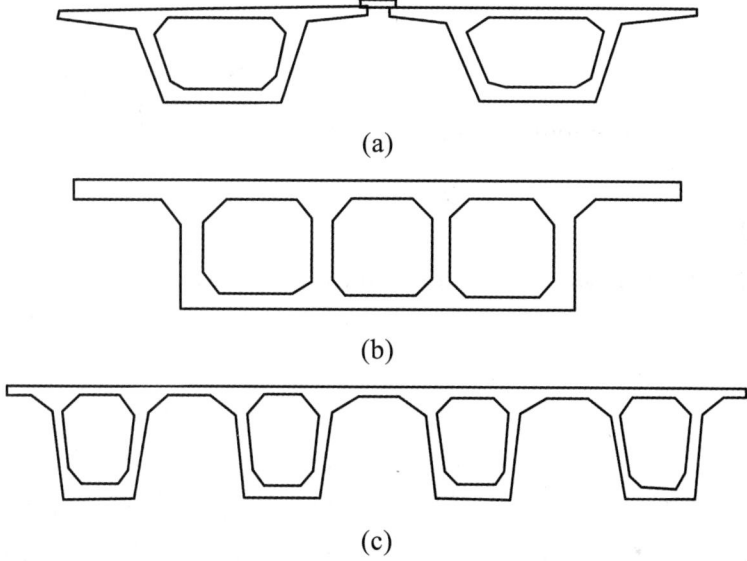

Figure 4.6 Box-shape cross-sections of highway reinforced concrete girder bridge: (a) separated box section; (b) multi-cell box section; (c) multi-box section.

4.3 Design calculation of deck slabs

4.3.1 The load dispersion patterns

For highway bridges, the wheel loads are not truly concentrated loads, instead they are distributed over the tire contact areas. In the design of the deck slab, the distributed wheel load is assumed to be transferred from the contact area to the top surface of the deck slab following the 45° line of load dispersion (Figure 4.7). Thus, the dispersed area of the wheel loads on the top surface of the deck slab is $a_2 \times b_2$, which are calculated from the contact area $a_1 \times b_1$ as

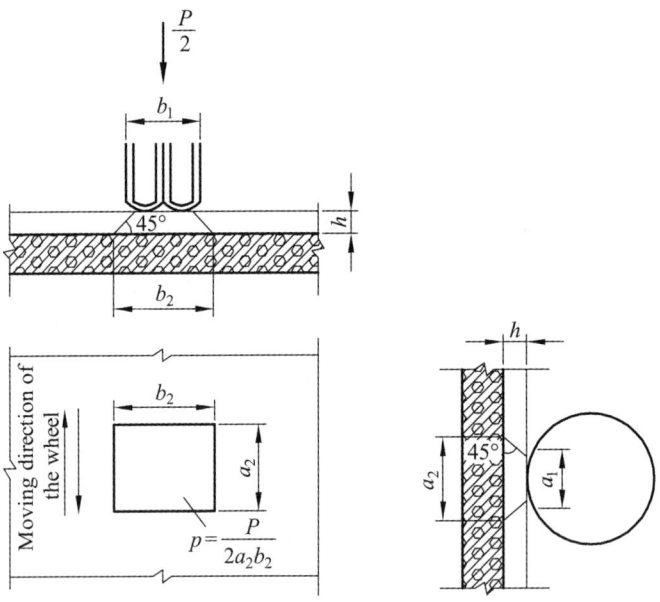

Figure 4.7 The wheel load dispersion pattern for highway bridge deck.

$$a_2 = a_1 + 2h \tag{4.1a}$$

$$b_2 = b_1 + 2h \tag{4.1b}$$

where, a_1 and b_1 are the dimensions of the load distribution area on the deck slab in the driving direction and the transverse direction, respectively. If there is one wheel acting on the deck with the wheel load of $P/2$, in which P is the axle load, the load intensity p in the loading area is

$$q = \frac{P}{2a_2 b_2} \tag{4.2}$$

For railway bridges, the wheel load is transferred from the rail to the tie and then to the deck slab through ballast. Load distribution is dependent on the tie and axle spacing, track modulus, and flexural strength of the rails. The dispersion of the wheel load from the bottom of the tie in the transverse direction is assumed to follow the 45° dispersion line. In the longitudinal direction, the load distribution length on the deck slab is assumed to be 1.2 m (Figure 4.8).

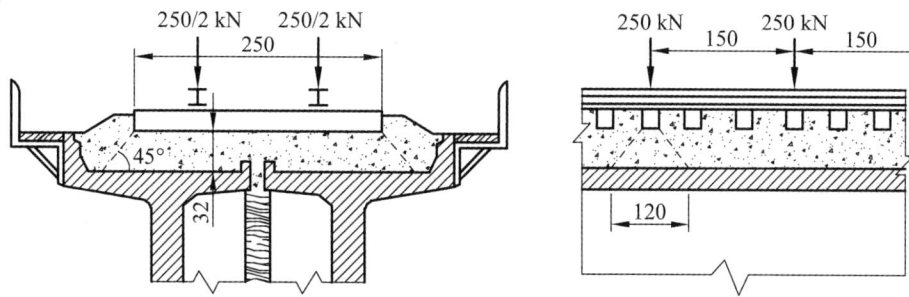

Figure 4.8 The wheel load dispersion pattern for railway bridge deck.

4.3.2 Effective working width of the deck slab

For concrete slab-and-girder bridges, the deck slab is connected with and supported on the girders and diaphragms. Strictly speaking, the structural behavior of the deck slab is two-dimensional and the thin plate theory can be used to obtain the internal forces in the slab. However, analytical solutions for bridge deck slabs under the action of applied load are only available for a limited number of cases, and generally are impractical for use in design. According to the solutions from the elastic plate theory, for a rectangular plate that is simply supported on its four sides, if the ratio $l_a/l_b \geqslant 2$, where l_a and l_b are the lengths of long side and the short side of a rectangular plate, respectively, then most of the transverse load acting on the plate will be transferred along the short side. This type of slab is called one-way slab. Most of deck slabs in slab-and-girder bridges are one-way slabs, and the deck slab behaves like transverse bending element supported over several stringers (Figure 4.10). Therefore, the deck slab is subjected to positive moment in its middle portion between the stringers and to negative moment in the portion near the stringers (Figure 4.11).

Design of one-way slabs is based on the bending moment and shear forces in a unit width slab supported on adjacent stringers. It is noted that the deflection at a point on the deck slab reduces with distance of the point from the loading area (Figure 4.12). To determine the maximum bending moment for which the slab is designed, an effective working width is introduced by

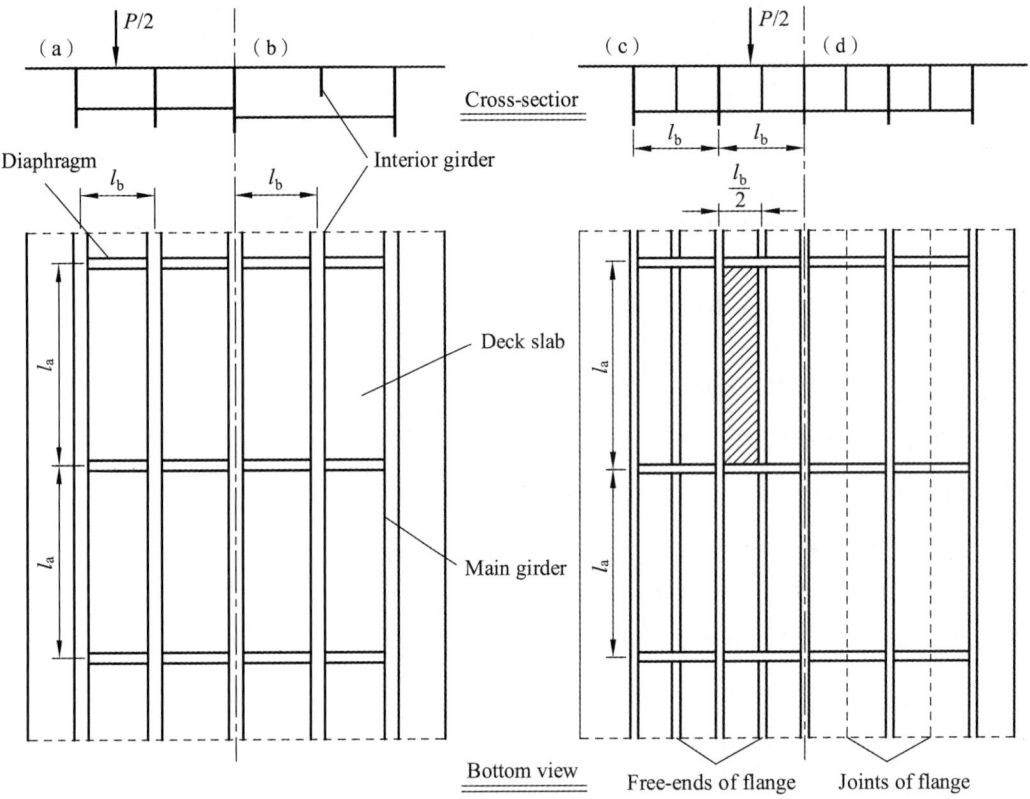

Figure 4.9 Supports of the deck slab on the stringers: (a) simply supported on four sides; (b) simply supported on four sides; (c) simply supported on three sides with one side free; (d) supported on three sides with one sides pin-jointed.

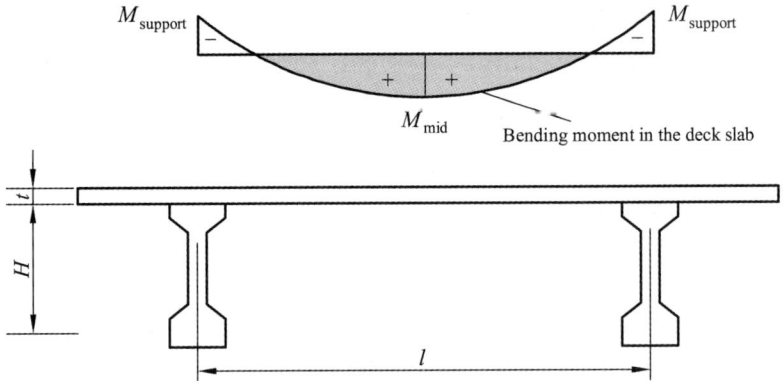

Figure 4.10 The bending moment distribution in the deck slab.

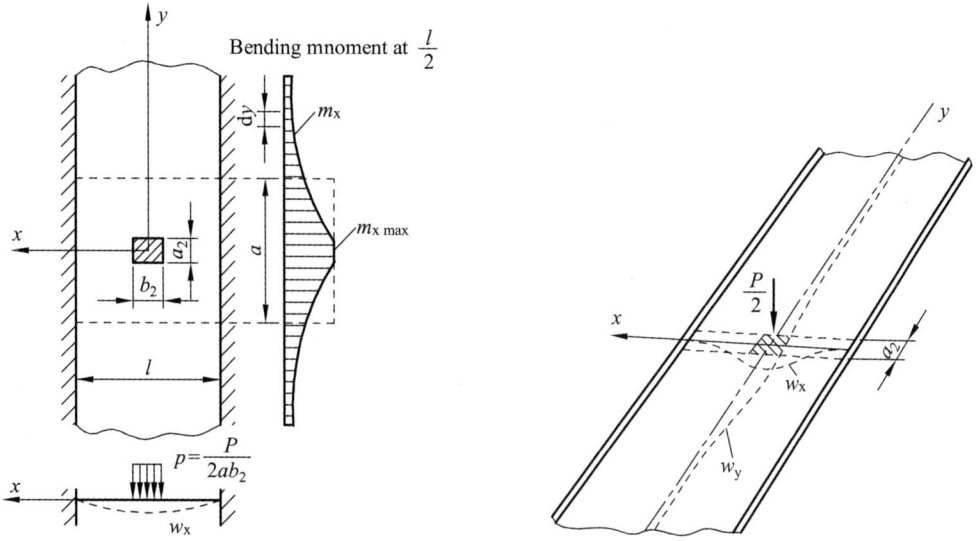

Figure 4.11 The equivalent working width of the deck slab.

$$a \times m_{x,\max} = \int m_x dy \tag{4.3}$$

$$a = \frac{\int m_x dy}{m_{x,\max}} \tag{4.4}$$

where, a represents the effective working width of the slab, $\int m_x dy$ represents the total bending moment at the mid-span of the slab due to the wheel load, $m_{x,\max}$ is the maximum bending moment at the mid-span.

The China's highway bridge design code JTG 3362 specifies the effective working width for the one-way deck slab under different support conditions as follows:

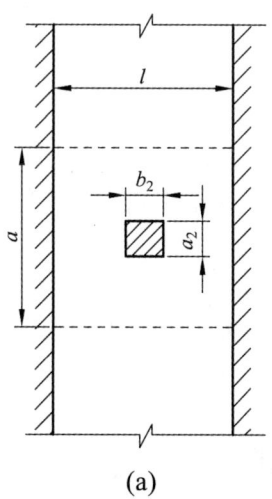

(a)

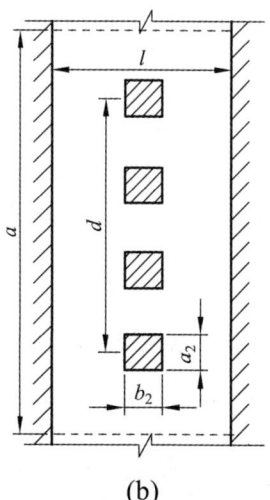

(b)

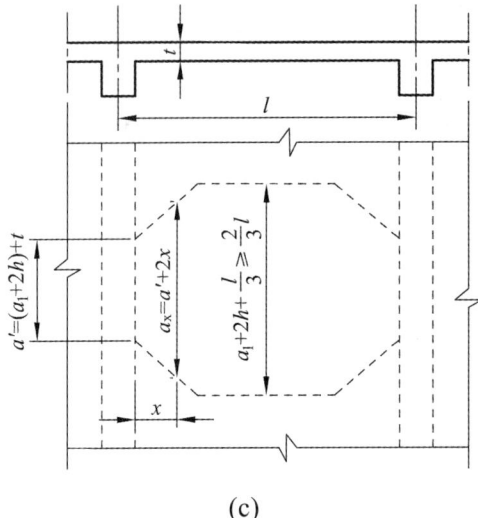

(c)

Figure 4.12 The equivalent working width of the deck slab when the wheel load is at different positions on the slab: (a) one wheel load at midspan; (b) multiple wheel loads at midspan; (c) equivalent working width of the slab for wheel loads at different positions along the slab span length.

1. For the one-way slab supported at adjacent stringers

For one wheel load acting on the midspan of the slab [Figure 4.12(a)].

$$a = a_1 + 2h + \frac{l}{3} \geqslant \frac{2l}{3} \tag{4.5}$$

where, l is the span length of the slab, which can be the center-to-center spacing of the adjacent girders.

(2) For multiple wheel loads acting on the midspan of the slab [Figure 4.12(b)].

$$a = a_1 + 2h + d + \frac{l}{3} \geqslant \frac{2l}{3} + d \tag{4.6}$$

where, d is the distance between the two outmost wheels.

(3) For one wheel load acting at the supports of the slab.

$$a = a_1 + 2h + t \tag{4.7}$$

(4) For one wheel load acting near the supports of the slab

$$a = a_1 + 2h + t + x \tag{4.8}$$

where, x is the distance of the wheel load away from the edge of the support.

The change of the effective working width of the slab when the wheel load is located at different locations between the support and the midspan of the slab is illustrated in Figure 4.12(c).

2. For the one-way cantilever slab

For overhanging deck slabs, the effective working width of the slab is approximately two times the cantilevering length (Figure 4.13). If the wheel load is located between the fixed end and the free side of the deck slab, the effective working width is

$$a = a_1 + 2h + 2c \tag{4.9}$$

where, c is the distance of the outer edge of the wheel from the fixed end of the slab.

If the wheel is near the near the free side of the slab, the distance c turns out to be span length of the slab, and the effective working width becomes

$$a = a_1 + 2h + 2l_0 \tag{4.10}$$

where, l_0 is the overhanging length of the slab.

Note that Eq. (4.9) and Eq. (4.10) only apply to the cases in which $c \geqslant 2.5$ m. If $c > 2.5$ m the bending moment calculated at the fixed end of the cantilevering slab based on the above equations need to be increased by 15% ~ 30%.

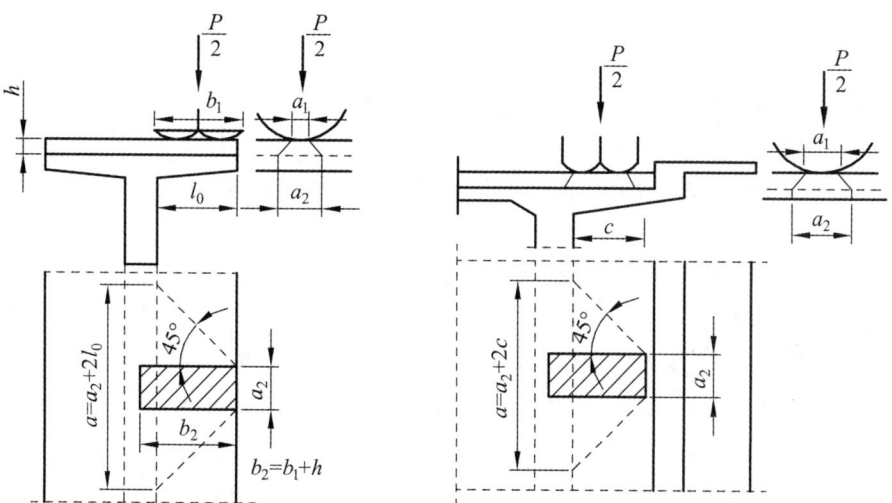

Figure 4.13 The effective working width of the overhanging deck slab.

For tracked vehicle loads, the contact area between the track and the deck is a long, narrow region. Thus it is common practice to assume that the distributed vehicle load will only be resisted by the part of the slab just below the loading area. In design, wherever the vehicle is located between the support and the midspan, a unit width slab strip along the direction of the track in the loading are is taken for analysis (Figure 4.14). The load acting on the strip is the actual distributed vehicle load. This method applies to the analysis of the deck slab of railway bridges subjected to the distributed load transferred from the track and ties through ballast.

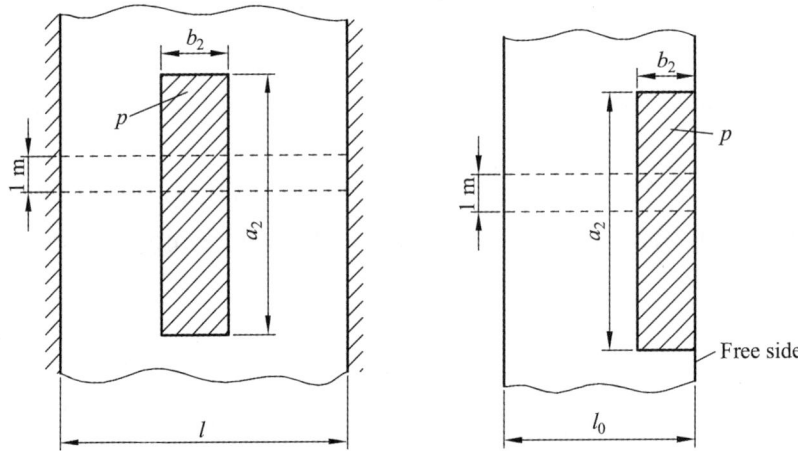

Figure 4.14 The effective working width of the deck slab loaded by tracked vehicles.

4.3.3 The internal forces in the deck slab

Once the effective working width of the deck slab is determined, the bending moments and shear forces in the deck slab can be calculated. Usually, a unit width slab is taken for calculating the internal forces.

<u>1. Continuously supported one-way slab</u>

For the one-way deck slab that continuously supported on the stringers, the torsional stiffness of the stringer affects the deformation of the deck slab and in turn the bending moment in it. The constraint on the deck slab put by the stringer depends on the way that the two parts are connected. Also, the support condition of the deck slab is affected by the torsional stiffness of the stringer (Figure 4.15). In practical design, the support of the deck slab can neither be treated as fixed nor hinged; instead it is treated as elastic. The bending moment in the continuously supported deck can be obtained by multiplying the bending moment in a simple beam of the same span length with a modification factor:

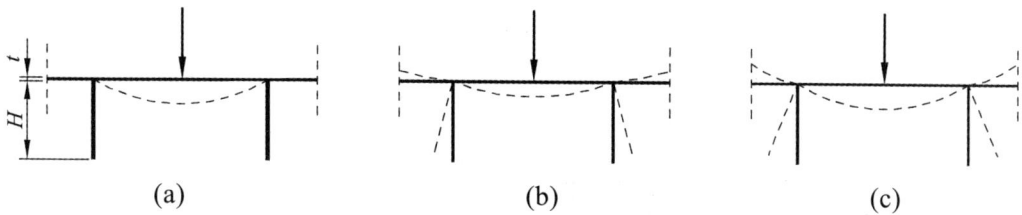

Figure 4.15 Influence of the torsional stiffness of the stringer on the support condition of the deck slab: (a) large torsional stiffness; (b) medium torsional stiffness; (c) small torsional stiffness.

(1) For $\dfrac{t}{H} < \dfrac{1}{4}$, which means the girder's torsional stiffness is large,

$$M_{mid} = 0.5 M_0 \tag{4.11a}$$

$$M_{support} = -0.7 M_0 \tag{4.11b}$$

where, t is the thickness of the deck slab; H is the depth of the stringer.

(2) For $\dfrac{t}{H} \geqslant \dfrac{1}{4}$, which means the girder's torsional stiffness is small,

$$M_{mid} = 0.7 M_0 \tag{4.12a}$$

$$M_{support} = -0.7 M_0 \tag{4.12b}$$

where, M_{mid} and $M_{support}$ are the bending moments at the midspan and the support of the deck slab, respectively (Figure 4.10); M_0 is the bending moment at the midspan of the deck slab with simply supported ends. Arrangement of the distributed wheel loadings on the unit width deck slab is shown in Figure 4.16.

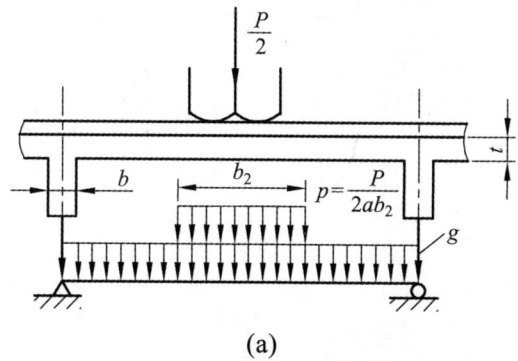

(a)

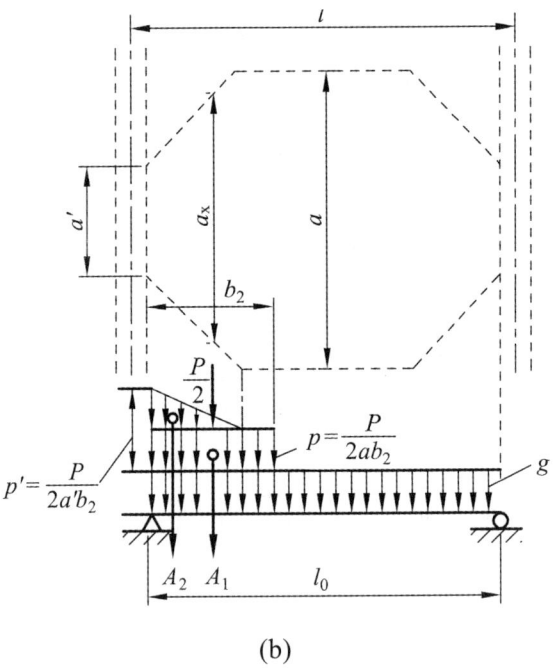

(b)

Figure 4.16 The loading pattern of the continuous deck slab for generating maximum bending moments and shear forces: (a) for maximum bending moments at the midspan; (b) for maximum shear forces at the supports.

2. Overhanging or hinged girder flange

For overhanging deck slab or the deck slab formed by hinged top flanges of T-girders, the maximum bending moment occurs at the fixed end of the slab. Usually, the wheel load is put at the free end of the cantilevering slab or cross the flange hinge to generate maximum bending moment at the fix end (Figure 4.17).

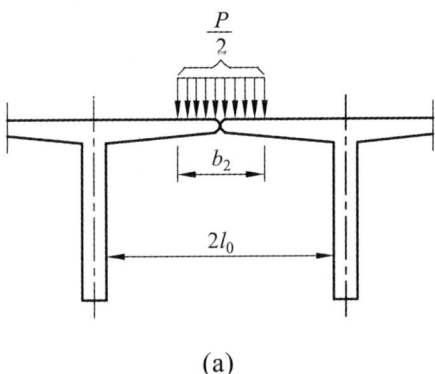

(a)

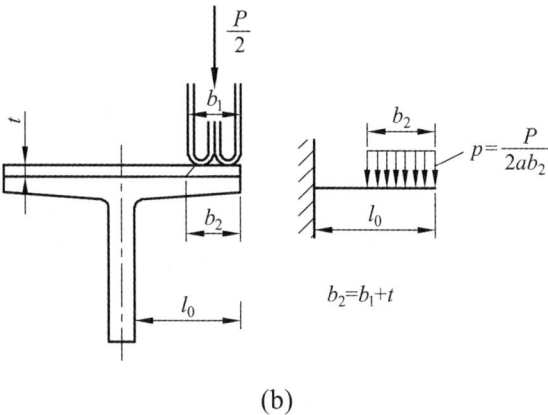

(b)

Figure 4.17 The loading patterns of the overhanging and the hinged girder flange for generating maximum bending moments: (a) hinged deck slab; (b) overhanging deck slab.

4.4 Transverse load distribution

A bridge is a three-dimensional structure comprising many components. In order to design these components, the forces and deformations in these individual components under the design loads have to be known. The purpose of structural analysis is to determine the internal forces within each member of the structure so as to proportion the size of the member and to check if the member can safely to carry the loads. Although many rigorous methods, such as finite strip method and finite element method are available to carry out accurate analysis of the load distribution, the substantial cost and time for building the model and conducting the analysis make those methods not realistic for design of short to medium span regular bridges. As a general practice, the influence lines are used to find the distribution of the maximum internal forces along the longitudinal direction of a bridge, and a factor- termed the load distribution factor is used to determine the distribution of the loadings in the transverse direction. This design practice is equivalent to analyzing bridge response by treating the longitudinal and transverse effects of loading as uncoupled phenomena.

The Eurocodes, EN 1992-1-1: 2004 and EN 1992-2: 2005 for design of concrete structures, do not give specific guidance on how to calculate live load distribution factors for multi-girder bridges. Other bridge codes, such as

AASHTO LRFD bridge design codes and Canadian highway bridge design code CAN/CSA S6, specify comprehensive methods for determining load distribution factors for various types of cross-sections. Like the Eurocodes, the Chinese design codes do not recommend the methods for calculating the live load distribution factors, however, several methods are widely used in the design of highway bridges. In this section, the principles of these methods are briefly introduced and discussed.

4.4.1 Definition of the load distribution factor

Consider a multi-girder bridge shown in Figure 4.18 and assume that a truck with two axle loads, P_1 and P_2, each including two wheel loads, acts on the roadway of the bridge deck. If the bending moments and shear forces in girder No.3 are to be analyzed, we can assume that the girder No.3 will carry the axle loads at the same positions, say A and B, in the longitudinal direction, as that the truck loads act on the roadway, but with different magnitude. The transverse load distribution factor $m_{i,j}$ is thus defined as

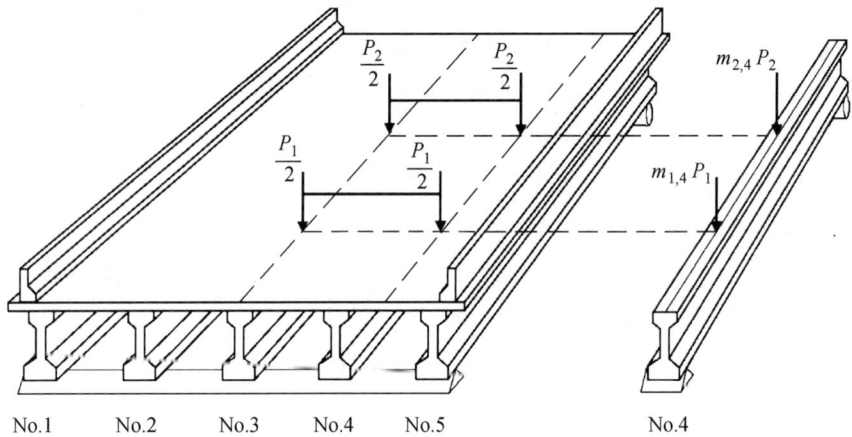

Figure 4.18 Definition of the transverse load distribution factor.

$$m_{i,j} = \frac{P_{i,j}}{P_i} \tag{4.13}$$

where, $m_{i,j}$ is the transverse load distribution factor of the axle load P_i at position i for the girder No. j of the beam; $P_{i,j}$ is the axle load carried by the girder No. j. Since the axle load P_i is carried by all the girders, the following relations hold

$$P_i = \sum_{j=1}^{n} P_{i,j} = \sum_{j=1}^{n} m_{i,j} P_i \qquad (4.14)$$

In which, n is the number of girders comprising the beam.

It should be pointed out that treatment of the loadings acting on individual girders as concentrated is only an approximate method for design convenience. As a matter of fact, the actions of the truck loads on the girders are not concentrated; instead they are distributive. However, the loads for design of a highway bridge involve lot of truck loads placed in the longitudinal and transverse directions, therefore the differences between the effects of concentrated and distributive loadings on individual girders are very small.

In practical design, the transverse load distribution factor m is the maximum fraction of an axle loading carried by a girder in the transverse direction. So, for calculating m, the wheel loads are placed at a critical position in the transverse direction to generate maximum action on the girder considered. For a multiple lane bridge, a number of wheel loads are placed across the deck width so that maximum load effect is generated on the girder concerned. Usually, the influence lines for transverse load distribution are used for this purpose.

The slab-girder bridges are the most common types of bridges. The major load carrying components of a slab-girder bridge include the deck slab, girders, and transverse beams or diaphragms. The girders and diaphragms in these bridges are usually made up of steel or concrete. The girders usually have cross-sections of T- or I-shape, such as shown in Figure 4.19, and the diaphragms usually have rectangular cross-sections. The deck slabs are generally made up of reinforce concrete or composite materials. The principal function of the slab is to provide the roadway surface and to transmit the applied loads to the girders. The diaphragms help the deck slabs distribute the live load in the transverse direction. If linear behavior is assumed, the load carried by each girder is related to its displacement. The load carried by each girder is a function of the relative stiffness of the components that comprise the slab-girder system. If the deck slab and the diaphragms have good stiffness, the girder near the location of the load application carries more load than those away from the applied load [Figure 4.21(a)]. If the slab are relatively flexible compared to the girders and no diaphragms are provided, the largest deflection occurs in the girder under the load and the deflections in other girders are relatively small [see Figure 4.21(b)]. If several diaphragms of large stiffness are constructed in the longitudinal direction, the load is distributed to the girders more evenly. If the diaphragm is rigid and the torsional stiffness of the slab-girder system is infinite, the load will be equally distributed to each girder [see Figure 4.21(c)].

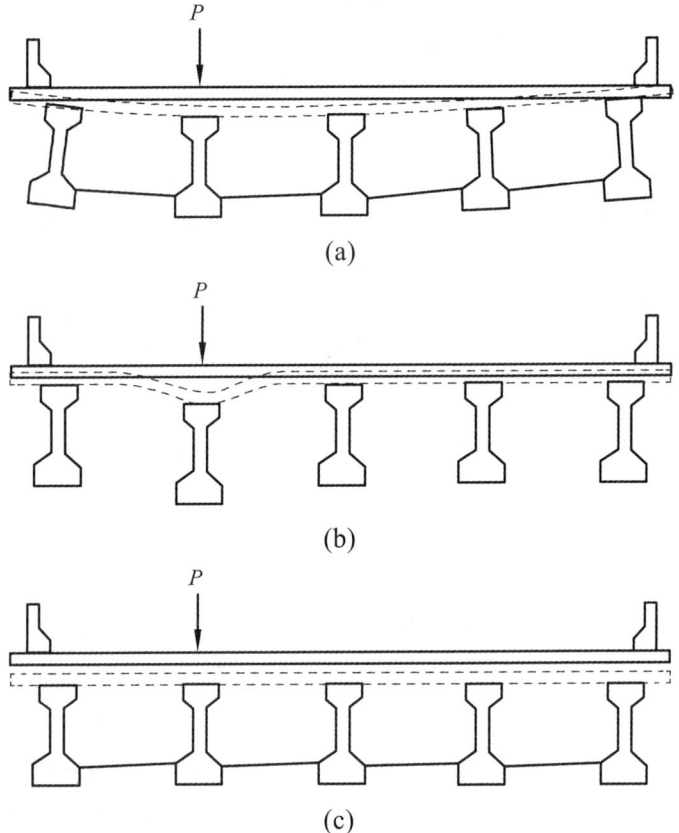

Figure 4.19 Transverse distribution of the wheel loads: (a) deflection of a cross-section with normal transverse stiffness; (b) deflection of a transversely flexible cross-section; (c) deflection of transversely stiff cross-section.

4.4.2 The lever rule method

The level rule method is a simple method to find the load distribution factors for a slab-girder bridge. In this method, it is assumed that the deck is simply supported by each girder and the effects of diaphragms and transverse connections are ignored. The load transferred to each girder can be determined by balancing the moments about the top-center of adjacent girders. This method is frequently used for the girder bridges having weak transverse stiffness.

Consider a slab-girder bridge with a cross-section shown in Figure 4.20. When an axle load P, consisting of two equal wheel loads $P/2$, is acting on the deck, the girder No.2 will be subjected to the reactions R_2 and R_2', which are calculated as

$$R_2 = \frac{Pa}{2(a+b)} \tag{4.15a}$$

$$R_2' = \frac{Pd}{2(c+d)} \tag{4.15b}$$

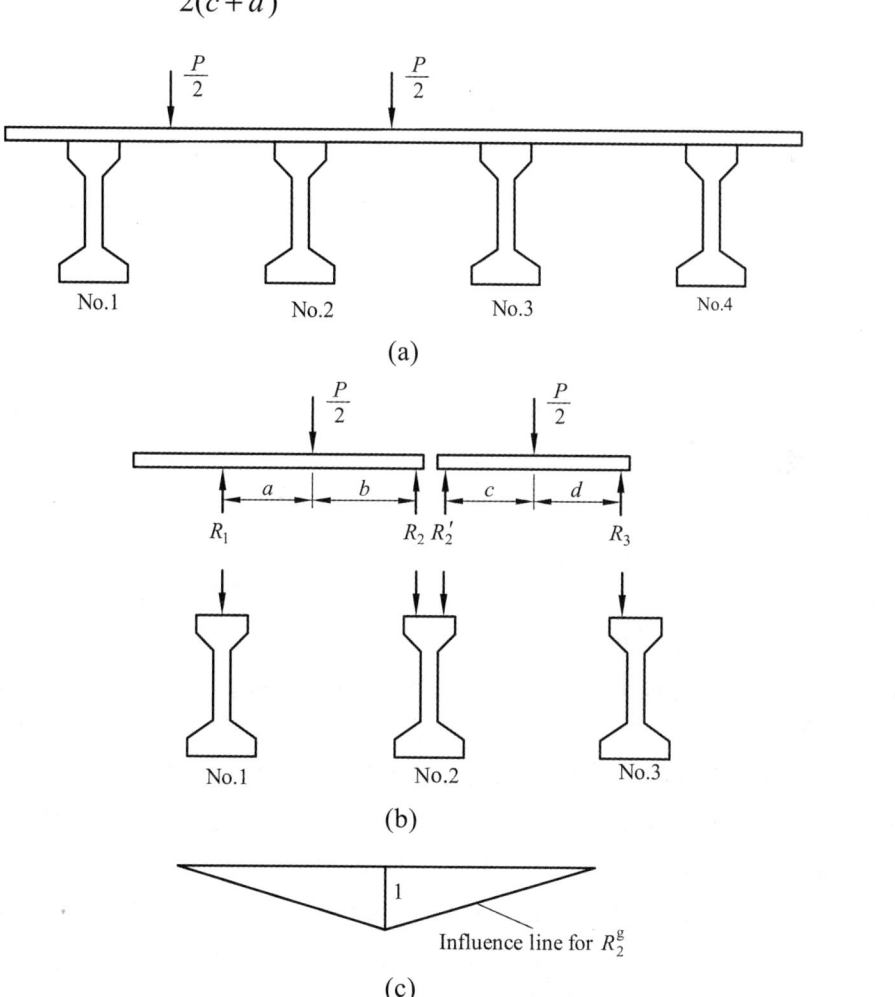

Figure 4.20 Transverse distribution of the wheel loads by the level rule: (a) the cross-section of a slab-girder beam; (b) transfer of the wheel loads by the level rule; (c) transverse load distribution influence line.

The total load R_2^g supported by the girder No.2 can be obtained as

$$R_2^g = R_2 + R_2' \qquad (4.16)$$

The load distribution factor for girder No.2 with this specific loading position can be calculated as

$$m = \frac{P}{R_2^g} = \frac{a}{2(a+b)} + \frac{d}{2(c+d)} \qquad (4.17)$$

To find the maximum load transferred to the girder, an influence line – termed transverse load distribution influence line — for the girder is necessary. Figure 4.21(c) shows the transverse load distribution influence line for R_2^g. The maximum load transferred to the girder No.2 can be obtained by placing the wheel loads at a critical position of the influence line. Note that when moving the wheel loads transversely, the spacing of the wheel loads for the same truck are fixed, but the spacing between different trucks can be varied, without exceeding the required minimum clear distance, to generate maximum load effect.

4.4.3 The eccentric compression method

Some reinforced and prestressed concrete bridges are provided with intermediate diaphragms to improve the distribution of the loads to the supporting girders. If the ratio of the bridge width to span length is less than 0.5, the deflection of the diaphragms is very small compared with that of the girder. The straight diaphragm remains straight while the bridge is deforming under the live loads [see Figure 4.23(a) ~ (c)]. This is to say that the behavior of the intermediate diaphragm is like that of a rigid beam. For this type of slab-girder bridges, the transverse distribution of the deflection of the girders is analogous to the deformation of an eccentrically compressed member [Figure 4.21(c)]. Since the girders are assumed to behavior elastically, the load thus distributed to each girder is proportional to its deflection. In the following, we develop the equations for calculating the transverse load distribution factor for a unit load acting at the mid span. It is assumed that the diaphragm has infinite stiffness and the girders are symmetrically arranged with respect to the centerline of the bridge.

First, let consider a unit load $P=1$ acting on the center of the cross-section [Figure 4.21(d)]. In this case, the deflections of the girders are the same due to the symmetry of the geometry of the cross-section. Thus, we have

$$\delta_1' = \delta_2' = \cdots = \delta_n' \tag{4.18}$$

If the load assigned to the girder i is assumed to be a concentrated load R_i', then the deflection δ_i' is related to R_i' by

$$R_i' = \alpha E I_i \delta_i' \tag{4.19}$$

where, α is a constant related to the span length and type of the supports, and I_i is the moment of inertia of the girder i. For simply-supported beam, $\alpha = 48/L^3$. The static equilibrium of the forces acting on the deck slab require that

$$\sum_{i=1}^{n} R_i' = 1 \tag{4.20}$$

Inserting Eq. (4.19) into Eq. (4.20) yields

$$\alpha E \delta_i' = \frac{1}{\sum_{i=1}^{n} I_i} \tag{4.21}$$

By substituting Eq. (4.21) into Eq. (4.19), we obtain

$$R_i' = \frac{I_i}{\sum_{i=1}^{n} I_i} \tag{4.22}$$

which means that the concentrated load carried by each girder is proportional to its moment of inertia. If $I_i = I_i = \cdots = I_n$, the load carried by each girder is the same, i.e.,

$$R_1' = R_2' = \cdots = R_2' = \frac{1}{n} \tag{4.23}$$

where n is the number of the girders.

Second, consider the deflection of the beam under the torque $M = 1 \cdot e$. Since the cross-section is symmetric, the deck-slab will rotate about the center O an angle θ. The deflection of each girder becomes

$$\delta_i'' = a_i \tan \theta \tag{4.24}$$

By Eq. (4.19), the reaction R_i'' can be expressed as

$$R_i'' = \alpha E I_i a_i \tan\theta = \lambda I_i a_i \quad (4.25)$$

where

$$\lambda = \alpha E \tan\theta \quad (4.26)$$

Since the torsional moment generated by the girder reactions R_i'' should balance the applied moment $M = 1 \cdot e$, there exists

$$\sum_{i=1}^{n} R_i'' a_i = \lambda \sum_{i=1}^{n} a_i^2 I_i = e \quad (4.27)$$

Thus, λ can be obtained as

$$\lambda = \frac{e}{\sum_{i=1}^{n} a_i^2 I_i} \quad (4.28)$$

Substituting Eq. (4.28) into Eq. (4.25) gives

$$R_i'' = \frac{e a_i I_i}{\sum_{i=1}^{n} a_i^2 I_i} \quad (4.29)$$

Note that when the girder and the unit load $P=1$ are located on the same side with respect to the center of the beam, R_i'' is positive, otherwise, R_i'' is negative.

The total reaction R_i generated by the eccentric load unit load is the sum of R_i' and R_i''. By summing Eq. (4.22) and Eq. (4.29), we obtain

$$R_i = \frac{I_i}{\sum_{i=1}^{n} I_i} + \frac{e a_i I_i}{\sum_{i=1}^{n} a_i^2 I_i} \quad (4.30)$$

To calculate the transverse load distribution factor for the girder i, a group of wheel loads should be placed at a critical position to generate the maximum load effect on the girder. An influence line for R_i needs to be constructed to find the critical position for wheel loads. Eq. (4.30) is actually the equation of the influence line for R_i in terms of e as a variable. Since Eq. (4.30) is a linear equation with respect to e, we can calculate the influence value at the position of each girder first and then connecting the obtained data points to generate the entire influence line. If the e is replaced with a_j, which represents the horizontal distance of the girder j away from the center of the beam O, Eq. (4.30) can be rewritten as

$$R_{ij} = \frac{I_i}{\sum_{i=1}^{n} I_i} + \frac{I_i a_i a_j}{\sum_{i=1}^{n} I_i a_i^2} \tag{4.31}$$

where R_{ij} represents the load transferred to girder i by the unit load acting at the position of girder j. Figure 4.21(f) shows the transverse load influence line for the 5-girder beam. Since the five girders have the same moment of inertia, i.e. $I_1 = I_2 = \cdots = I_5$, it is easy to obtain

$$R_{11} = \frac{1}{5} + \frac{a_1^2}{\sum_{i=1}^{5} a_i^2} \tag{4.32}$$

$$R_{15} = \frac{1}{5} - \frac{a_1^2}{\sum_{i=1}^{5} a_i^2} \tag{4.33}$$

The critical position for the maximum load effect can be obtained by the influence line.

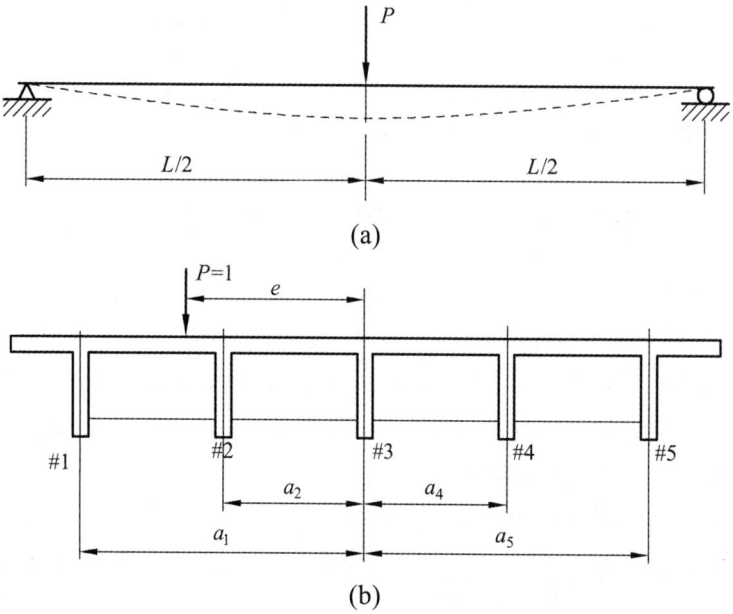

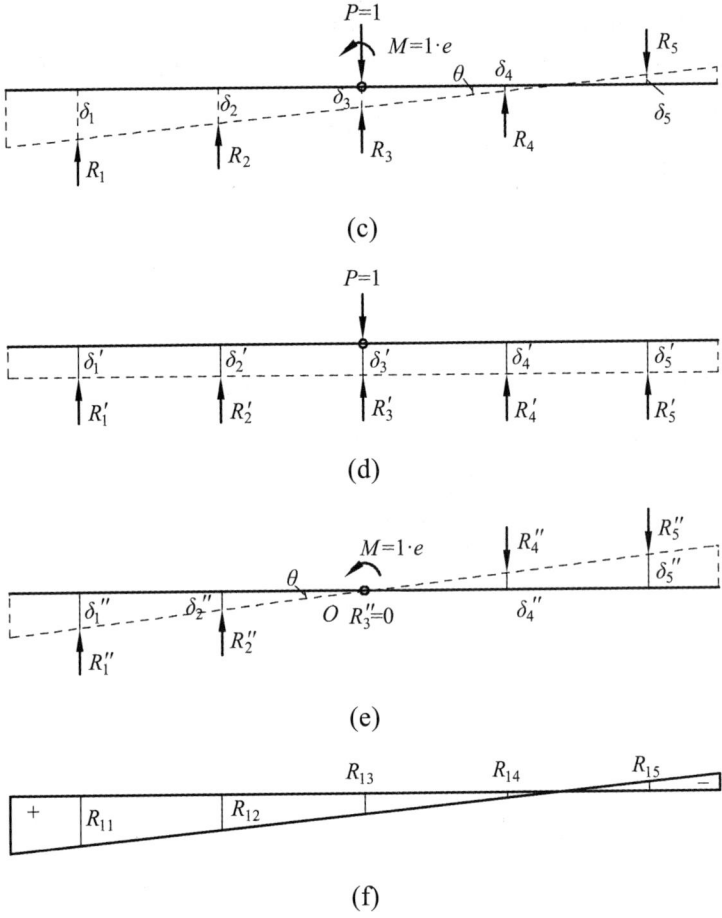

Figure 4.21 Transverse distribution of the wheel loads by the eccentric compression method: (a) the deflection of the bridge; (b) the cross-section of a slab-girder beam; (c) deflected shape of the deck slab under eccentric unit load; (d) deflected shape of the deck slab under concentric load; (e) deflected shape of the deck slab under unit torque; (f) transverse load influence line.

4.4.4 The modified eccentric compression method

In the eccentric compression method, the torsional stiffness of the girders is neglected. This will result overestimation of the loads transferred to the girders located at the side of the beam. To improve this method, the torsional stiffness of the girders has to be considered, which leads to the following modified eccentric compression method.

Consider the equilibrium of the cross-section of a slab-girder bridge under a unit torsional moment $M = 1 \cdot e$, as shown in Figure 4.22. The cross-section rotates an angle θ around the beam center O under M. If the torsional stiffness of the girder is considered, Eq. (4.27) for the equilibrium of torsional moments becomes

$$\sum_{i=1}^{n} R_i'' a_i + \sum_{i=1}^{n} M_{Ti} = e \qquad (4.34)$$

For a simply supported girder i subjected to a vertical concentrated load R_i'' and torsional moment M_{Ti} at mid span, the vertical deflection δ_i'' and torsional anger θ can be calculated, respectively, as

$$\delta_i'' = \frac{R_i'' L^3}{48 E I_i} \quad \text{and} \quad \theta = \frac{M_{Ti} L}{4 G I_{Ti}} \qquad (4.35)$$

where, I_{Ti} is the torsional constant (the polar second moment of the cross-sectional area) of the girder; G is shear modulus of the girder.

It is assumed that the entire cross-section is rotated rigidly around the center of the deck slab O and the deformation is small, the δ_i'' and θ have the following relation

$$\tan \theta \approx \theta = \frac{\delta_i''}{a_i} \qquad (4.36)$$

For the girder i and j, Eq. (4.36) results in

$$\frac{\delta_i''}{a_i} = \frac{\delta_j''}{a_j} \qquad (4.37)$$

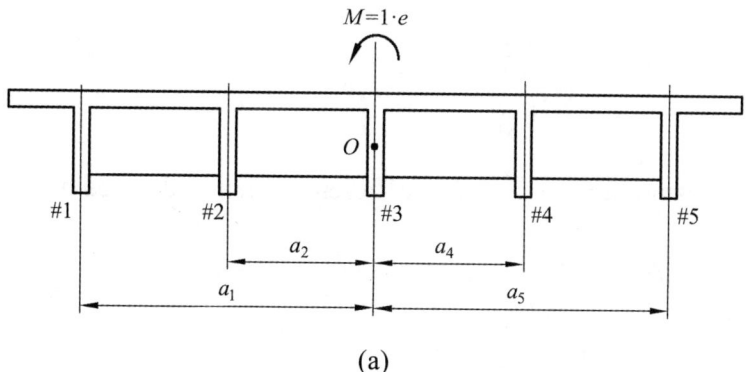

(a)

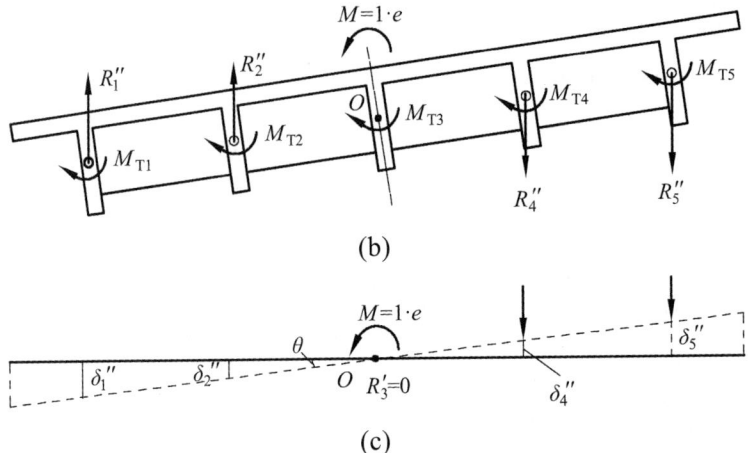

Figure 4.22 Transverse distribution of the wheel loads considering torsional stiffness of the girder: (a) the cross-section of a slab-girder beam; (b) equilibrium of the torsional moments on the cross-section; (c) deformed deck slab.

By substituting Eq. (4.35) into Eq. (4.37), we obtain

$$R_i'' = R_j'' \frac{a_i I_i}{a_j I_j} \tag{4.38}$$

Combining Eq. (4.59) with Eq. (4.60) yields

$$M_{Ti} = R_i'' \frac{GI_{Ti} L^2}{12 a_i E I_i} \tag{4.39}$$

By substituting Eq. (4.38) and Eq. (4.39) into Eq. (4.34), we arrive at

$$R_j'' \sum_{i=1}^{n} \frac{a_i^2 I_i}{a_j I_j} + R_j'' \sum_{i=1}^{n} \frac{a_i I_i}{a_j I_j} \cdot \frac{L^2 GI_{Ti}}{12 a_i E I_i} = e \tag{4.40}$$

Rearranging the terms in Eq. (4.40), one can obtain the load distributed on girder j as

$$R_j'' = \beta \frac{a_j I_j e}{\sum_{i=1}^{n} a_i^2 I_i} \tag{4.41}$$

where, β is termed the torsional coefficient which is defined as

$$\beta = \frac{1}{1 + \dfrac{L^2 G \sum_{i=1}^{n} I_{Ti}}{12 E \sum_{i=1}^{n} a_i^2 I_i}} < 1 \tag{4.42}$$

If $I_1 = I_2 = \cdots = I_n = I$, and $I_{T1} = I_{T2} = \cdots = I_{Tn} = I_T$, then

$$\beta = \frac{1}{1 + \dfrac{nL^2 GI_T}{12EI \sum_{i=1}^{n} a_i^2}} < 1 \tag{4.43}$$

If the spacing between the girders are the same, the following relation hold

$$\frac{n}{12 \sum_{i=1}^{n} a_i^2} = \frac{\xi}{B^2} \tag{4.44}$$

where, B is the width of the bridge;

ξ is a parameter related to the number of the girders which is listed in Table 4.1.

Table 4.1 The relation between ξ and the number of girders

n	4	5	6	7
ξ	1.067	1.042	1.028	1.021

By substituting Eq. (4.44) into Eq. (4.43), we can write

$$\beta = \frac{1}{1 + \xi \dfrac{GI_T}{EI} \left(\dfrac{L}{B}\right)^2} < 1 \tag{4.45}$$

We can see from the above equation that the larger the L/B, the smaller the β.

In practical design, the shear modulus of concrete, G, can be approximated taken as $0.425E$. For the T-type or I-type girders made up of narrow rectangular subsections, the torsional constant can be calculated approximately as

$$I_T = \sum_{i=1}^{m} c_i b_i t_i^3 \tag{4.46}$$

where, b_i and t_i are the width and length of the ith rectangular subsection (see Figure 4.23);

c_i is the torsional stiffness coefficient which can be found in Table 4.2;

m is the total number of rectangles comprising the cross-section.

Table 4.2 The torsional stiffness coefficient c

t/b	1	0.9	0.8	0.7	0.6	0.5	0.4	0.3	0.2	0.1	<0.1
c	0.141	0.155	0.171	0.189	0.209	0.229	0.250	0.270	0.291	0.312	1/3

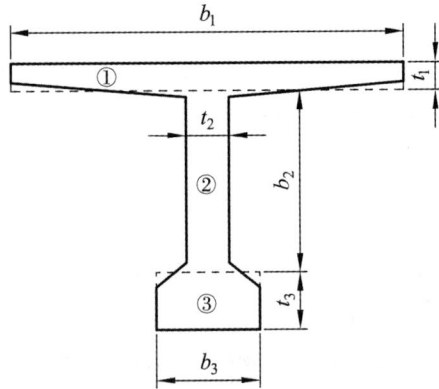

Figure 4.23 The division of the cross-section of the T-type girder for calculation of the torsional constant.

By summation of R_j'' obtained from Eq. (4.65) and R_j' obtained from Eq. (4.46) (the dummy index i in the equation is replaced with j), we can obtain the total load transferred to the girder j as

$$R_j = \frac{I_j}{\sum_{i=1}^{n} I_i} + \beta \frac{ea_j I_j}{\sum_{i=1}^{n} a_i^2 I_i} \tag{4.47}$$

If the girders have the same cross-sections, i.e., $I_1 = I_2 = \cdots = I_5$, the above equation can be written as

$$R_j = \frac{1}{n} + \beta \frac{ea_j}{\sum_{i=1}^{n} a_i^2} \tag{4.48}$$

The Eq. (4.48) is the function of the influence line for the load carried by girder i. For the side girder No.1 shown in Figure 4.24, the influence value R_{11} and R_{15} can be calculated as

$$R_{11} = \frac{1}{5} + \beta \frac{a_1^2}{\sum_{i=1}^{5} a_i^2} \tag{4.49}$$

$$R_{15} = \frac{1}{5} - \beta \frac{a_1^2}{\sum_{i=1}^{5} a_i^2} \qquad (4.50)$$

The influence values at other positions can be obtained through linear interpolation with R_{11} and R_{15}.

4.4.5 The Guyon-Massonnet method

Although the eccentric compression method and the modified eccentric compression method are easy to understand and to use in the design, the disadvantage of these method is that the diaphragm assumed to be is rigid. This will underestimate the load carried by the central girder and overestimate the load on the side girder. To give more accurate estimation of the load distribution, the stiffness of the diaphragm should be considered.

A refined method based on orthotropic plate theory was presented by a French Engineer, Guyon, in 1946, for computing transverse distribution of loads in a slab and beam floor system by neglecting the torsional stiffness of the beams. This method was further extended by Massonnet in 1950 by including the effects of torsion. The combined work of Guyon and Massonnet is referred to as the Guyon-Massonnet load distribution theory and has been extended by others.

In this method, a slab-girder structure is transformed into an elastic orthotropic plate whereby customary plate solutions are utilized to obtain certain distribution coefficients. These coefficients are the ratio of the deflection of a certain point on the plate under action of concentrated force to the mean deflection of the plate under uniform load. A series of design curves are provided that give the proper distribution coefficients for any known set of flexural and torsional stiffnesses and given load positions.

The basic assumptions of the Guyon-Massonnet load distribution theory is that:

(1) The actual bridge system, for the purpose of calculation, is replaced by an elastically equivalent structure with different stiffnesses in the two orthogonal directions. In each of the two directions, the equivalent structure has the same average flexural and torsional stiffnesses everywhere, as the actual bridge (Figure 4.24).

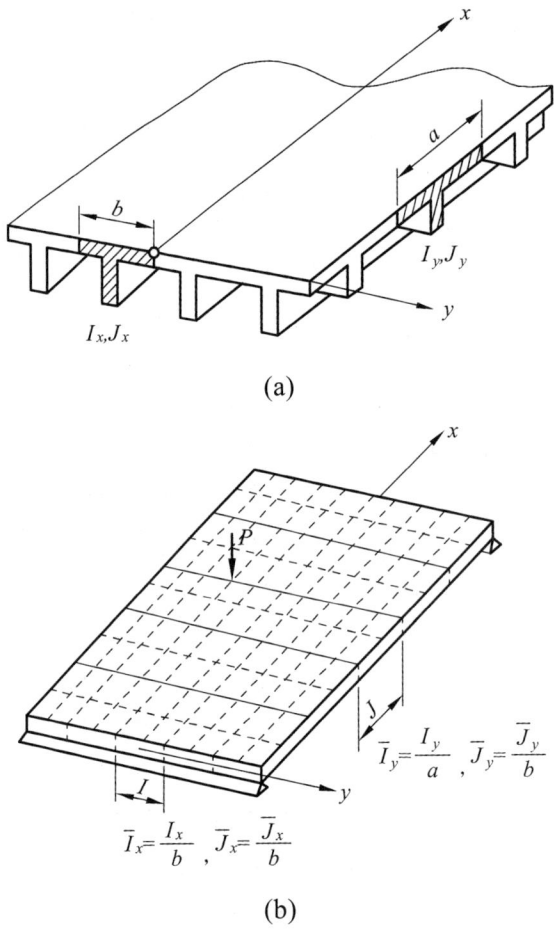

Figure 4.24 The orthotropic plate equivalent to a slab-girder bridge: (a) the slab-girder bridge with diaphragms; (b) the equivalent orthotropic plate.

(2) The equivalent structure can be treated as an orthotropic plate, and all the assumptions normally used in the derivation of the plate equation are valid.

Consider the slab-girder bridge shown in Figure 4.24(a). It is assumed that the longitudinal (x-direction) girders and the transverse girders (y-direction, i.e. the diaphragms) are equally spaced. The spacing between the longitudinal (x-direction) girders and that between the transverse girders (y-direction, i.e. the diaphragms) are b and a, respectively. The moment of inertia of the x- and y-direction girders are I_x and I_y, respectively. The torsional constants of the x- and y-direction girders are J_x and J_y, respectively. An equivalent orthotropic plate is such that the flexural stiffnesses and torsional stiffnesses per unit width of the plate in x- and y- direction are defined as

$$D_x = E\bar{I}_x; \quad D_y = E\bar{I}_y; \quad H = \alpha E\sqrt{\bar{I}_x \bar{I}_y} \tag{4.51}$$

where, $\bar{I}_x$, $\bar{I}_y$, $\bar{J}_x$ and $\bar{J}_y$ are moment of inertia and torsional constants per unit width in x- and y- direction, which are defined as

$$\bar{I}_x = \frac{I_x}{b}; \quad \bar{I}_y = \frac{I_y}{a}; \quad \bar{J}_x = \frac{J_x}{b}; \quad \bar{J}_y = \frac{J_y}{a} \tag{4.52}$$

The parameter α is related to the ratio of the torsional stiffness to the flexural stiffness and is given by

$$\alpha = \frac{G(\bar{J}_x + \bar{J}_y)}{2E\sqrt{\bar{I}_x \bar{I}_y}} \tag{4.53}$$

The governing differential equation for the equilibrium of the orthotropic plate is expressed as

$$D_x \frac{\partial^4 w}{\partial x^4} + 2H \frac{\partial^4 w}{\partial x^4} + D_y \frac{\partial^4 w}{\partial y^4} = p(x, y) \tag{4.54}$$

where, w is the deflection of the orthotropic place at point (x,y); $p(x,y)$ is load function depending on live load on the bridge deck.

Once w is obtained, the bending moments and torsional moments in x- and y-direction of the plate can be calculated by

$$M_x = -E\bar{I}_x \frac{\partial^2 w}{\partial x^2}; \quad M_y = -E\bar{I}_y \frac{\partial^2 w}{\partial y^2} \tag{4.55}$$

$$T_x = -E\bar{J}_x \frac{\partial^2 w}{\partial x \partial y}; \quad T_y = -E\bar{J}_y \frac{\partial^2 w}{\partial x \partial y} \tag{4.56}$$

Guyon and Massonnet developed the solution to the differential equation (4.54) for the bridge with a concentrated load P acting at midspan. The distribution coefficients K were defined as the ratio of the actual deflection of a longitudinal strip of a bridge under some loading system to the deflection of the bridge with the same load distributed uniformly across the bridge width (Figure 4.25), i.e.,

$$K = \frac{w}{\bar{w}} \tag{4.57}$$

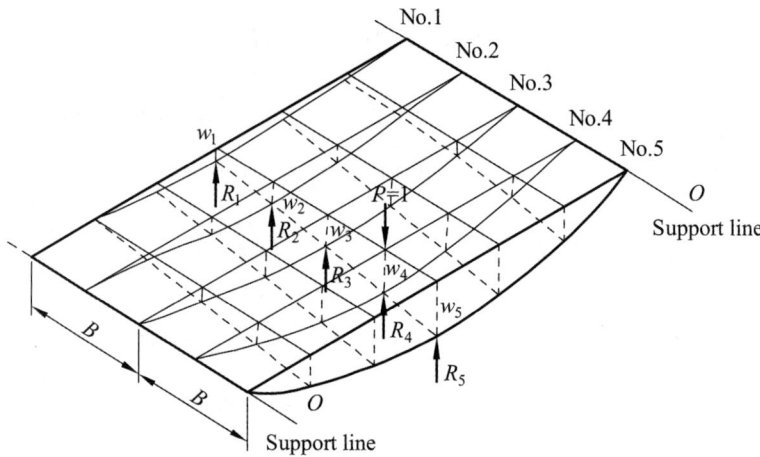

Figure 4.25 Deformation of the equivalent orthotropikc plate and load distribution.

Since the load carried by each longitudinal strip is proportional to the deflection of the strip, the ratio of the load transferred to a unit width of the strip to the total applied load is given by

$$\bar{K} = \frac{K}{2B} \tag{4.58}$$

It has been known that distribution coefficient K depends on many parameters, such as the span length and width of the bridge, flexural and torsional stiffnesses of the girders and diaphragms, and the load position. It has been found that K can be expressed as

$$K = g(\alpha, \theta, y_i, y_j) \tag{4.59}$$

where, $g(\ldots)$ denoted a function, y_i is the position of the point to which the load is to be transferred and y_j is the position of the point on which the load is acting. α is defined by Eq.(4.53) and θ are defined as

$$\theta = \frac{B}{L} \sqrt[4]{\frac{\bar{I}_x}{\bar{I}_y}} \tag{4.60}$$

The results of K for no-torsion structure ($\alpha = 0$), i.e. K_0, and those of K for torsion structure ($\alpha = 1$), i.e. K_1, for a wide and continuous range of values of θ have been developed in the form of graphs which may be used for practical design (see Appendix). It has been found that the required values of K_α for an actual beam and slab bridge in which α has a value other than 0 or 1 can be determined with sufficient accuracy by the interpolation

$$K_\alpha = K_0 + (K_1 - K_0)\sqrt{\alpha} \tag{4.61}$$

Each group of curves in Figures A.1 to A.11 gives the value of K for a given transverse position f under loads whose eccentricity e varies from $-B$ to B. It is important to note that both f and e are expressed in terms of the effective width $2B$. The actual load transferred to girder i is calculated as

$$R_i = \overline{K}_i b = \frac{K_i}{2B} b \tag{4.62}$$

where, R_i is the load transferred to the girder i, and K_i is the distribution coefficient for girder i. Obviously, Eq. (4.62) is the equation of the influence line for R_i (see Figure 4.25). If there are totally n girders equally spaced, then

$$b = 2B/n \tag{4.63}$$

Thus, we have

$$R_i = \frac{K_i}{n} \tag{4.64}$$

which means that for the slab-girder bridge with equally spaced girders, the load transferred to the girder i is equal to the load distribution coefficient K_i divided by the total number of the girders.

The established graph for K_i shown in Figures A.1 ~ A.11 only give the K_i for the transverse positions $f = 0$, $\pm\frac{1}{4}B$, $\pm\frac{1}{2}B$, $\pm\frac{3}{4}B$, and $\pm B$. If the girder i is not just located on any of this dividing points, interpolation using the adjacent data points have to be carried out to determine K_i. For example, if $f = -\xi B$ and $(3/4) < \xi < 1$, then $K_{-\xi B}$ can be determined by interpolation between $K_{-(3/4)B}$ and K_{-B} (Figure 4.26).

The calculation of moment of inertia of the girder and diaphragm, I_x and I_y, should consider the effective flange width, especially for the diaphragm. Usually the spacing of the diaphragm is large in the longitudinal direction, so the compressive stress distribution is no longer uniform in the flange (Figure 4.27). As a result, the assumption of plane cross-section is not valid any more. The effective flange width is define as the flange width with which the compressive

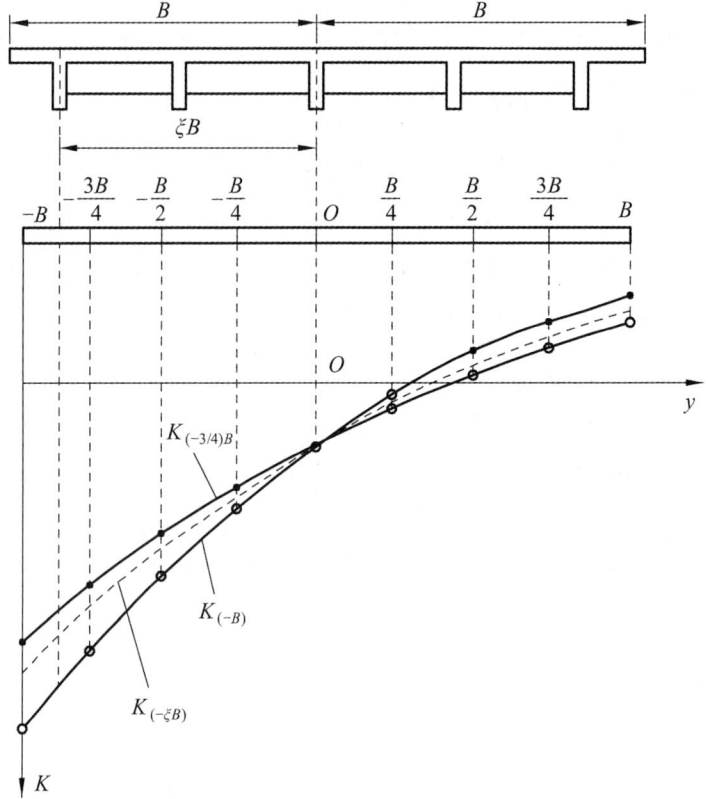

Figure 4.26 Calculation of distribution coefficient when $f=\pm\xi B$

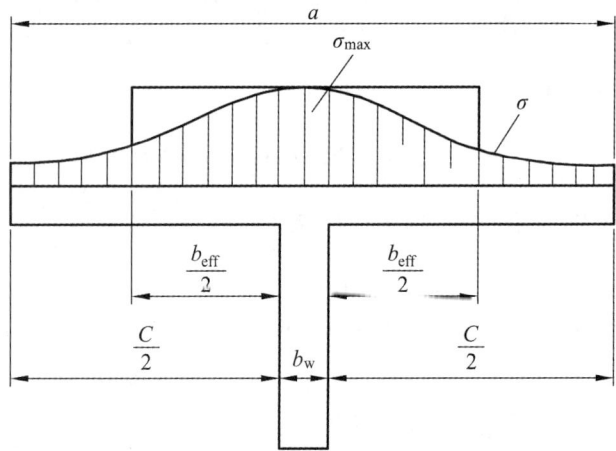

Figure 4.27 the effective flange width

stress is assumed to be uniform and equal to the maximum stress at the girder center such that the resultant compressive force within the effective flange width is equivalent to the resultant force between the adjacent centers of the girders. For the girders shown in Figure 4.28, the effective flange width $(b_{eff}+b_w)$ can be taken the value listed in Table 4.3, where b_w is width of the web and b_{eff} is the effective width of flange excluding the width of the web, and l is the span length of the girder or diaphragm.

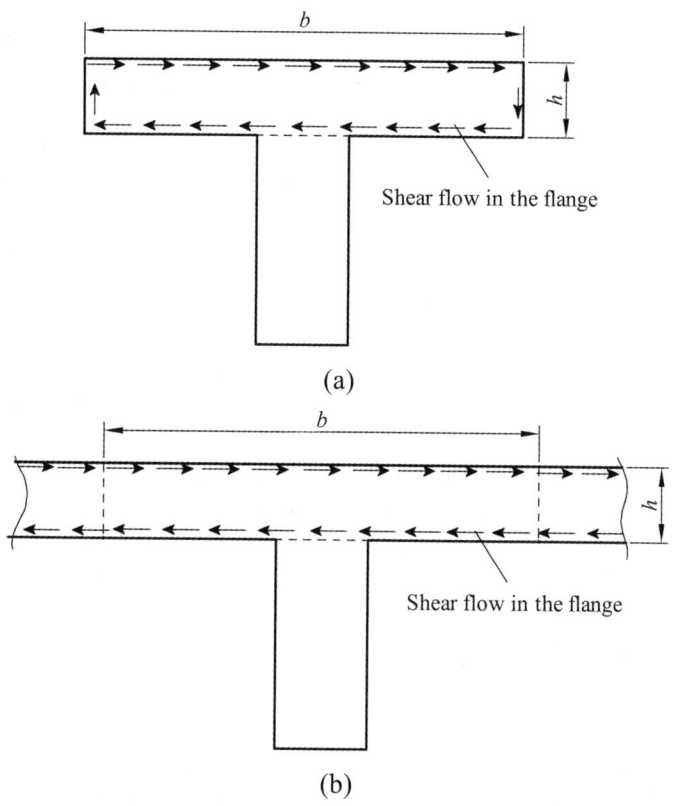

Figure 4.28 The shear flow in the flange of: (a) the T-girder; (b) the diaphragm.

Table 4.3 The ratio of the effective flange width to the spacing of the girder

c/l	0.1	0.2	0.3	0.4	0.5	0.6	0.7	0.8	0.9	1.0
b_{eff}/c	0.983	0.936	0.867	0.789	0.71	0.635	0.568	0.509	0.459	0.416

Calculation of the torsional constant J should consider the continuality of the deck slab. For the cross-section of a T-girder shown in Figure 4.28(a), the torsional constant is the sum of the those of the flange and the web. Since the thickness of the flange is much smaller relative to its width, the torsional constant of the flange per unit width, $\bar{J}^f$, can be calculated as

$$\bar{J}^f = \left(\frac{1}{3}bh^3\right)\bigg/b = \frac{1}{3}h^3 \qquad (4.65)$$

where, h is the thickness of the flange. The total torsional constant of the cross-section is

$$\bar{J} = \bar{J}^f + \bar{J}^w \qquad (4.66)$$

where $\bar{J}^w$ is the torsional constant of the web per unit width of b.

However, the flange of a diaphragm is usually the deck slab which is continuous in the longitudinal direction [Figure 4.28(b)]. Based on the theory of the elastic plate [Ref], the torsional constant per unit width of the continuous flange is

$$\bar{J}^f = \frac{1}{6}h^3 \qquad (4.67)$$

This is because the shear flow in the continuous flange does not form a closed loop. Thus, for a slab-girder bridge whose deck slab is continuous in the longitudinal and transverse directions, and the deck slab also serves as the flange of both the girder and diaphragm, the sum of $(\bar{J}_x + \bar{J}_y)$ in Eq. (4.53) can be calculated as

$$\begin{aligned}\bar{J}_x + \bar{J}_y &= 2 \cdot \frac{1}{6}h^3 + \frac{1}{b}J_x^w + \frac{1}{a}J_y^w \\ &= \frac{1}{3}h^3 + \frac{1}{b}J_x^w + \frac{1}{a}J_y^w\end{aligned} \qquad (4.68)$$

where, J_x^w and J_y^w are the torsional constants of the girder (the x-directional beam) and diaphragm (the y-directional beam).

Example A 5-girder reinforced concrete bridge is shown in Figure 4.29. The span length of the bridge is $L = 19.50$ m. The flanges of the girders are rigidly connected in the transverse direction. Find the load distribution factor of the side girder No.1 under the wheel loads shown in Figure 4.29(c).

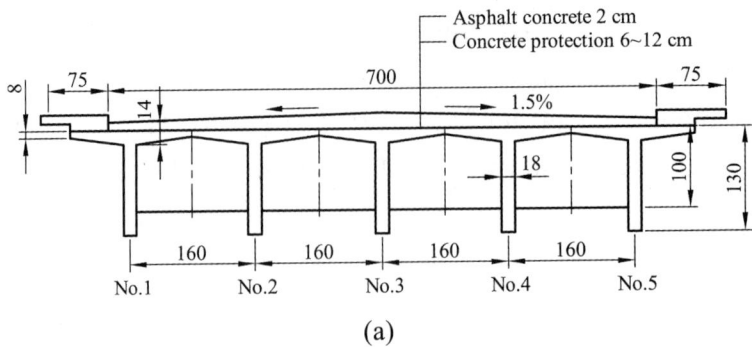

(a)

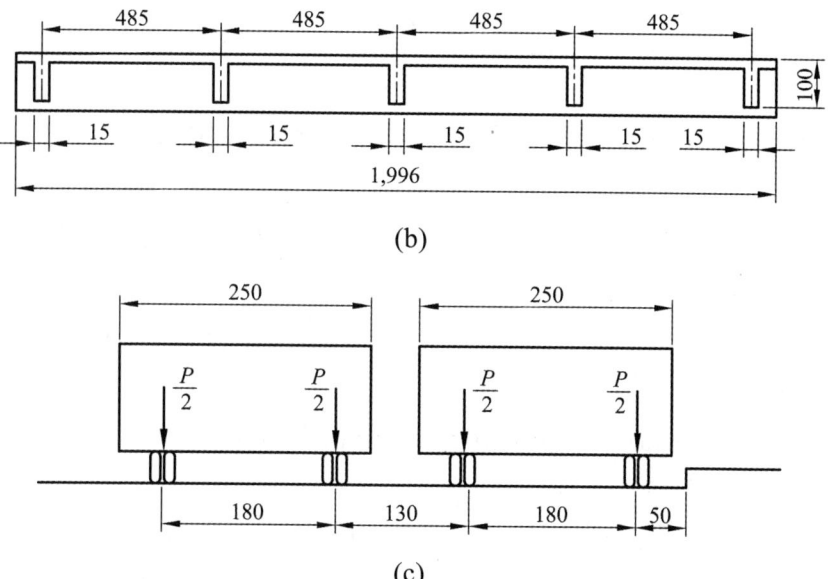

(b)

(c)

Figure 4.29 A slab-girder bridge loaded with truck load (units: cm): (a) the cross-section; (b) the layout of the diaphragms; (c) wheel loads.

Solution

(1) Calculation of moments of inertia.

The dimensions of the cross-section of the girder are shown in Figure 4.30. The averaged thickness of the girder flange can be calculated as

$$h = \frac{8+14}{2} = 11 \text{ (cm)}$$

Figure 4.30 The dimensions of the cross-section of the girder (units: cm).

Then the distance of neutral axis from the top of the flange is

$$a_x = \frac{(160-18)\times 11\times \frac{11}{2} + 130\times 18\times \frac{130}{2}}{(160-18)\times 11 + 130\times 18}$$

$$= \frac{8{,}591+152{,}100}{1{,}562+2{,}340} = \frac{169{,}691}{3{,}902} = 41.2 \text{ (cm)}$$

The moment of inertia of the girder I_x is calculated as

$$I_x = \frac{1}{12} \times (160-18) \times 11^3 + (160-18) \times 11 \left(41.2 - \frac{11}{2}\right)^2 +$$

$$\frac{1}{12} \times 18 \times 130^3 + 18 \times 130 \left(\frac{130}{2} - 41.2\right)^2 = 6.26 \times 10^3 \text{ (cm}^4\text{)}$$

The moment of inertia per unit width can be obtained as

$$\overline{I}_x = \frac{I_x}{b} = \frac{6{,}626 \times 10^3}{160} = 41{,}410 \text{ (cm}^4\text{/cm)}$$

The dimensions of the diaphragm is shown in Figure 4.33. To determine the effective length of the flange of the diaphragm, the span length of the diaphragm, l' is taken as

$$l' = 4 \times b = 4 \times 160 = 640 \text{ (cm)}$$

$$c/l' = 470/640 = 0.736$$

By Table 4.3, we can find that $b_{\text{eff}}/c = 0.547$ for $c/l' = 0.736$. Then we have

$$b_{\text{eff}} = 0.547 \times 470 \text{ cm} = 256 \text{ (cm)}$$

$$b_{\text{eff}}/2 = 128 \text{ (cm)}$$

The position of neutral axis, a_y, for the diaphragm, is thus obtained as

$$a_y = \frac{2 \times 128 \times 11 \times \frac{11}{2} + 15 \times 100 \times \frac{100}{2}}{2 \times 128 \times 11 + 15 \times 100} = 21.0 \text{ (cm)}$$

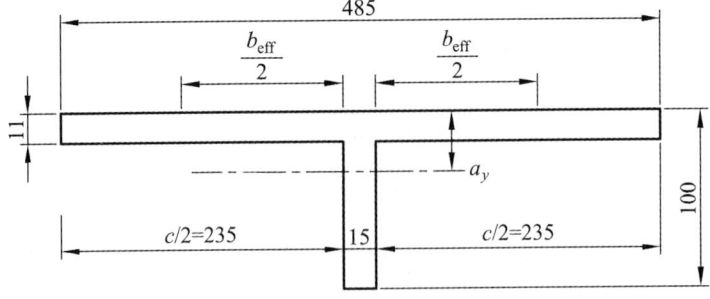

Figure 4.31 The dimensions of the diaphragm (units: cm).

The moment of inertia of the diaphragm is calculated as

$$I_y = \frac{1}{12} \times 2 \times 128 \times 11^3 + 2 \times 128 \times 11 \times \left(21 - \frac{11}{2}\right)^2 +$$

$$\frac{1}{12} \times 15 \times 100^3 + 15 \times 100 \times \left(\frac{100}{2} - 21\right)^2$$

$$= 3,220 \times 10^3 \text{ (cm}^4\text{)}$$

The moment of inertia of the diaphragm per unit width is

$$\bar{I}_y = \frac{I_y}{a} = \frac{3,220 \times 10^3}{485} = 6,640 \text{ (cm}^4/\text{cm)}$$

(2) Calculation of torsional constants.

Since the T-girders are rigidly connected in the transverse direction, the torsional constant can be calculated by Eq. (4.68). The averaged thickness of the T-girder is

$$h_1 = \frac{8+14}{2} = 11 \text{ (cm)}$$

The ratio of thickness of the web of the T-girder to the height is

$$t/b_w = 18/(130-11) = 0.151$$

From Table 4.2, we can find that $c = 0.301$. Then the torsional constant for the T-girder is

$$J_x = cbt^3 = 0.301 \times (130-11) \times 18^3 = 209 \times 10^3 \text{ (cm}^4\text{)}$$

For the diaphragm, we have

$$t/b_w = 15/(100-11) = 0.167$$

By Table 4.2, we find that $c = 0.298$, Then we have the torsional constant for the diaphragm as

$$J_y = 0.298 \times (100-11) \times 15^3 = 89.51 \times 10^3 \text{ (cm}^4\text{)}$$

The sum of the torsional constants per unit width in x- and y- direction is

$$\bar{J}_x \times \bar{J}_y = \frac{1}{3}h_1^3 + \frac{1}{b}J_x + \frac{1}{a}J_y$$

$$= \frac{1}{3} \times 11^3 + \frac{209{,}000}{160} + \frac{89{,}510}{485}$$

$$= 444 + 1{,}306 + 185 = 1{,}935 \ (\text{cm}^4/\text{cm})$$

(3) Calculation of α and θ for Eq. (4.77) and Eq. (4.84)

$$\alpha = \frac{G(\overline{J}_x + \overline{J}_y)}{2E\sqrt{\overline{I}_x \overline{I}_y}} = \frac{0.425E \times 1\,935}{2E\sqrt{41\,410 \times 6\,640}} = 0.024\,79$$

$$\sqrt{\alpha} = \sqrt{0.02479} = 0.1574$$

Noting that B in Eq.(4.77) is the half of the bridge width, then we have

$$B = \frac{5 \times 160}{2} = 400 \text{ cm}$$

$$\theta = \frac{B}{L}\sqrt[4]{\frac{\overline{I}_x}{\overline{I}_y}} = \frac{400}{1\,950}\sqrt[4]{\frac{41{,}410}{6{,}640}} = 0.324$$

(4) Determination of the influence line of transverse load distribution on girder No.1

Given $\theta = 0.324$, the K_0 and K_1 can be found from the Figure A.1 ~ A.11 for the standard transverse points of $f = 0$, $\pm\frac{1}{4}B$, $\pm\frac{1}{2}B$, $\pm\frac{3}{4}B$, and $\pm B$, as shown in Table 4.4.

Table 4.4 The distribution coefficients at the standard transverse positions

Distribution Coefficient	Position of Girder	Position of Load									Check
		B	$3B/4$	$B/2$	$B/4$	0	$-B/4$	$-B/2$	$-3B/4$	$-B$	
K_1	0	0.94	0.97	1.00	1.03	1.05	1.03	1.00	0.97	0.94	7.99
	$B/4$	1.05	1.06	1.07	1.07	1.02	0.97	0.93	0.87	0.83	7.93
	$B/2$	1.22	1.18	1.14	1.07	1.00	0.93	0.87	0.80	0.75	7.98
	$3B/4$	1.41	1.31	1.20	1.07	0.97	0.87	0.79	0.72	0.67	7.97
	B	1.65	1.12	1.24	1.07	0.93	0.84	0.74	0.68	0.60	8.04
K_0	0	0.83	0.91	0.99	1.08	1.13	1.08	0.99	0.91	0.83	7.92
	$B/4$	1.66	1.51	1.35	1.23	1.06	0.88	0.63	0.39	0.18	7.97
	$B/2$	2.46	2.10	1.73	1.38	0.98	0.64	0.23	-0.17	-0.55	7.85
	$3B/4$	3.32	2.73	2.10	1.51	0.94	0.40	-0.16	-0.62	-1.13	8.00
	B	4.10	3.40	2.44	1.64	0.83	0.18	-0.54	-1.14	-1.77	7.98

The correspondence of the positions of the girders to the standard positions of the equivalent orthotropic plate is shown in Figure 4.32.

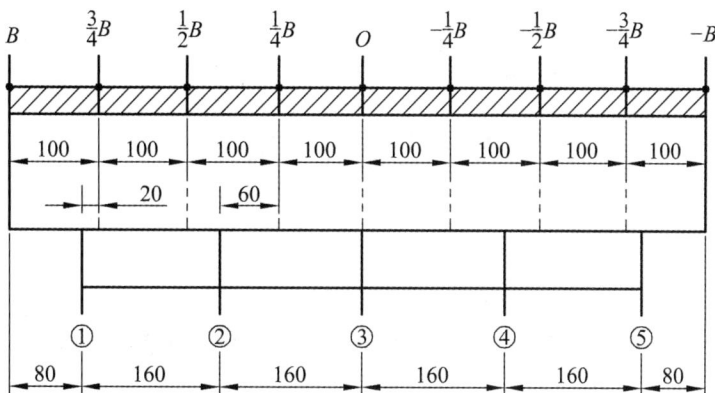

Figure 4.32 The correspondence of the positions of the girders to the standard positions of the equivalent plate.

Since the position of the girder No.1 is not just located at one of the standard positions, interpolation between K_0 and K_1 is necessary. From Figure 4.33, we can write the following interpolations equation for the distribution factor at girder No.1 as

$$K' = K_{\frac{3}{4}B} + (K_B - K_{\frac{3}{4}B}) \times \frac{20}{100} = 0.2K_B + 0.8K_{\frac{3}{4}B}$$

The influence value for the transverse load distribution is listed in the row of the Table 4.5, and also is drawn in Figure 4.33.

(5) Placement of the wheel loads on the critical position.

By trial and error, it is easy to find that two trucks placed on the position shown in Figure 4.34 can generate the largest load effect on the girder No.1. Note that the clear distance of the wheel load from the curb is 50 cm, and the clear distance between trucks is 130 cm.

(6) Calculation of the load distribution factor.

For the two trucks each having axle load P, the load distribution factor for girder No.1 is defined as

$$m_{P,1} = \frac{\sum_{j=1}^{k} \frac{P}{2} R_{1,j}}{P} = \frac{1}{2} \sum_{j=1}^{k} R_{1,j} \tag{4.69}$$

Table 4.5 Influence values for the transverse load distribution

N of Girder	Equation for Interpolation	Position of Load								
		B	$\frac{3}{4}B$	$\frac{1}{2}B$	$\frac{1}{4}B$	0	$-\frac{1}{4}B$	$-\frac{1}{2}B$	$-\frac{3}{4}B$	$-B$
1	$K'_1 = 0.2K'_{1B} + 0.8K'_{1\frac{3}{4}B}$	1.458	1.332	1.208	1.070	0.962	0.864	0.780	0.712	0.656
	$K' = 0.2K'_{0B} + 0.8K'_{0\frac{3}{4}B}$	3.476	2.864	2.168	1.536	0.918	0.356	−0.236	−0.724	−1.258
	$K'_1 - K'_0$	−2.108	−1.532	−0.960	−0.466	0.044	0.508	1.016	1.436	1.914
	$(K'_1 - K'_0)\sqrt{\alpha}$	−0.318	−0.242	−0.152	−0.074	0.007	0.080	0.161	0.227	0.302
	$K'_\alpha = K'_0 + (K'_4 - K'_0)\sqrt{\alpha}$	3.158	2.622	2.016	1.462	0.925	0.436	−0.075	−0.497	−0.956
	$R_1 = \dfrac{K'_\alpha}{5}$	0.632	0.524	0.403	0.292	0.185	0.087	−0.015	−0.099	−0.191

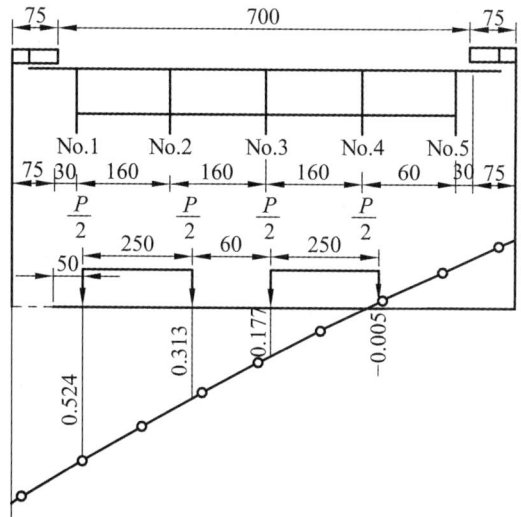

Figure 4.33 Transverse load distribution influence line for the girder No.1.

where, j is the wheel load number and k is the total number of the wheel loads; $R_{1,j}$ is the ordinate of the transverse load distribution influence line for R_1 at the wheel load position j.

Thus

$$m_{P,1} = \frac{1}{2}(0.524 + 0.313 + 0.177 - 0.005) = 0.504 \qquad (4.70)$$

(7) Check on the correctness of the distribution coefficient K_α.

To check if the K_α's obtained from the graph and by interpolation is correct, let consider an equivalent orthotropic plate under a unit load acting on any of the nine standard points, as shown in Figure 5.36(a). The actual deflection of the plate under the unit load is shown in Figure 5.36a. If the unit load is divided into eight concentrated loads such that the plate deflects uniformly, as shown in Figure 5.36(b), then application of the Betti-Maxwell reciprocal theorem results in

$$1 \cdot \overline{w} = \frac{1}{8}\sum_{i=2}^{8} w_i + \frac{1}{16}(w_1 + w_9) \qquad (4.71)$$

Rearranging the terms in the equation leads to

$$\sum_{i=2}^{8} \frac{w_i}{\overline{w}} + \frac{1}{2}\left(\frac{w_1}{\overline{w}} + \frac{w_9}{\overline{w}}\right) = 8 \qquad (4.72)$$

119

In terms of the definition of K, we have

$$\sum_{i=2}^{8} K_i + \frac{1}{2}(K_1 + K_9) = 8 \tag{4.73}$$

The above equation can be used to check the correctness of the results for K. The last column of the Table 4.4 gives the results of the check in terms of Eq. (4.72).

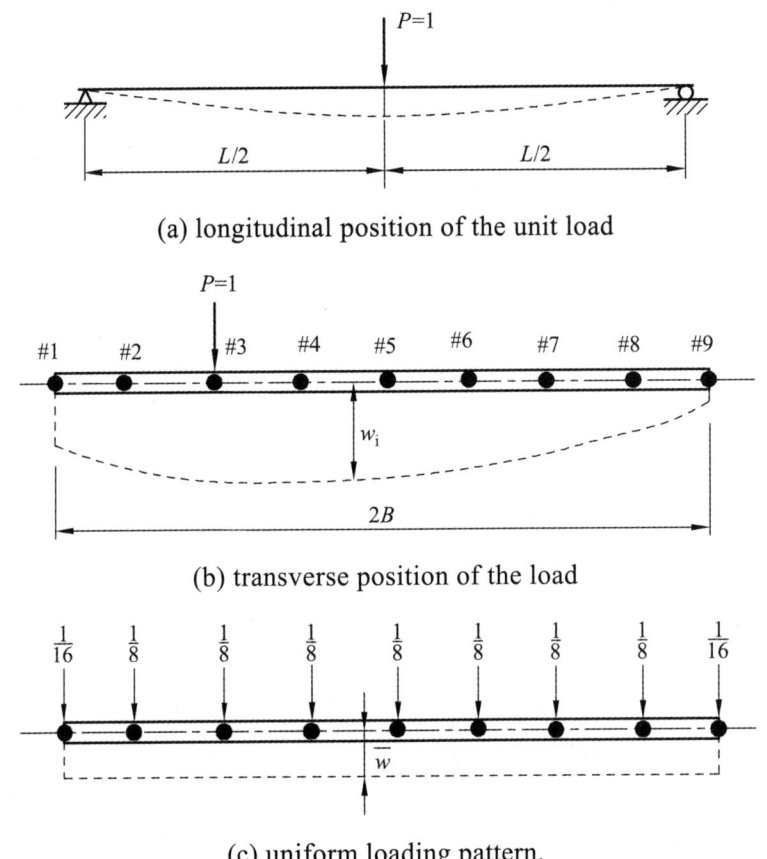

(a) longitudinal position of the unit load

(b) transverse position of the load

(c) uniform loading pattern.

Figure 4.34 The transverse deflection of the orthotropic plate under two equivalent loads: (a) longitudinal position of the unit load; (b) transverse position of the load; (c) uniform loading pattern.

References

[4.1]   Li Y.-D., ed., Introduction to Bridge Engineering (in Chinese), 3rd ed., Southwest Jiaotong University Press, Chengdu, China, 2005.
李亚东. 桥梁工程概论. 3 版. 成都：西南交通大学出版社，2014.

[4.2] Yao L.-S, ed., (Xiang H.-F., Gu A.-B., reviewers), Bridge Engineering, 2nd ed., China Communications Press, Beijing, China, 2008.

[4.3] 姚玲森. 桥梁工程. 2 版. 项海帆，顾安邦，主审. 北京：人民交通出版社，2008.

[4.4] Tang J.-S., ed., (Yang, J. reviewer), Railway Bridges, China Railway Press, Beijing, 2015.

唐继舜. 铁路桥梁. 杨进，主审. 北京：中国铁道出版社，2015.

[4.5] Morice P. B., and Little, G, "Load Distribution in Prestressed Concrete Bridge Systems," *the Structural Engineer*, Vol. 32, No. 3. 1954.

[4.6] Zokaie T. L, T. A. Osterkamp T. A., and R. A. Imbsen, R. A., Distribution *of Wheel Loads on Highway Bridges*, Final Report Project 12-26/1, National Cooperative Highway Research Program, Transportation Research Board, National Research Council, Washington, DC., 1991.

[4.7] Hołowaty J., "Live Load Distribution for Assessment of Highway Bridges in American and European Codes," *Structural Engineering International* , Vol. 22, No.4, 2012.

[4.8] Sanders W. W. Jr., and Elleby, H. A., *Distribution of Wheel Loads On Highway Bridges*, Engineering Research Institute, Iowa State University, Ames, Iowa, 1970.

[4.9] AASHTO, *LRFD Bridge Design Specifications*, 5th ed., American Association for State Highway and Transportation Officials, Washington, DC., 2014.

[4.10] TB 10092-2017 (J 462-2017), *Code for Design of Concrete Structures of Railway* Bridges *and Culverts*, China National Railway Bureau, 2017.

[4.11] JTG 3362-2018, *Specifications for Design of Highway Reinforced Concrete and Prestressed Concrete Bridges and Culverts*, China's Transportation Ministry, 2018.

[4.12] Guyon Y., "Calcul des Ponts Larges a pouters multiples Solidarisses par les Entretoies." Ann. Des Ponts et Chaussess, 116, pp. 553-612. 1946.

[4.13] Massonnett C., "Methods of Calculation of Bridges with Several Longitudinal Beams, Taking into Account Their Torsional Resistance." International Associaion of Bridge and Structural Engineers Publications, Zurich, Vol. 10, pp. 147-182, 1950.

Chapter 5 Reinforced Concrete Girder Bridges

5.1 Introduction

Bridges made of concrete and reinforcement steel bars, without prestress, are called reinforced concrete bridges. Since concrete is strong in compression but weak in tension, cracks develop when the applied loads or restrained temperature and shrinkage changes introduce tensile stresses exceeding the tensile strength of concrete. The steel reinforcement bars are thus provided in concrete to develop the tension forces necessary for moment equilibrium after the concrete has cracked.

Concrete can also be prestressed to prevent cracking under live loads. In this case, we speak of prestressed concrete. The bridges made of prestressed concrete are called prestressed concrete bridges. In these bridges, structural elements are prestressed through high strength steel tendons or bars such that compressive stresses developed in concrete before live loads are applied can cancel the tensile stress caused by the live loads.

Reinforced concrete girder bridges are widely used for small spans. For railway bridges, the span-lengths of the reinforced concrete girders can be up to 20 m; for highway bridges, the span-lengths can reach 25 m. When the span length is longer than 20 m, prestressed concrete girders or other types of bridges are preferred alternatives. On modern high-speed railways and highways, even the girders of span-length less than 20 m are often made of prestressed concrete to prevent cracking of concrete and to increase the stiffness of the girder. In North America, reinforced concrete bridges were the preferred types for spans of between 6 m and 18 m before the advent of prestressed concrete technology, according to the data between the years 1950-1989, and they are still built in that span range in many cases.

Concrete girder bridges have many advantages over other types. They may consist of precast concrete elements, which are cast in a production plant or casting yard and then transported to the construction site for fabrication and erection, or cast-in-place concrete, which is cast and formed in the formwork set up at the elements' finished position. Cast-in-place structures are continuous and monolithic, having the attributes of easy construction, low costs, and good earthquake-resistance performance. However, when the project is on a fast-track construction schedule or when the clearance for the opening of the falsework is limited, precast construction method may be a better choice. The shapes and sizes of the reinforced concrete girders can be standardized for typical span-lengths, which make the girders easy to be replaced once they have deteriorated or damaged.

In this chapter, configurations and design considerations of concrete girder bridges are discussed. Design examples are also presented to illustrated the functions and arrangement of steel reinforcement. All design specifications referenced in this chapter are those used in design of Chinese railway or highway bridges.

5.2 Design methods

5.2.1 Dimensioning of the cross-section

1. Slab bridges

The design of a girder bridge usually starts with the selection or estimation of the shape and size of the cross-section of the girder, so that self-weight can be estimated and the proportioning of reinforcement can be carried out according to the given concrete cross-section. The most important dimension of a girder cross-section is its depth. This is generally estimated by design experience or selected from a group of standard cross-sections specified in a design manual. For simply supported railway reinforce concrete slab bridges, the depth of the slab is constant and the depth-to-span ratios are about 1/8 to 1/9. For highway slab bridges, the economical depth-to-span ratios of the monolithic slabs are about 1/12 to 1/16; while the fabricated slabs have the depth-to-span ratios of between 1/16 and 1/22. The longer the span length, the smaller the depth-to-span ratio. Table 5.1 lists the range of depths of typical slab bridge for usual span lengths of Chinese highway bridges.

Table 5.1 Depths of the reinforced concrete slab highway bridges

Cross-section type	Span length L/m	Depth h/m
Solid slab	< 8	0.16 ~ 0.36
Voided slab	6 ~ 13	0.4 ~ 0.8

2. T-girder bridges

The depth-to-span ratios of simply supported reinforce concrete T-girder railway bridges in China are in the range of 1/6 and 1/9. For simply supported reinforced concrete T-girder highway bridges, the economical depth-to-span ratios are about 1/11 to 1/18 for span length of 8 m to 20 m. When the span length is larger than 20 m, prestressed concrete are generally used to build the girder. Generally speaking, if the bridge under clearance allows, increasing the depth of the girder can reduce usage of the reinforcing steel. This is usually an economical way to proportion the cross-section, since, as the depth of the girder is increased, only the height of the web is increased, resulting in a small increase of concrete usage and self-weight.

The thickness of the web depends on the tensile stress in concrete and amount and layout of reinforcement steel bars. For railway girder bridges, the web thickness is in the range of 0.2 m (at the mid-span) to 0.6 m (at the end of the girder). The center-to-center spacing of the webs is 1.8 m. For monolithic girder highway bridges, the web thickness is usually from 0.6 m to 1.2 m (Figure 5.2), while for the fabricated girder bridge, the web thickness is between 0.15 m and 0.18 m (Figure 5.3). The center-to-center spacing of the girders is between 1.5 m and 2.5 m. For standard highway girder bridges, the center-to-center spacing of girders is 1.6 m (Figure 5.3).

The thickness of the top flange depends on the center-to-center spacing of the girders, since the top flange behaves as a one-way slab in the transverse direction when the wheel load is positioned in-between the girders or at the overhang. The wider the girder spacing, the thicker the top flange. For the railway bridge, the minimum thickness of the top flange is 0.12 m (see Figure 5.1). For highway bridges, the thickness should not be less than 1/10 of the girder depth at the top of the web and, at the same time, should not be less than 0.1 at the the free ends. For monolithic deck slab serving as the top flange of the girder, the thickness of the slab at the edge should not be less than 0.14 m (see Figure 5.2). Figure 5.3 shows the cross-section of a typical five-girder fabricated highway reinforced concrete girder bridge.

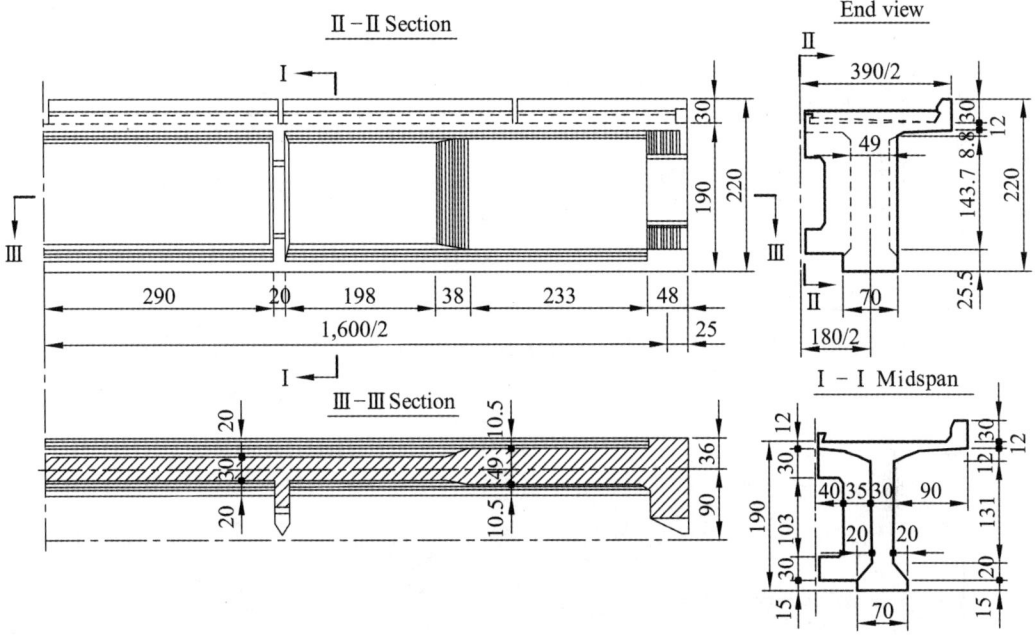

Figure 5.1 The standard reinforced concrete girder used in Chinese railway bridge for span length of 16 m.

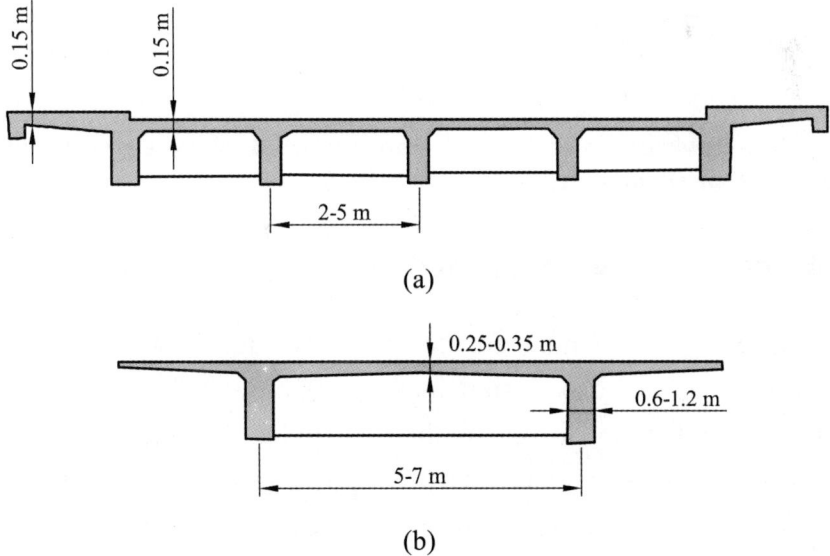

Figure 5.2 The cross-section of the monolithic reinforced concrete girder: (a) multi-girder bridge; (b) double-girder bridge.

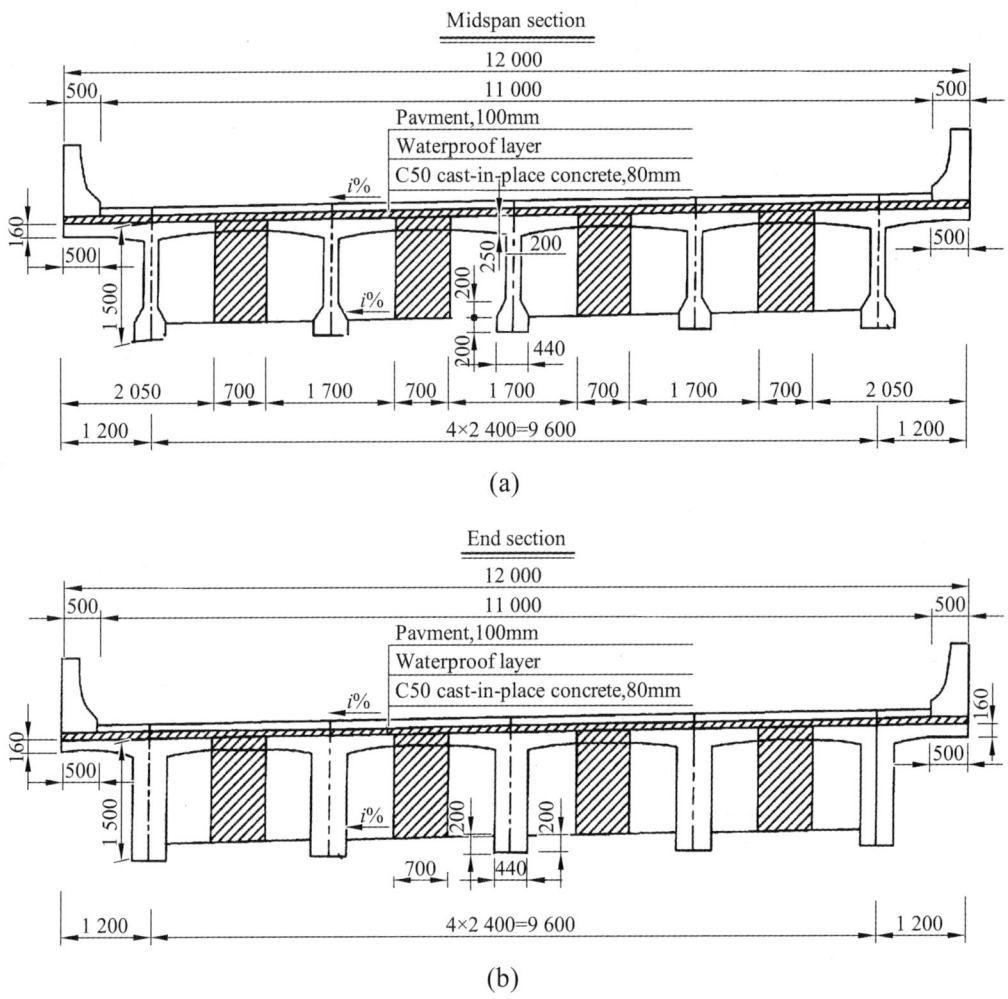

Figure 5.3　The cross-section of the fabricated reinforced concrete girder (units in mm): (a) midspan section; (b) end section.

5.2.2　Allowable stress design method

Railway bridges in China are designed by the allowable stress design method or the service load design method. Although the new design code based on the limit state design method is under development for railway bridges, the current design code TB 10092 for railway bridges is still founded on the allowable stress design. One of the reasons is that the railway live loads are much heavier than highway live loads, therefore the allowable stress design method is simple to use and is thought to be conservative to ensure the safety of the designed bridge. Another reason is that the railway bridges designed with the allowable stress design method have been performing safely up to now. This classical design method treats concrete as an elastic material working together with reinforcing steel bars, both behaving in the linear-elastic region. Designs are based on the allowable stresses of the concrete and steel induced by the working loads or service loads. The safety of the member is represented by a safety factor which is defined as the ratio of strength of material to the allowable stress. The fundamental assumptions of the allowable stress method are:

(i) Plane Section before bending will remain plane after bending;

(ii) Steel and concrete behave as linear elastic materials under working load;

(iii) Bond between steel and concrete is perfect within elastic limit of steel;

(iv) All tensile stresses are taken by reinforcement and none by concrete after cracking;

All of the formulas developed for design calculations in the allowable stress design method are based on the above assumptions.

5.2.3 Limit state design method

The Chinese design code for highway reinforced concrete bridges JTG 3362 and the provisions on the design for strength of railway prestressed concrete bridges TB 10092 are based on the state limit design method. Unlike the working stress design method, the limit state design method classifies the safety of a bridge into different levels that correspond to different failure criteria. For design of reinforced concrete bridges, there are generally four design limit states: service limit state, fatigue limit state, extreme limit state, and strength limit state.

The design for service limit state design is to controls the crack width of concrete and deflections; the design for fatigue limit state is to control the stress in concrete and reinforcement under dynamic service loads, so as to prevent the bridge from fatigue failure. The design for extreme event limit state is to ensure that the bridge will not collapse during natural or man-made disasters, such as earthquakes and collisions by a vessel; design for strength limit state is to provide sufficient strength and stability to resist the statistically-significant load combinations during the lifetime of the bridge. The basic difference between the allowable stress design and the state limit design lies in the calculation of the beam strength. The limit state design accounts for the full-strength potential of the concrete on the compressive side of the neutral axis, thus, the design strength comes from a more realistic distribution of stresses in concrete allowed by inelastic deformation at or near the ultimate load. Because of differences in the variability of loads involved, design for different limit states uses different load combinations and different load factors.

5.3 Detailing of reinforcement

Detailing of reinforcement is the process of determining from the required area the number, shape and location of the reinforcing bars. This will be governed by considerations of structural efficiency and construction requirements, such as minimum reinforcement ratio and the clear spacing between bars to allow effective placing and compaction of the concrete. Requirements for detailing of reinforcement for highway and railway concrete bridges are covered in their respective design specifications.

5.3.1 Flexural reinforcement

1. <u>Minimum reinforcement ratio</u>

The railway bridge design code TB 10092 requires that at any section of a flexural member, the minimum reinforcement ratio ρ_{min} in tension zone shall not be less than the values listed in Table 5.2.

Table 5.2 The minimum reinforcement ratio for flexural members (from TB 10092)

Type of steel bar	Grade of concrete	
	C25 ~ C45	C50 ~ C60
HPB300	0.20	0.25
HRB400	0.15	0.20
HRB500	0.14	0.18

2. <u>Spacing limits</u>

(1) The tension bars are permitted to be placed in bundles with each bundle

consisting of one, two, or three bars.

(2) The minimum clear space provided between bundles shall be equal to the diameter of a single, round bar having an area equivalent to the area of the bundle, and shall be not less than 30 mm (Figure 5.4).

(3) Where bars or bundled bars are placed in three or more layers, the horizontal clear distance between the bars shall not be less than 1.5 times the nominal diameter of the bars and shall not be less than 45 mm; the vertical clear distance shall not be less than the nominal diameter of the bars and shall not be less than 30 mm.

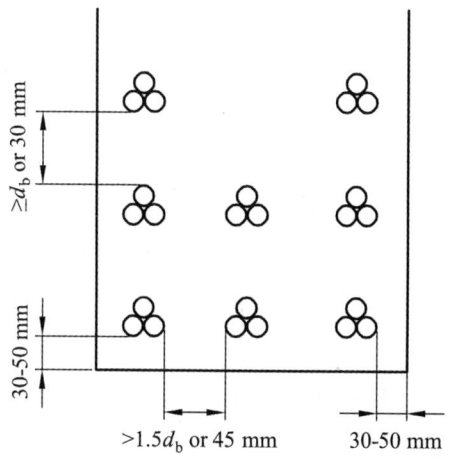

Figure 5.4 Clear spacing of reinforcing bars.

3. Hooks and bends

To anchor the reinforcing bars firmly in concrete, standards hooks shall be used at the ends of bars. In general, there are three types of hooks: the 180-degree hook, the 90-degrees hook, and the 135-degree hook (Figure 5.5). These hooks consist of a 180° or a 90° or a 135° hook, plus an extension. For plain round bars, all of these hooks are allowed to be used; for deformed round bars, only the 90-degrees hook and the 135-degree hook are permitted.

(1) For plain round bars, the 180-degree hook consists of a 180-degree bend of diameter not less than $2.5\,d_b$ measured on the inside of the bar, plus an extension not less than $3.0\,d_b$ at the free end of the bar [Figure 5.5(a)], where d_b is diameter of a reinforcing bar

(2) For plain or deformed round bars, the required dimensions of the 90-degree and the 135-degree hooks are shown in Figures 5.5(b) and (c).

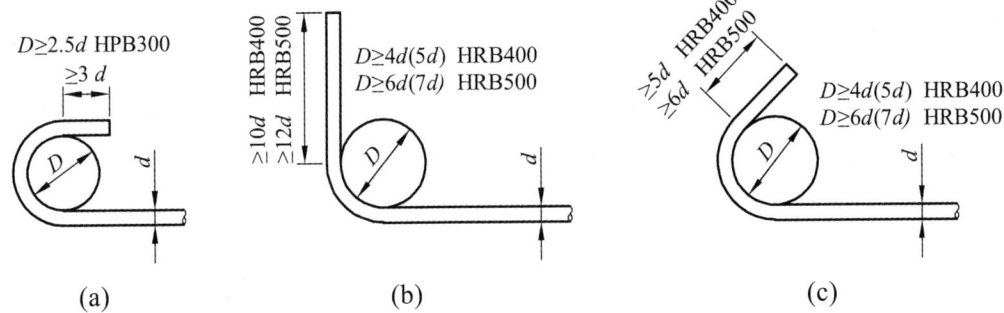

Figure 5.5 Dimensions of standard hooks: (a) the 180-degree hook; (b) the 90-degree hook; (c) the 135-degree hook.

4. Development length

The development length is defined as the shortest length of embedment of a reinforcing bar necessary to develop the full strength of the steel, controlled by either pullout or splitting [Figure 5.6(a)]. The development lengths are different in tension and compression, because a bar loaded in tension transfers stress into concrete by bonding stress and hence requires longer development length. But if the bar is loaded in compression, the bearing stress at the end of the bar will transfer part of the compression into the concrete. According the TB 10092, the anchorage or development length of a reinforcing bar shall meet the following requirements:

(1) The anchorage length of a reinforcing bar shall not be less than that specified in Table 4.3.

(2) At each end of a beam, reinforcement shall be extended beyond the support for a distance not less than $10\,d_b$ with a standard hook at the free end [Figure 5.6(b)(c)].

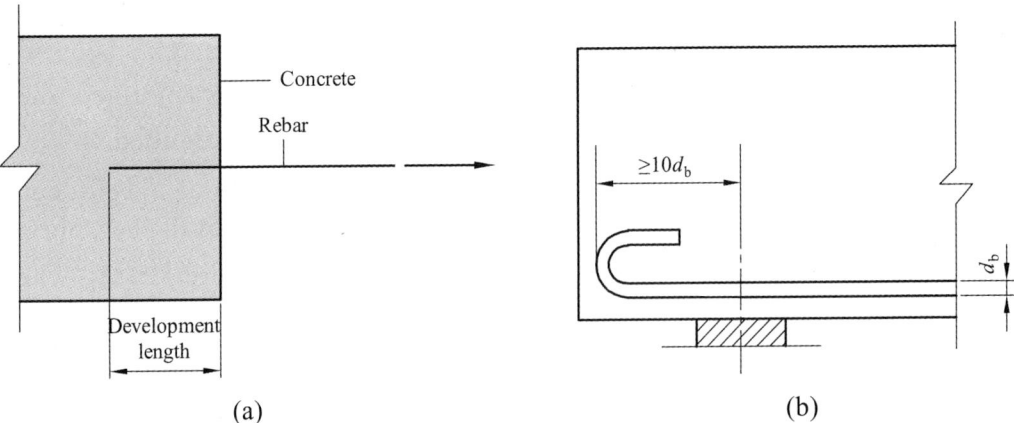

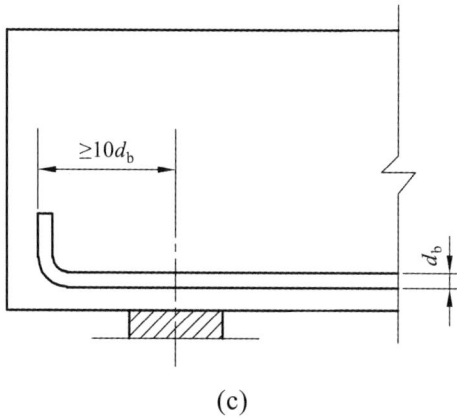

(c)

Figure 5.6 The development and anchorage lengths: (a) the development length of a bar; (b) the anchorage length of a plain round bar at the end of a beam; (c) the anchorage length of a deformed round bar at the end of a beam.

(3) The minimum radii of curvature of reinforcing bars shall be $10d_b$ for steel type HPB300, $14d_b$ for steel type HRB400, and $18d_b$ for steel type HRB500 (Figure 5.7).

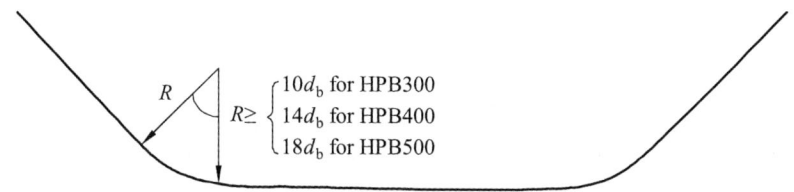

Figure 5.7 The radius of curvature of reinforcing bars.

Table 5.3 The minimum anchorage lengths of reinforcing bars (mm)

Type of steel		HPB300			HRB400			HRB500		
Grade of Concrete		C25	C30、C35	≥C40	C25	C30、C35	≥C40	C25	C30、C35	≥C40
Steel in compression (without hooks)		30d	25d	20d	35d	30d	25d	40d	35d	30d
Steel in tension	Without hooks	—	—	—	45d	40d	35d	50d	45d	40d
	With hooks	25d	20d	20d	30d	25d	20d	35d	30d	25d

Note: (i) For the deformed bars of diameter larger than 25 mm, the values shall be increased by 10%;
(ii) Cutoff points of the tension bars shall not be in the tension zone. The values in the table should be used when it is difficult to do so.
(iii) For epoxy-coated reinforcing bars, the values for the tension steel shall be increased by 25%.
(iv) If the concrete is liable to disturbance, the values shall be increased by 10%.

5. Bar splices

The required continuity of reinforcing bars can be provided by bar splices. The bar splices include the lap splice (Figure 5.8), welded splice (Figure 5.9), and the mechanical splice (Figure 5.10), their use depending on the diameter of the bars and the detailing requirements. According to the railway design code, the following requirements shall be met:

(1) Lap splices shall not be used for the main reinforcement required by analysis, but may be used for secondary reinforcement.

(2) Lap splices in adjacent reinforcing bars of the same member shall be staggered. The length of lap L_s shall not be less than that specified in Table 5.4.

(3) For the welded splice, the length of lap shall be determined by test with the requirement that the strength of the welded splice shall be larger than that of the joining bars.

(4) For the mechanical splice, the thread pitch of the coupler shall be 2.0 mm, 2.5 mm, and 3.0 mm for bar diameters of 16 mm to 20 mm, 22 mm to 25 mm, and 28 mm to 32 mm, respectively.

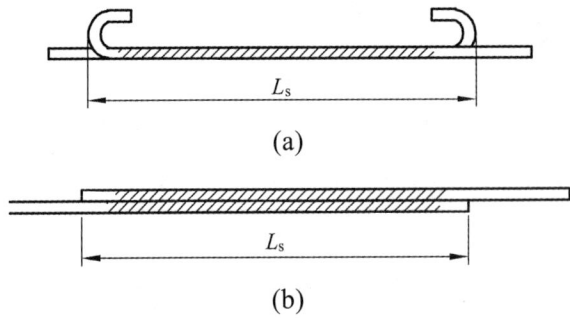

Figure 5.8 The lap splice: (a) for plain round bars; (b) for deformed round bars.

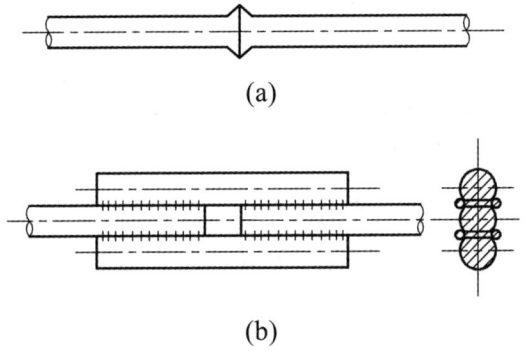

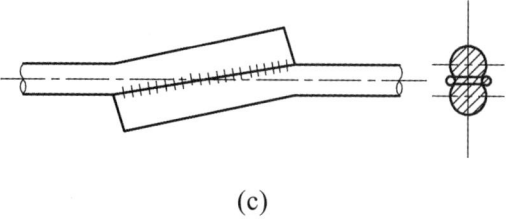

(c)

Figure 5.9 The welded splice: (a) direct butt joint; (b) indirect butt joint with two splice bars; (c) direct lap joint.

Figure 5.10 The mechanical splice.

Table 5.4 The lengths of lap for lap splices

Type of steel	Grade of Contrete		
	C25	C30、C35	⩾C40
HRB400	63d	56d	49d
HRB500	70d	63d	56d

6. Concrete Protection for Reinforcement

Corrosion of the reinforcing steel is caused carbonation or sulphation, chloride attack, cracks, and inadequate cover. Corrosion of the reinforcing steel can result in reduction of effective cross-sectional area of the bars, and in turn results in serious degradation of reinforced concrete bridges. Reinforcing steel is also more sensitive to high temperatures than concrete. At high temperatures the strength of steel decreases sizably and as a consequence the load-carrying capacity of reinforced concrete members is substantially reduced.

To provide the steel with adequate concrete protection against fire and corrosion, a sufficient thickness of concrete cover over the reinforcing bars must be maintained outside of the outermost steel. The thickness required will vary, depending upon the type of member and conditions of exposure. According to the Chinese railway design code TB 10092, the thickness of clear concrete cover over reinforcement shall not be less than 35 mm and greater than 50 mm (Figure 5.11). For reinforced concrete deck slab, the clear concrete cover thickness shall not be less than 30 mm.

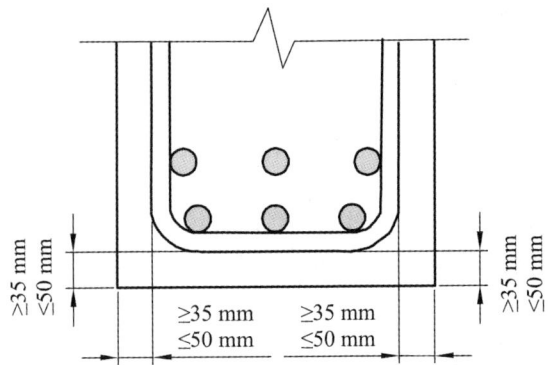

Figure 5.11 Clear cover over reinforcement.

5.3.2 Transverse reinforcement

The Chinese railway design code stipulates that stirrups of diameter not less than 8 mm long shall be provided for the reinforced concrete beam along with the following requirements:

(1) To support reinforcing bars in tension, the stirrups shall be spaced at not greater than $3/4h$ and not greater than 300 mm, where h is the depth of the beam.

(2) To support reinforcing bars in compression, the stirrups shall be spaced at not greater than 15 times the diameter of the main reinforcing bars and not greater than 300 mm.

(3) In the region within the distance of $h/2$ from the support, the spacing of stirrups shall not be greater than 100 mm. The numbers of tension and compression bars enclosed in a stirrup shall not be greater than 5 and 3 in each row, respectively.

(4) If the beam may be subjected to torsion, the stirrups shall be closed ones.

5.3.3 Skin and distribution reinforcements

For relatively deep flexural members, some reinforcement should be placed near the vertical faces in the tension zone to control cracking in the web. Without such auxiliary steel, the width of the cracks in the web may greatly exceed the crack widths at the level of the flexural tension reinforcement. The contribution of the skin steel to flexural strength is usually disregarded, although it may be included in the strength calculations if a strain compatibility analysis is used to establish the stress in the skin steel at the flexural failure load.

According to the Chinese railway design code, if the total depth of the beam h exceeds 1.0 m, longitudinal skin reinforcement shall be uniformly distributed along both side faces of the web (Figure 5.12). The spacing of the skin reinforcement shall be between 100 mm and 150 mm and the diameter of the skin reinforcement bars shall be not less than 8 mm.

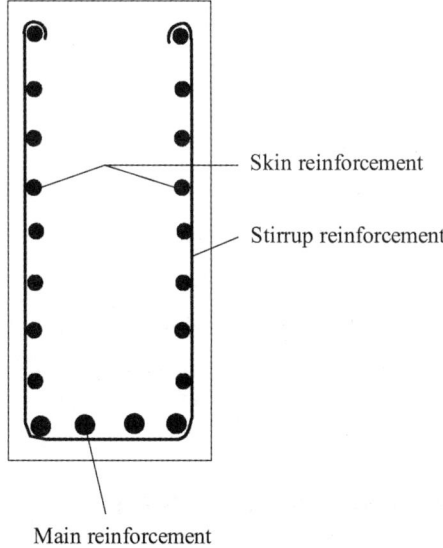

Figure 5.12   Skin reinforcement.

For the flange of T-beam, the distribution reinforcement shall be placed in the top of the slab to help distribute wheel loads in the longitudinal direction of the bridge to the primary reinforcement in the transverse direction (Figure 5.13). The spacing of the distribution reinforcement shall not be large than 300 mm and the bar diameter shall not be greater 8 mm. Longitudinal distribution reinforcement in the flange or deck slab contributes to resistance and should be included in computing ultimate moment capacity.

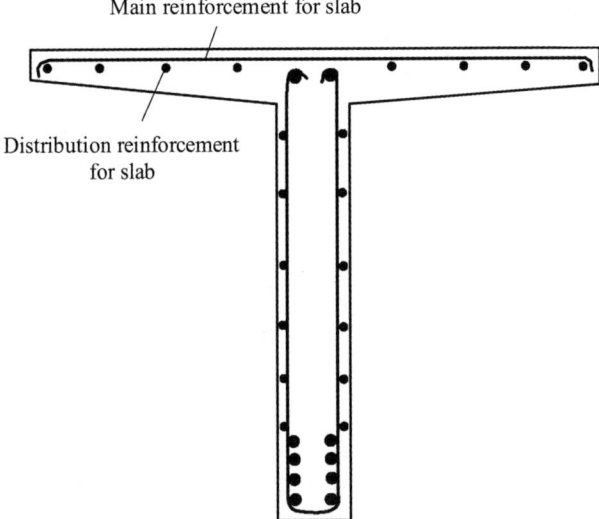

Figure 5.13   Distribution reinforcement.

5.4   Bridge examples

In this section, several examples of simply-supported reinforced concrete bridges are presented to illustrate the reinforcement details in a reinforced concrete bridge. These bridges are selected from the inventory of the standard railway and highway concrete bridges in China, and they are used in short- to medium-span length. However, for medium span length, these bridges are often replaced by prestressed concrete bridges.

5.4.1   Railway reinforced concrete bridges

<u>1. The slab bridge</u>

Figure 5.14 shows a typical railway reinforced concrete slab bridge for the span length of 8 m. In the midspan section, there are totally 23 main reinforcing bars, designated by N1, N2 … N7, which are designed to resist the normal stresses produced by bending moments. These bars are bent up in turn at some locations, where they are no longer needed, to serve as web reinforcement to resist shear forces and prevent diagonal cracking. The N21 bars are stirrups to resist diagonal tension. The N34 bars are secondary reinforcing bars to form rebar frames with the N21 stirrups and the main

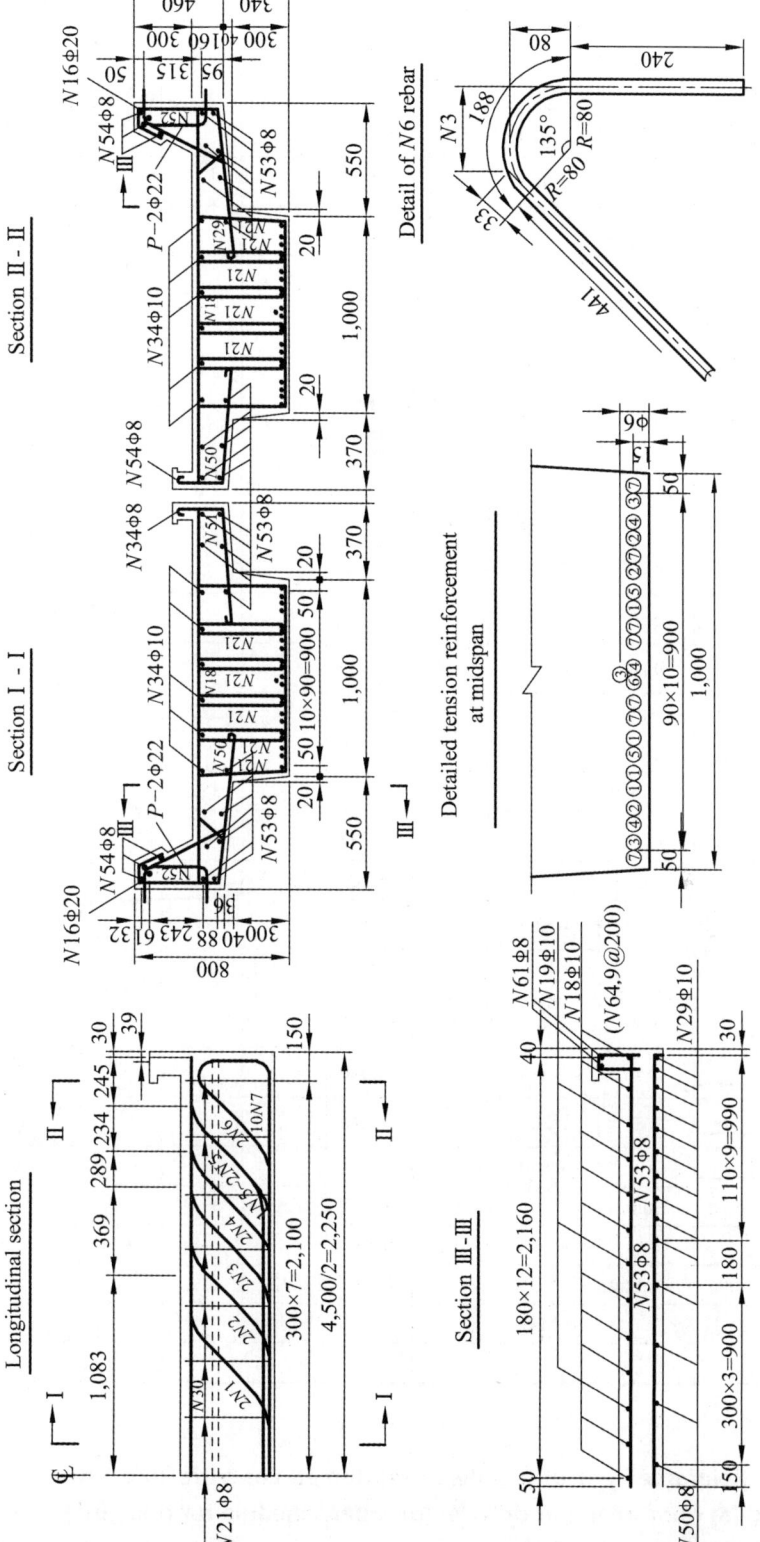

(a)

Bar No.	Shape	Diameter /mm	Length of each bar /m	No..of Bars	Total Length /m	Unit Weight /(kg/m)	Total Weight /kg	Notes
1		φ16	2.478	2	4.956			Main rebars in the loghitudinal direction
2		φ16	3.216	2	6.432			Main rebars in the loghitudinal direction
3		φ16	3.794	2	7.588			Main rebars in the loghitudinal direction
4		φ16	4.262	2	8.524			Main rebars in the loghitudinal direction
5 (5′)		φ16	4.752 (4.736)	2 1	9.504 (4.736)			Main rebars in the loghitudinal direction
6		φ16	5.292	2	10.584			Main rebars in the loghitudinal direction
7		φ16	4.576	10	45.760			Main rebars in the loghitudinal direction
	φ16	Subtotal			98.084	1.578	154.8	
16		φ20	2.205	2	4.410	2.466	10.9	Distribution rebars inside U-shaped bolts
18		φ10	1.965	20	39.300			Main rebars in top of deck slab
19		φ10	2.019	6	12.114			Main rebars in top of deck slab
29		φ10	0.835	20	16.700			Special rebars in bottom of deck slab
30		φ10	0.871	20	17.420			Special rebars in bottom of deck slab
	φ10	Subtotal			85.534	0.617	52.8	
21		φ8	1.200	75	90.000			Stirrups in web
	φ8	Subtotal			90.000	0.395	35.6	
34		φ10	4.460	6	26.760			Secondary rebars to form rebar frame
	φ10	Subtotal			26.760	0.617	16.5	
50		φ8	0.850	8	6.800			Rebars in the bottom of deck slab
51		φ8	0.889	8	7.112			Rebars in the bottom of deck slab
52		φ8	1.484	26	38.584			Rebars in the ballast retaining wall
53		φ8	4.470	12	53.640			Distribution rebars in the deck slab
54		φ8	2.205	4	17.640			Distribution rebars in the inside ballast retaining wall
61		φ8	1.880	4	7.520			Rebars in the end wall
	φ8	Subtotal			131.296	0.395	51.9	
64		φ6	0.476	18	8.568			Rebars in the end wall
	φ6	Subtotal			8.568	0.222	1.9	
Total			16Mn			254.1 kg		
			A3			70.3 kg		

(b)

Figure 5.14 Reinforcement of a railway reinforced concrete slab bridge with a span length of 8 m: (a) reinforcement details; (b) rebar schedule for one girder (units: mm).

tension reinforcing bars N1, N2 ... N7. The N1 to N5 rebars are extended to and anchored in the compressive zone with enough anchorage length. But N6 rebars have to bend downwards to meet the development requirement.

The N18 and N19 rebars are main reinforcing bars in the transverse direction for the deck slab to resist the bending stress caused by the wheel loads acting on the deck. Since the top of the deck slab is subjected to tension under the wheel loads, the main reinforcing bars are placed at the top of the slab. The rebars N29, N30, N50, and N51 are secondary reinforcing bars for the slab. These bars are placed at the bottom of the slab to resist the bending stress in the bottom of the deck slab produced by casual negative bending moments. The rebars N53 and N54 are distribution reinforcement in the longitudinal direction serving to form rebar frame with other main rebars. Details of the rebars are shown in the rebar schedule [Figure 5.14(b)].

2. The T-shaped girder bridge

Figure 5.15 shows the reinforcement details of a standard T-shaped railway concrete girder bridge which has a span-length of 16 m. There are totally 43 $\phi 20$ main reinforcing bars, designated by N1, N2 ... N16, among which the bars from N1 to N12 are in turn bent-up at the locations where they are no longer needed. The bars N1 to N10 are directly anchored in the compressive zone without hooks, while bars N11 and N12 have to be bent again upwards at the girder end to be anchored in the compression zone. The bars N13 and N14 are straight bars and are anchored in the tension zone with hooks at the free ends. The bars N15 and N15a are extended over the support and anchored at the girder ends with hoops at the bar ends.

To reduce the size of the bottom flange, the main rebars are arranged in groups of two or three bars. There are totally 132 $\phi 20$ stirrups, designated by N21 and N22. Since the width of the web is 0.3 m in the area adjacent to the midspan and 0.49 near the support, the N21 stirrups are placed within the thin web, while the N22 stirrups are placed in the thick web. The spacing of the stirrups are all 0.25 m. The N27 and N28 rebars are skin reinforcement steel, which are placed on the two sides of the web to distribute cracks. The N65 and N66 $\phi 6$ rebars serve as spacers to maintain the distance between the two legs of stirrups, so that stirrups would not dbe displaced during of concrete.

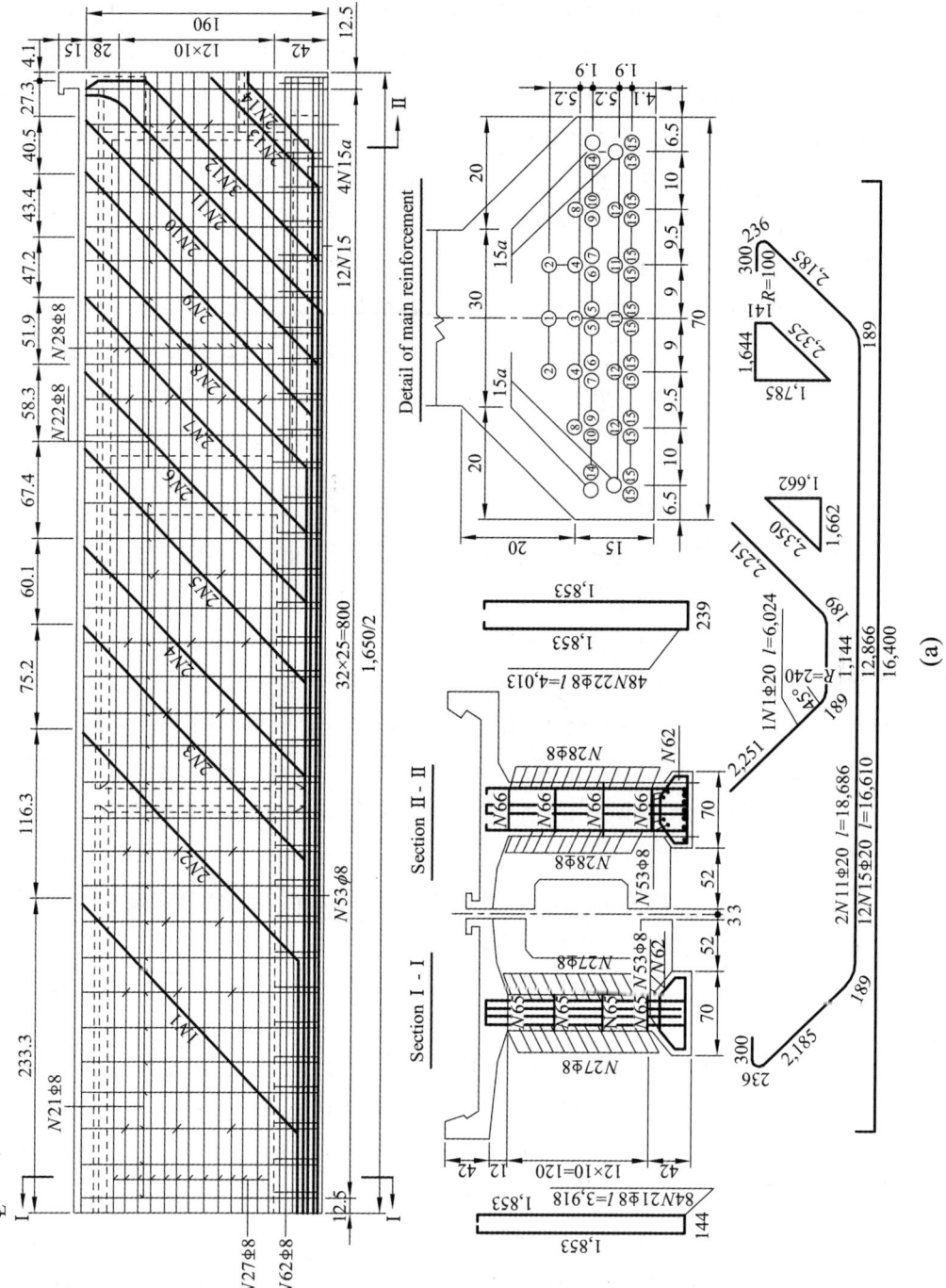

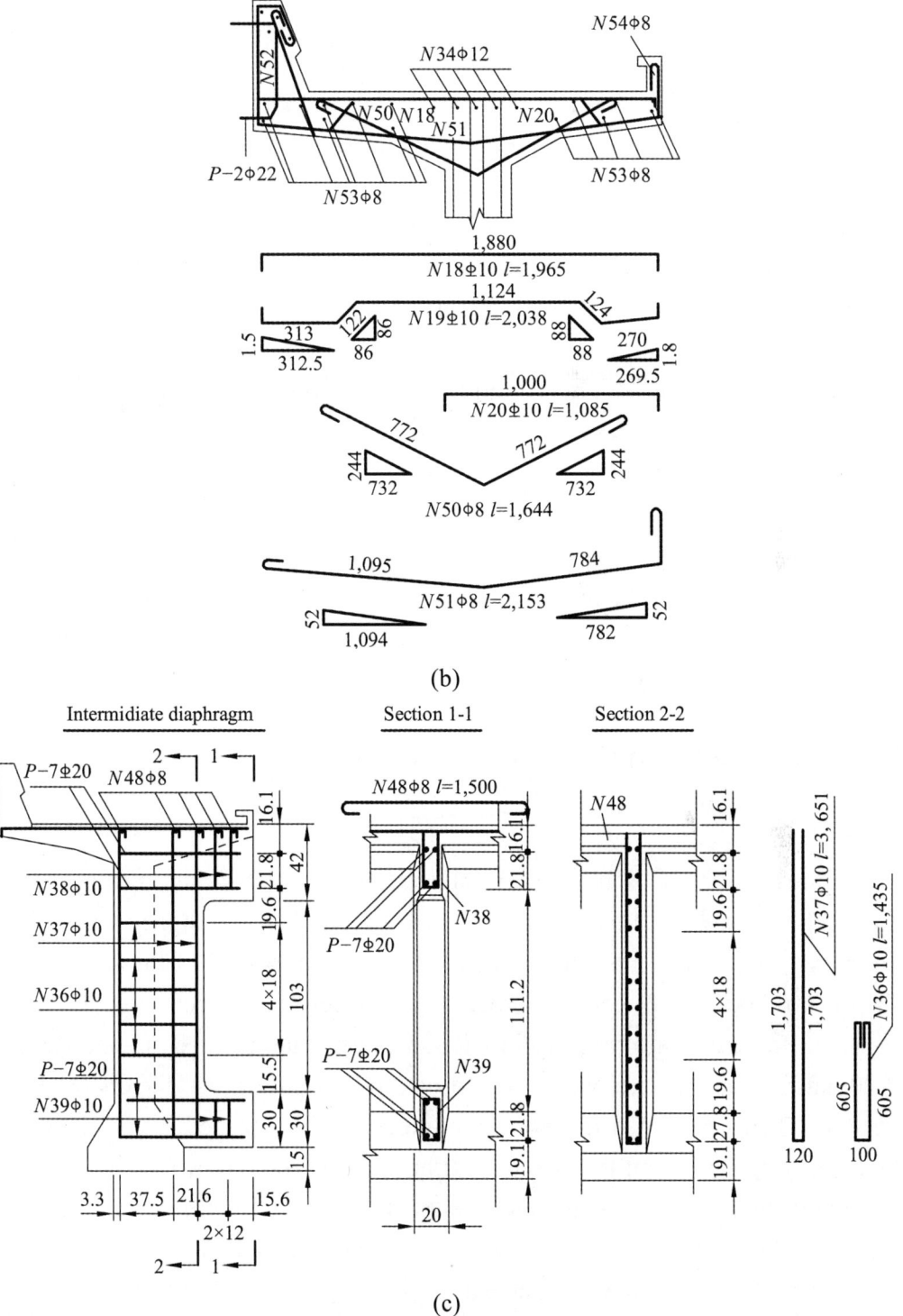

Figure 5.15 Reinforcement details of a railway reinforced concrete T-girder bridge (units: cm): (a) Reinforcment in the web; (b) Reinforcement in deck slab; (c) Rcinforccmcnt in diaphragm.

The N18, N19, and N20 rebars are placed at the top of the deck slab to resist bending stresses in the overhanging slab. In some circumstances, such as that happens during transportation and installation, the slab may be accidentally bent upwards to produce tensile stress in the bottom of the deck slab. Thus, the rebar N50 and N51 are placed in the bottom of the slab to resist the casual tensile stress. The N34 and N53 $\phi 8$ rebars that are placed on the top of the deck slab are distribution reinforcement whose function is to transfer the wheel loads acting on the deck to the main reinforcing bars N18 to N20. The N53 rebars in the enlarged bottom flange are secondary reinforcement whose function is to form the rebar frame with the N62 stirrups and the main rebars N1 to N16, so that the main rebars are hold in place during casting.

The rebars N48 and N49 are short longitudinal rebars placed in the top of the deck slab above the diaphragm to resist longitudinal tension stress in the slab. In the diaphragm, the P- $7\phi 20$ rebars are the main rebars to resist the transverse forces due to distribution of the wheel loads in the transverse direction. The rebars N36 to N39 are the secondary reinforcement designed to resist the stresses that are usually difficult to predict by the design formulas.

5.4.2 Highway reinforced concrete bridges

1. The slab bridge

Figure 5.16 shows a highway reinforce concrete slab bridge having a span length of 8 m and the clear width of 11 m. The bridge is designed for Chinese Highway-I class. The slab thickness is 0.45 m which is 1/17 of the span length. The main reinforcement consists of the rebar frames and N1 rebars of 25 mm in diameter. These bars are made from HRB335 steel. The inclined N2 and N3 bars of 20 mm in diameter, are placed at a spacing of 0.3 m to resist diagonal stress in the slab. There are also distribution reinforcement bars placed in the transverse direction at the bottom of the slab to distribute the wheel loads to the main rebars. The distribution reinforcement bars have the diameter of 16 mm and are placed at a spacing of 0.12 m, which meets the requirement that the area of the distribution reinforcement in unit length of the slab in the longitudinal direction shall not be less than 15% of the main rebar area in unit width of the slab. The layouts of the reinforcement bars in Figure 6.48 are easy to understand.

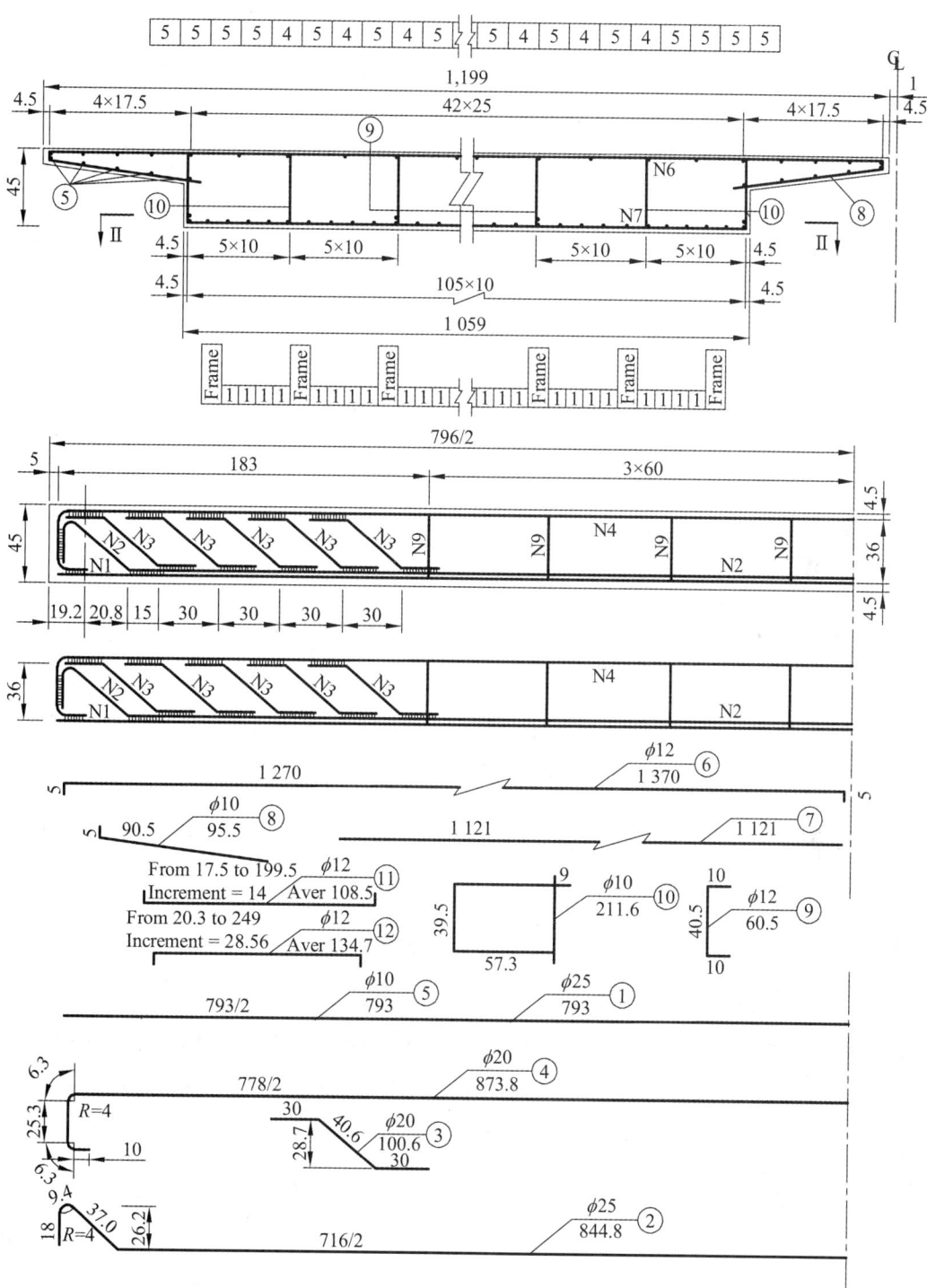

Figure 5.16 Reinforcement details of a highway reinforced concrete slab bridge (units: cm).

2. The T-shaped girder bridge

Figure 5.17 shows a prefabricated reinforced T-girder concrete highway bridge having a span length of 20 m. The bridge is designed based on an old design vehicular loads Truck-15 and Trailer-80 stipulated by the highway design code published in 1981. The bridge is 19.96 m long in total length. Each girder is provided with 8 $\phi 32$ and 2 $\phi 16$ longitudinal reinforcing steel bars which are required by analysis. These main reinforcing bars are designated as N1, N2 ... and N5, among which 2 N1 rebars are placed at the bottom of the girder and extended over the support center, and other rebars are in turn bent up at the locations where they are no longer required.

The N6 rebars are the secondary reinforcement to form bar frame with stirrups and main rebars. The N6 rebars have a diameter of 32 mm, and they are bent down at the beam ends to be welded to the N1 bars. The N12 bars are U-shaped stirrups which are plain round bars of 8 mm in diameter. These stirrups are placed at a spacing of 0.24 m. Note that in the area far from the support, one U-shaped stirrups are placed in a section (see Section I-I in Figure 5.17); however in the area adjacent to the support, double U-shaped stirrups are used in a section to resist the increased shear force near the support (see Section II-II in Figure 5.17). The N11 $\phi 8$ bars are skin reinforcement, sometimes also called distribution reinforcement in China, to control cracking. These bars are densely distributed near the bottom of the girder and sparsely distributed in the area far from the bottom flange. The additional inclined bars N7, N8, N9, and N10 are web reinforcement designed to strengthen the resistance to the diagonal tension in the web. The reinforcement details in the diaphragm are shown in Figure 5.18, in which the functions of the rebars are similar to those for the diaphragms of the railway concrete girders.

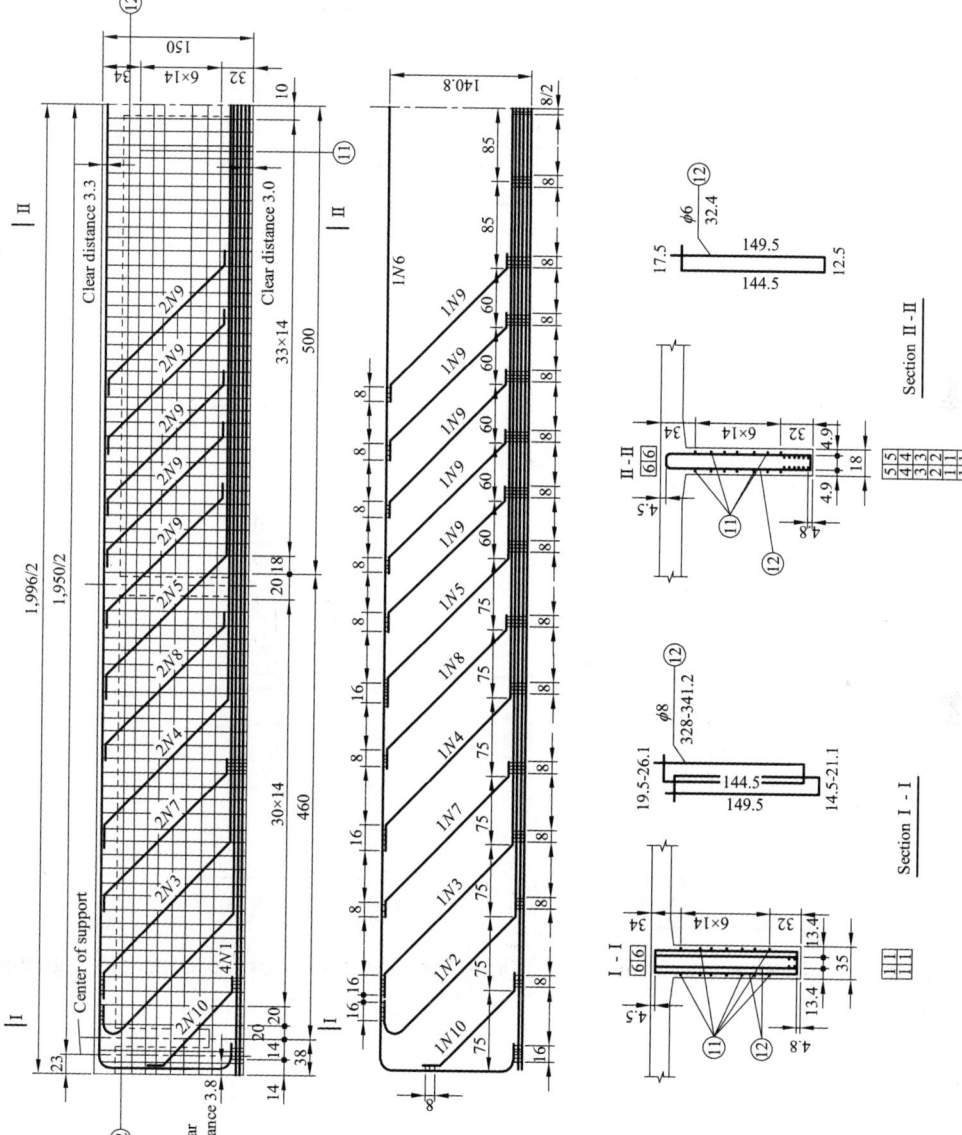

Figure 5.17 Reinforcement details of a highway reinforced concrete T-girder bridge (units: cm).

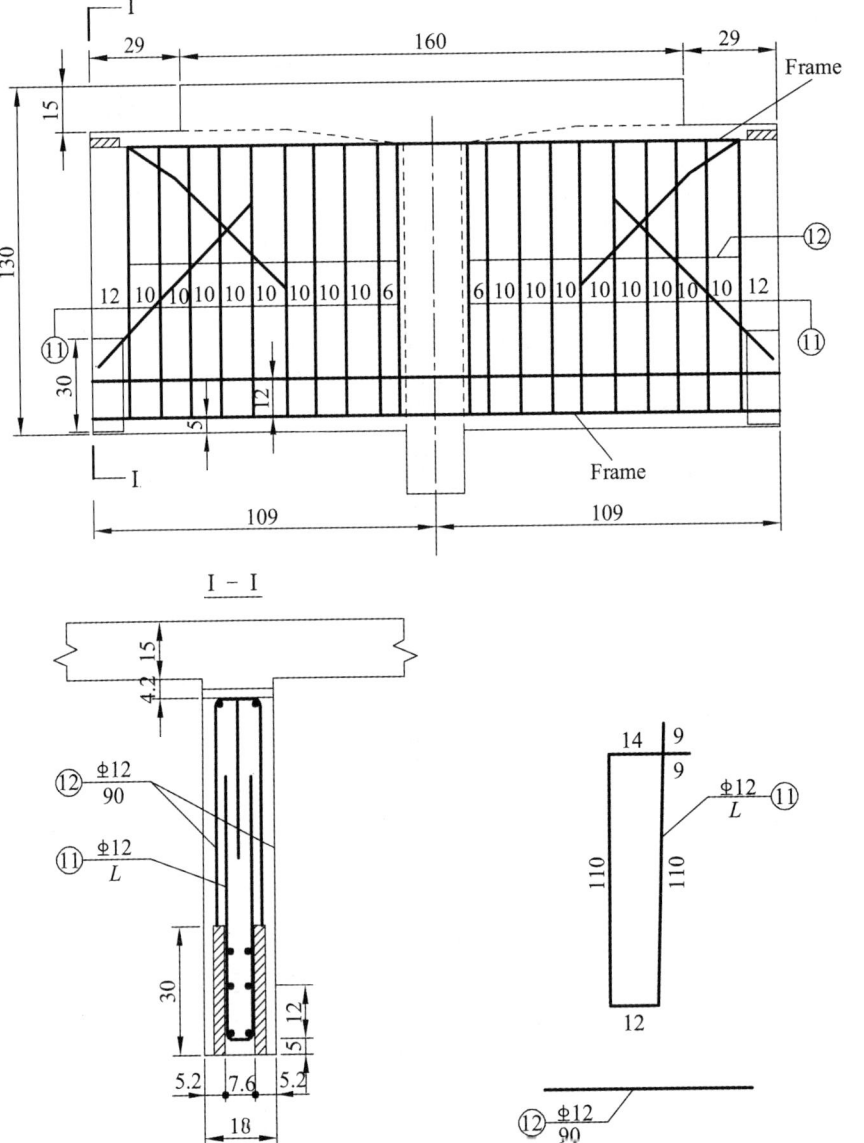

Figure 5.18 Reinforcement details in a diaphragm for a reinforced concrete T-girder (units: cm).

References

[5.1] Yao, L.-S., ed., (Xiang, H.-F., Gu, A.-B., reviewers), Bridge Engineering, 2nd ed., China Communications Press, Beijing, China, 2008.
姚玲森. 桥梁工程. 2 版. 项海帆, 顾安邦, 主审. 北京：人民交通出版社, 2008.

[5.2] He G.-H., Che, H.-M., and Xie, Y.-F., Railway Reinforced Concrete Bridges, China Railway Press, Beijing, 1986.

何广汉, 车惠民, 谢幼藩. 铁路钢筋混凝土桥. 北京：中国铁道出版社, 1986.

[5.3] Tang J.-S., ed., (Yang, J. reviewer), Railway Bridges, China Railway Press, Beijing, 2015.

唐继舜. 铁路桥梁. 杨进, 主审. 北京：中国铁道出版社, 2015.

[5.4] Shao X.-D., ed., (Gu, A.-B., reviewer), Bridge Engineering, 4th ed., China Communications Press Co., Ltd., Beijing, China, 2018.

邵旭东. 桥梁工程. 4 版. 顾安邦, 主审. 北京：人民交通出版社股份有限公司, 2018.

[5.5] TB 10092-2017 (J 462-2017), *Code for Design of Concrete Structures of Railway Bridges and Culverts*, China National Railway Bureau, 2017.

[5.6] JTG 3362-2018, Specifications *for Design of Highway Reinforced Concrete and Prestressed Concrete Bridges and Culverts*, China's Transportation Ministry, 2018.

Chapter 6 *Prestressed Concrete Girder Bridges*

6.1 Introduction

It is has been well known that concrete is strong in compression but weak in tension. Usually, its tensile strength is around 1/10 to 1/15 of its compressive strength. As a result, cracks develop at early stages of loading. The reinforced concrete combines concrete and steel bars by simply putting them together to let them work together as wished. A member made from reinforced concrete thus takes advantage of the compressive strength of concrete and tensile strength of steel to resist loading. However, for the reinforcing steel bars to take substantial effect, the stress in concrete around the bars has to reach or exceed its tensile strength, resulting in cracking of concrete. With increase of the stress in the steel bars, the cracks grow in width and number, and propagate across the depth of the member; at the same time, the deflection of the beam rises. Consequently, the serviceability of the structure is limited by severe cracking and undue deflection.

In order to reduce or prevent such cracks from developing, compressive stresses can be generated in concrete by means of some techniques before application of external loadings, so that the tensile stresses in concrete to be produced by external loadings can be cancelled out by the pre-existing compressive stresses. Such a pre-existing compressive stress is called a prestress, and the method for generating the prestress in concrete is called a prestressing technique. The concrete with prestress is termed prestressed concrete.

Application of the prestressing technique in construction of concrete bridges and building structures resulted from the availability of high-strength steel and high-strength concrete. In 1926 through 1928, Eugene Freyssinet, a

French engineer, proposed methods to overcome prestress losses by using high-strength steel wires. In 1940, he developed the well-known Freyssinet system which has two coupled steel cones to anchor the prestressing tendons by wedge action. During World War II and thereafter, many bridges destroyed in the war in western and central Europe were reconstructed by application of the concept and technique of prestressing. Over the history of the prestressed concrete, P. W. Abeles of England, F. Leonhardt of Germany, V. Mikhailov of Russia, and T. Y. Lin of the United States made great contributions to the art and science of the design and construction of prestressed concrete structures. T. Y. Lin's load-balancing method considerably simplified the design process, especially for continuous bridge structures. By the 1950s, manufacturing techniques for steel had developed sufficiently to such an extent that stress-relieved steel wires with high strength and ductility were produced at costs that were economically suitable for wide use in prestressed concrete structures. With advent of low-relaxation prestressing strands, prestressed concrete has become a commonly used material for building long-span bridges and other civil structures.

In China, the research and development of prestressed concrete started in 1950s. The first prestressed concrete girder in China was experimentally produced in 1955. It was a simply supported girder of 12 m long used to carry railway loads. In 1956, the first prestressed concrete railway bridge, the Xinyi river bridge, was built in Lanzhou-Lianyungang railway, with 28 spans, each 24 m long. In 1957, the first prestressed concrete highway bridge in China was built in the town of Zhoukoudian near the City of Beijing. It was a single-span simply supported girder bridge of 20 m long. Since then, the prestressing technique has been extensively used in China to build long-span bridges, including continuous bridges, rigid frame bridges, and cable-stayed bridges. Currently, a simply supported prestressed concrete box girder can span a maximum distance of 64 m. For continuous prestressed concrete bridges, the maximum span length has been 180 m (Figure 6.1), while the span length of the continuous rigid frame bridge has reached 330 m (Figure 6.2).

Figure 6.1 The Min River bridge, a continuous prestressed concrete box girder bridge with the span arrangement of 100.4m+3×180m+100.4m, located on Leshan-zigong high-speed highway.

Figure 6.2 The Chongqing Shibanpo highway bridge (the new one), a continuous rigid frame prestressed concrete bridge with the span arrangement of 87.75m+4×138m+ 330m+133.75m, located in City of Chongqing.

6.2 Principles of prestressing

6.2.1 The general principle of prestressing

The general principle of prestressed concrete can be stated as follows: the prestressing introduces internal stresses of such magnitude and distribution in a structural member that the stresses resulting from given external loads are counteracted to the desired degree. Prestressing of concrete members is achieved by transferring forces between the prestressing tendons and the concrete. The prestressing tendons can be placed within the concrete member as internal tendons or alongside the concrete as external tendons.

To illustrate this principle, let consider a simply supported rectangular beam prestressed with a straight tendon that is placed eccentrically with respect to the centroid of the concrete section (Figure 6.3). The construction procedure of the beam is as follows: first, the concrete beam is cast with a duct placed in the design position of the tendon; second, after the beam has been cured to the design strength, the prestressing tendon is threaded through the duct and is tensioned against the ends of the beam to the design force P by a hydraulic jack; finally the tendon is anchored at the ends of the beam such that the force in the tendon is maintained at the constant value P. Note that the space between the duct and the tendon is not grouted after prestressing. As a general convention for discussing prestressed concrete, compressive stresses are assigned positive signs, and tensile stresses negative signs.

The stresses at the top and bottom fiber of the concrete due to the prestressing force P can obtained by

$$\sigma_{c,top}^{P} = \frac{P}{A_c} - \frac{Pec_t}{I_c} \tag{6.1}$$

$$\sigma_{c,bot}^{P} = \frac{P}{A_c} + \frac{Pec_b}{I_c} \tag{6.2}$$

where, $\sigma_{c,top}^{P}$ is the stress at the top fibers of concrete produced by the prestressing force;

$\sigma_{c,bot}^{P}$ is the stress at the bottom fibers of concrete produced by the prestressing force;

c_t is the distance from the top surface to the centroid of the concrete beam;

c_b is the distance from the bottom surface to the centroid of the beam;

A_c is the cross-sectional area of the beam without the area occupied by the duct;

I_c is the moment of inertia of the cross-section of the beam without the area occupied by the duct.

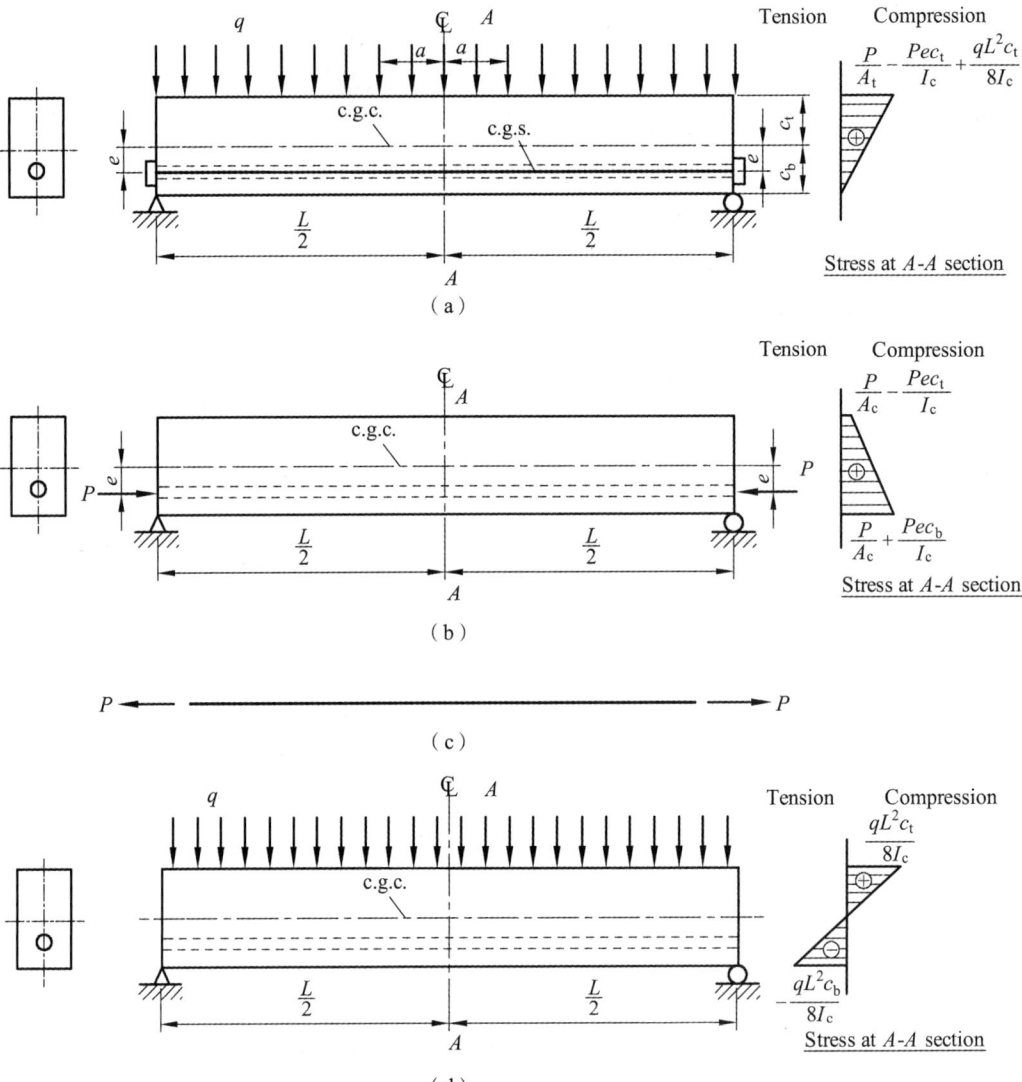

Figure 6.3 Stress distributions in an eccentrically prestressed concrete beam: (a) total stress in concrete; (b) stress in concrete due to prestressing force; (c) prestressing force in the steel tendon; (d) stress in concrete due to self-weight.

The uniform load q, representing the self-weight of the beam, causes a maximum bending moment M_q at the midspan:

$$M_q = \frac{qL^2}{8} \tag{6.3}$$

The stresses at the top and bottom fibers of the concrete produced by M_q become

$$\sigma_{c,top}^q = \frac{M_q c_t}{I_c} = \frac{qL^2 c_t}{8I_c} \quad (6.4)$$

$$\sigma_{c,bot}^q = -\frac{M_q c_b}{I_c} = -\frac{qL^2 c_b}{8I_c} \quad (6.5)$$

where, $\sigma_{c,top}^q$ and $\sigma_{c,bot}^q$ denote the stresses at the top and bottom fibers caused by the self-weight q. The total stresses in the concrete are the superposition of the stresses caused by the prestressing force and the self-weight, i.e.,

$$\sigma_{c,top} = \sigma_{c,top}^P + \sigma_{c,top}^q = \frac{P}{A_c} - \frac{Pec_t}{I_c} + \frac{qL^2 c_t}{8I_c} \quad (6.6)$$

$$\sigma_{c,bot} = \sigma_{c,bot}^P + \sigma_{c,bot}^q = \frac{P}{A_c} + \frac{Pec_b}{I_c} - \frac{qL^2 c_b}{8I_c} \quad (6.7)$$

Since the prestressing force causes compressive stresses at the bottom fiber of the concrete, and the self-weight of the beam causes tensile stresses, the sums of the two systems of stresses at the midspan can be made zeros if the prestressing force is set to be

$$P = \frac{qL^2}{8} \frac{c_b}{I_c} \bigg/ \left(\frac{1}{A_c} + \frac{ec_b}{I_c} \right) = \frac{qL^2}{8} \frac{c_b}{r_c^2} \bigg/ \left(1 + \frac{ec_b}{r_c^2} \right) \quad (6.8)$$

$$r_c^2 = \frac{I_c}{A_c} \quad (6.9)$$

where, r_c is the radius of gyration of the cross-section of concrete. If the prestressing force P is kept unvaried, the eccentricity e can be adjusted to make the total stress at the bottom fiber zero. The distributions of stresses at the midspan for the two actions and the combinations of the stresses are shown in Figure 6.4.

After completion of the prestressing, the duct has to be filled with corrosion-inhibiting materials or grouted. For prestressed concrete girder, the duct is usually grouted with Portland cement-based material, by which the prestressing tendon is bonded to the concrete before application of the service loads. For this reason, the transformed section should be used to calculate the stresses and strains in the girder under service loads. In the transformed section, the holes are considered to be filled with concrete and the prestressing steel replaced with an equivalent area of concrete.

Assume that the live loadings F acts on the beam after the strength of the grout has reached the design strength (Figure 6.4). Then, the stresses at the top and bottom fibers of the concrete caused by the live loads F, denoted by $\sigma^F_{c,top}$ and $\sigma^F_{c,bot}$, are

$$\sigma^F_{c,top} = \frac{Fac'_t}{I_t} \tag{6.10}$$

$$\sigma^F_{c,bot} = -\frac{Fac'_b}{I_t} \tag{6.11}$$

where, I_t is the moment of inertia of the transformed cross-section. The total stresses in the concrete are the combinations of stresses produced by the prestressing force, the self-weight, and the live loads:

$$\sigma_{c,top} = \frac{P}{A_c} - \frac{Pec_t}{I_c} + \frac{qL^2 c_t}{8I_c} + \frac{Fac'_t}{I_t} \tag{6.12}$$

$$\sigma_{c,bot} = \frac{P}{A_c} + \frac{Pec_b}{I_c} - \frac{qL^2 c_b}{8I_c} - \frac{Fac'_b}{I_t} \tag{6.13}$$

The stress in the prestressing steel becomes

$$\sigma_{s,bot} = \frac{P}{A_p} + n\frac{Fae}{I_t} \tag{6.14}$$

where, $n = E_s / E_c$ is the modular ratio of the prestressing steel to concrete, and the A_p is the cross-sectional area of the prestressing steel. Note that the prestress loss is not considered in Eq. (6.14). The bottom fiber of the concrete in the section is subjected to tension under the live loads and the stress in the prestressing steel increases due to the live loads. If the tensile stresses in concrete caused the live loads are below the tensile strength, cracks will not occur. In practical design, the stress at the bottom fiber of the concrete before application of the live loads is usually set to be compressive to counteract the tensile stress to be produced by the live loads. Consequently, the concrete will not crack under service loads. Figure 6.4 shows the final stress distribution in the prestressed concrete girder shown in Figure 6.3, after application of service loads.

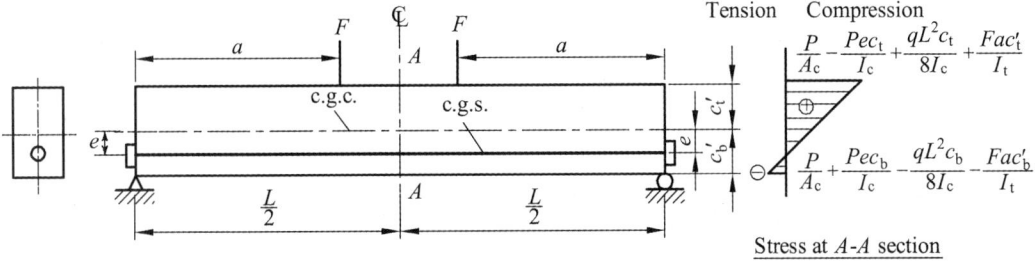

Figure 6.4 Final distribution of the stress in concrete of an eccentrically prestressed concrete beam, due to effects of the prestressing force, the self-weight of the beam, and the live loads.

6.2.2 The effects of prestressing tendons with variable eccentricity

In general, for a simply girder bridge, the bending moments caused by the self-weight and live loadings are maximum at the midspan and minimum at the supports. To counteract the load-induced moment, the best arrangement of the prestressing tendon would be such that a counter-moment is produced in the opposite direction to the load-induced moment. This can be achieved by giving the tendon an eccentricity that varies linearly or quadratically, from zero at the supports to maximum at midspan.

As a simplest case, let's consider a prestressed concrete beam with eccentricity of the tendon linearly varied from zero at the supports to e at midspan [Figure 6.5(a)]. The free body diagram of the concrete is shown in Figure 6.5(b). The action of the prestressing tendon on the concrete beam can be looked upon as a system of external loads: at the ends of the beam, the tendon applies force P at the centroid of the concrete section with angle θ; at the midspan, the change of the slope of tendon introduces a transverse force $2P\sin\theta$ acting upward. The bending moment at the midspan is easily obtained as

$$M_{P, 0.5L} = P\sin\theta \frac{L}{2} \qquad (6.15)$$

$$\sin\theta = \frac{e}{\sqrt{e^2 + (L/2)^2}} \tag{6.16}$$

where, $M_{P,0.5L}$ represent the bending moment produced by prestressing force at the midspan. Since e is very small compared to $L/2$, i.e., $e \ll L/2$, we can have

$$\sin\theta \approx \frac{e}{L/2} \tag{6.17}$$

Substituting Eq. (6.17) into Eq. (6.15) gives

$$M_{P,0.5L} = Pe \tag{6.18}$$

Since the eccentricity of the tendon is linearly varied between the support and the midspan, the prestressing moment at any cross-section x can be written as

$$M_{P,x} = Pe_x \tag{6.19}$$

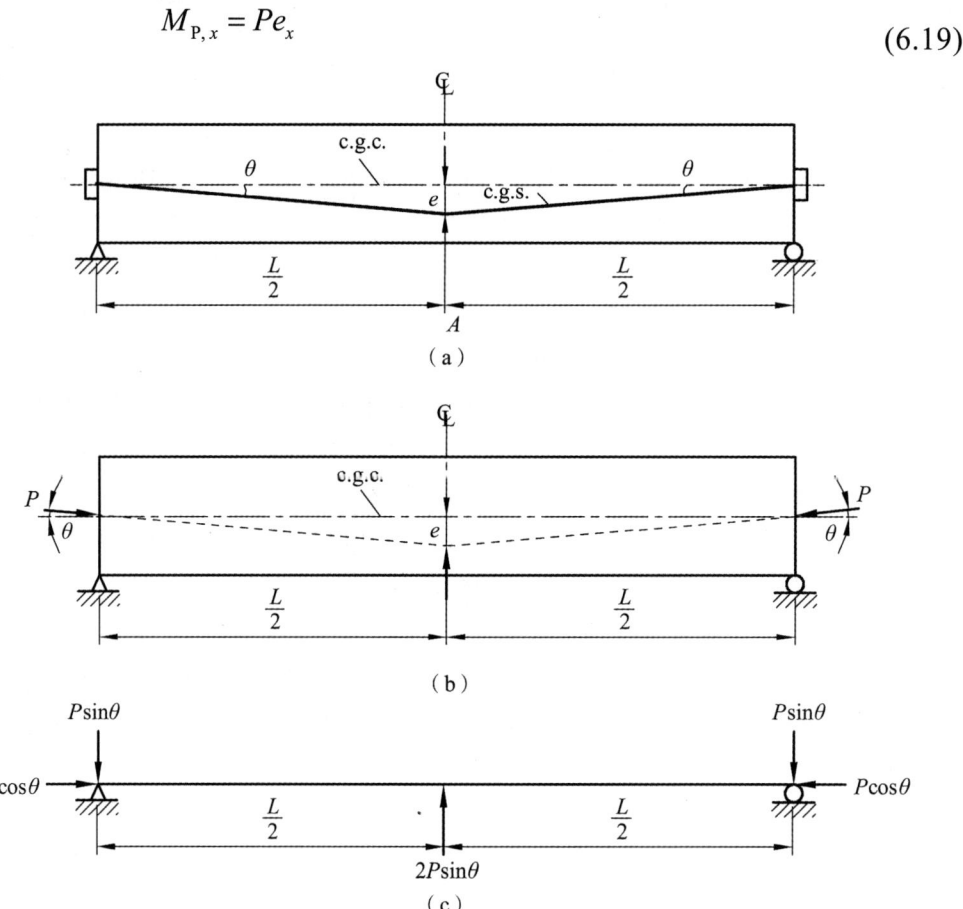

156

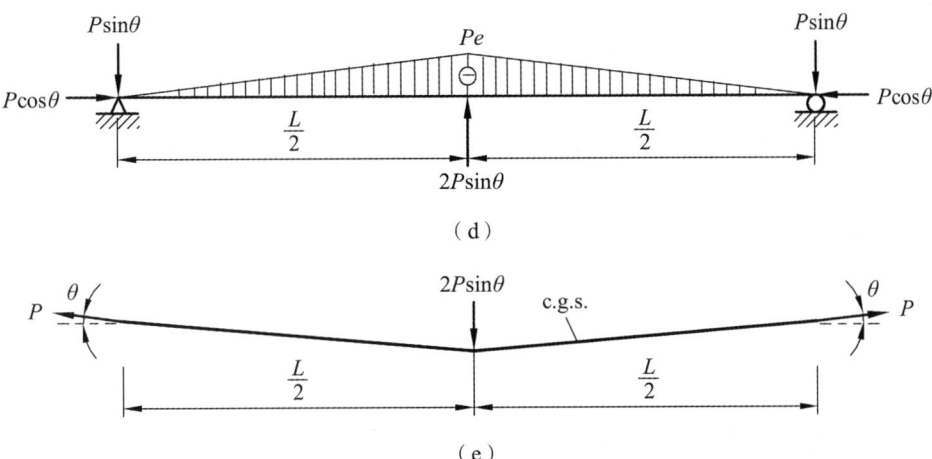

Figure 6.5 Free body diagram and moment diagram for a prestressed beam with linearly varied eccentricity of the tendon: (a) the beam with varied eccentricity of tendon; (b) free body diagram of the concrete beam; (c) equivalent loads on the beam; (d) moment diagram of the beam due to prestressing force; (e) free body diagram of the tendon.

Since the distributions of bending moment of girder bridges caused by self-weights and live loads are usually quadratic along the longitudinal axes of the girders, most frequently a bridge girder is prestressed with parabolically curved tendons to counteract the load-induced moments. Figure 6.6(a) shows a simple beam prestressed with a parabolic tendon. The eccentricity of the tendon is e_0 at the midspan, and is zero at the two supports. The free body diagrams of concrete beam and the tendon are shown in Figures 6.6(b) and 6.6(c). To find the distribution of the force acted on the concrete by the prestressing tendon, a segment of tendon of differential length, ds, is taken as a free body. The forces acting on the tendon segment is shown in Figure 6.6(d). Equilibrium of forces on the tendon segment in the direction passing through OC, which subdivides the angle $d\theta$ into equal parts, requires that

$$2P\sin\left(\frac{d\theta}{2}\right) = q_s ds \tag{6.20}$$

where, q_s is the load intensity acting on the tendon by the concrete in the direction normal to the axis of the tendon. Generally, q_s is a function of its location. The θ is the slope of the tendon. Since $d\theta$ is infinitesimal,

$\sin\left(\dfrac{d\theta}{2}\right) \approx \dfrac{d\theta}{2}$. Then Eq. (6.20) becomes

$$q_s = P\dfrac{d\theta}{ds} = \dfrac{P}{R} \tag{6.21}$$

where, $R = \dfrac{ds}{d\theta}$ is the radius of curvature of the tendon, which can be expressed by

$$\dfrac{1}{R} = \dfrac{|e_x''|}{(1+e_x'^2)^{\frac{3}{2}}} \tag{6.22}$$

where, e_x denotes the eccentricity of the tendon at the location x along the beam axis, e_x' and e_x'' denote the first- and second-order derivative of e_x. Substituting Eq. (6.22) into Eq. (6.21) gives

$$q_s = \dfrac{P|e_x''|}{(1+e_x'^2)^{\frac{3}{2}}} \tag{6.23}$$

Usually the slope of the tendon is very small, leading to $e_x' \ll 1$. Thus, q_s can be approximately expressed as

$$q_s = P|e_x''| \tag{6.24}$$

The equation for the parabolic tendon shown in Figure 6.7c is given by

$$e_x = -\dfrac{4e_0}{L^2}\left(x - \dfrac{L}{2}\right)^2 + e_0 \tag{6.25}$$

Substituting Eq. (6.25) into Eq. (6.24) yields

$$q_s = \dfrac{8Pe_0}{L^2} \tag{6.26}$$

It obvious that q_s is also the force intensity acted on the concrete by the prestressing tendon but in the opposite direction. The vertical component of q_s, denoted by q_y, is given by

$$q_y = q_s \cos\theta \tag{6.27}$$

Due to the small slope of the tendon, $\cos\theta \approx 1$. The q_y can be approximately equals to q_s, i.e.,

$$q_y = q_s = \frac{8Pe_0}{L^2} \tag{6.28}$$

Consequently, the effect of the parabolic prestressing tendon is approximately equivalent to a uniform load acting vertically upwards on the beam [Figure 6.6(e)]. For other curved prestressing tendon profiles, the equivalent load may not be uniform.

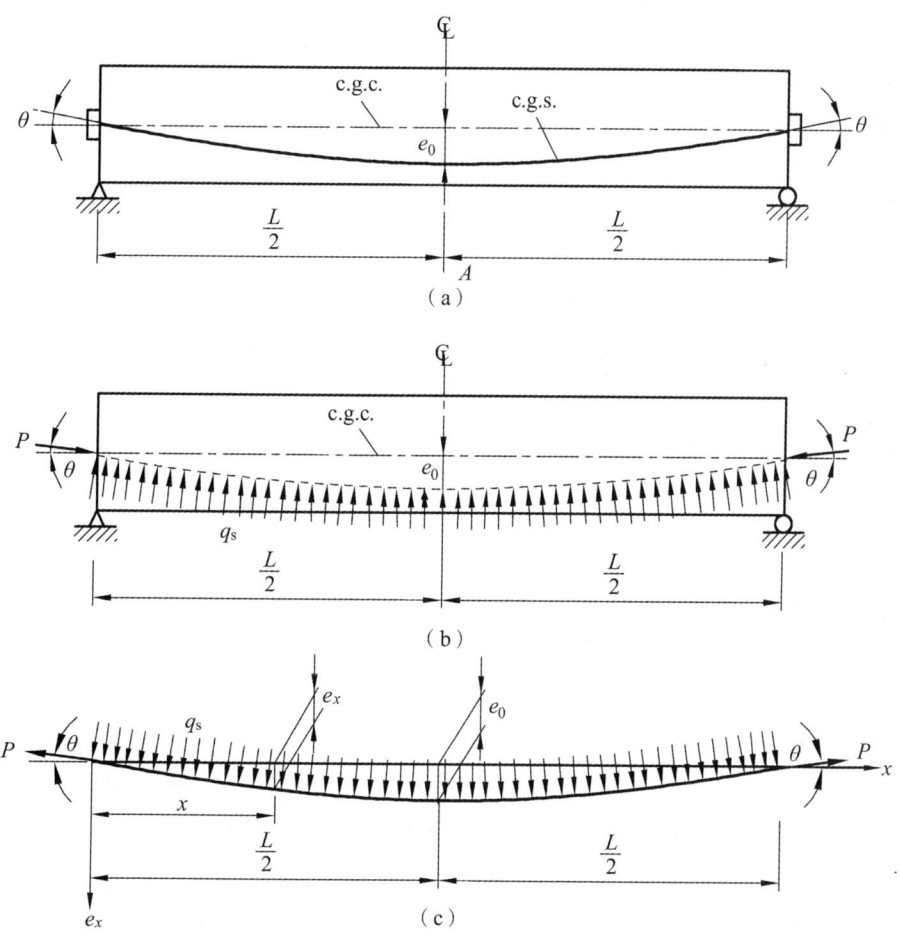

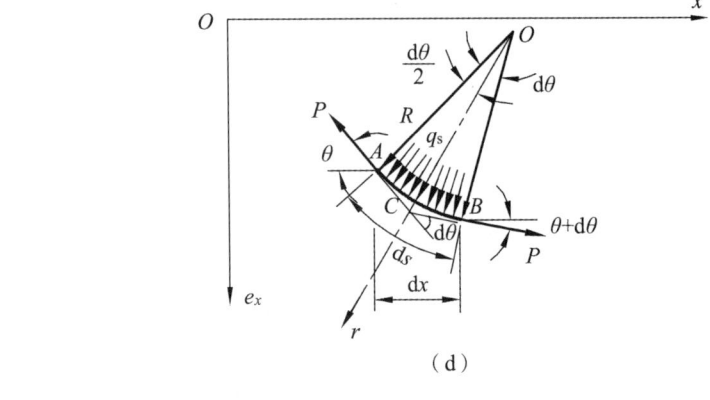

Figure 6.6 Free body diagram and equivalent loads for a prestressed beam with a parabolically curved tendon: (a) the beam with the parabolic tendon profile; (b) free body diagram of the concrete; (c) free body diagram of the tendon; (d) free body diagram of an infinitesimal section of the tendon; (e) Equivalent loads on the concrete beam by the prestressing tendon.

The bending moment at the location x produced by the prestressing force can be easily calculated from the equivalent load q_y:

$$M_{p,x} = \frac{q_y L x}{2} - \frac{q_y x^2}{2} \qquad (6.29)$$

Inserting Eq. (6.28) into Eq. (6.29) and rearranging the terms in the resulting equation, we arrive at

$$M_{p,x} = P\left[-\frac{4e_0}{L^2}\left(x - \frac{L}{2}\right)^2 + e_0\right] = Pe_x \qquad (6.30)$$

The Eq. (6.30) implies that the prestress moment is the multiplication of the prestressing force in the tendon by the eccentricity of the tendon.

This conclusion can also be verified from the free body diagram of a portion of prestressed concrete beam to the left of a vertical cutting plane x-x, as shown in Figure 6.7(a). The prestressing force P at the left end of the beam acts on the concrete through the tendon anchorage, while the force P on the concrete at the cutting plane x-x, is exerted by the portion of the beam to the right of the vertical plane x-x. In addition, the curved prestressing tendon applies a distributed load q_s on the concrete over the contact area between the tendon and concrete [Figure 6.7(b)]. The resultant of the q_s, denoted by N, and the two forces P at the beam end and the cutting plane x-x maintain the concrete portion in a state of equilibrium, as illustrated by the force triangle shown in Figure 6.7(c). The prestressing force P can be decomposed into horizontal and vertical components. The horizontal component is $P_\mathrm{H} = P\cos\theta_x$, and the vertical component is $P_\mathrm{V} = P\sin\theta_x$, where θ_x is the angle of

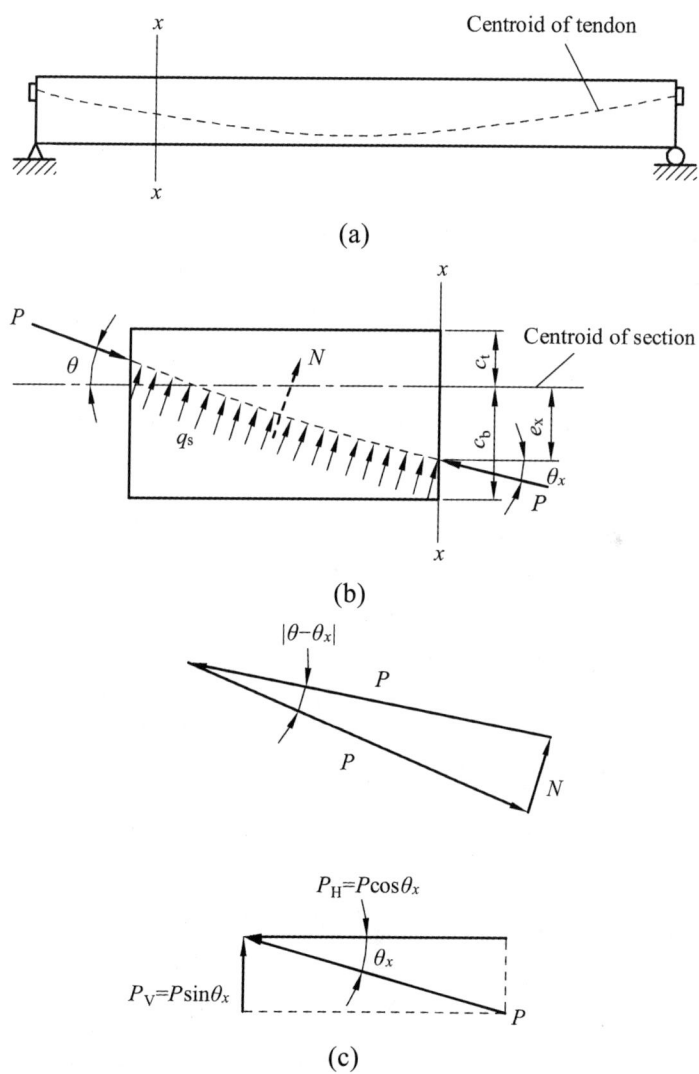

Figure 6.7 Free body diagram of a portion of a prestressed concrete beam: (a) the prestressed concrete beam; (b) the prestressing force acting on the portion of concrete to the left of the cutting place x-x; (c) the force triangle.

inclination of the tendon at the location x-x. Since the θ_x is normally quite small, the cosine of θ_x is very close to unity and, for most calculations, it is sufficient to take $P_H = P$. Consequently, the bending moment produced by the prestressing tendon at the location x-x becomes $M_{p,x} = P_H e_x = Pe_x$, which is just the same as Eq. (6.30).

6.3 Prestressing systems

There are two ways of introducing prestress into a concrete member: pretensioning and post-tensioning.

6.3.1 Pretensioning systems

Pretensioning is a method of prestressing concrete whereby steel strands are pretensioned between abutments before the concrete is placed in the forms (Figure 6.8). After the concrete has hardened, force in the strands is transferred to the concrete by releasing anchors at the abutments. The transfer of force occurs through the bond between concrete and steel. The term "pretensioning" applies to the steel only, and it is therefore incorrect in the strict sense to speak of 'pre-tensioned beams' or 'pre-tensioned concrete'.

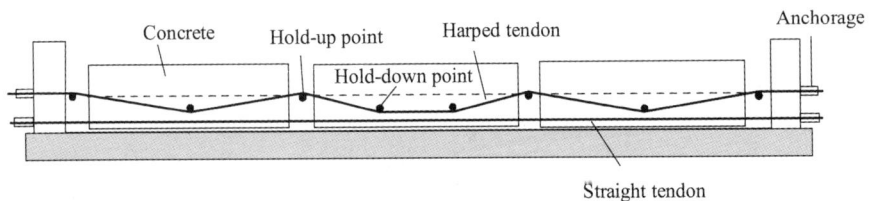

Figure 6.8 The pretensioning bed.

Pretensioning is normally performed at precasting plants or casting yards, where a precast stressing bed of a reinforced concrete slab is constructed on the ground with vertical anchor walls at its ends to resist prestressing force. The steel strands are stretched, individually or all at one jacking operation, and anchored to the vertical walls. For harped tendon profiles, the prestressing bed is provided with hold-down and hold-up devices. Since the bed can be more than one hundred meters long, several precast prestressed members can be produced in one operation, and the exposed prestressing strands between the members can be cut after the concrete hardens.

6.3.2 Post-tensioning systems

Post-tensioning is another method of prestressing concrete whereby steel strands or bars are tensioned against the concrete after the concrete has hardened (Figure 6.9). The prestressing force is transferred to the concrete by means of end anchorages at the time when the steel is tensioned. Cement grout is usually pumped to fill the duct after completion of prestressing.

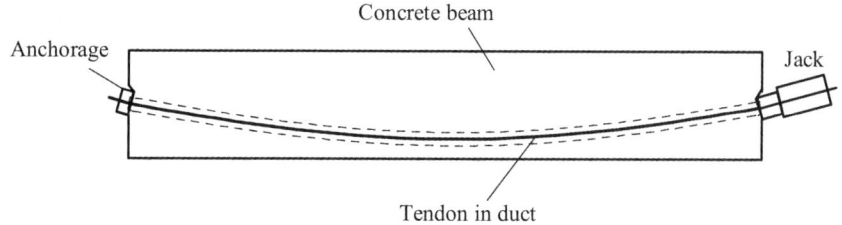

Figure 6.9 A concrete beam prestressed with the post-tensioning method.

6.3.3 Prestressing steel wires and strands

Prestressing reinforcement can be in the form of single wires, strands composed of several wires twisted to form a single element, and high-strength bars. Individual wires are sometimes used in pre-tensioning construction but have become less common in favour of strand, which has better bond characteristics. The wire is cold-drawn from hot-rolled rods of high-carbon steel, and is stress-relieved to give the required properties. The diameters and properties of prestressing steel used in China are described in the design specifications. Figure 6.10(a) and (b) shows several types of prestressing wires and strands for illustration purpose.

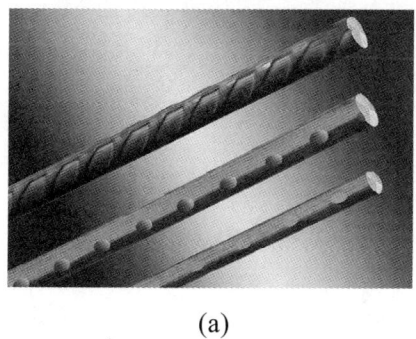
(a)

(b)

Figure 6.10 The prestressing steel: (a) the prestressing wires; (b) the prestressing strands.

6.3.4 Anchorage systems

Transfer of the prestressing force from a tendon to the concrete is critical to effective prestressing. For pretensioned strands the force transfer is by means of bond and friction between the bare strand and the concrete, while for post-tensioned tendons the force transfer is achieved by using mechanical anchor blocks.

1. <u>Strand Chucks</u>

A strand chuck is a mechanical device to grip the wire or strand through wedge friction while stressing to hold the strands until the force is transferred to the concrete (Figure 6.11). Strand chucks are only used for short periods of time and not intended to be long-term anchors. The chuck consists of a barrel, a set of two or three wedges, and in some cases a cap and a spring. The wedges have machined serrations or "teeth" that bite into and grip the strand, distributing the radial load to the barrel. The cap is spring loaded to push the wedges forward in the barrel and keep the wedges in place during jacking or tensioning. Strand chucks are typically used in pretensioned construction and are intended to be reusable.

Figure 6.11 A strand chuck and its components.

2. <u>Multi-strand Anchors</u>

Anchors for post-tensioned strand generally use wedges similar to strand chucks. These anchors are embedded in the concrete prior to stressing, and are reinforced to resist the bursting stresses associated with high localized concentrated loads. A stressed anchor is known as 'live', while unstressed anchors are known as 'dead'. Each strand at the live-end is locked to the anchor by hardened steel wedges that fit into conical holes. The strands at dead anchors may also be locked by wedges that are pushed home before the tendon is stressed. Figure 6.12 shows a typical live-end anchorage for a multi-strand tendon after the strands have been stressed and locked into the anchor. The strands and wedges are seated in holes formed in the anchor block, which rests against the bearing plate and trumpet, cast into the concrete. The hole in the bearing plate of the anchor is for the grout to flow through.

Figure 6.12 A multistrand anchor.

There are also a type of multistrand anchors, which have flat shapes, called the "flat" anchors, as shown in Figure 6.13. The flat anchor is used mainly in floor slabs, bridge decks, transfer beams, thin-wall members, and other structural members which have limited space accommodating large round anchors. The flat anchor system connects bare strands which run through a

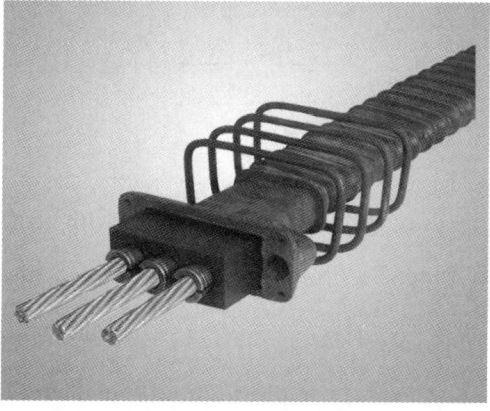

Figure 6.13 A flat multistrand anchor.

steel or plastic oval duct. The strands are stressed individually using a monostrand jack.

3. Tendon couplers

Prestressing tendons can be coupled to extend their length during construction. Figure 6.14 shows a coupler system for multi-strand tendons. A special anchor block and a coupler is used to enable the tendon to be extended after it has been stressed. The bearing plate is cast into concrete in the first stage of concreting, with the tendon being placed and stressed after concrete has hardened. In the next stage of construction and before concreting, the next length of tendon is positioned with the ends of the strands fixed into the coupling head. After concrete hardens, the new length of tendon is stressed and the force is transferred to the first tendon through the coupler.

(a) the photo of a typical coupler

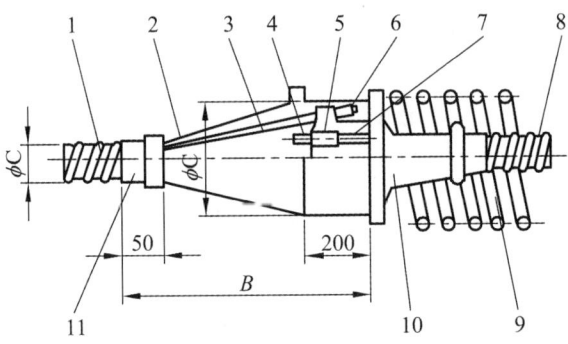

(b) the drawing of a typical coupler with captions

1—Corrugated metal pipe; 2—Protection sleeve; 3, 4—Strands to be connected; 5—Wedges; 6—Strand chucks; 7—Coupling head; 8—Corrugated metal pipe; 9—Spring; 10—Bearing plate; 11—Constraining ring.

Figure 6.14 A tendon coupler: (a) the photo of a typical coupler; (b) the drawing of a typical coupler with captions.

6.3.5 Ducts

Post-tensioned tendons are normally placed inside ducting to allow them to be stressed inside the hardened concrete and to provide protection to the tendons. For internal tendons, ducts are usually formed by sheath left in place, not permitting the entrance of cement paste. The duct should be able to transfer bond stresses as required and should retain their shape under the weight of the concrete stresses as required and should retain their shape under the weight of the concrete. Ducts are traditionally formed by corrugated galvanized steel pipes [Figure 6.15(a)]. More recently, plastic ducting systems have been used to provide a watertight barrier around the tendon as protection against corrosion [Figure 6.15(b)], in addition to the cement grout that fills the ducts after the tendons have been stressed. The post-tensioned tendon profile is achieved by fixing the ducts to temporary supports at appropriate intervals within the formwork.

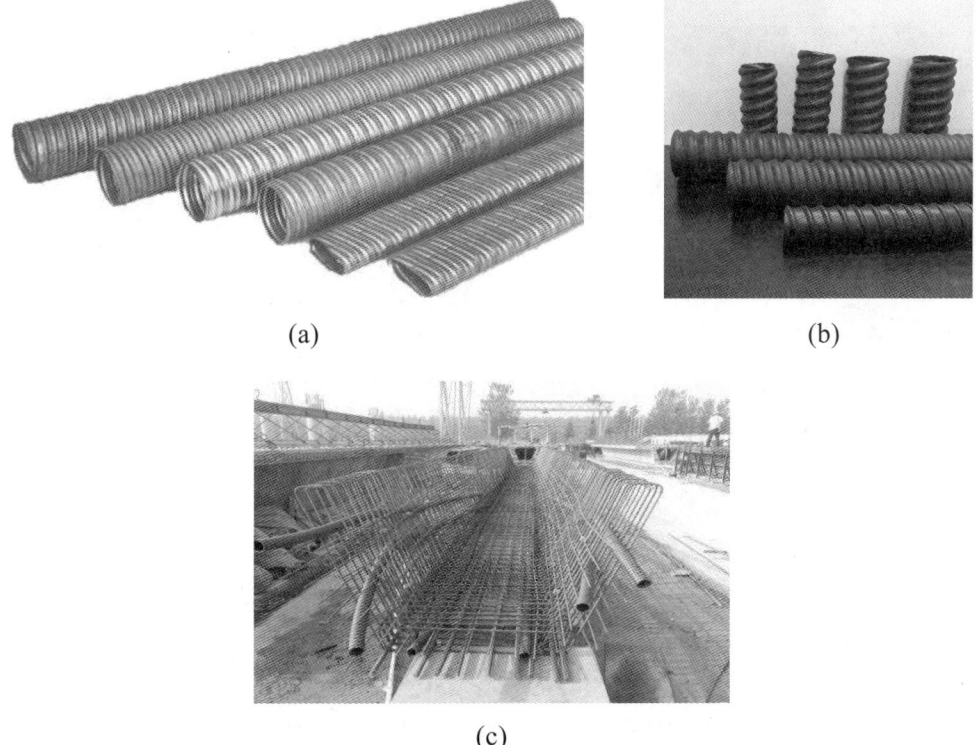

Figure 6.15 Post-tensioning ducts: (a) corrugated steel pipe; (b) corrugated plastic pipe; (c) the layout of the ducts for a prestressed concrete box girder.

All ducts should have grout openings at both ends. For draped cables, grout vents should be set at all high points except where the cable curvature is small. Grout vents or drain holes should be provided at low points if the tendon is to be placed, stressed, and grouted in a freezing climate. All grout openings or vents should include provisions for preventing grout leakage.

6.3.6 Jacking systems

Typical jacks for stressing of mono-strand and multi-strand tendons are shown in Figures 6.16. They are hollow core hydraulic jacks with capacity of 30 tons and 500 tons for stressing a single strand and multiple strands, respectively. These jacks are hydraulically operated, with oil pumped into the piston to apply load to the tendon. The larger jacks can generate a pulling force in excess of 1500 tonnes. The design and detailing of a prestressed components of a bridge should always take into account the access needed to set up and operate the jacks and associated equipment.

(a)   (b)

Figure 6.16   The jacking system: (a) the mono-strand jack; (b) the multi-strand jack.

6.3.7 Grouting of post-tensioned tendons

Post-tensioned tendons that are mechanically anchored to the concrete can be unbounded or bonded. In bonded construction the ducts containing the strands are filled with cement grout after stressing of the tendons. The grout serves two important functions: (i) the grout bonds the strand to the duct and hence to the surrounding concrete, facilitating the transfer of force between the tendon and the concrete; (ii) the grout provides a cementitious cover that protects the post-tensioned steel against corrosion.

The grout must be fluid enough to fill the gaps in the tendon and to be easily pumped over long distances in confined spaces without excessively high pumping pressure that could damage the ducts and the structure. Most grouts used in post-tensioned construction are simple mixtures of Portland cement and water with typical water/cement ratio of 0.47 to 0.53. In some instances, expansive and non-bleeding admixtures are used.

The mixing and pumping of the grout into the duct is carried out in a continuous operation. The grout is pumped in at the low end and steadily pushed through until the duct is full. Grout vents need to be placed at regular intervals along the duct and at all high and low points to ensure that all the air is expelled and the ducts filled (Figure 6.17).

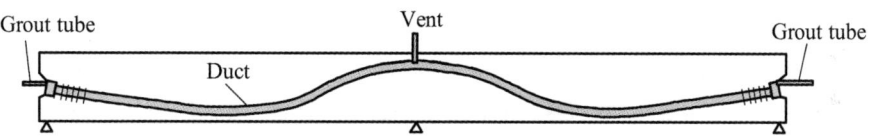

Figure 6.17   Grouting of post-tensioned tendons

6.4   Loss of prestress

All prestressed concrete members are subject to losses of prestress due to elastic shortening of the member, shrinkage and creep of concrete, and relaxation of prestressing steel. In addition, post-tensioned members are subject to losses of prestress resulting from anchorage seating and friction between the tendon and the duct.

Estimation of loss of prestress plays a significant role in design. First, a reasonable estimate of the loss is needed immediately following transfer of prestress to avoid overstressing the concrete beam; second, an estimate of effective prestress under long-term service conditions is required to ensure that the stresses in the concrete are below the limits prescribed by the specifications.

The losses of prestress can be essentially grouped into two categories:

(i) The instantaneous losses during the fabrication or construction process, including elastic shortening of the member, anchorage losses, and frictional losses.

(ii) The time-dependent losses such as those due to creep and shrinkage of concrete, temperature effects, and steel relaxation.

Accurate determination of these losses -- particularly the time-dependent ones -- is difficult, since they depend on many interrelated factors. Thus empirical methods of estimating losses are provided and recommended in design specifications and codes. Some organizations, such as the AASHTO and post-tensioning institute (PTI), also suggest the lump-sum estimates of the losses. However, lump-sum losses may be used only for preliminary design purposes. In the formal design stage of a bridge, refined estimates of losses are always necessary to meet the requirement of the serviceability.

According to the Chinese railway design code TB 10092, the sources of prestress losses listed in Table 6.1 shall be considered in the design of prestressed concrete bridges. The symbols of representing separate prestress losses are also shown in the table. Note that the notation used for the prestress losses in this textbook is different from that used in the Chinese design code, so that different types of losses can be easy to identify and remember.

Table 6.1 Type of prestress losses

Type of prestress loss	Notation in TB 10092	Notation in this textbook
Friction between tendon and duct	σ_{L1}	σ_{LF}
Anchor set, tendon retraction, compression of construction joints	σ_{L2}	σ_{LA}
Thermal effect due to temperature difference between stressing bed and tendons	σ_{L3}	σ_{LTH}
Elastic shortening of concrete	σ_{L4}	σ_{LES}
Relaxation of tendons	σ_{L5}	σ_{LR}
Creep and shrinkage of concrete	σ_{L6}	σ_{LCS}

The total losses of prestress for pretensioned and post-tensioned members can be calculated as follows:

$$\sigma_{LTT} = \sigma_{LTH} + \sigma_{LES} + \sigma_{LR} + \sigma_{LCS} \quad \text{for pretensioned members} \quad (6.31)$$

$$\sigma_{LTT} = \sigma_{LF} + \sigma_{LA} + \sigma_{LES} + \sigma_{LR} + \sigma_{LCS} \quad \text{for post-tensioned members} \quad (6.32)$$

where σ_{LTT} denotes the total prestress loss.

6.5 Design methods

6.5.1 General considerations

Analysis and design of a prestressed concrete bridge are two different processes. The analysis is to determine the stresses and strains in the steel and concrete in a member based on the given geometric and material properties of the member and the applied loads. The design, however, is to determine the geometrical shape and size of the concrete cross section and the amount and alignments of the prestressing strands under the given loading conditions to meet the requirements on the stresses in the concrete and steel in the service and strength limit states. From a mathematical point of view, analysis and design are two mathematical problems that are reverse to each other.

In actual practice, the design usually starts with a preliminary choice of the shape and size of the section, and proceeds with analysis to determine whether the section can safely carry the prestressing forces and the required external loads. By trial and adjustment, the section geometry and the size and the layout of the prestressing tendons converge to satisfying solutions. In this sense, a design process includes iterative analysis processes.

A prestressed concrete bridge is required to meet the requirements of the service level stresses as well as the strength requirements, whereas the reinforced concrete is mostly designed on the basis of the strength requirements. This makes the analysis and design processes of prestressed concrete bridges slightly more complicated than those of reinforced concrete bridges. A logical sequence in the design process is to perform first the service-load design of the section required in flexure, including determination of the level of prestress and the layout of the tendons, and then to conduct the analysis of the moment strength of the section in the limit state at failure.

Compared with the reinforced concrete bridges, the distinguishing features of the prestressed concrete bridges are as follows:

(i) The stresses in concrete and prestressing steel and deformation of the members at the stages of prestressing, erection, and service can be determined on the basis of elastic theory.

(ii) The dead loads and live loads are applied to the prestressed concrete member at varying concrete strengths at various loading stages.

(iii) The prestressing force is determined by concrete stress limits under service load.

(iv) Flexural and shear capacities are determined by the ultimate strength theory.

Evolution of the stress distribution across the depth of a critical cross-section of a prestressed concrete beam throughout the loading history is shown in Figure 6.18.

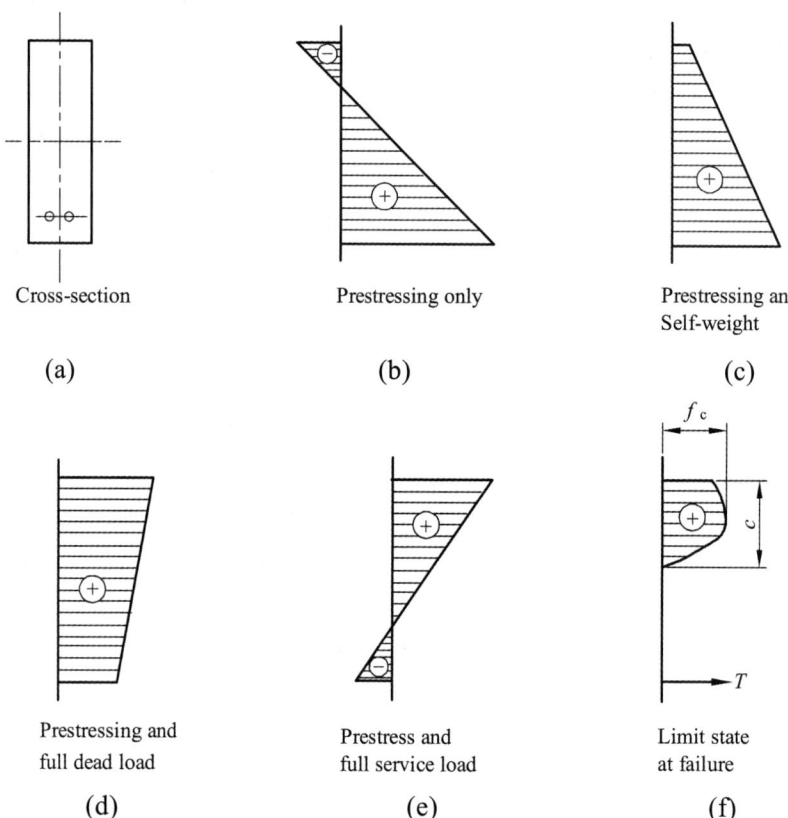

Figure 6.18　Stress distributions in concrete across the depth of a cross-section of a prestressed concrete beam: (a) cross-section; (b) prestresing only; (c) prestressing plus self-weight; (d) prestressing plus full dead load; (e) prestressing plus full service load; (f) limit state at failure.

6.5.2　Cross-sections

Almost all types of cross-sections for reinforced concrete bridges can be used for prestressed concrete bridges. These cross-sections include solid-slab, voided-slab, I-shape, T-shape, and box-shape, which are shown in Figure 6.4 through Figure 6.6. The major difference between the cross-sections used for reinforced and prestressed concrete bridges lies in the depths of the cross-sections. For the same span length, the depth of the cross-section of the prestressed concrete bridge is smaller than that of the reinforced concrete bridge. In addition, the bottom flange of the T-shape cross-section is enlarged to accommodate the prestressing tendons and anchors. The I-shape, T-shape, and box-shape sections are mostly used for the medium- to long-span prestressed concrete bridges. Figure 6.19 shows the three typical sections.

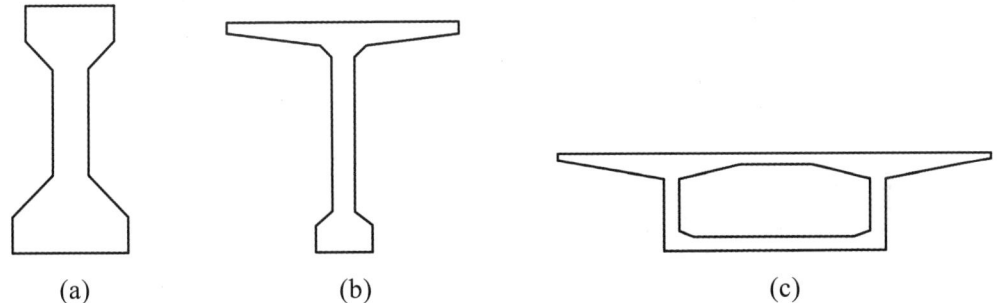

Figure 6.19 **The typical sections of prestressed concrete bridges: (a) I-shape; (b) the T-shape; (c) the box shape.**

For highway bridges that are simply supported, the prestressed concrete is used for the span length equal or larger than 20 m. The depth-to-span ratios of the simply supported prestressed concrete girder usually range from 1/15 to 1/25, and the longer the span length, the lower the depth-to-span ratios. The standard designs are available for the fabricated prestressed concrete highway bridges for the span length of 25 m, 30 m, 35 m, and 40 m, whose section depths are 1.25 ~ 1.45 m, 1.65 ~ 1.75 m, 2.00 m, and 2.30 m, respectively. The width of the web is traditionally between 0.14 m and 0.16 m. But recent chinese highway bridge design code JTG 3362 requires that the web width shall not be less than 0.16 m.

For railway bridges, the prestressed concrete is used when the span length is equal or larger than 16 m. The depth-to-span ratios of the girder usually range from approximately 1/10 to 1/12. The standard designs of prestressed concrete T-shaped girder bridges for main line railways are available for the span lengths of 16 m, 20 m, 24 m, 32 m, 40 m, and 48 m. For high speed railways, standard designs of prestressed T-shaped girders are available for span length of 12 m and 16 m in 250 km/h railways. Figure 6.20 shows the cross-section of a multiple-girder bridge for double-track passenger railways. Standard designs of prestrssed concrete girders with box-shape cross-sections are available for span lengths of 20 m, 24 m, 32 m, and 40 m. Figure 6.21 shows a typical single-cell box cross-section for the prestressed concrete girders on double-track high-speed railways. The web width cannot be less than 0.15 m according to the Chinese railway bridge design code TB 10002.3, and is usually varied between the mid span and the support. But a legacy prepensioned concrete railway bridge has a minimum web width of 0.14 m in the mid span for the span length of 16 m. Generally, the web width is 0.24 ~ 0.3 m in the mid span and is 0.3 ~ 0.6 m in the support.

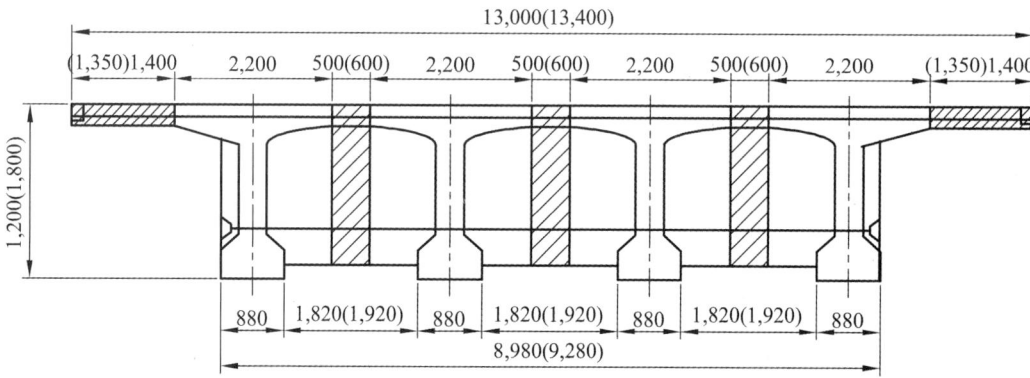

Figure 6.20 The typical T-shaped section of prestressed concrete bridges in the 250 km/h high-speed railways (units: mm).

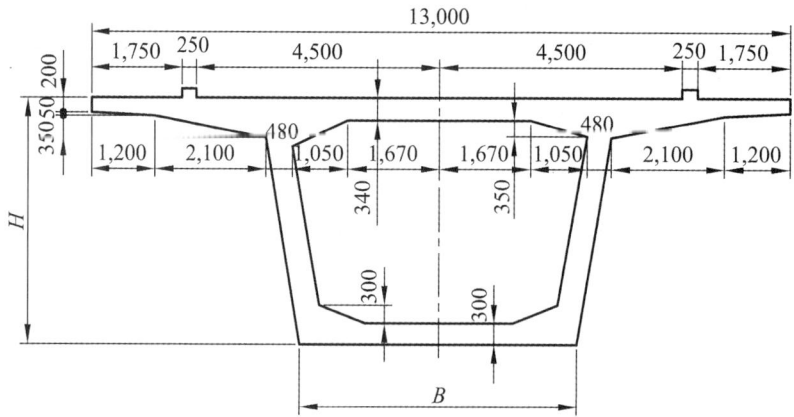

Figure 6.21 The typical box section of prestressed concrete bridges in the 250 km/h high-speed railways.

6.5.3 Design for flexure

The common practice in the design of prestressed concrete bridge is first to choose a concrete cross section from available cross-section shapes, then to determine the dimensions of the section and the layout of the prestressing tendons according to the requirements on stress limits under service loads, and finally to check the stresses in concrete and steel at all stages. If the stress limits are not satisfied, then the trail section has to be revised and the above process is repeated. In this trail-and-error method, the dimensions of the section must meet the requirement for the minimum modulus which is determined from the concrete stress limits under the service load.

1. Minimum section modulus

As stated previously, the behavior of the prestressed concrete bridge is assumed to be linearly elastic under service loads. Thus the service level stresses in concrete are calculated by

$$\sigma_c = \frac{P}{A} \mp \frac{Pey}{I} \pm \frac{M_G y}{I} \pm \frac{(M_D + M_L)y}{I}$$

$$= \frac{P}{A}\left(1 \mp \frac{ey}{r^2}\right) \pm \frac{M_G y}{I} \pm \frac{(M_D + M_L)y}{I} \qquad (6.33)$$

where, σ_c is the concrete stress in a section at a distance y from the neutral axis; P is the prestressing force; A is the cross-sectional area; I is the moment of inertia; e is the tendon eccentricity at the section; M_G, M_D, M_L are the moments due to the girder self-weight, the superimposed dead load, and the live load, respectively. The r is the radius of gyration of the section defined by $I = Ar^2$. The sign $\mp$ or $\pm$ denotes that the upper sign is used when the stress is calculated at a location above the neutral axis, and the lower sign is used if the location of the stress is below the neutral axis.

The section properties, the cross-sectional area A and the moment of inertia I in Eq.(6.33), are dependent on the prestressing method. For the pretensioned tendons, the properties of the transformed cross-section in which the area occupied by tendons are transformed into equivalent concrete area used. For post-tensioned tendons, before grouting, the properties of net cross-section excluding the area of ducts are used. After grouting, the transformed cross-section is used. In general, the gross cross-sectional area of the concrete section is adequate for use in the service-load design. While some designers prefer refining their designs through the use of the transformed section, the accuracy gained in accounting for the contribution of the area of the reinforcement to the stiffness of the concrete section is normally not warranted.

The solutions obtained with gross section properties are usually acceptable in terms of engineering accuracy.

At transfer of prestressing, if the allowable tensile and compressive stresses concrete is f_{ti} (negative) and f_{ci} (positive), respectively, the stresses in the concrete at the top and bottom of the section are required to be

$$\sigma_c^t = \frac{P_i}{A_g} - \frac{P_i e c_t}{I_g} + \frac{M_G c_t}{I_g} \geqslant f_{ti} \tag{6.34a}$$

$$\sigma_c^b = \frac{P_i}{A_g} + \frac{P_i e c_b}{I_g} - \frac{M_G c_b}{I_g} \leqslant f_{ci} \tag{6.34b}$$

where, σ_c^t and σ_c^b represent the concrete stresses in the top and bottom faces of the section, respectively. The P_i is the initial prestressing force. Although the accurate value to use should be the horizontal component of P_i, it is acceptable for practical purposes to use P_i instead of its horizontal component. The c_t and c_b are the distances of the top and the bottom faces of the section from the neutral axis, respectively.

At the service load stage, after all the losses have finished, the requirements for the concrete stresses become

$$\sigma_c^t = \frac{P_e}{A} - \frac{P_e e c_t}{I} + \frac{M_T c_t}{I} \leqslant f_{cs} \tag{6.35a}$$

$$\sigma_c^b = \frac{P_e}{A} + \frac{P_e e c_b}{I} - \frac{M_T c_b}{I} \geqslant f_{ts} \tag{6.35b}$$

in which,

$$M_T = M_G + M_D + M_L \tag{6.36}$$

In Eq. (6.35), P_e is the effective prestress after all losses; the f_{ts} (negative) and f_{cs} (positive) are the allowable tensile and compressive stresses at service load stage, respectively.

If the compressive prestress in concrete at the gravity center of the steel is reduced to zero under additional loads, the stress increment in concrete caused the external loads would be

$$\sigma_c^{decomp} = \frac{P_e}{A} + \frac{P_e e^2}{I} = \frac{P_e}{A}\left(1 + \frac{e^2}{r^2}\right) \tag{6.37}$$

where, the stress σ_c^{decomp} is called decompression stress.

(1) Beams With Variable Tendon Eccentricity.

For the beams with either draped or harped tendons, the maximum eccentricity is usually at the midspan section for the simply supported case. Assuming that the effective prestressing force is

$$P_e = \zeta P_i \tag{6.38}$$

where, ζ is the effectiveness ratio of prestress, the loss of prestress is

$$\Delta P = (P_i - P_e) = (1-\zeta)P_i \tag{6.39}$$

If, at transfer stage, the prestressing force is such that

$$\sigma_{ci}^t = \frac{P_i}{A_g} - \frac{P_i e c_t}{I_g} + \frac{M_G c_t}{I_g} = f_{ti} \tag{6.40a}$$

$$\sigma_{ci}^b = \frac{P_i}{A_g} + \frac{P_i e c_b}{I_g} - \frac{M_G c_b}{I_g} = f_{ci} \tag{6.40b}$$

then, after all losses, the stresses become

$$\sigma_{ce}^t = \frac{P_e}{A_g} - \frac{P_e e c_t}{I_g} + \frac{M_G c_t}{I_g} \tag{6.41a}$$

$$\sigma_{ce}^b = \frac{P_e}{A_g} + \frac{P_e e c_b}{I_g} - \frac{M_G c_b}{I_g} \tag{6.41b}$$

Since $\sigma_{ce}^t > \sigma_{ci}^t$ and $\sigma_{ci}^b > \sigma_{ce}^b$, the increment of concrete stress at the top and bottom faces of the section are

$$\Delta \sigma_c^t = \sigma_{ce}^t - \sigma_{ci}^t = -(1-\zeta)\left(\frac{P_i}{A_g} - \frac{P_i e c_t}{I_g}\right)$$

$$= (1-\zeta)\left(\frac{M_G c_t}{I_g} - f_{ti}\right) \qquad (6.42a)$$

$$\Delta\sigma_c^b = \sigma_{ci}^b - \sigma_{ce}^b = (1-\zeta)\left(\frac{M_G c_b}{I_g} + f_{ci}\right) \qquad (6.42b)$$

At the service stage, the inequalities in Eq. (6.35a) and Eq. (6.35b) can be written as

$$f_{ti} + \Delta\sigma_c^t + \frac{(M_D + M_L)c_t}{I_g} \leq f_{cs} \qquad (6.43a)$$

$$f_{ci} - \Delta\sigma_c^b - \frac{(M_D + M_L)c_b}{I_g} \geq f_{ts} \qquad (6.43b)$$

Substituting Eq. (6.42a) and Eq. (6.42b) into the above equations leads to

$$S_g^t \geq \frac{(1-\zeta)M_G + M_D + M_L}{f_{sc} - \zeta f_{ti}} \qquad (6.44a)$$

$$S_g^b \geq \frac{(1-\zeta)M_G + M_D + M_L}{\zeta f_{ci} - f_{st}} \qquad (6.44b)$$

where, $S_g^t = I_g/c_t$ and $S_g^b = I_g/c_b$, which are top and bottom section modulus of concrete section, respectively.

From Figure 6.22, the concrete stress at the centroid of the section, denoted by f_{ci}^{cgc}, at transfer of prestressing force P_i, is given by

$$f_{ci}^{cgc} = f_{ti} + \frac{c_t}{h}(f_{ci} - f_{ti}) \qquad (6.45)$$

Thus, the initial prestressing force P_i can be determined by

$$P_i = f_{ci}^{cgc} A_g \qquad (6.46)$$

The required eccentricity of the prestressing tendon at a section can be determined by Eq. (6.34a) as

$$e = (f_{ci}^{cgc} - f_{ti})\frac{S_g^t}{P_i} + \frac{M_G}{P_i} \qquad (6.47)$$

Note that throughout the derivation from Eq. (6.34) to Eq. (6.47), the tensile stress is designated as negative and compressive stress positive.

The cross section must be selected to provide at least these values of S_g^t and S_g^b. Since $I_g = S_g^t c_t$ and $I_g = S_g^t c_t$, the centroidal axis must be located such that

$$\frac{c_t}{c_b} = \frac{S_g^b}{S_g^b} \tag{6.48}$$

or in terms of $h = c_t + c_b$

$$\frac{c_t}{h} = \frac{S_g^b}{S_g^b + S_g^b} \tag{6.49}$$

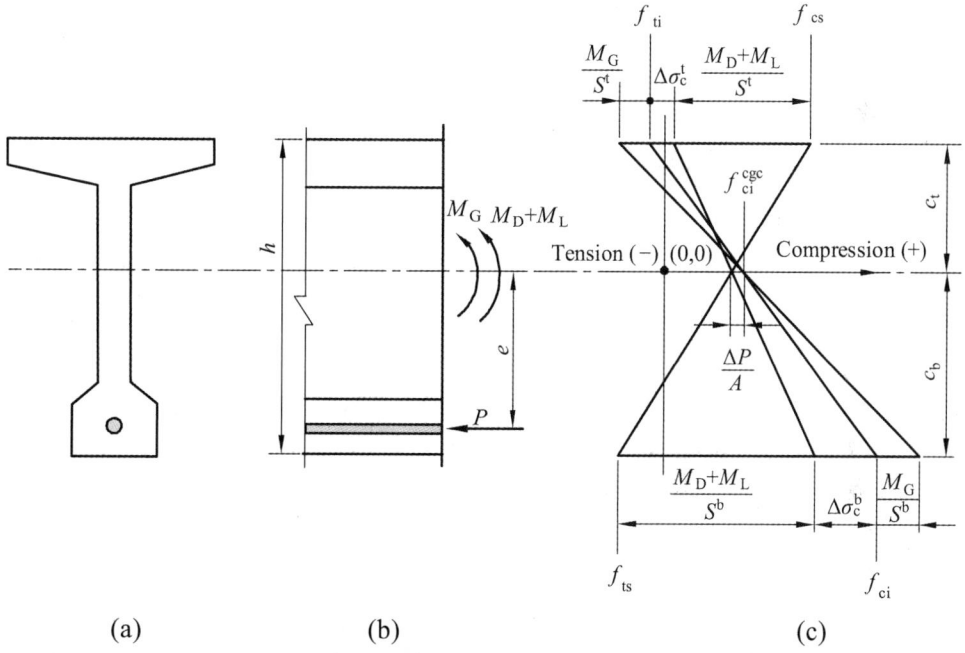

Figure 6.22 The stress distribution across a section of a prestressed concrete beam: (a) the beam cross-section; (b) the forces acting on the section; (c) the stress distribution.

In practical design, the section is acceptable only if the section properties of a member exceed the minimum requirements for S_g^t and S_g^b set by Eq. (6.44a) and Eq. (6.44b). Rounding concrete dimensions upward, providing broad flanges for functional reasons, or using standardized cross-sectional shapes can result in required solutions. In such a case, the stresses in the concrete at the full service load stage will stay within the allowable limits.

However, an infinite number of combinations of prestress force and eccentricity can satisfy the requirements. Usually, a design that has the lowest value of prestress force and the largest practical eccentricity is the most economical.

The stress distributions shown in Figure 6.22, on which the design equations are based, apply at the section whose bending moment is a maximum. Elsewhere, M_G, M_D and M_L are less, and, consequently, the prestressing force or eccentricity must be reduced if the concrete stress limits are not to be exceeded. In many cases, tendon eccentricity is reduced to zero at the support sections, where bending moments due to transverse load are zero. In this case, the stress in the concrete is uniformly equal to the centroidal value f_{ci}^{cgc} at the transfer of initial prestress and f_{ce}^{cgc} after losses.

(2) Beams with Constant Tendon Eccentricity.

If the prestressing force P_i and eccentricity e are held constant along the span, as is often the case in pretensioned construction, then the stress limits f_{ti} and f_{ci} will be exceeded elsewhere along the span, where M_G is less than its maximum value. To avoid this condition, the constant eccentricity must be less than that given by Eq. (6.47). Its maximum value will be controlled by conditions at the support where M_G is zero. The stress distribution in the support section is shown in Figure 6.23. After all losses, the change of the concrete stresses at top and bottom faces of the support section are given by

$$\Delta\sigma_c^t = -(1-\zeta)f_{ti} \tag{6.50a}$$

$$\Delta\sigma_c^b = (1-\zeta)f_{ci} \tag{6.50b}$$

At other sections where M_G is non-zero, the requirements for the stresses at the top and bottom faces under service load are given by

$$f_{ti} + \Delta\sigma_c^t + \frac{(M_G + M_D + M_L)c_t}{I_g} \leqslant f_{cs} \tag{6.51a}$$

$$f_{ci} - \Delta\sigma_c^b - \frac{(M_G + M_D + M_L)c_b}{I_g} \geqslant f_{ts} \tag{6.51b}$$

Substitution of Eq. (6.50a) and Eq. (6.50b) into Eq. (6.51a) and Eq. (6.51b) results in

$$S_g^t \geqslant \frac{M_G + M_D + M_L}{f_{sc} - \zeta f_{ti}} \qquad (6.52a)$$

$$S_g^b \geqslant \frac{M_G + M_D + M_L}{\zeta f_{ci} - f_{st}} \qquad (6.52b)$$

The concrete stress at the centroid of section may be found by Eq. (6.45) and the initial prestress force by Eq. (6.46) as before. The required eccentricity can be obtained from the Eq. (6.47) by taking $M_G = 0$ as

$$e = (f_{ci}^{cgc} - f_{ti})\frac{S_g^t}{P_i} \qquad (6.53)$$

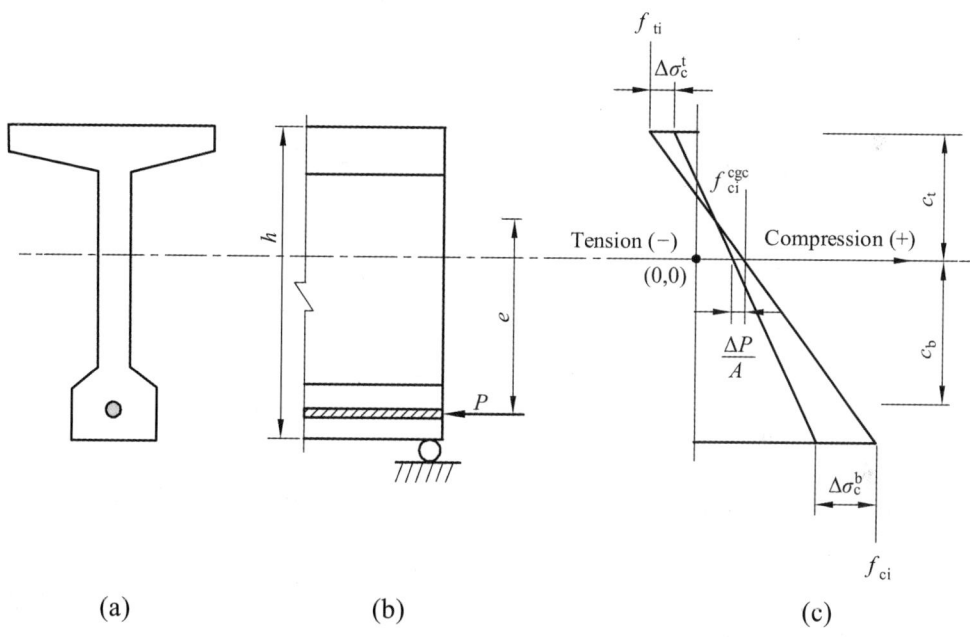

(a) (b) (c)

Figure 6.23 The stress distribution at support section of a prestressed concrete beam: (a) the cross-section; (b) the forces acting on the support section; (c) the stress distribution.

The significant difference between beams with variable eccentricity and those with constant eccentricity can be noted by comparing Eq. (6.44a) and Eq. (6.44b) with the corresponding Eq. (6.52a) and Eq. (6.52b). In the first case, the section modulus requirement is controlled mainly by the superimposed load moments M_D and M_L, and almost all of the self-weight is carried by simply increasing the eccentricity along the span by the amount of M_G/P_i. In the second case, however, the eccentricity is determined by conditions at the supports, where $M_G=0$, and the full moment M_G due to self-weight is involved in determining section moduli.

2. Tendon profiles

The purpose of applying prestress to concrete beam is to counteract the tensile stress in concrete induced by external loads. To achieve this purpose, the tensile stresses in the extreme concrete fibers under construction and service-load conditions are required not to exceed the maximum stress specified by the design code. It is therefore necessary to establish the envelope within which the prestressing force can be applied without causing tension in the extreme concrete fiber.

It is well known that when a compressive point load is exerted on a special region of a section, the whole section will be set in compression. This special region is called the "kern" of the section. From Eq.(6.34a) and Eq.(6.35a), it is easy to obtain the upper and lower limits of the kern (as shown in Figure 6.25), whose distances k_t and k_b from the centroid of the section are given by

$$k_t = \frac{r^2}{c_b} \tag{6.54a}$$

$$k_b = \frac{r^2}{c_t} \tag{6.54b}$$

It is obvious that when the prestressing force acts above the upper kern point, the tensile stress will develop at the bottom face of the section; similarly, when the prestressing force acts below the lower kern point, the tensile stress will develop at the top face of the section.

The Eq. (6.44) to Eq. (6.47) developed for members with variable tendon eccentricity establish the requirements for section modulus, prestress force, and eccentricity at the maximum moment section of the member. If the amount of the tendons is maintained constant along the span length, the eccentricity of the tendon must be reduced along the span to be in accordance with the reduced external moment. Since the concrete at the top and bottom faces of the section is not allowed to crack, the minimum and maximum eccentricities of the tendon centroid are required to determined, which constitute the envelope of the tendon placement.

At the transfer of prestressing force, the only external load is the self-weight which causes the compressive stress at the top face and the tensile stress at the bottom face of the section. Thus the point of application of the prestressing force are allowed to move downward a distance Δe_G to counteract the self-weight induced bending moment. The Δe_G can be calculated as

$$\Delta e_G = \frac{M_G}{P_i} \tag{6.55}$$

The lower limit of the eccentricity is

$$e_{max} = k_b + \Delta e_G = k_b + \frac{M_G}{P_i} \tag{6.56}$$

At the service load stage, the external loads include M_G, M_D and M_L, which cause substantial additional tensile stresses at the bottom face of the section. Thus the point of application of the prestressing force has to move downward a distance Δe_T from the kern points to counteract the service-load induced bending moment. The Δe_T is given by

$$\Delta e_T = \frac{M_G + M_D + M_L}{P_e} \tag{6.57}$$

The upper limit of the eccentricity is thus

$$e_{min} = -k_t + \Delta e_T = -k_t + \frac{M_G + M_D + M_L}{P_e} \tag{6.58}$$

Some design codes allow limited tensile stresses f_{ti} and f_{ts} to occur at transfer and at service-load stages, respectively. In such cases, it is possible to allow the centroid of steel tendons to fall slightly outside the two limiting envelopes described in Eq. (6.56) and Eq. (6.58). The additional eccentricities can be obtained as

$$\Delta e_{max} = -\frac{f_{ti} I_g}{P_i c_t} = -\frac{f_{ti} A_g k_b}{P_i} \tag{6.59a}$$

$$\Delta e_{min} = \frac{f_{ts} I_g}{P_i c_b} = \frac{f_{ts} A_g k_t}{P_i} \tag{6.59b}$$

The upper and lower limits of the centroid of the steel tendons are given by

$$e'_{max} = e_{max} + \Delta e_{max} = k_b + \frac{M_G}{P_i} - \frac{f_{ti} A_g k_b}{P_i} \qquad (6.60a)$$

$$e'_{min} = e_{min} + \Delta e_{min} = -k_t + \frac{M_G + M_D + M_L}{P_e} + \frac{f_{ts} A_g k_t}{P_i} \qquad (6.60b)$$

Figure 6.24 shows the envelopes of the centroid of prestressing tendons. It should be pointed that it is only the tendon centroid that shall be within the zone enclosed by upper and lower limits; individual strands may be outside of it.

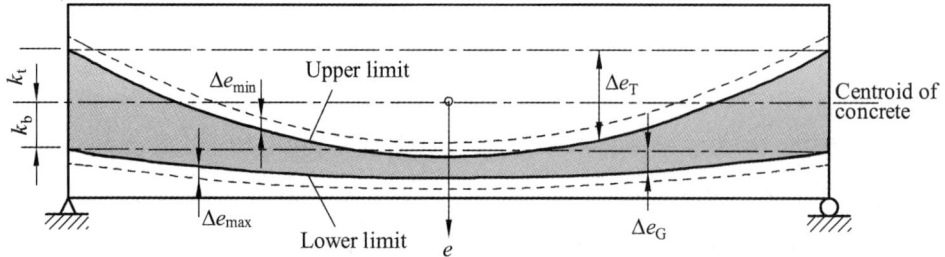

Figure 6.24 The envelopes for the centroid of prestressing tendons.

The tendon profile actually used in a post-tensioned beam is often a parabolic curve or a catenary. In pretensioned beams, deflected or harped tendons are often used. In practical design, it is often not necessary to create a diagram for the zone of the tendon centroid, as is shown in Figure 6.24. The tendon centroid at midspan is usually determined first by Eq.(6.53) or other approaches. At support, the tendon centroid can be located at or close to the concrete centroid. By placing the tendon centroid in a near-parabolic shape between these controlling points, satisfaction of the limiting stress requirements is ensured.

3. <u>Lin's method for preliminary elastic design</u>

A simple and quick method was proposed by Lin and Bums to give preliminary estimations of prestressing force and the cross-sectional area of the concrete. This method is based on the concept of the internal *C-T* force couple acting in the section, where *C* denotes the total compressive force and *T* the total tensile force. At the service-load stage, the lever arm of this couple varies approximately between $0.30h$ and $0.8h$, depending on the shape of the section.

The average value of the lever arm can be taken as $0.65h$, as shown in Figure 6.25. Given the total moment M_T, the effective prestressing force P_e can be estimated by

$$P_e = T = \frac{M_T}{0.65h} \tag{6.61}$$

If the effective prestress in the prestressing steel is f_{pse}, the area of steel required is

$$A_{ps} = \frac{P_e}{f_{pse}} = \frac{M_T}{0.65h f_{pse}} \tag{6.62}$$

Since the total compressive force in concrete is equal to the prestressing force, i.e. $C = T = P_e$, the area of the concrete section is

$$A_c = \frac{P_e A_{ps}}{f_{cs}} = \frac{M_T}{f_{cs}} \tag{6.63}$$

where f_{cs} is the allowable compressive stresses at the service load stage.

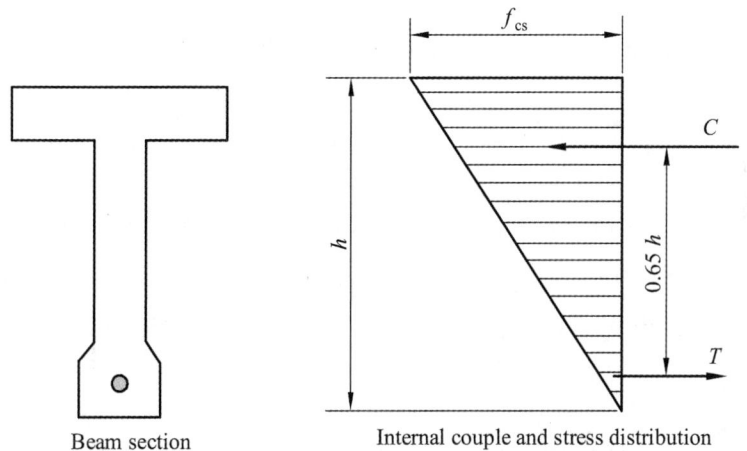

Figure 6.25 Assumed stress distribution for preliminary elastic design.

In the above procedure, the only approximation made is the coefficient 0.65. This coefficient depends on the shape of the section. In design of bridge superstructures, the total design moment is known for a given span length, and the shape and size of the girder are generally chosen based on experience. Hence, this procedure can be used to give preliminary estimates of the prestressing force and the cross-sectional area of concrete. Refined method, described in Section 6.5.2, can be used to check the preliminary estimates and to give accurate estimations of the prestressing force and the corresponding eccentricities.

4. <u>Preliminary design based on ultimate flexural strength</u>

A preliminary design can also start with the ultimate flexural strength required by the design moment. For a given prestressed concrete beam with bonded prestressing tendons, in the strength limit state, the ultimate resisting moment is

$$M_r = A_{ps} f_{ps} Z_r \tag{6.64}$$

where, Z_r is the lever arm between the centroid of the steel and the point of application of the resultant compressive force in concrete; f_{ps} is the calculation strength of prestressing steel. For the known design moment M_T, the flexural strength design requires that

$$KM_T \leqslant M_r \tag{6.65}$$

where, K is the strength safety factor. By substituting Eq. (6.65) into Eq. (6.64), the minimum area of prestressing steel can be obtained as

$$A_{ps} = \frac{KM_T}{f_{ps} Z_r} \tag{6.66}$$

The arm lever Z_r varies with the shape of section and generally ranges between $0.6h$ and $0.9h$, with a common value of $0.8h$. The calculation strength of prestressing tendon is $f_{ps} = 0.9 f_{pk}$. Then the area A_{ps} of prestressing tendons is

$$A_{ps} = \frac{KM_T}{0.9 f_{pk}(0.8h)} = \frac{KM_T}{0.72 f_{pk} h} \tag{6.67}$$

Assuming that the concrete stress in the equivalent compressive block is $0.85 f_c$ in the strength limit state, then, from the equilibrium condition $C = T$, the required concrete area under compression can be estimated by

$$A_c' = \frac{KM_T}{0.85 f_c (0.8h)} = \frac{KM_T}{0.68 f_c h} \tag{6.68}$$

which is supplied by the compression flange if the I-shaped and T-shaped beams are chosen. Once the depth of the beam is known, the area of web and the tension flange can be designed based on the shear requirement.

5. The cracking moment

One of fundamental properties of prestressed concrete beam is the continuous shift of the center of pressure line away from the gravity center of the steel tendons toward the compression side of the beam as the load increases. In other words, the lever arm of the internal couple continues to increase with the load without any appreciable change of the stress in the prestressing steel. As bending moment continues to increase, a loading stage is reached where the concrete compressive stress in the bottom extreme fibers becomes zero. This stage is called the limit state of decompression. Starting from this state, any additional external load will result in tensile stress at the bottom face. Cracking occurs at the locations where tensile stress reaches the tensile strength f_{ct}. The minimum bending moment causing occurrence of cracking is called cracking moment, denoted by M_{cr}. Once concrete cracks, a sudden increase in the steel stress takes place and the tension is transferred from the concrete to the steel.

It is important to evaluate the cracking moment, since the section stiffness is reduced by cracking and an increase in deflection follows. Also, the crack width has to be controlled in order to prevent reinforcement corrosion. The concrete stress at the extreme tension fibers is

$$\sigma_c^b = \frac{P_e}{A_g}\left(1+\frac{ec_b}{r^2}\right) - \frac{M_{cr}}{S_b} = f_{ct} \qquad (6.69)$$

where the cracking moment M_{cr} is the moment due to all the loads in the service load stage. From Eq. (6.69), the cracking moment is given by

$$M_{cr} = P_e\left(e+\frac{r^2}{c_b}\right) - f_{ct}S_b \qquad (6.70)$$

where f_{ct} is the tensile strength of concrete, treated as negative. It is noted that $r^2/c_b = k_t$, so that $P_e[e+(r^2/c_b)]$ is the elastic moment required to raise the center-of-compression line from the prestressing steel level to the upper kern point, giving zero tension at the bottom fibers. Therefore, the term $-f_{ct}S_b$ is the additional moment required to cause the development of the first crack at the extreme tension fibers.

6. Flexural strength

When the bending moment of a prestressed concrete beam exceeds the cracking moment and the beam is further loaded, the beam starts to behave like a reinforced concrete beam. The ultimate strength theory for reinforced concrete is applicable to the determination of the flexural strength of the prestressed concrete beam. The principles and equations for the flexural strength of prestressed concrete beam have been described in Section 6.3.3 of Chapter 6. Also the design formulas used for Chinese railway prestressed concrete bridges are presented in Section 6.3.3. It should be emphasized that the flexural strength of the prestressed concrete is independent of the prestress level in the prestressing steel. Instead the flexural strength depends on the area and strength of the prestressing and non-prestressing steel, as well as the dimension and strength of the concrete cross-section. Since the prestressing wires or strands are made of high-strength steel which has not obvious yield plateau, the tension-controlled failure of the prestressed concrete beam is a little bit brittle. This is one of the disadvantages of prestressed concrete bridges.

6.5.4 Design for shear

The shear in a prestressed concrete beam comprises the effect of the prestressing force that a reinforced concrete beam does not have and that of the externally applied load. The action of the vertical component of the prestressing force reduces the vertical shear force caused by the external load (Figure 6.27). Consequently, the net shear force is markedly less in a prestressed concrete beam than in a reinforced concrete beam.

Furthermore, the compressive stress in concrete caused by the prestressing tendon considerably reduces the effect of the tensile flexural stress generated by external loads, so that flexural cracking is prevented or under control. As a result, the principal stress in a prestressed concrete beam is considerably lower than that in a reinforced concrete beam with the same geometrical configuration and loading condition.

The design equations for prestressed concrete in shear are identical to those developed for reinforced concrete and described in detail in Figure 6.26 shows the contributions of the vertical component of the prestressing force in counteracting the vertical shear V caused by the external load. The net shear force V_c carried by the concrete is

$$V_c = V - V_{pb} \tag{6.71}$$

where, V_{pb} denotes the shear force caused by the longitudinal prestressing tendons.

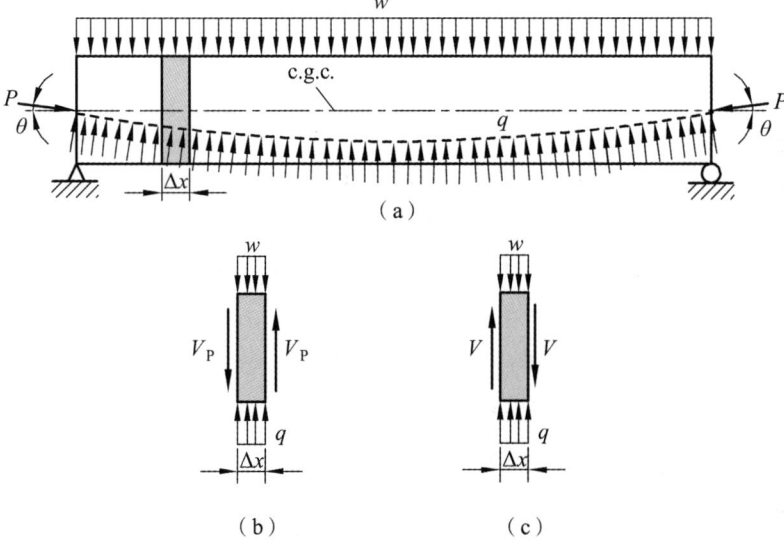

Figure 6.26 Shear forces in a prestressed concrete beam: (a) the shear force caused by the prestressing force; (b) the shear force caused by the external load.

The shear stress τ_c at any depth of the section is thus

$$\tau_c = \frac{V_c Q}{bI} \tag{6.72}$$

The normal stress caused by the prestressing force and external bending moment is

$$\sigma_c = \frac{P_e}{A_g} \mp \frac{P_e ec}{I_g} \pm \frac{Mc}{I_g} \tag{6.73}$$

and the principal stresses are obtained as

$$\genfrac{}{}{0pt}{}{\sigma_{c1}}{\sigma_{c2}} = \frac{\sigma_c}{2} \mp \sqrt{\frac{\sigma_c^2}{4} + \tau_c^2} \qquad (6.74)$$

6.5.5 Detailing of prestressed and non-prestressed reinforcement

Detailing of prestressing tendons is to arrange the prestressing tendons in accordance with the required amounts, layouts, and locations in the cross-section and along the member axis, to meet the design requirements. Requirements for detailing of prestressing steel are covered in Chinese highway and railway design codes. Here, only the detailing requirements for railway bridges are presented.

1. Spacing of tendons and ducts

For post-tensioning ducts, if the duct diameter is equal or less than 55 mm, the clear distance between post-tensioning ducts shall not be less 40 mm; if the duct diameter is greater than 55 mm, the clear distance shall not be less than 0.8 times the duct external diameter. The cross-sectional area of the duct shall not be less than 2 times the area of the tendon.

For pre-tensioned tendons, the clear distance between tendons or steel bars shall not be less 1.5 times the tendon or bar diameter or 30 mm.

2. Clear concrete cover

The clear concrete cover over the prestressing steel or ducts shall not be less than the duct external diameter and not less than 50 mm on the top and sides of the member. On the bottom of the member, the clear cover shall not be less than 60 mm.

3. The anchorage length of bonded strands

The anchorage length of a prestressing strand in pretensioned construction shall not be less than 130 times the diameter of the strand. If the nominal diameter and the tensile strength of the strand exceed the values specified in the design code, experiments should be conducted to determine the anchorage length.

4. Anchorage zones of post-tensioned members

In the anchorage zone of the post-tensioned members, resistance to bursting forces shall be provided by non-prestressed or prestressed reinforcement or in the form of spirals or closed hoops or grids of steel bars. This reinforcement shall resist the total bursting and spalling forces. The non-prestressed bars should be in relatively small diameter and closely spaced, as shown in Figure 6.27. The closed hoop stirrups are usually used, looping around non-prestressing longitudinal bars at the beam corners to improve anchorage.

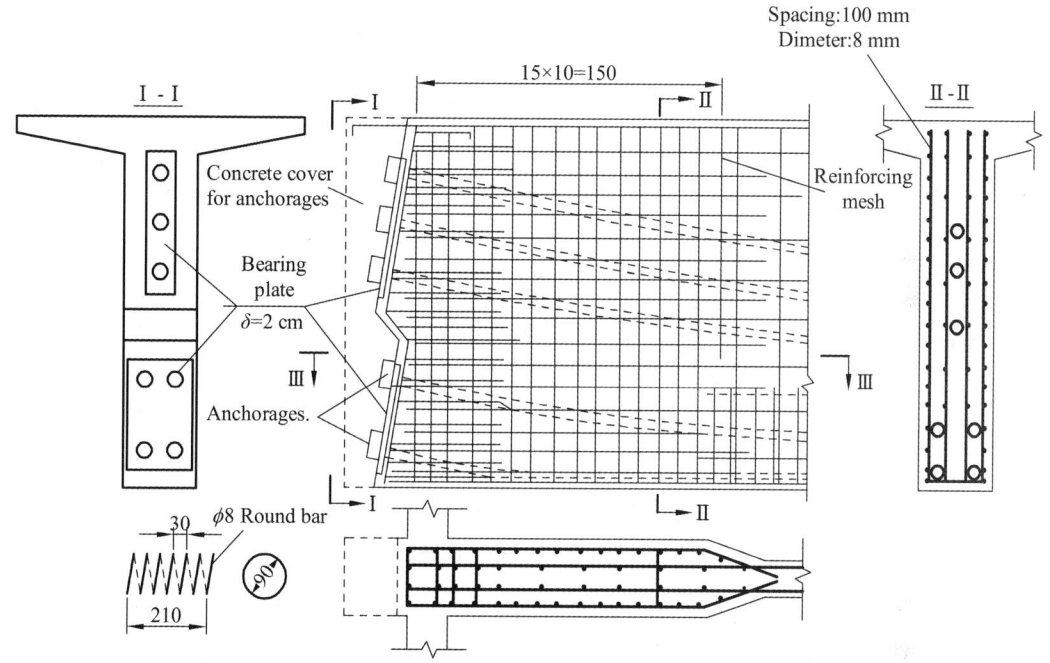

Figure 6.27 Anchorage zone reinforcement for post-tensioned beams.

5. Curved tendons

For post-tensioned beams with curved prestressing tendons, if the diameter of the strands or wires that comprise the tendon is equal or less than 5 mm, the radius of curvature of the tendon shall not be less than 4 m. If the wire diameter is greater than 5 mm, then the radius of curvature of the tendon shall not be less than 6 m.

For pretensioned beams with harped prestressing tendons, deviators shall be used and the diameter of the guiding wheels should be greater than 20 mm.

6. Non-prestressed stirrups

Stirrups shall be provided in the prestressed concrete beams in accordance with requirements for shear resistance. If non-prestressing stirrups are used, the following requirements shall be satisfied:

(i) The diameter of the stirrup steel bar shall not be greater than 8 mm;

(ii) In the web, the spacing of the stirrups shall not be greater than 200 mm, and hot-rolled ribbed rebars should be used.

(iii) In the flange with longitudinal prestressing tendons, the stirrups shall be provided in closed hoop or spiral form with spacing of not greater than 100 mm. In the region within 500 mm from the beam end, the spacing of the stirrups in the flange shall be 80 to 100 mm.

(iv) If the width of the flange is greater than 500 mm, four-leg stirrups shall be used.

(v) For members subjected to torsion, closed stirrups shall be used.

7. Non-prestressed longitudinal reinforcement

On the tension sides of a prestressed beam under service loads, non-prestressing reinforcement shall be provided according to the following requirements:

(i) For the members not allowed to subjected to tension stresses, the diameter of the non-prestressing bars shall not be less than 8 mm, and the spacing of the bars shall not be greater than 100 mm;

(ii) For the members allowed to have tension stresses and to crack, hot-rolled deformed bars shall be used. The area of the bars shall be determined based on strength requirements and shall not be less than 0.3% area of concrete in tension. Small diameter reinforcing bars at small spacing should be used.

6.6 Example bridges

Two standard prestressed concrete girders, one for railway bridges and another for highway bridges, are presented to illustrate the detailing of prestressing tendons and non-prestressing reinforcement. These girders are designed to the Chinese design codes, and are typical of simply supported girders widely used in medium- to long-span bridges. The design live load is the Chinese railway standard live loading Type-ZK (see Chapter 2)

6.6.1 The railway prestressed concrete girder

Figure 6.28 shows the reinforcement details of a standard T-shaped railway prestressed concrete girder of 24 m in span length. The shape of the cross-section and the structural configuration of the girder in the longitudinal direction are similar to those of reinforced concrete girder (Figure 6.7), but with a smaller web thickness depth (240 mm). The total length of the girder is 24.60 m. The girder can be used in straight or curved bridges. If the girder is used in straight bridges, the C43 concrete is used and there are totally 14 prestressing tendons used. If the girder is used in curved bridges, the C48 concrete is used and 14 prestressing tendons are provided. Each prestressing tendon consists of 24 cold-drawn high-carbon 5-mm diameter wires. The prestressing tendons are raised gradually from the region near the midspan to end surface of the girder where they are diffusely anchored.

The non-prestressed stirrups are made up of 10-mm diameter steel bar at spacing of 200 mm in the region near midspan and at spacing of 100 mm in the region close to the beam end. Longitudinal non-prestressing bars of 8 mm in diameter are placed in the bottom flange and the web to prevent cracking due to concrete shrinkage and thermal stress. To prevent splitting stress in the bottom flange due to application of prestressing force, closed stirrups of 8 mm in diameter are provided in the bottom flange at spacing of 100 mm.

Each anchor chuck is supported on a steel bearing plate of 16 mm thick. A helical spring, 57 mm in spring diameter and 210 mm in length, made up of a 3-mm diameter steel wire, is cast in concrete under each bearing plate to confine the concrete so to increase the local strength of the concrete.

6.6.2 Highway prestressed concrete bridges

Figure 6.29 shows a prefabricated prestressed concrete highway T-girder bridge, which is a standard design for span length of 30 mm. The span length of a highway concrete girder bridge usually refers the distance between centers of piers. The calculational span length of the bridge, which is distance between the bearing centers of the bridge, is 29.44 m. The total length of each girder is 29.92 m. The bridge consists of 12 pieces of prestressed concrete T-girders and the deck width of the bridge is 25.5 m, as shown in Figure 6.29(a). The bridge is designed for the Chinese Highway Class-I live loading.

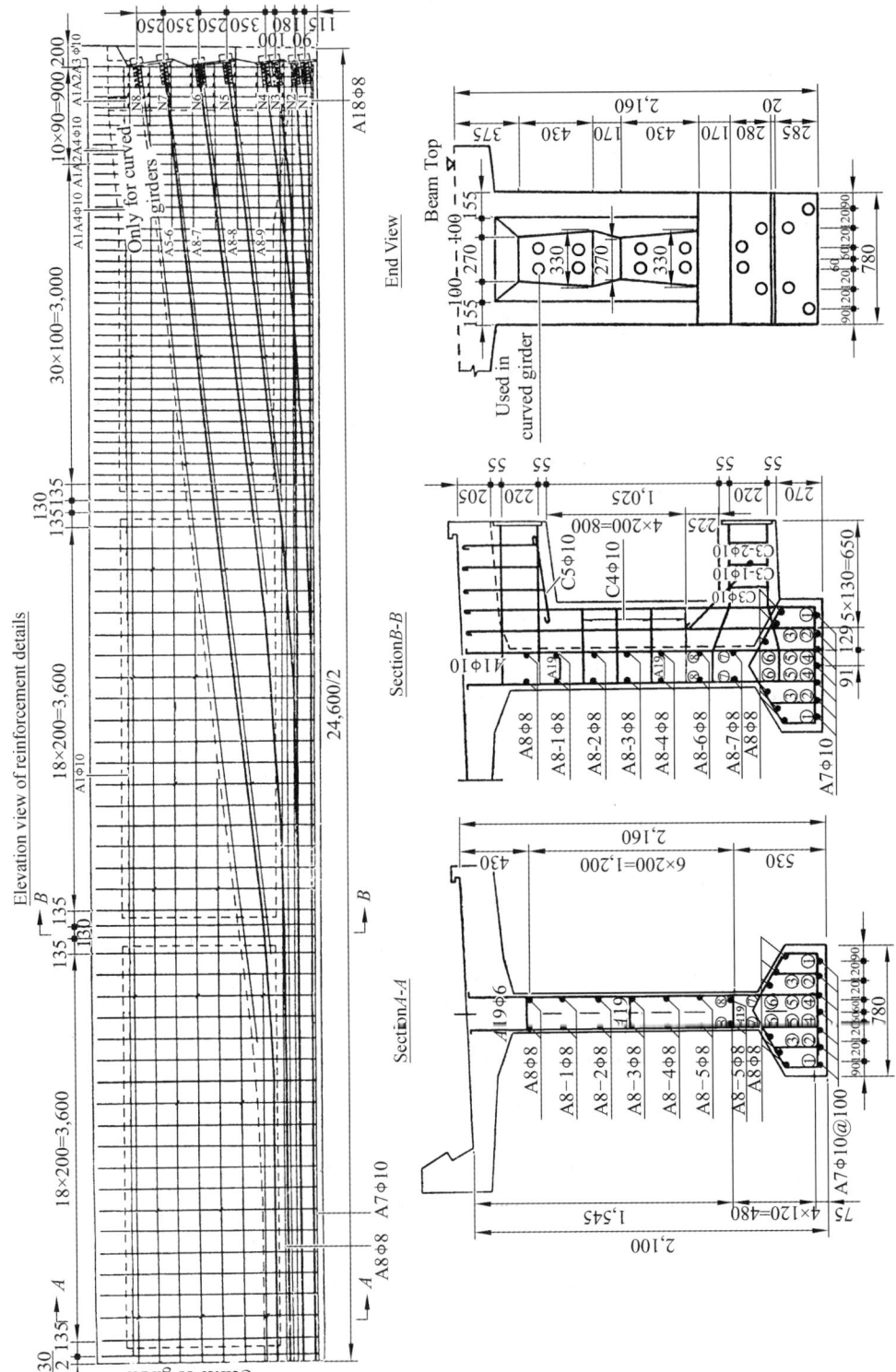

Figure 6.28 Reinforcement details of a railway prestressed concrete T-girder of 24 m in span length (units in mm).

The girder is made from C50 concrete. The depth of the girder is 2.0 m with the depth-to-span ratio of 1/15. The thickness of the web is 200 mm. At the girder end, the web thickness is increased to 500 mm, which equals to the width of bottom flange. This is to provide the sufficient space for anchoring the prestressing tendons. There are totally three tendons provide in each girder, each tendon comprises 15.2-mm diameter high-strength low relaxation strands [Figure 6.29(b)]. The N1 tendon has 10 stands. The N1 and N3 tendons both have 9 strands. The yield strength of the strand is f_{pk} = 1 860 MPa. To have the anchors distributed uniformly on the girder end, the tendons are gradually raised from some locations so that they can smoothly reach their anchoring positions. To meet this requirement, N2 and N3 tendons have to be bent smoothly in the horizontal plane to reach the symmetrical center of the web. The prestressing force is applied after the concrete has gained 90% of the compressive strength and not earlier than 7 days of curing. Corrugated steel pipes of 87 mm and 97 mm in diameter are used as tendon ducts.

Non-prestressed reinforcement in the girder has similar arrangements to those in the reinforced concrete girder [Figure 6.29(c)]. In the web, the N3 and N3' longitudinal bars of 10 mm in diameter are placed along the two sides of the web to serve as skin reinforcement controlling the cracking of concrete. The N4, N5, and N6 bars are closed stirrups of 12-mm diameter which are placed in the web to resist the shear force. In the bottom flange, the N7 and N8 closed hoops of 12-mm diameter are placed to resist bursting stress due to prestress. There are also 5 non-prestressing N1 bars of 25-mm diameter provided in the bottom flange to control flexural cracking and to meet the strength requirement. It is noted that no inclined non-prestressed reinforcing bars are provided in the girder. Reinforcement details of the diaphragms are not shown in the figure.

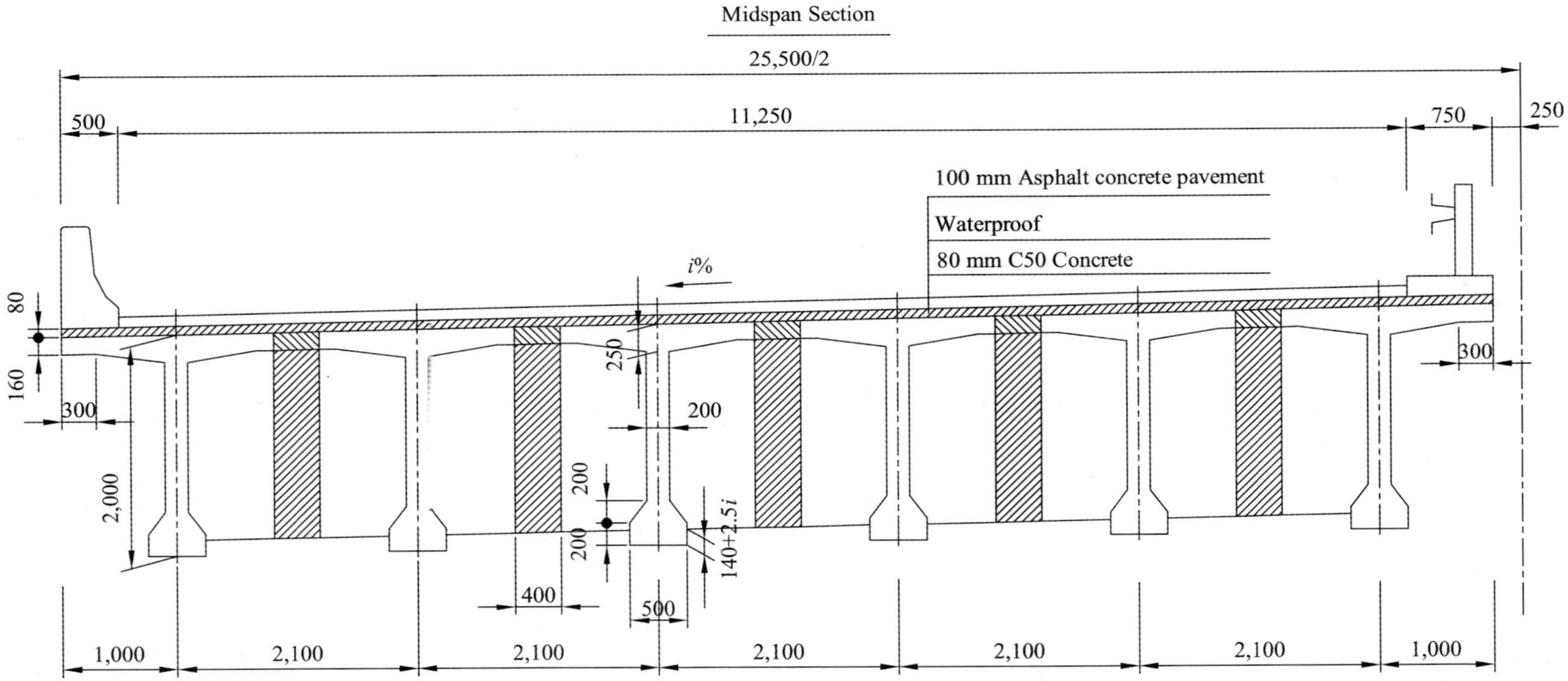

Midspan Section
25,500/2
500
11,250
750
250
100 mm Asphalt concrete pavement
Waterproof
80 mm C50 Concrete
i%
80
160
300
250
200
2,000
200
200
140+2.5i
400
500
300
1,000
2,100
2,100
2,100
2,100
2,100
1,000

(a)

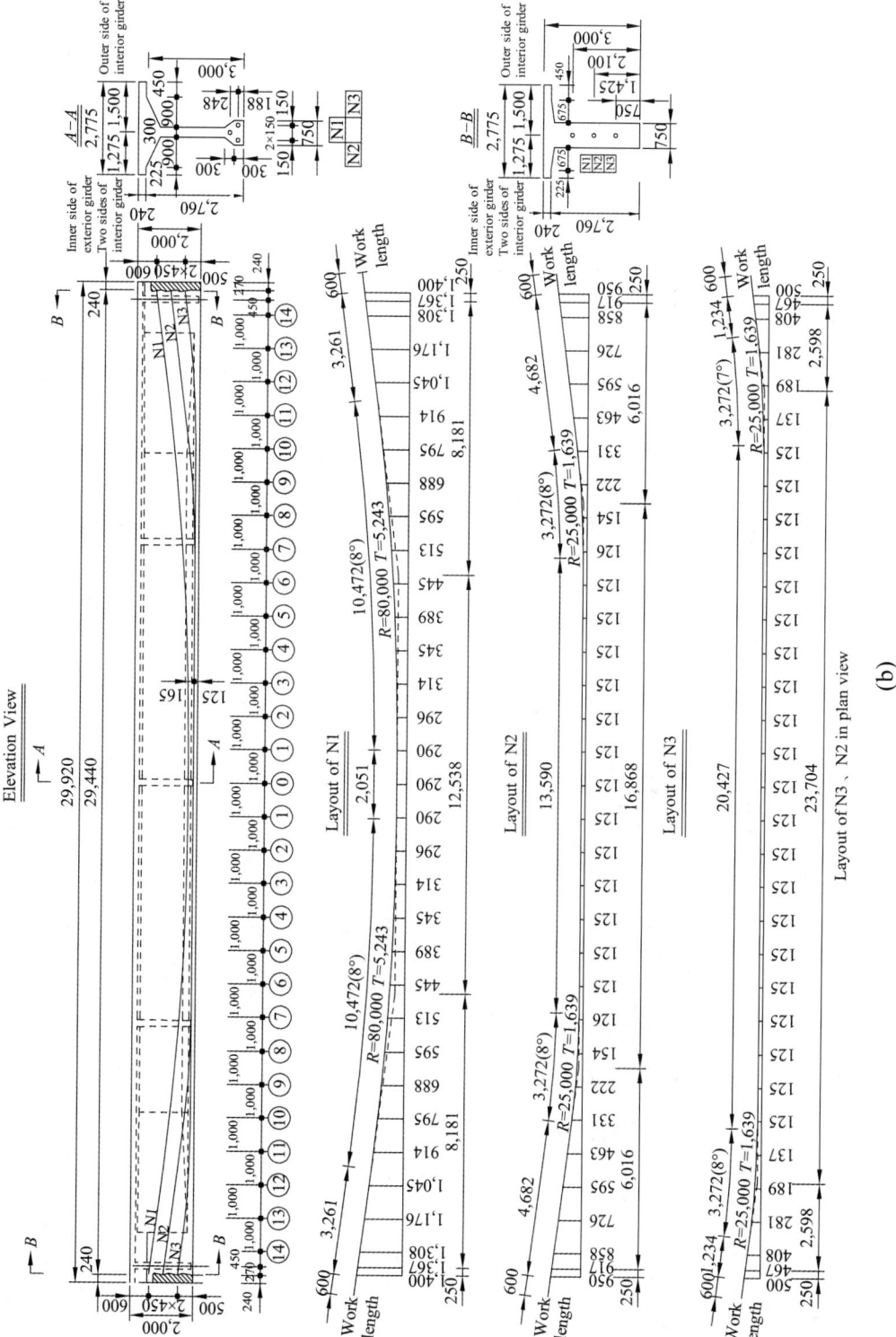

(b)

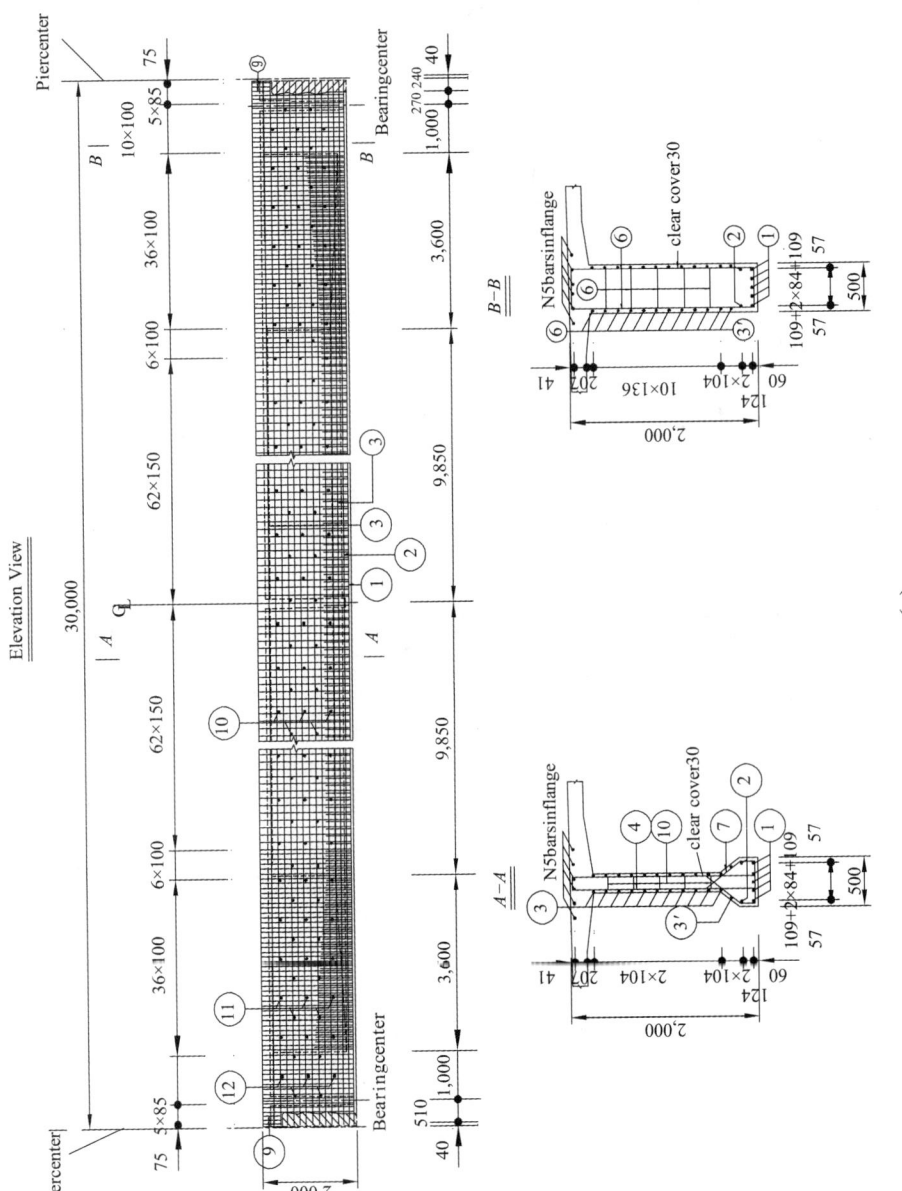

Figure 6.29 A highway prestressed concrete T-girder bridge of 30 m in span length (units: mm): (a) cross-section; (b) layout of prestressing tendons; (c) details of non-prestressed reinforcement.

References

[6.1] Lin, T. Y., Burns, N. H., *Design of Prestressed Concrete Structures*, 3rd ed., John Wiley & Sons, New York, 1981.

[6.2] Nawy, E. G., *Prestressed Concrete– A Fundamental Approach*, 5th ed., Prentice Hall, Upper Saddle River, New Jersey, 2010.

[6.3] Dolan, C. W., Hamilton, H. R. (Trey), *Prestressed Concrete Building – Design, and Construction*, Springer Nature Switzerland AG 2019.

[6.4] Benaim, R., *The Design of Prestressed Concrete Bridges–Concepts and Principles*, Taylor & Francis, New York, 2018.

[6.5] Hewson, N., *Prestressed Concrete Bridges– Design and Construction*, 2nd ed., ICE Publishing, London, 2012.

[6.6] Nilson, A. H., *Design of Prestressed Concrete*, 2nd ed., John Wiley & Sons, New York, 1987.

[6.7] Yao, L.-S, ed., (Xiang, H.-F., Gu, A.-B., reviewers), *Bridge Engineering*, 2nd ed., China Communications Press, Beijing, China, 2008.

姚玲森. 桥梁工程. 2 版. 项海帆，顾安邦，主审. 北京：人民交通出版社，2008.

[6.8] Fan, L.-C., ed., *Bridge Engineering*, 2nd ed., China Communications Press, Beijing, China, 1988.

范立础. 桥梁工程. 2 版. 北京：人民交通出版社，1988.

[6.9] Shao, X.-D., ed., (Gu, A.-B., reviewer), *Bridge Engineering*, 4th ed., China Communications Press Co., Ltd., Beijing, China, 2018.

邵旭东. 桥梁工程. 4 版. 顾安邦，主审. 北京：人民交通出版社，2018.

[6.10] Qiang, S.-Z., ed., Shao, X.-D., assoc. ed., *Bridge Engineering*, 2nd ed., Higher Education Press, Beijing, 2011.

强士中. 桥梁工程. 2 版，北京：高等教育出版社，2011.

[6.11] Li, Y.-D., ed., *Introduction to Bridge Engineering* (in Chinese), 3rd ed., Southwest Jiaotong University Press, Chengdu, China, 2005.

李亚东. 桥梁工程概论. 3 版. 成都：西南交通大学出版社，2014.

[6.12] Tang, J.-S., ed., (Yang, J. reviewer), *Railway Bridges*, China Railway Press, Beijing, 2015.

唐继舜. 铁路桥梁. 杨进，主审. 北京：中国铁道出版社，2015.

[6.13] Li, Q., ed., Principles of Concrete Structures, 3rd ed., China Railway Press, Beijing, 2013.

李乔. 混凝土结构设计原理. 3 版. 北京：中国铁道出版，2013.

[6.14] TB 10092-2017 (J 462-2017), *Code for Design of Concrete Structures of Railway Bridges and Culverts*, China National Railway Bureau, 2017.

[6.15] JTG 3362-2018, *Specifications for Design of Highway Reinforced Concrete and Prestressed Concrete Bridges and Culverts*, China's Transportation Ministry, 2018.

[6.16] AASHTO, LRFD *Bridge Design Specifications*, 5th ed., American Association for State Highway and Transportation Officials, Washington, DC., 2014.

Chapter 7 Concrete Continuous and Rigid Continuous Bridges

7.1 Introduction

To characterize the size of a bridge, it is customary to classify bridges into short-span, medium-span, long-span, and extra long-span bridges, depending on the span lengths. There are not consistent criteria among the bridge design codes to define the range of spans for the different classifications. The Chinese highway design code classifies the bridge size by the span lengths as follows:

Short-span bridges: $\quad$ 5 m $\leqslant L_k <$ 10 m
Medium-span bridges: $\quad$ 20 m $\leqslant L_k <$ 40 m
Long-span bridges: $\quad$ 40 m $\leqslant L_k <$ 150 m
Extra long-span bridges: $\quad L_k >$ 150 m

where, L_k is the span length of a single span. For multi-span bridges, L_k is the maximum span length among all the spans. In North America, the common practice of the classification by span lengths is:

Short-span bridges: $\quad$ 6 m $\leqslant L_k <$ 38 m
Medium-span bridges: $\quad$ 38 m $\leqslant L_k <$ 120 m
Long-span bridges: $\quad L_k >$ 120 m

Bridges with span length less than 6 m are classified as culverts. The Chinese railway design code classifies the size of a bridge by the total length of the bridge. This type of classification identifies the bridge sizes as:

Short-span bridges: $\quad L_T <$ 20 m
Medium-span bridges: $\quad$ 20 m $\leqslant L_T <$ 100 m
Long-span bridges: $\quad$ 100 m $\leqslant L_T <$ 500 m
Extra long-span bridges: $\quad L_T >$ 500 m

where L_T is the total length of a bridge, which is generally the distance between the front walls of the two abutments on the two ends of a bridge, or, alternatively, the summation of all span lengths plus the center-to-center distances between adjacent bearings on the piers.

The significance of the classification of bridges by span lengths is related to the selection of bridge types. Design and construction practice has shown that certain types of bridges are only suitable for a certain range of span lengths. Thus, if the span length of a bridge is in a particular size category, some bridge types can be automatically eliminated from consideration. For example, a suspension bridge is usually used for long span lengths, thus will not be considered as an alternative for a short-span or medium-span bridge. Similarly, simply supported girder bridges are typically suited for short to medium span lengths in the sense of Chinese classification of the bridge sizes, and generally are not used for long-spans.

Generally, the bridge types for long spans include continuous bridges, arch bridges, cable-stayed bridges, and suspension bridges. This does not means that these bridge types can not be used for medium span lengths; instead it means that using these bridge types for medium span lengths is not appropriate from an economic standpoint. Arch bridges can be used for short to medium span lengths, but most modern arch bridges are used for long spans in the form of the steel trussed arch or tied arch. In the National Bridge Inspection Standards (NBIS) of the U.S. Federal Highway Administration, cable-stayed and suspension bridges are defined as complex bridges.

In this chapter, the structural configurations of the prestressed concrete continuous bridges are briefly introduced with discussions of design issues and construction methods of this type of bridges.

7.2 Overview of prestressed concrete continuous bridges

In China, prestressed continuous bridges represent about 75% of the long span bridges. The maximum span length of prestressed concrete continuous bridges has reached 200 m. For rigid continuous bridges, the maximum span length has been 300 m.

The main advantages of the prestressed concrete continuous bridges are in the following:

(1) Bending moments are smaller in continuous beams than in simple beams of the same span length. This is due to the negative bending moments at intermediate supports cancelling out part of the positive bending moments along the spans between supports (Figure 7.1). As a result, continuous beams are shallower, and hence lighter, than simply supported bridges of the same span length. This is the reason that the continuous bridges are suitable for long spans.

(2) Continuous bridges require fewer piers than simply supported bridges. At each interior support, only single bearings are required, thus reducing the width of piers compared to simple spans. Costs of the piers and foundations are thus reduced.

(3) Continuous bridges require fewer expansion joints, thus resulting in good riding quality and causing less noise.

(4) The prestressed concrete continuous bridges have better vertical, lateral, and torsional stiffnesses than simply supported concrete bridges. Deflections are smaller in continuous girders than in comparable simple spans.

(5) Continuous bridges allow stress redistribution under overload conditions, leading to higher reserve strength against collapse.

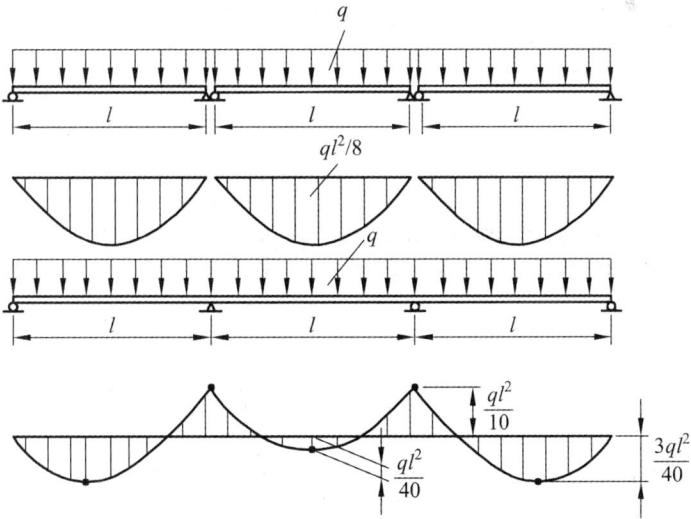

Figure 7.1 Comparison of the distributions of bending moments between a three-span continuous bridge and a comparable simple bridge under the dead load.

7.3 Layout of span lengths with girder depths

1. Conventional continuous bridges

The interior-to-exterior span ratio L_1/L_2 is usually from 1.25 to 1.67 (Figure 7.2). For continuous and rigid-continuous bridges, the depth-to-span ratios are generally in the following range:

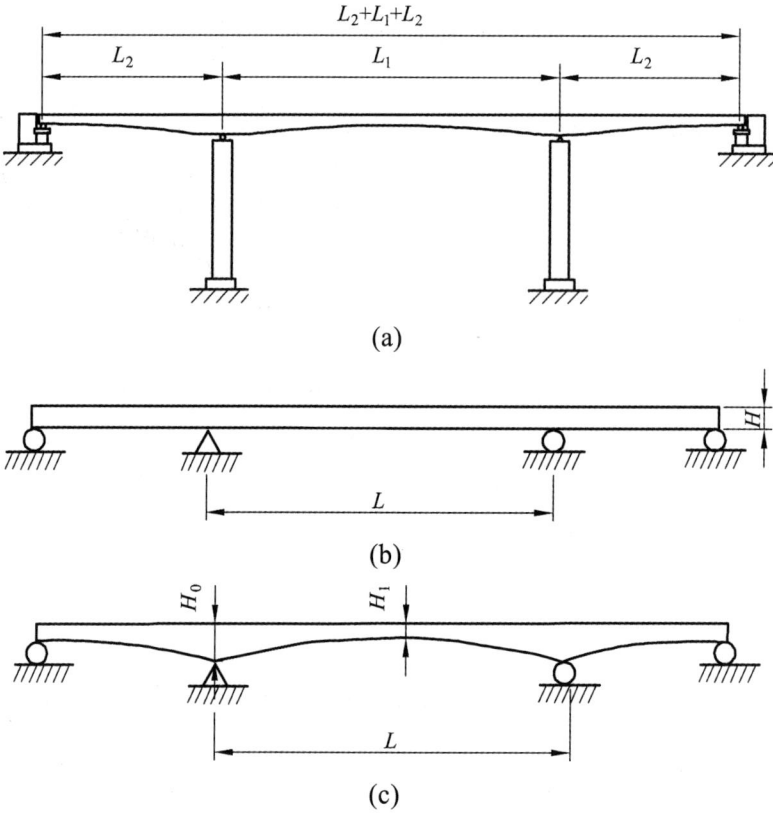

Figure 7.2 Arrangement of spans and the variation of depth along the spans: (a) layout of a three-span continuous bridge; (b) constant-depth girder; (c) variable-depth girder.

For variable-depth girders
$$\begin{cases} \dfrac{H_1}{L} = \dfrac{1}{30} \sim \dfrac{1}{50} & \text{at midspan} \\ \dfrac{H_0}{L} = \dfrac{1}{16} \sim \dfrac{1}{25} & \text{at support for highway bridges} \\ \dfrac{H_0}{L} = \dfrac{1}{12} \sim \dfrac{1}{16} & \text{at support for railway bridge} \end{cases}$$

For constant-depth girders
$$\begin{cases} \dfrac{H}{L} = \dfrac{1}{15} \sim \dfrac{1}{25} \text{ for highway bridges} \\ \dfrac{H}{L} = \dfrac{1}{16} \sim \dfrac{1}{18} \text{ for railway bridges} \end{cases}$$

where, H denotes the depth of the constant-depth girder; H_0 and H_1 are the depths of the section at midspan and support, respectively. The ratios of the depth at mid span to the depth at the support are 2.0 ~ 3.0 and 1.5 ~ 2.0 for highway and railway bridges, respectively.

2. Rigid continuous bridges

The rigid continuous bridge is a type of bridge in which the continuous girder is rigidly connected with the intermediate piers to act as a continuous unit (Figure 7.3). Compared to the conventional continuous bridge, the rigid continuous bridge has the following advantages:

(i) Intermediate bearings are removed to reduce construction and maintenance cost;

(ii) Deflection of the continuous girder under live loads is smaller and the riding quality is better;

(iii) The rigid continuous bridge is more suitable for cantilever construction method.

The disadvantages are that (i) the piers are subjected to bending moments, and the deformation of piers have considerable influence on the distributions of internal forces in the continuous girder; and (ii) shrinkage of concrete and change of temperature in the piers can cause secondary shear and moment in the girder, and these secondary forces usually can't be neglected.

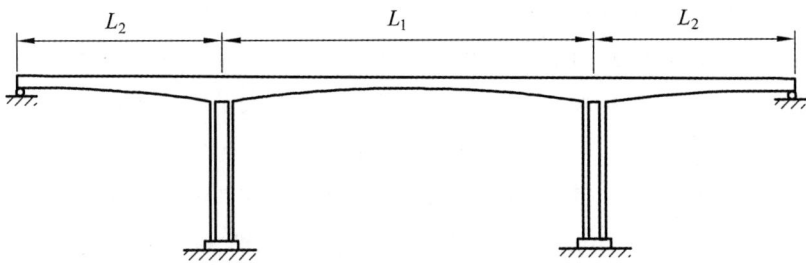

Figure 7.3　A typical three-span rigid continuous bridge.

7.4 Cross-sections

The cross-sections for prestressed continuous concrete bridges of medium- or long-spans are generally T-shaped or box-shaped (Figure 7.4). For medium-span continuous highway bridges, the T-shaped girders are most commonly used. For long-spans highway and railway continuous bridges, the box cross- section are popular, since the cross-cross has excellent flexural and torsional stiffness, and is capable of maintain integrity of the structure under overloads.

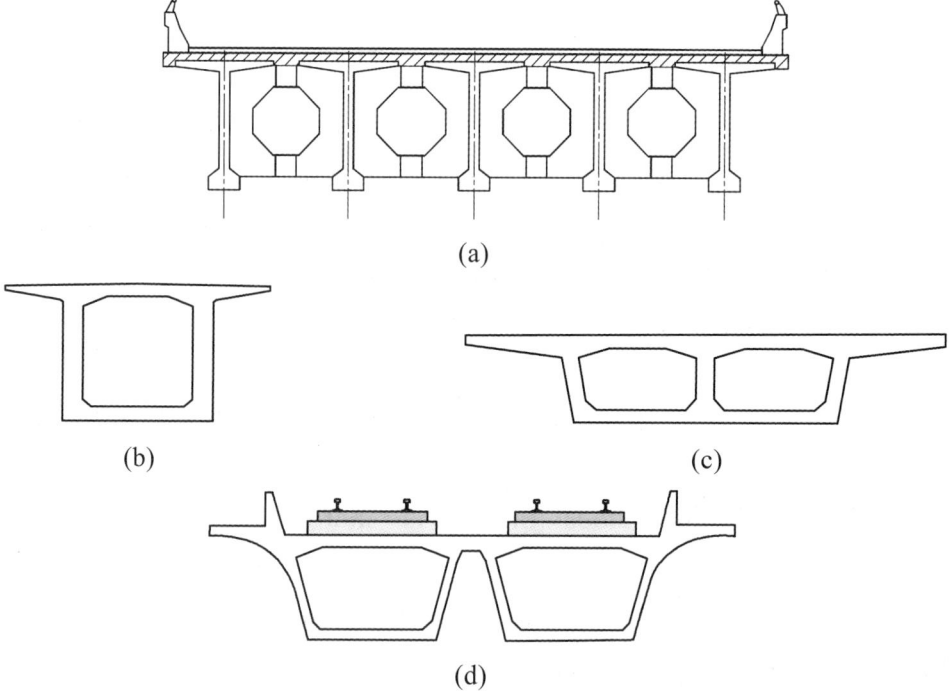

Figure 7.4 Cross-sections for prestressed concrete continuous bridges: (a) T-shaped; (b) single cell box; (c) single box with tow cells; (d) two box each with single cell.

To increase the torsional resistance of the girder, diaphragms are usually provided for the continuous girder along the spans. Generally, the diaphragm is provided at the supports, at midspan, at the fourth points, and at the girder ends. The diaphragms can improve the load distribution in the transverse direction, but can cause difficulties in construction. There have been some research results suggesting elimination of intermediate diaphragms. In some long span concrete continuous bridges, diaphragms were provided only at supports. Figure 7.5 shows a typical arrangement of diaphragms along the span of a continuous box girder.

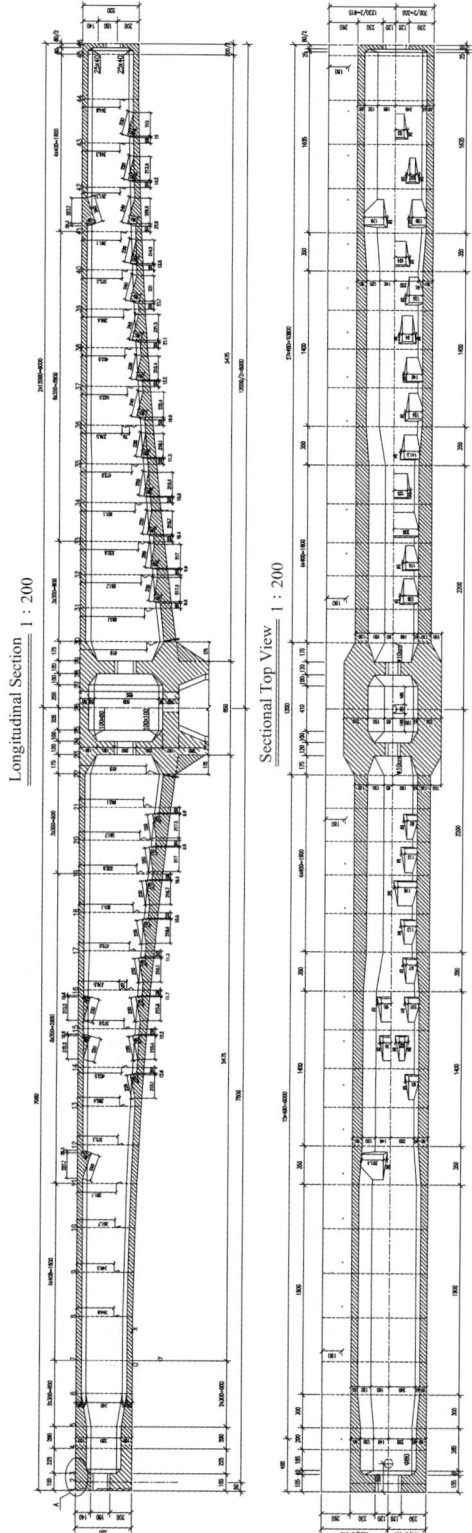

Figure 7.5 A typical arrangement of diaphragms in a continuous box girder.

7.5 Layouts and detailing of prestressing tendons

In the long-span prestressed concrete continuous bridges, the prestressing force are usually applied in the longitudinal, lateral, and vertical directions. Thus, longitudinal, lateral, and vertical prestressing tendons are provided in the continuous girders.

7.5.1 The longitudinal prestressing tendons

The layout of the longitudinal prestressing tendons is closely related to the construction method. Several layouts of prestressing tendons in continuous girders are illustrated in Figure 7.6.

Figure 7.6(a) shows the layout of the tendons in the continuous girder of a constant depth constructed by the incremental launching method. The tendons are laid out in straight form at the top and bottom of the girder, extending over the entire span to resist the reversed cyclic moments during launching. After erection, additional tendons are provided in the midspan section and the support sections. Sometimes, temporary tendons are provided at the top of the midspan section and the bottom of the support sections to provide temporary constraints. After the erection is completed, the temporary prestressing tendons are removed.

Figure 7.6(b) shows the tendon layouts for the constant depth girder constructed by the simple-then-continuous construction method. Continuity is achieved at the support sections through cast-in-place concrete in conjunction with local post-tensioning tendons.

Figure 7.6(c) (d) shows the tendon layouts for the continuous girder of variable depth. The curved prestressing tendons are provided in the regions of positive and negative moments, respectively. In addition, straight tendons are also provided in the top and bottom slabs of the girder in the negative and positive moment regions. The tendons can be anchored within the depth of the girder [Figure 7.6(c)] or outside the top or bottom slabs of the girder [Figure 7.6(d)].

In Figure 7.6(e), the prestressing tendons are continuously run through the girder and anchored at the girder ends. This type of layout can lead to considerable frictional loss of prestress.

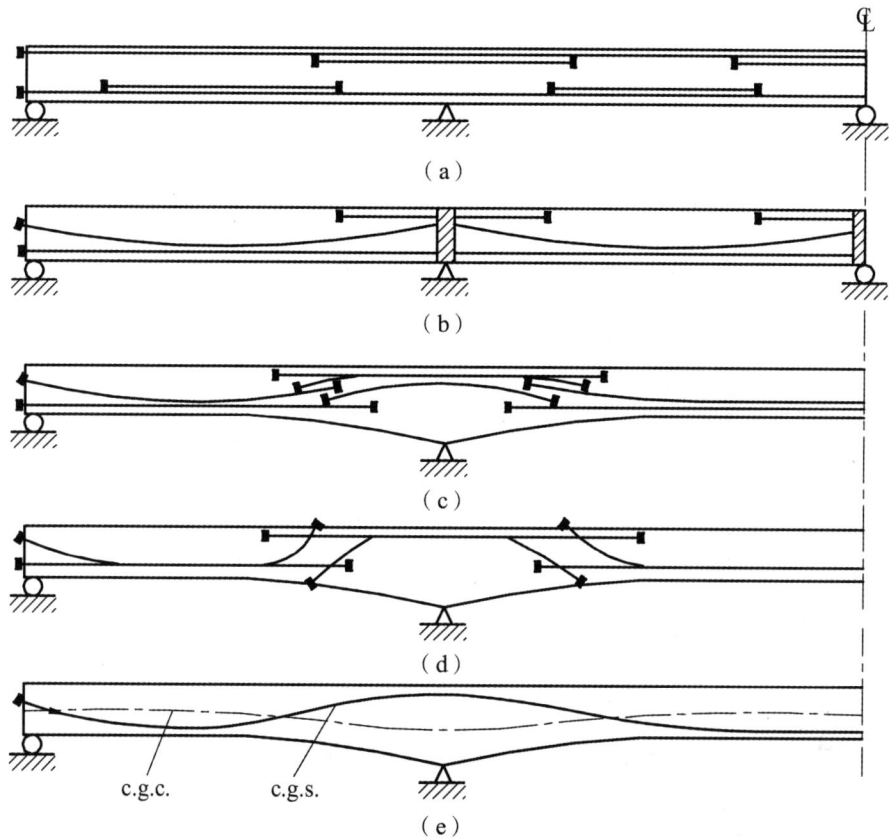

Figure 7.6 Several layouts of prestressing tendons in continuous concrete girders: (a) for the incremental launching method; (b) for the simple-then-continuous construction method; (c) for the cantilever methods; (d) for the cantilever methods; (e) for the cantilever methods.

Long span prestressed concrete continuous bridges are usually constructed by the balanced cantilever method. The layouts of the prestressing tendons must meet the construction as well as design requirements. With balanced cantilever construction there are two distinct sets of prestressing tendons, as illustrated in Figure 7.7. The first are the cantilever tendons that are installed in the top slab and web to resist the negative moments as the girder is being cantilevered out. The second are the tendons placed in the bottom slab and web to take the positive moments over the mid-span region or over the side span after the cantilevered girders are connected in the main span and supported in the side span. Figure 7.8 shows the separate layouts of the cantilever tendons and the draped tendons to resist positive moments.

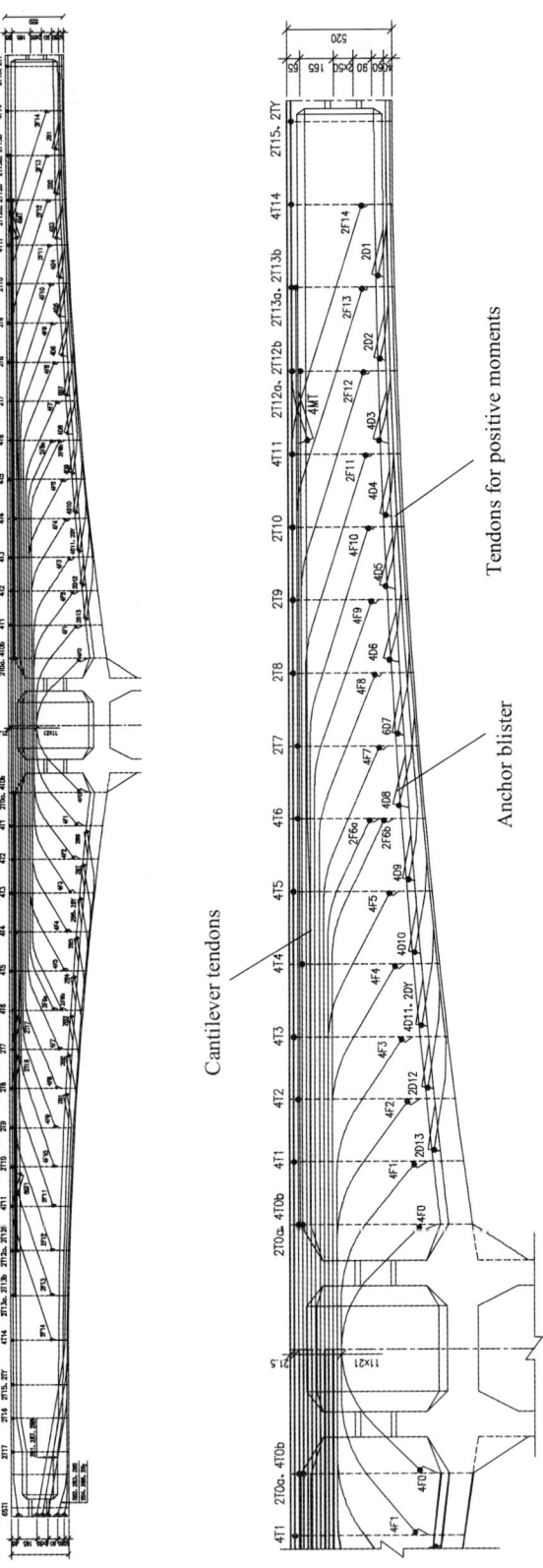

Figure 7.7 Tendon layout in a rigid continuous girder for balanced cantilever construction.

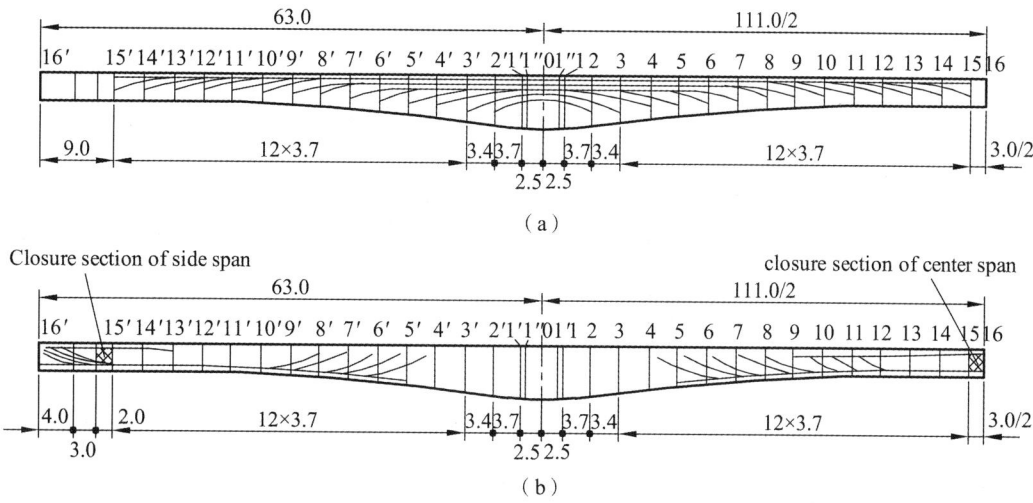

Figure 7.8 Layout of tendons in positive and negative moment regions: (a) in negative moment region; (b) in positive moment regions.

7.5.2 Lateral and vertical prestressing steel

Lateral prestressing steel is designed to resist the moment in the top slab of the box girder, and the vertical prestressing steel is designed to resist the shear forces in the web. When the span length of the top slab is large, lateral prestressing becomes necessary. The lateral prestressing reinforcement is generally provided in the form of prestressing strands or wires, while the vertical prestressing reinforcement is most often in the form of high-strength bars. The vertical prestressing bars can also be used as the anchoring device for the form travelers in the balanced cantilever construction. Figure 7.9 illustrates the layout of the lateral and vertical prestressing reinforcement in a box girder cross-section.

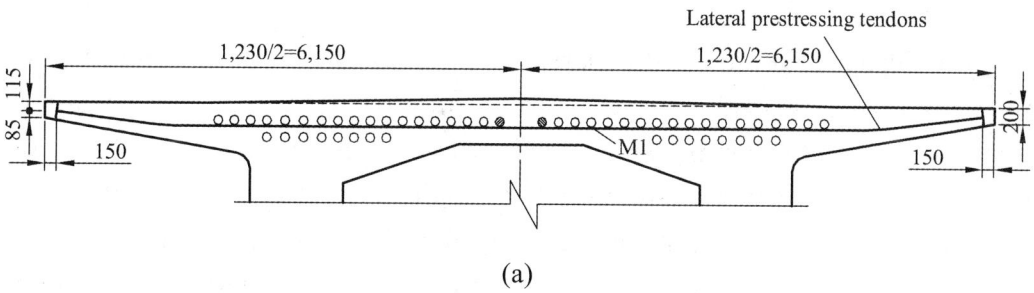

(a)

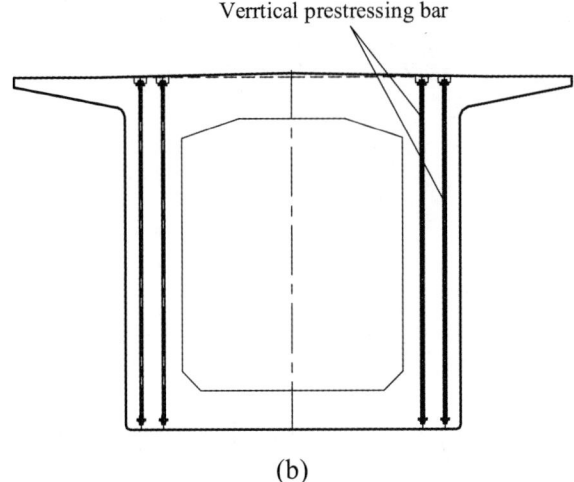

(b)

Figure 7.9 Layouts of lateral and vertical prestressing reinforcement in a box girder cross-section.

7.5.3 Anchor blister

For prestressed continuous box girders, the straight tendons run through the top and bottom slabs are anchored in recesses on the slab face inside the box. The curved cantilever tendons are anchored in the recesses on the face of the segments. The tendons resisting positive moments are anchored, inside the box, on blisters on the bottom slab or on the web. Figure 7.10 shows a typical anchor blister on the bottom slab of a box girder.

7.6 Design issues

7.6.1 Secondary forces

The design of prestressed concrete continuous girders differs from that of the simple prestressed concrete girder, in that secondary moments are introduced when the continuous girder is stressed. The secondary moments are the result of restrained deformation in statically indeterminate structures. Although we call these moments "the secondary", their magnitude cannot be neglected, and instead must be accounted for in the design. Differential shrinkage of concrete, temperature gradients over a cross section, creep of concrete, and differential settlement of supports will all result in secondary

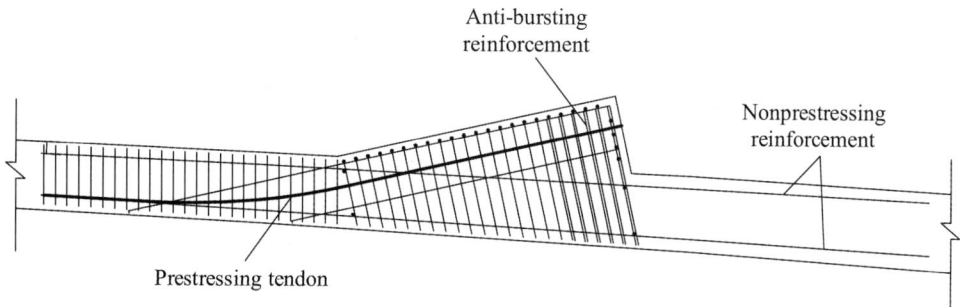

Figure 7.10 A typical anchor blister on the bottom slab of a box girder.

forces in continuous girders. Figure 7.11 illustrates how the secondary moments are generated in a two-span continuous girder under a prestressing force. When an eccentric prestressing force is applied to the continuous girder, the girder will deflect upward. Since the intermediate support B tends to constrain the upward deflection, a downward reaction R_B will be generated at the support during application of the prestressing force. The total moment M in the girder is the sum of the prestress moment M_P and the secondary moment M_s caused by the reaction R_B:

$$M = M_P + M_s$$

Since the secondary moments are generated by the reaction R_B, variation of the secondary moment between supports is linear.

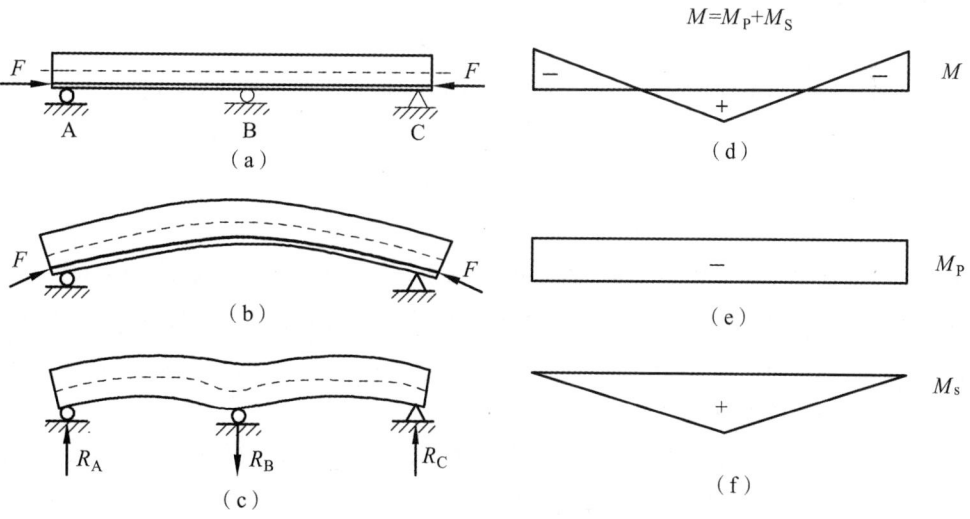

Figure 7.11 The secondary moment in a prestressed concrete continuous girder.

7.6.2 Transformation of structural systems during construction

The erection of the prestressed concrete continuous bridges involves many stages and the structural system may change from one to another during erection. Determination of internal forces in a continuous girder must consider the transformation of the structural system caused by the change of construction stages. Accordingly, the determination of the deformation of the continuous girder must consider the construction process.

Figure 7.12 illustrates the transformation of the structural form during the balanced cantilever construction, and shows the bending moment in the girder in different construction stages.

In stage 1 [Figure 7.12(a)], the girder is built outward from the adjacent piers to form cantilevers. In this stage, the self-weight of the girder acts on the cantilevers and the moments are easy to determine, since the cantilevers are determinate structures.

In stage 2 [Figure 7.12(b)], the end sections of the side spans are cast in situ. In this stage, two processes need to be considered in calculating the moment. First, before concrete hardens, the self-weight of concrete is transferred to the girder and the end supports by formwork, which is equivalent to applying concentrated forces to the girder ends and the supports. In this phase, the structure is still determinate. Second, after concrete hardens the formwork is removed, the end sections are jointed to the cantilevers, the determinate structure transforms to an indeterminate structure. In this phase, removing the formwork is equivalent to removing the concentrated forces applied in the first phase from the indeterminate structure and applying uniformly distributed self-weight to the structure.

In stage 3 [Figure 7.12(c)], the fixed joints between the girder and piers are removed and roller supports are installed. In this stage, the indeterminate structures transform to simply supported structures. This is equivalent to applying the unbalanced moments at the intermediate supports of the resulting determinate structures.

In stage 4 [Figure 7.12(d)], the closure section in the middle span is cast in situ and the cantilevers are stitched together. This stage has similar features to the stage 2. When the concrete of the closure section has not hardened, the equivalent effect is the application of concentrated forces to the ends of the cantilevers. After concrete has hardened, removing the formwork is equivalent to removing the concentrated forces from, and applying the uniform self-weight of closure section to, the resulting indeterminate structure.

The final moment in the completed continuous girder is the superposition of the moments produced in all the construction stages. The final moment diagram is shown in Figure 7.12(e).

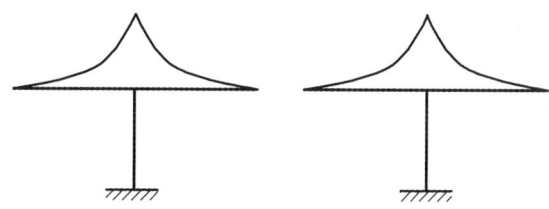

(a) Stage 1: Cantilever completed

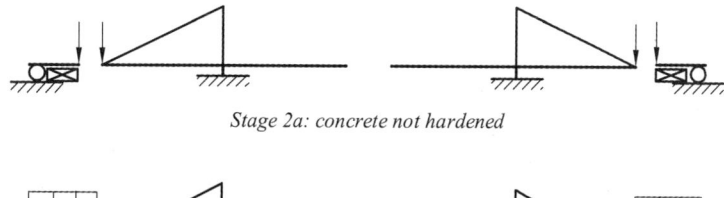

Stage 2a: concrete not hardened

Stage 2b: Formwork removed

(b) Stage 2: End span connencted

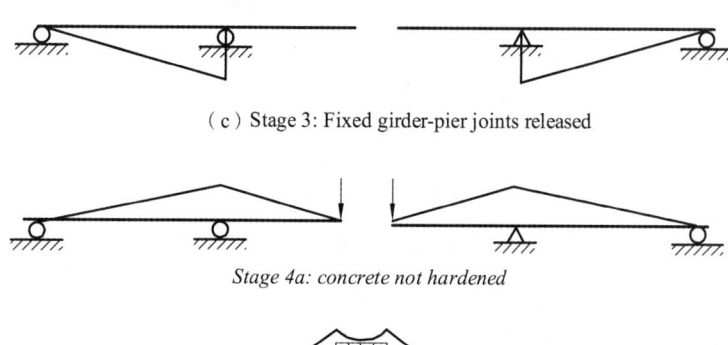

(c) Stage 3: Fixed girder-pier joints released

Stage 4a: concrete not hardened

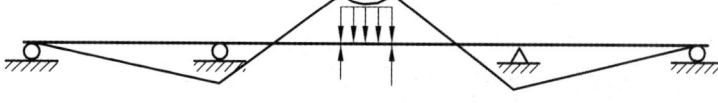

Stage 4b: Formwork removed

(d) Stage 4: Central span stitched

(e) Final moment diagram

Figure 7.12 Transformation of the structural system and the bending moments in different construction stages: (a) Stage 1: Cantilevers completed; (b) Stage 2: End span connencted; (c) Stage 3: Fixed girder-pier joints released; (d) Stage 4: Central span stitched; (e) Final moment diagragm.

7.6.3 Deformation and stress analyses of the box girder

Most of long-span continuous prestressed concrete bridges are built with box girders, because the box girders has excellent torsional resistance. Analysis of the deformations and stresses in box girder under torsional loads plays an important role in the design of box girder bridges.

Generally, the dead loads are uniformly distributed on the bridge deck. However, the live loads may be eccentrically acted on the deck. To analyze the distortion, the eccentric load can be decomposed into a symmetric components [Figure 7.13(b)] and an antisymmetric component [Figure 7.13(c)]. The symmetric component causes vertical bending of the whole box-girder and thus-produced stresses and deformations can be calculated by the beam flexure theory. The antisymmetric component cause not only the pure torsion shear flows [Figure 7.13(e)] but also the distortion shear flows [Figure 7.13(f)]. The torque involved in the pure torsion is equal to the torque of the antisymmetric loading, while the distortion shear flows balance each other and have no net resultant.

Since the continuous box-girder is constrained at supports, the out-of-plane deformation of the cross-section under torsion, termed "the warping", is constrained. Longitudinal warping stresses would develop in the top and bottom slabs and the webs of the box girder (Figure 7.14).

In the design calculation of the continuous box girder bridges, the total stress in the box girder should include the stresses caused by the bending, torsion, and warping actions. In addition, the stress in the top slabs should include the bending stress of the slab under local wheel loads.

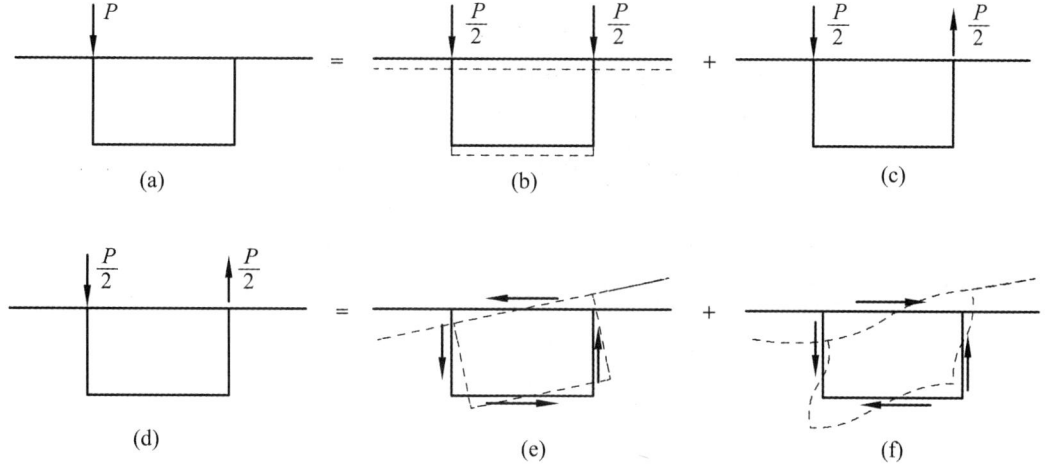

Figure 7.13 Decomposition of the eccentric load applied to the box girder: (a) the eccentric load; (b) symmetric load; (c) antisymmetric load; (d) antisymmetric load; (e) pure torsion; (f) distortion.

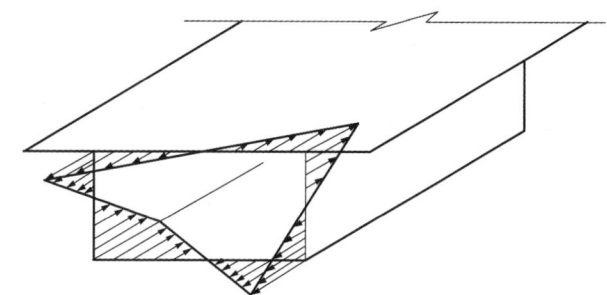

Figure 7.14 The longitudinal warping stresses in the box girder.

References

[7.1] Taly N., *Design of Modern Highway Bridges*, McGraw-Hill, New York, 1998.

[7.2] Benaim R., *The Design of Prestressed Concrete Bridges-Concepts and Principles*, Taylor & Francis, New York, 2018.

[7.3] He G.-H., Che, H.-M., and Xie, Y.-F., *Railway Reinforced Concrete Bridges*, China Railway Press, Beijing, 1986.

[7.4] 何广汉, 车惠民, 谢幼藩. 铁路钢筋混凝土桥. 北京: 中国铁道出版社, 1986.

[7.5] Yao L.-S, ed., (Xiang, H.-F., Gu, A.-B., reviewers), Bridge Engineering, 2nd ed., China Communications Press, Beijing, China, 2008.
姚玲森. 桥梁工程. 2 版. 项海帆, 顾安邦, 主审. 北京：人民交通出版社, 2008.

[7.6] Fan L.-C., ed., Prestressed Concrete Continuous Bridges, China Communications Press, Beijing, 1988.
范立础. 预应力混凝土连续梁桥. 北京：人民交通出版社，1988.

[7.7] Li, Y.-D., ed., *Introduction to Bridge Engineering* (in Chinese), 3rd ed., Southwest Jiaotong University Press, Chengdu, China, 2005.
李亚东. 桥梁工程概论. 3 版. 成都：西南交通大学出版社，2014.

[7.8] Zhao R.-D., ed., (Gao, Z.-Y., reviewer), Long-Span Railway Bridges, China Railway Press, Beijing, 2012.

[7.9] 赵人达. 大跨度铁路桥梁. 高宗余，主审. 北京：中国铁道出版社，2012.

Chapter 8 *Construction of Concrete Girder Bridges*

8.1 Introduction

There are many methods available for construction of concrete bridges. These construction methods can be classified from different perspectives. Based on if the concrete is cast at the site in the formwork or not, the construction methods can be classified into cast-in-place method and precast method. On the other hand, in terms of the erection technique of the bridge superstructure, the construction methods can be classified into the full-span cast-in-place, the span-by-span, the balanced cantilever, the incremental launching, and the full-span erection. Since each of these erection techniques can involve cast-in-place or precast concrete elements, the above classifications are overlapped.

8.2 Construction of concrete elements

8.2.1 Cast-in-place method

Cast-in-place method is a method of constructing concrete elements in which concrete is cast and cured in the formwork at the concrete component's finished position (Figure 8.1). The advantage of this method is in its ability to produce large-scale structures cast as a single unit without any connecting elements and to produce complex and unusual geometrical shapes. Thus, the cast-in-place method allow for greater flexibility and adaptability than precast method.

The major disadvantages of this method are these: (i) the form work required for on-site concrete pouring is both time and space intensive; (ii) on-site curing requires leaving forms in place for extended periods of time; (iii) quality control is difficult, particularly if weather conditions are not favorable; (iv) the construction process is labor intensive, resulting in much more labor costs.

Figure 8.1 A concrete bridge constructed by the cast-in-place method.

8.2.2 Precast method

The precast method is a method of construction by which concrete elements are cast and cured in a controlled factory environment, transported to the construction site, and lifted into place and fabricated at the components' design positions (Figure 8.2). There are many advantages to the precast method: first, the element's shape, geometry, dimensions, position and location of the reinforcement, as well as the processes related to concrete placement, compaction and curing, are preformed under precise quality control; second, the precast concrete casting can be carried on simultaneously with other works on site such as earthwork, construction of the foundations, and construction of other parts of the structure; third, the forms used in a precast plant can be reused hundreds to thousands of times before they have to be replaced, thus making construction cost effective.

(a)

(b)

(c)

Figure 8.2 The precast method: (a) precast girders; (b) transportation; (c) erection of the precast girders.

However, there are some disadvantages to this method: (i) a high initial investment in heavy equipment, such as cranes or gantries, for lifting and moving precast units, is required; (ii) transportation of heavy precast members from the precast concrete plant to the construction site requires special and heavy-duty transporter, which incurs high expenses; (iii) it becomes difficult to produce satisfactory connections between the precast members; (iv) if not properly handled, the heavy and large precast units may be damaged during transport. In many cases, the economy achieved in precast construction is partially balanced by the amount spent in transport and handling of precast members.

8.3 Temporary works

Construction of concrete bridges by cast-in-place method involves two types of temporary works: falsework and formwork. Falsework is considered to be any temporary structure which supports structural elements of concrete, steel, masonry, or other materials during their construction or erection. Formwork is the total system of the temporary molds which retain the plastic or fluid concrete and withstand the forces due to its placement and consolidation. Formwork may in turn be supported on falsework.

8.3.1 Falsework

It is essential that falsework be strong enough to support the weight of three things: the forms, the fresh concrete, construction equipment and tools, and workers. Thus, falsework usually include steel or timber beams, girders, bracing, columns, piles and foundations, and any proprietary equipment including modular shoring frames, post shores, and horizontal shoring. Most stationary falsework today consists of standardized or proprietary steel components used in supporting columns, frames and girders. The size and configuration of these standardized components are readily available in construction manuals.

Falsework shall be founded on a solid footing, safe against undermining, protected from softening, and capable of supporting the loads imposed on it. The bracing components must have sufficient strength and stiffness to resist lateral loads and buckling. Falsework also must be capable of maintaining the correct elevations. To do this, jacks, wedges or other approved devices must be used as part of the falsework. These devices also will permit the falsework to be lowered gradually. The probable settlement of falsework during the placement of concrete should be compensated by the built-in precamber. To avoid cracking of the semi-hardened during adjustment of elevation, mechanical jacks such as screw jacks, wedge-type jacks or sandpots are suitable. Simple hydraulic jacks that cannot be locked are generally not suitable for supporting long-term loading, because of possible leakage. Figure 8.3 shows typical falsework for a concrete bridge.

Figure 8.3 False work for a concrete bridge.

8.3.2 Formwork

The formwork must be strong enough to resist the fluid pressure and the weight of the fresh concrete and any construction loads such as finishing equipment and workers. In addition, the forms shall be capable of withstanding the dynamic loads caused by vibrators that are used for consolidation.

Traditional timber formwork is built out of timber and plywood or moisture-resistant particleboard, but modern formwork for concrete bridge is mostly made from steel. Aluminum, glass-fibre reinforced plastics (GRP) and other materials are also used in formwork. The modern engineered formwork is built out of prefabricated modules with a metal frame and covered on the inside with material having the wanted surface structure, such as steel, aluminum, or timber. Compared to traditional timber formwork, the modern formwork system has advantages of easy and quick construction and lower life-cycle costs. Also, metal formwork is better protected against rot and fire than traditional timber formwork.

There are two types of formwork: vertical forms and horizontal forms. The vertical forms are used to form vertical concrete surfaces, such as the vertical faces of girder and deck slab, while the horizontal forms are used to form bottom surface of the concrete elements, such as the bottom faces of deck slab and the overhang of the girder flange. Obviously, vertical forms are used to hold pressure while horizontal forms hold weight.

Typical vertical forms consist of the following components (Figure 8.4):

(i) sheathing to provide the concrete finish, (ii) studs to support the sheathing, (iii) wales to support the studs and align the forms, (iv) bracing to prevent shifting of the forms during construction and wind loading; (v) form ties and spreaders to hold forms under pressure of fluid concrete. Figure 6.49 shows typical vertical formwork.

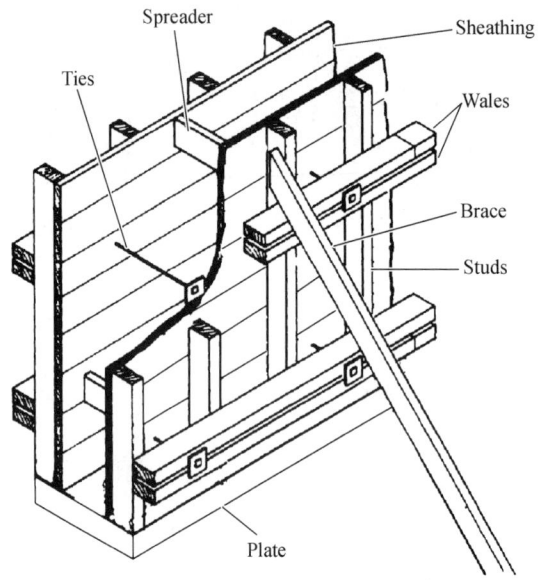

Figure 8.4 Vertical formwork.

Typical horizontal forms include sheathing, joists, stringers, shores, and diagonal bracings for improved stability (Figure 8.5). The joists and stringers are used to support the weight of fresh concrete, and transfer the weight to the ground. Figure 8.5 shows typical horizontal formwork.

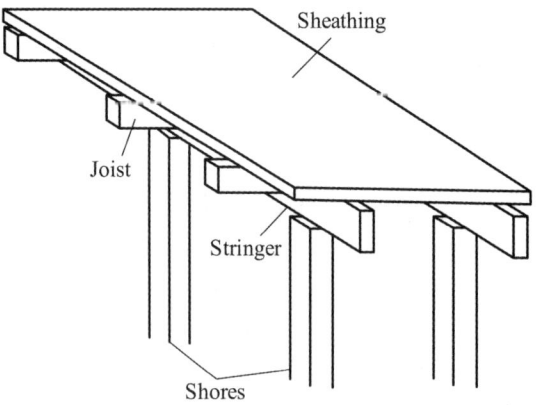

Figure 8.5 Horizontal formwork.

In construction of modern concrete bridges, modularized forms are widely used in the formwork. The modular formwork consists of metal modular panels to form the square or rectangular sides of bridge components, and standardized shores and braces to support pressure and weight of the fresh concrete. The advantages of the modular formwork are that it has well- designed stiffness and strength and is easy to install and uninstall. Figures 8.6 and Figure 8.7 show the modern formwork for concrete T-shaped girders and box girders, respectively.

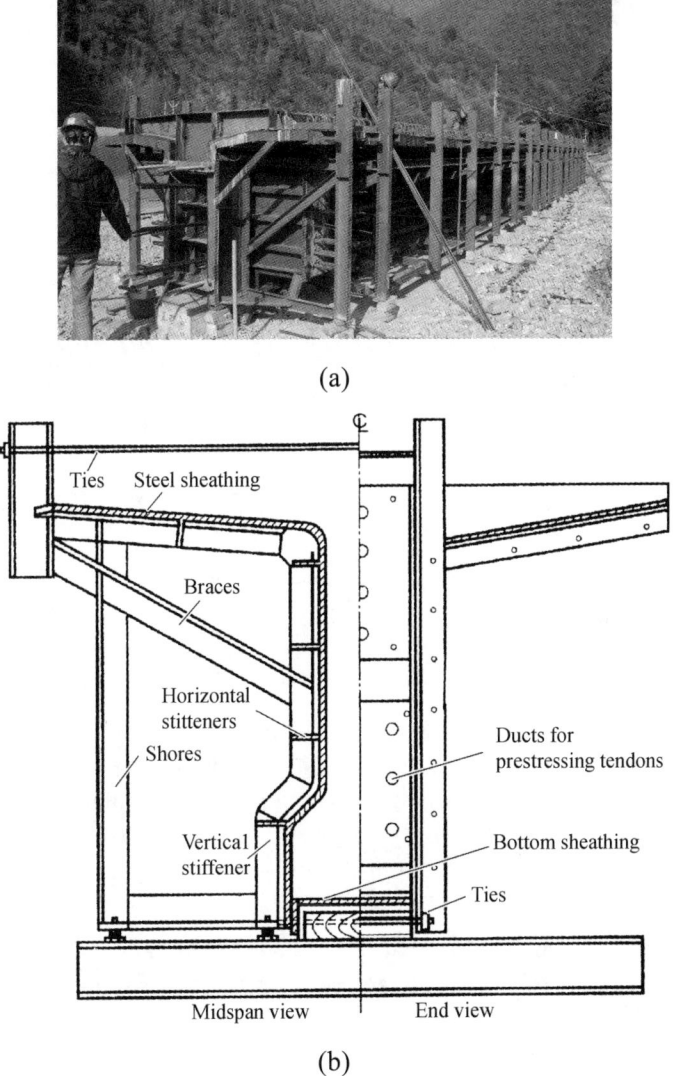

Figure 8.6 Formwork for concrete T-shaped girders: (a) finished formwork; (b) cross-sectional view of the formwork.

(a)

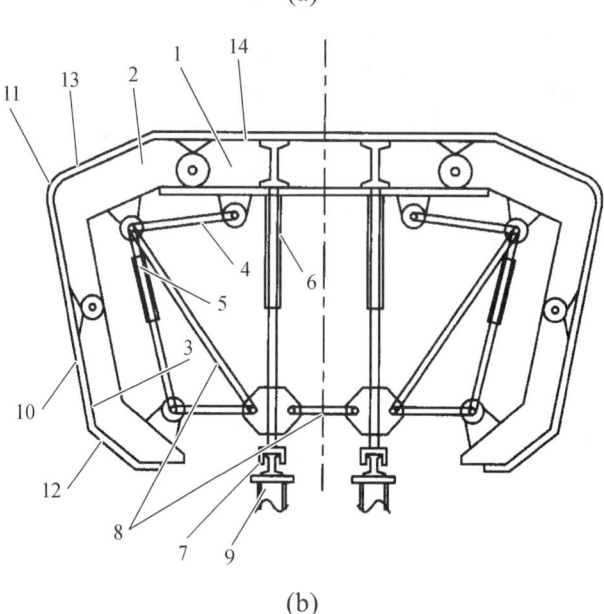

(b)

1—fixed frame; 2—the 2nd rotational lever; 3—the 1st rotational lever; 4—the 2nd hydraulic jack; 5—the 1st hydraulic jack; 6—the hydraulic jack for lifting and lowering; 7—wheels; 8—struts; 9—shores; 10—sheathing for inside wall; 11—curved sheathing; 12—sheathing for upper chamfer; 13—sheathing for lower chamfer; 14—sheathing for slab.

Figure 8.7 Formwork for segmental concrete box girders: (a) finished formwork; (b) structure of the inner forms for retracting from the cast segment.

8.4 Erection methods

There are many erection methods available for construction of concrete bridges. However, it is difficult to classify these erection methods in a clear way. Roughly speaking, these methods fall into five categories: the full-span cast-in-place method, the span-by-span method, the balanced cantilever method, the incremental launching method, and the full-span erection method. Each of these methods may involve cast-in-place or precast methods in manufacturing concrete components.

Selection of a construction method depends on many factors, including engineering constraints, costs, and environmental impacts. The same bridge may require completely different construction methods simply due to site restrictions and accessibility. For example, one site may have unrestricted areas for stockpiling of materials, equipment staging, and traffic control while another site may have limited access and require unrestricted traffic flow during construction. The former may be suitable for cast-in-place method while the latter would probably require precast method.

Although there are many variations of these methods currently in use, only the five erection methods are introduced here briefly.

8.4.1 Full-span cast-in-place method

This method is the traditional method for construction of concrete bridges. In this method, stationary falsework is supported directly on ground and the entire span is constructed at one time. This method is most frequently used in construction of single-span concrete bridges (Figure 8.8). Some multi-span bridges of short span-lengths are also constructed by this method.

Figure 8.8 The full-span cast-in-place method.

This construction method can be used for concrete continuous bridges. In this method, concrete is cast in situ in the formwork that is in turn supported on the temporary stationary falsework. When the concrete has attained 70% of the design strength, the prestress tendons are installed and stressed. Then the falsework can be unloaded and removed.

Because of the possible settlement of formwork and falsework during placement of concrete, the entire girder cannot be cast at a time, instead it generally cast cast in segments, from the midspan or the side span towards the pier supports. The joint sections between segments are cast last and only after settlement of the falsework is finished (Figure 8.9).

The benefit of the full-span cast-in-place method for continuous bridges is that no transformation of the structural systems happens during construction, and the prestress can be arranged in an efficient manner. The disadvantages are that it requires a lot of falsework, formwork and labour resources to achieve a good construction rate.

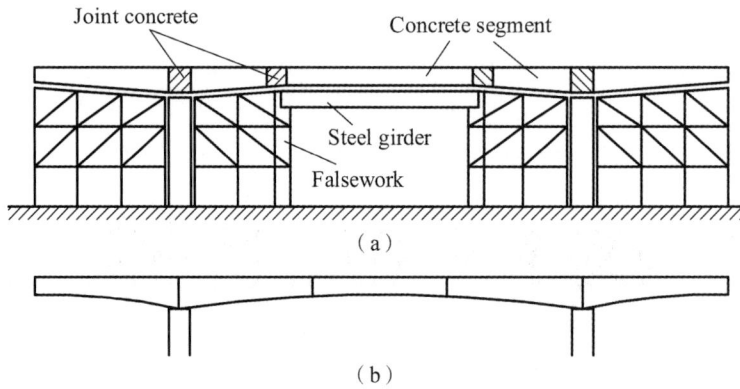

Figure 8.9 The full-span cast-in-place method for continuous concrete bridges: (a) girder under construction; (b) completed girder.

8.4.2 The span-by-span method

The span-by-span method for concrete bridges, by definition, refers to the construction process in which concrete girders are erected or cast at site between piers or between a pier and an abutment to create each span in a sequential way. The span-by-span method may use the precast method or cast-in-place method to manufacture concrete segments as units of erection. If the concrete segments are cast at site on scaffolding, transferring falsework is used. Thus, this method belongs to the segmental construction method.

The precast span-by-span construction method offers a very high speed of construction. It is used in conjunction with an erection truss under the bridge segments or an overhead erection gantry to guide the precast elements into position (Figure 8.10). The method consists of the following primary steps:

(1) Erecting the precast bridge segments onto a temporary erection girder spanning between a pair of adjacent supports;

(2) Installing and stressing longitudinal prestressing tendons enabling the segments to span on their own;

(3) Advancing the erection girder into place to erect the adjacent span.

The span-by-span casting is a popular alternative to precast span-by-span construction. In this method, the bridge segments are cast in situ in the movable scaffolding system which can be seen as a system of moving formwork supported by the previously finished bridge span and the next pier (Figure 8.11). One of the advantages of the span-by-span casting is that the resulting superstructure is a joint-less monolithic structure. The span-by-span casting is compatible with simply-supported and continuous spans, and with different types of cross-section. It offers a similar productivity to that of the incremental launching, assures more flexibility in the geometric design of the bridge, and is much faster than balanced cantilever construction.

Figure 8.10 The precast span-by-span construction method.

Figure 8.11 The span-by-span casting method.

8.4.3 Balanced cantilever method

The balanced cantilever method is a segmental construction method in which the superstructure is erected segmentally by cantilevering out from opposite sides of the pier. In this method, the deck section directly above the pier is first constructed, which is usually termed the #0 block, then, other sections, either precast, or cast-in-place in the traveling formwork, are symmetrically added to the opposite ends of the cantilevers to maintain a balanced system.

The balanced cantilever method is suitable for long-span bridges and where access beneath the deck is difficult. There exist two types of cantilever construction method: the balanced cantilever in situ casting and the precast segmental balanced cantilever erection.

1. The balanced cantilever in situ casting

With this technique the girder is cast in short lengths within a pair of form travelers attached to the ends of completed girders which connected to rigidly a pier rigidly to form two cantilevers (Figure 8.12). The girder section over the pier is cast first and fixed with the pier rigidly, then cantilevering sections are cast progressively in segments, usually symmetrically about the pier to minimize the out-of-balance moment on the pier. When the cantilevers from adjacent piers have been completed and face each other at the midspan, the closure stitch is concreted and the prestressing tendons installed to make the girder continuous. The end section of the side span is usually cast on falsework in front of the abutment and stitched with the completed section with prestressing tendons. Figure 8.12 briefly illustrates the construction process of the balanced cantilever method, and Figure 8.13 shows the configuration of a form traveler.

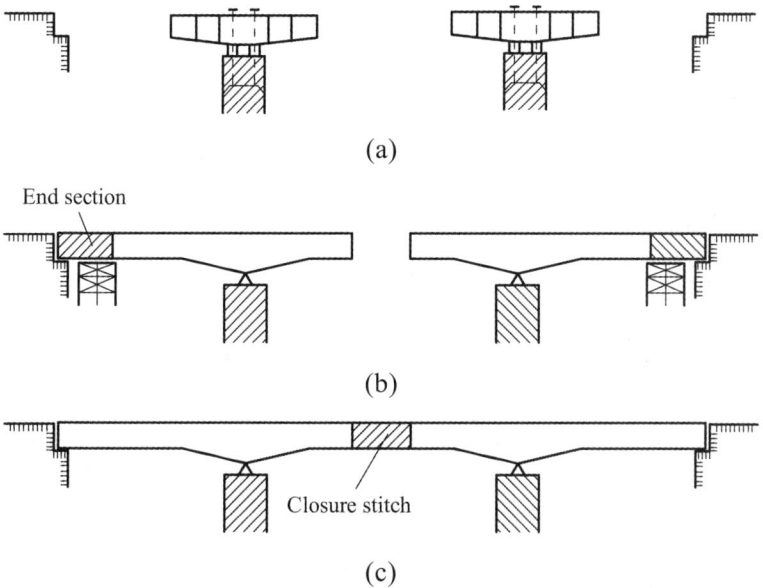

Figure 8.12 Construction process of the balanced cantilever method: (a) Casting cantilevered sections; (b) Casting end sections; (c) Casting closure stitch.

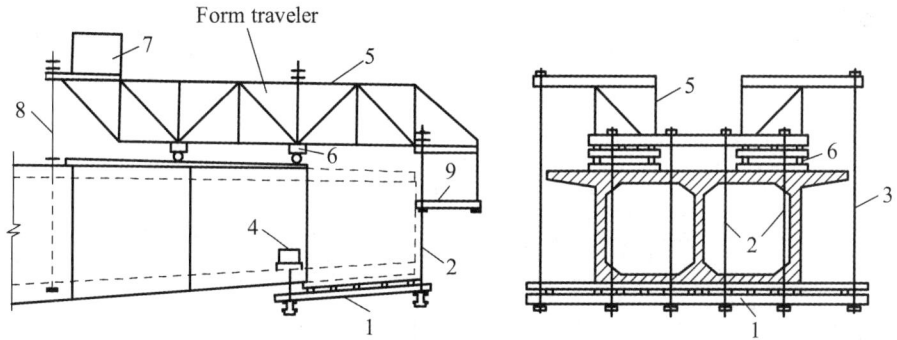

1—Bottom formwork; 2, 3, 4—Hanging structures; 5—Support frame; 6—Wheels;
7—Counterweight; 8—Anchoring system; 9—Work platform.

Figure 8.13 Configuration of a form travelers.

2. The precast segmental balanced cantilever erection

With this method, the girder segments are cast and fabricated in a casting yard and then are transported to the construction site. These segments are erected in the site, commencing with the section over the pier and proceeding by cantilever method from both sides of the piers symmetrically (Figure 8.14).

Concrete segments are cast in specially designed formwork, employing either the short-line or the long-line methods. In the short-line match-casting method, each segment is cast next to the previously cast segment in an adjustable casting machine [Figure 8.15(a)]. This ensures that the interface between the two segments matches exactly when erected. In the long-line method, formwork matching the shape of the soffit of a complete cantilever or the span between field closures is erected on the ground [Figure 8.15(b)]. The segments are cast one at a time in the long formwork until all the segments in the span section are finished.

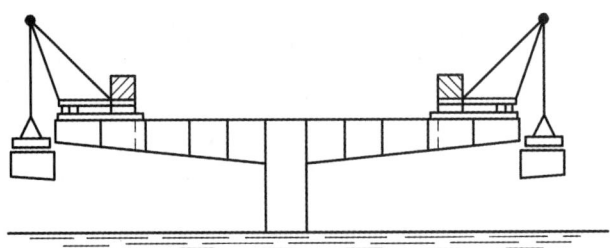

Figure 8.14 The precast segmental balanced cantilever erection using a rail car mounted derrick crane.

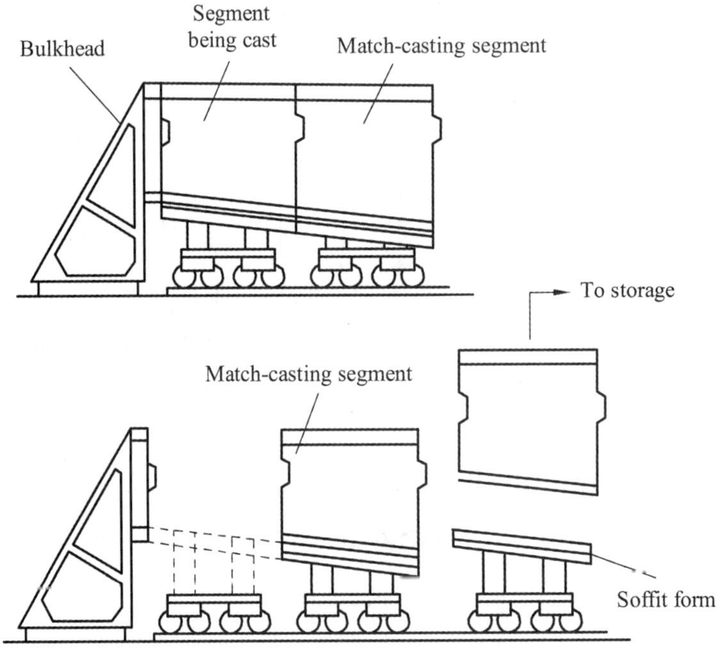

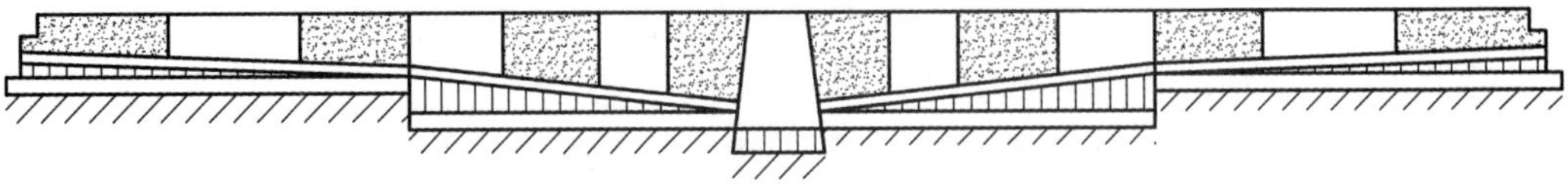

Figure 8.15 Precasting of segments: (a) the short-line method; (b) the long-line method.

3. The types of segment joints

In general, there are three types of joints between segments of the concrete girder: the cast-in-place joints, dry joints, and epoxy joints. The cast-in-place joints belong to the wide joints, and are formed by casting in situ concrete in a narrow section of 100 to 200 wide between the segments to be connected. Before casting of concrete, the adjacent concrete surfaces should be roughened and kept thoroughly wet, and the reinforcement steel can be spliced [Figure 8.16(a)]. This type of joints is usually used in the connection of the segments over piers. The dry joint is a match-cast joint. With a dry joint, the adjacent segments are joined by prestressing force without any bonding agents applied to the connecting surfaces. For the dry joints, shear keys are formed on the concrete faces of the segment joints to assist in lining up adjacent segments and to transfer the shear across the joint [Figure 8.16 (b)]. However, dry joints are not watertight, and thus water leakage from the deck can happen, which makes the grouting and protection of internal tendons difficult. For this reason, the dry joints have no longer been used. The epoxy joints are similar to the dry joints except that epoxy is applied in the segment faces being connected [Figure 8.16 (c)]. The epoxy in the joint creates a strong bond between the segments. The epoxy joint is watertight and has greater strength than the concrete on either sides, and therefore are most widely used joints in segmental construction.

The balanced cantilever method is the most economical for span lengths greater than about 50 m. It is the often appropriate and cost-effective for the construction of long span concrete bridges, especially for the bridges where height, topography or geotechnical conditions render the use of conventional formwork and other construction methods uneconomical.

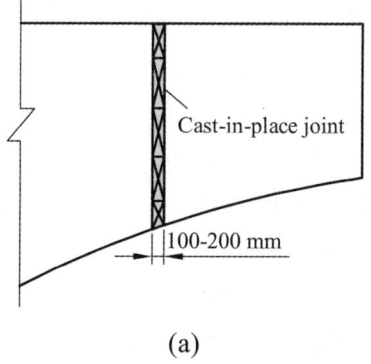

(a)

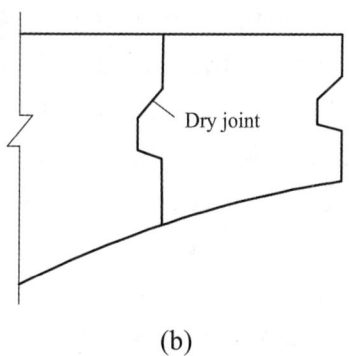

(b)

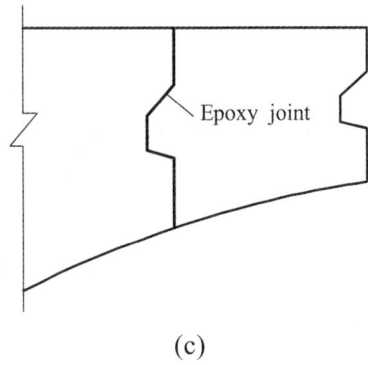

(c)

Figure 8.16 The segment joints: (a) the cast-in-place joint; (b) the dry joint; (c) the epoxy joint.

8.4.4 The incremental launching method

The incremental launching method involves casting sections of the bridge superstructure, which are usually 15 ~ 30 m long, in a stationary formwork behind an abutment, and pushing the completed sections forward in succession with jacks or friction launching system along the bridge axis. After the segment has been cast and cured to sufficient strength at the casting site, it is prestressed for the launching stage and the completed sections of the bridge launched over temporary sliding bearings on the piers. During launching, the section undergoes complete stress reversals as it travels from the first support to its final position. To keep the bending moment in the superstructure low during launchong, a launching nose is attached to the front of the bridge deck (Figure 8.17). To use this method, the concrete bridge profile should be constant, preferably straight, but horizontal and vertical curvature of constant radius can be accommodated within limits. The deck slab should have a constant superelevation.

The main advantages of the incremental launching method, compared with other traditional construction methods, are these: (i) minimal disturbance to environmentally sensitive areas; (ii) smaller assembly zone required; (iii) economy of transportation and reduction in construction elements; (iv) ease of access to restricted or limited sites – such as rivers, deep valleys, or environmentally protected areas.

One disadvantage is that this method is only suitable for erection of straight continuous girder with the constant depth. Another disadvantage is that during launching, the girder section undergoes complete stress reversals as it progresses from a cantilever to a continuous beam, and the girder designed for this erection sequence requires much longitudinal prestressing and non-prestressing steel reinforcement at both top and bottom of the cross-section. The box cross-section should has large wall thicknesses.

1—Casting yard; 2—Girder segment; 3—Launching nose; 4—Hydraulic jack;
5—Sliding bearings; 6—Temporary pier.

Figure 8.17　The incremental launching method.

8.4.5　The full-span erection method

The full-span erection method is a modern construction method for concrete bridges. With this method, entire bridge spans are produced in a casting yard, then transported, and lifted to their final positions using a heaving lifting machine. This method has seen a great rise in popularity over the past two decade for the construction of high-speed railway bridges in many countries. In China, most of the railway concrete bridges which have the standard span lengths of 24 m and 32 m are erected using the full-span erection method. This method not only shortens the construction time, but also allows the concrete girders to be built with much less disruption to the public than would have been possible with other construction methods. For traditional erection methods, cycle times vary from a minimum of two days, such as that with the span-by-span segmental erection method, up to 14 days, such as that with the cast-in-place method with a movable scaffolding system, With the full-span erection method, erection cycle time of less than one day per span is common.

Different types of erection equipment for the full-span erection method have been developed. Basically, if the precast full-span girder is to be delivered over the finished spans, the erection equipment can be classified into three major types:

Type 1: Launching gantry with self-propelled transporter. The launching gantry is capable of unloading the precast girder from the self-propelled transporter and place it at its final position (Figure 8.18). This type is designed to work on the single-deck bridge only.

Type 2: Launching gantry with dual self-propelled transporter. The launching gantry is capable of unloading the precast girder from the transporter and place it at its final position (Figure 8.19). Unlike the type 1, the type 2 is configured to work across twin-deck bridges.

Type 3: Straddle launching carrier with self-launching support beam. The straddle launching carrier picks up the precast girder directly at the precast yard, transports it to the erection front over the erected deck, and places it at its final position by moving over the self-launching support beam (Figure 8.20).

Figure 8.18 The Type-1 bridge erection equipment.

Figure 8.19 The Type-2 bridge erection equipment.

Figure 8.20 The Type-3 bridge erection equipment.

References

[8.1] ICE, Bridge Deck Erection Equipment–A Best Practice Guide, ICE Publishing, London, 2018.

[8.2] Barker J. M., "Construction Techniques for Segmental Concrete Bridges," *PCI Journal*, July-August, 1980, pp. 66-86.

[8.3] Matt P., Status of Segmental Bridge Construction in Europe," *PCI Journal*, May-June, 1983, pp. 104–125.

[8.4] Rostam S., Design and Construction of Segmental Concrete Bridges for Service Life of 100 to 150 years, American Segmental Bridge Institute, ASBI 2005 Convention, Washington, DC.

[8.5] Liebenberg A. C., Concrete Bridges: Design and Construction, Longman Scientific & Technical, Essex, England, 1992

[8.6] Khan M. A., *Accelerated Bridge Construction–Best Practices and Techniques*, Butterworth-Heinemann, Waltham, MA, 2015.

[8.7] Benaim R., *The Design of Prestressed Concrete Bridges–Concepts and Principles*, Taylor & Francis, New York, 2018.

[8.8] Hewson N., *Prestressed Concrete Bridges– Design and Construction*, 2nd ed., ICE Publishing, London, 2012.

[8.9] Yao L.-S, ed., (Xiang, H.-F., Gu, A.-B., reviewers), Bridge Engineering, 2nd ed., China Communications Press, Beijing, China, 2008.

姚玲森. 桥梁工程. 2 版. 项海帆，顾安邦，主审. 北京：人民交通出版社，2008.

[8.10] Fan L.-C., ed., Prestressed Concrete Continuous Bridges, China Transportation Press, Beijing, 1988.

范立础. 预应力混凝土连续梁桥. 北京，1988.

[8.11] Li Y.-D., ed., *Introduction to Bridge Engineering* (in Chinese), 3rd ed., Southwest Jiaotong University Press, Chengdu, China, 2005.

李亚东. 桥梁工程概论. 3 版. 成都：西南交通大学出版社，2014.

Chapter 9 *Steel bridges*

9.1 Introduction

Steel is a material with high strength in tension, compression, and shearing. Due to its high strength-to-weight ratio and good workability, steel can be used to construct almost all forms of bridges. Many famous and historic bridges have been built with steel, such as the Brooklyn Bridge (a suspension bridge) in the United States, Forth Railway Bridge (a cantilever truss bridge) in Scotland, and the St. Lawrence Bridge (a continuous truss bridge) in Canada, to name a few. In China, one of historic bridges, the Luding Suspension Bridge, is made of wrought iron (Figure 9.1). The first modern steel bridge in China is the Qiantang River Bridge, which is a 16-span railway-highway bi-purpose steel truss bridge built in 1937 (Figure 1.33). In 1976, an inclined-leg rigid frame box girder steel railway bridge, Ankang Han River Railway Bridge, was built to cross the Han river (Figure 9.2). The span length of this bridge, which is 176 m, ranks the first among the bridges of the same type in the world. The Chaotianmen Yangtze River Bridge, located in city of Chongqing, China, is a continuous through-type steel trussed arch bridge (Figure 9.3). Its 1 741 m total length makes it world's longest through-type steel arch bridge up to 2018.

Figure 9.1 The Luding Suspension Bridge built in 1706, in Sichuan Province, China.

Figure 9.2 The Ankang Han River Railway Bridge built in 1982, in Shaanxi Province, China.

Figure 9.3 The Chaotianmen Yangtze River Bridge built in 2008, in city of Chongqing, China.

Main advantages of steel bridges can be summarized as follows:

(1) Because of the high strength-to-weight ratio of the material, steel bridges usually have lighter superstructures than comparable concrete bridges, and in turn result in smaller, economical foundations.

(2) A steel bridge can span a very long distance, supporting the imposed traffic loads with the minimum self weight. Steel bridges have the capability of spanning over 1 500 m, in the form of trusses, tied-arches, suspension bridges, and cable-stayed bridges.

(3) Steel bridges can be constructed faster than concrete bridges. Steel components are normally manufactured and prefabricated off-site in a factory environment under strict quality control, shipped to the site, and piece together in situ to form a complete bridge structure. This construction method results in minimal disruption to traffic, reducing on-site labor requirements and overall project costs.

(4) Steel bridges are easy to inspect, repair, and strengthen. Visual inspection can be carried out easily, as all major load-carrying components are accessible by inspectors. Repairs can be made more quickly than in concrete bridges. When necessary, components can be strengthened with additional steel components, or components can be removed and replaced with new ones without removing the bridge permanently from service.

(5) Steel is a material of good ductility. Thus, steel bridges have excellent earthquake resistance.

(6) Steel is the most recycled material. Almost 99 percent of steel from retired or demolished steel bridges can be returned to the steel-making process or reused as is.

However, steel bridges also have disadvantages compared with concrete bridges. These advantages should be taken into full consideration when deciding if steel should be used as a construction material of a bridge. In some situations, these disadvantages can counterbalance the advantages stated above. The major disadvantages of steel bridges include the following:

(1) Steel bridges are susceptible to corrosion, which is one of the major causes of deterioration of steel bridges. Thus, a steel bridge should be painted regularly, resulting in high maintenance cost. Application of weathering and corrosion-resistant steels may eliminate this problem.

(2) Steel bridges have very small resistance against fire in comparison with concrete.

The strength of steel is reduced by 50% when heated at temperatures between 600 °C and 700 °C. Also, steel conducts and transmits heat from a burning portion of the structure quite fast.

(3) Steel bridges are easy to generate noise under moving loads. For composite highway bridges, which are made up from steel girders and concrete deck slabs, the noise can be mitigated by concrete deck. However, steel railway bridges without ballast are sources of annoying railway noise, which is produced by the wheel-rail interactions. In urban areas, measures, such as sound absorber or noise protection walls, have to be taken to mitigate the noise, leading to increased construction cost of a steel bridge.

Evolution of modern steel bridges in China started with the development of modern railway network systems and provoked the development of the structural steel. The first modern grand steel bridge is the Wuhan Yangtze

River Bridge across the the Yangtze River in the city of Wuhan (Figure 1.34). The bridge is a railway–highway bi-purpose continuous steel truss bridge with main span lengths of 128 m. The bridge was built in 1957 and is a milestone in China's bridge history. The steel used in Wuhan Yangtze River Bridge is developed and produced by Chinese steel manufacturers. The steel is designated as Type-A3, which is a low-carbon structural steel with carbon of 0.14% ~ 0.22%. Its yield strength is only $f_y = 240$ MPa, equivalent to that of the current Q235q steel. After 1969, driven by need for building the Nanjing Yangtze River Bridge, Chinese steel manufacturers developed Type-16Mnq manganese steel (Currently Q345q) by adding 1.4% manganese to the low-carbon steel to increase the yield strength to $f_y = 320$ MPa. As a result, the span length of the Nanjing Yangtze River Bridge was increased to 160 m. But the toughness property of the Type-16Mnq steel is not good. To further increase the span length of steel bridges, Type-15MnVNq (currently Q420q) was developed in 1990s and was used in the construction of the Jiujiang Yangtze River Bridge. The Type-15MnVNq is a low-alloy steel containing 1.3% ~ 1.7% Manganese and about 0.08% Vanadium. Its yield strength reaches $f_y = 412$ MPa due to addition of Manganese and Vanadium, but with decreased low temperature toughness and weldability. Thanks to the increased steel strength, the main span length of the Jiujiang Yangtze River Bridge reaches 216 m. To improve the overall properties of the structural steel and to meet the need for building a longer railway-highway bi-purpose steel bridge, the Wuhu Yangtze River Bridge, Type-14MnNbq (currently Q370qE) steel was developed by adding 0.010% ~ 0.035% Niobium to the low-carbon steel in addition to Manganese and Vanadium. The Type-14MnNbq structural steel has excellent low temperature impact toughness and good weldability, and becomes the widely used construction material for steel bridges since completion of the Wuhu Yangtze River Bridge. The above four grand railway–highway bi-purpose steel bridges, the Wuhan Yangtze River Bridge, the Nanjing Yangtze River Bridge (Figure 1.35), the Jiujiang Yangtze River Bridge (Figure 9.4), and the Wuhu Yangtze River Bridge (Figure 1.39) mark the progress of design and construction of steel bridges in China.

Figure 9.4   The Jiujiang Yangtze River Bridge built in 1993, in city of Jiujiang, China.

To meet the need for building long-span high-speed railway bridges in China, a high strength weathering steel, Type-WNQ570 (Q420q) was successfully developed in 2007 to build the Nanjing Dashengguan Yangtze River Bridge, a though-type double truss-arch bridge with maximum span length of 336 m (Figure 9.5). The Nanjing Dashengguan Yangtze River Bridge proved to be another milestone in the Chinese steel bridge history, in that the bridge carries six high-speed railway tracks, has the longest span length among the similar multi-track high-speed railway steel bridges in the world, and carries the heaviest live loads. The high-strength materials, design method, and construction techniques used in this bridge laid solid foundation for building long-span high-speed railway and highway steel bridges in the following decade.

Figure 9.5   The Nanjing Dashengguan Yangtze River Bridge built in 2009, in city of Nanjing, China.

Over the last decade, a great number of long-span steel bridges were built in China, most of which are railway truss bridges, arched truss bridges, or truss-arch bridges. In addition, many long-span cable-stayed bridges and all suspension bridges are steel bridges. In the Hong Kong-Zhuhai-Macau Bridge completed in 2018, which consists of three cable-stayed bridges and two continuous bridges, all main girders crossing wide deep navigable waterways are steel box girders and only one continuous bridge in shallow waterways use steel-concrete composite girders. In July 2020, the Husutong Yangtze River Bridge, a cable-stayed bridge with steel truss girders, was open to traffic (Figure 9.6). The main span length of the bridge, which is 1092 m, ranks the first among the railway-highway bi-purpose cable-stayed bridges in the world at its completion.

Figure 9.6 The Husutong Yangtze River Bridge built in 2020, in the province Jiangsu, China.

The raid development of high-speed railway and highway networks in China need long-span bridges to cross wide waterways, valleys, and gorges. With their many advantages, the steel bridges are the most suitable for long spans. For sea-crossing bridges, steel is almost the unique construction material for the long-span superstructure. Before 1980s, due to limited supply and high price of structural steel in China, steel bridges were mainly built on railway lines; the number of highway steel bridges is very limited. Since 1990s, with rapid growth of steel industry in China, structural steel has been increasingly used to build long-span highway bridges, in particular, the cable-stayed bridges and the suspension bridges. In recent years, structural steel was gradually used to build medium-span highway bridges.

In the following decades, the need for longer and stronger railway and highway bridges will require high-strength and high-performance steel, new structural forms, and advanced construction techniques for steel structures. On high-speed passenger railways, steel bridges need greater transverse, vertical, and torsional stiffness than on the freight railways. Also, high durability is required for steel bridges to keep its required performance and functions during the service life, which is the major challenge faced by bridge engineers for years to come. Without doubt, advances and innovations in construction materials, design theories, and erection techniques will contribute to the development of longer span, more robust steel bridges in the future.

9.2 Types of steel bridges

Steel can be used to build various types of bridge for different span lengths. All types of bridges described in Chapter 1 can be constructed with steel. Typically, there are seven types of steel bridges for current construction in China:

(1) Girder bridges. This type of bridges uses girders as the means of supporting its deck [Figure 9.7(a)]. The two most common types of steel girders are the plate and box girders, which have I-shaped and box-shaped cross-sections, respectively. Each girder is fabricated by welding steel plate together. Usually, steel girders are used in simply supported railway bridges as load carrying members: the plate girders are used for the span length less than 40 m; when the span length is greater than 40 m, box girders or truss bridges are in order.

(2) Rigid frame bridges. This type of bridge consists of a longitudinal steel girder and two vertical or inclined supporting members that are rigidly connected at the joints to transfer bending moments, shear forces, and axial forces [Figure 9.7(b)]. This type of bridges is suitable for the span lengths between 25 m and 200 m.

(3) Truss bridges. A truss bridge comprises discrete members that are subjected primarily to axial loads [Figure 9.7(c)]. The members are generally arranged to form a series of triangles that act together to form the structural system. A truss behaves as a large beam to carry vertical loads: the upper and

lower chords behave as the flanges of a girder; diagonal and vertical members function in a manner similar to the web in a plate girder. Diagonal members generally provide the necessary shear capacity.

(4) Arch bridges. This type of bridges refers to the arch bridges whose ribs are made of steel [Figure 9.7(d)]. There are usually two types of arch rib: solid rib and trussed rib. The solid arch rib has I-shape or box-shape cross-section, while the trussed rib consists of axially loaded members like those in a truss bridge. Arches are classified into deck arches and through arches which refer to the arches located below and above the deck, respectively. Tied arches are normally constructed as through arches with the tie member at the deck level.

(a)

(b)

(c)

(d)

Figure 9.7 Structural form of steel bridges: (a) girder bridge; (b) rigid frame bridge; (c) truss bridge; (d) arch bridge.

(5) Combined truss-arch bridges (Figure 9.3). This type of bridges refers to the bridges with combined trusses and arches structures to carry loads, such as the structures used in the Jiujiang Yangtze River Bridge and the Chaotianmen Yangtze River Bridge.

(6) Cable-stayed bridges. This type of bridges refers to the cable-stayed bridge with main girders made of steel. The stay cables, of course, are made of high-strength steel, but the towers are not necessarily made of steel. There are three types of main girders: plate girders, box girders, and truss girders.

(7) Suspension bridges. Suspension bridges are classified as steel bridges, in that the main cables, hangers, and stiffening girders of a suspension bridge are made of steel, but the towers could be built with steel or concrete. Anchorages and foundations are built with concrete, reinforced or prestressed concrete.

Historically, there are only two types of steel bridges used to carry railway traffic in China: girder bridges and truss bridges. Only after 1993, following the completion of Jiujiang Yangtze River Bridge, the steel arch bridges and truss-arch bridges started going up in China's to meet the need for long-span bridges to carry railway traffic crossing wide waterways. Most of steel cable-stayed bridges and almost all suspension bridges are built to carry highway traffic. The design of steel arch bridges is similar to the design of concrete arch bridges, which is addressed in Chapter 10. Since the design of combined truss-arch bridges, cable-stayed bridges, and suspension bridges need advanced knowledge of engineering mechanics and involves complex calculations, they will not be addressed in this introductory textbook. Instead only the steel girder bridges and truss bridges are treated in this chapter.

9.3 Plate girder bridges

9.3.1 Configurations of bridge deck

1. Railway bridges

Generally, there are two types of deck for steel railway bridges: the open deck and the closed or ballasted deck. The open deck bridge is also divided into the deck girder bridge and the through girder bridge, depending on the position of the bridge deck.

The open deck plate girder railway bridge consists of two I-shape girders and transverse bracing frames [Figure 9.8(a)]. The sleepers are directly supported on the steel plate girders [Figure 9.8(b)] and rails are fastened to the sleepers by elastic fasteners. Traditionally, wooden sleepers are used in the open deck steel bridges, but recently, sleepers made of other materials have been used. The I-shape girder is fabricated by welding three steel plates together to form the top flange, the bottom flange, and the web [Figure 9.8(c)]. To prevent the web plate from buckling, longitudinal and transverse stiffeners are also welded to the web plate. In addition to the transverse bracing frames, there are also two lateral bracing frames, on the upper and lower parts of the girders, respectively, to resist the transverse forces (wind force, nosing and centrifugal forces) and to maintain the transverse stability of the girders. The two bracing systems, the transverse and the lateral, act together to resist torsional deformation of the bridge.

The open through plate girder bridge has two I-shape girders supporting the deck at the location near the bottom flanges of the girders through shallow floor-beams connecting the girders by means of knee braces [Figure 9.9(a)]. There are longitudinal stringers framed into the floor-beams to support the railway sleepers [Figure 9.9(b)]. Since railway trucks travel between the two girders, lateral bracings could not be set on the top of the girders. The through girder bridge is generally used in the sites where that superstructure depth is severely restricted. For a through plate girder bridge carrying a standard single railway track, the center-to-center spacing of the girders is normally 5.4 m. The through plate girder bridges are seldom used to for highways, because the highway bridge generally has wider deck than the railway bridge.

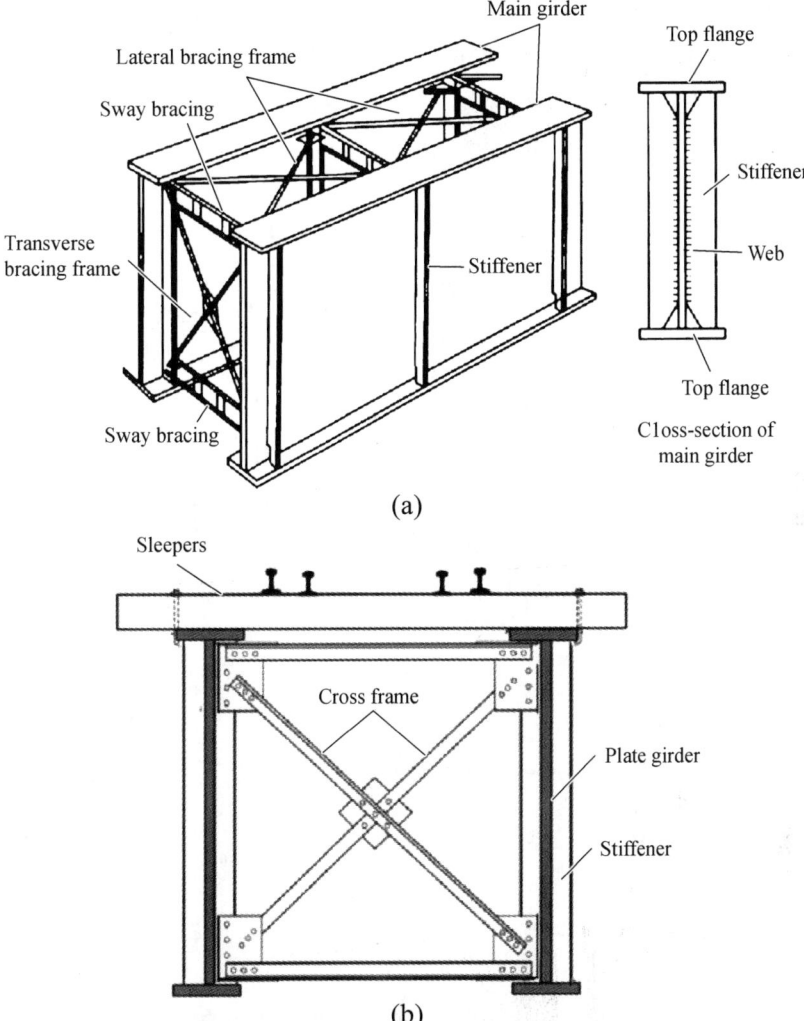

Figure 9.8 The open deck plate girder railway bridge: (a) the configuration of the girder; (b) the cross-section of the girder with sleepers.

The closed or ballasted steel plate or box girder bridge generally has a concrete deck slab placed on the top flanges of the girders to support the stone ballast section on which the track sleepers are laid (Figure 9.10). Although the dead load of the bridge is thus increased, dynamic effects of the moving traffic are reduced and train ride quality is improved due to the relatively constant track stiffness across the bridge. Since steel and concrete materials are both used in the ballasted steel bridge, this type of bridge is also termed steel-concrete composite bridge. Important components in this type of bridge are those called the shear connectors or shear keys, which are usually fixed at the top flange of the steel girder and embedded in the concrete slab to transfer horizontal shear force in between. The common issue with the composite bridges is the cracking of concrete around the shear connectors. which should be treated carefully through design.

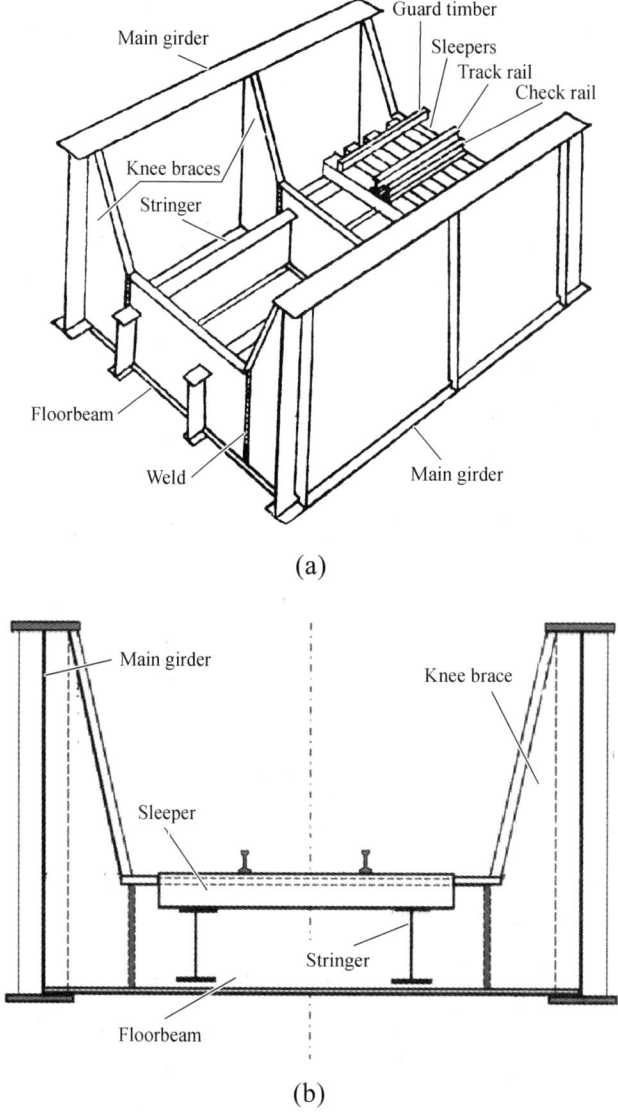

Figure 9.9 The open through deck plate girder railway bridge: (a) the configuration of the girder; (b) the cross-section of the girder with sleepers.

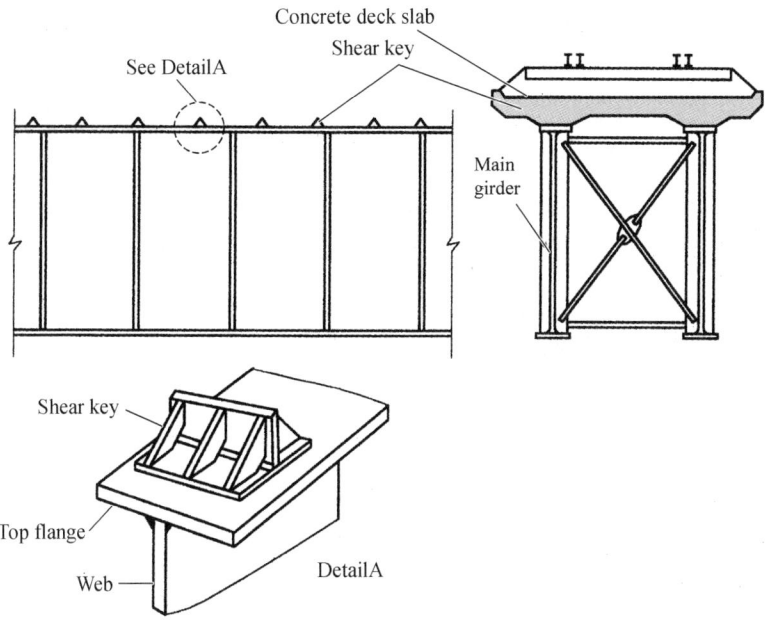

Figure 9.10 The ballasted deck plate girder railway bridge.

Ballasted decks generally require less maintenance and allow for easier track elevation changes on curved track geometry. But drainage must be carefully considered to prevent the steel girders from corrosion.

In 1980s, only a few composite steel-concrete railway bridges were built in China, with maximum span length of 48 m for simply supported girders. After 2003, due to their high stiffness and low noise, steel-concrete composite railway bridges were increasingly built to carry high-speed passenger railway traffic and became a favorite type of railway bridges. In the future, there will be more composite railway bridges to be built on high-speed railway lines (Figure 9.11).

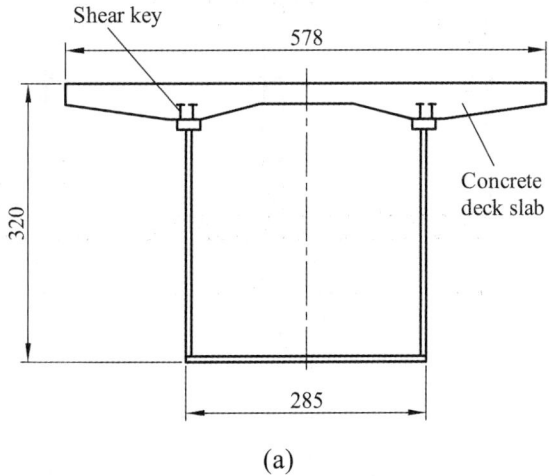

(a)

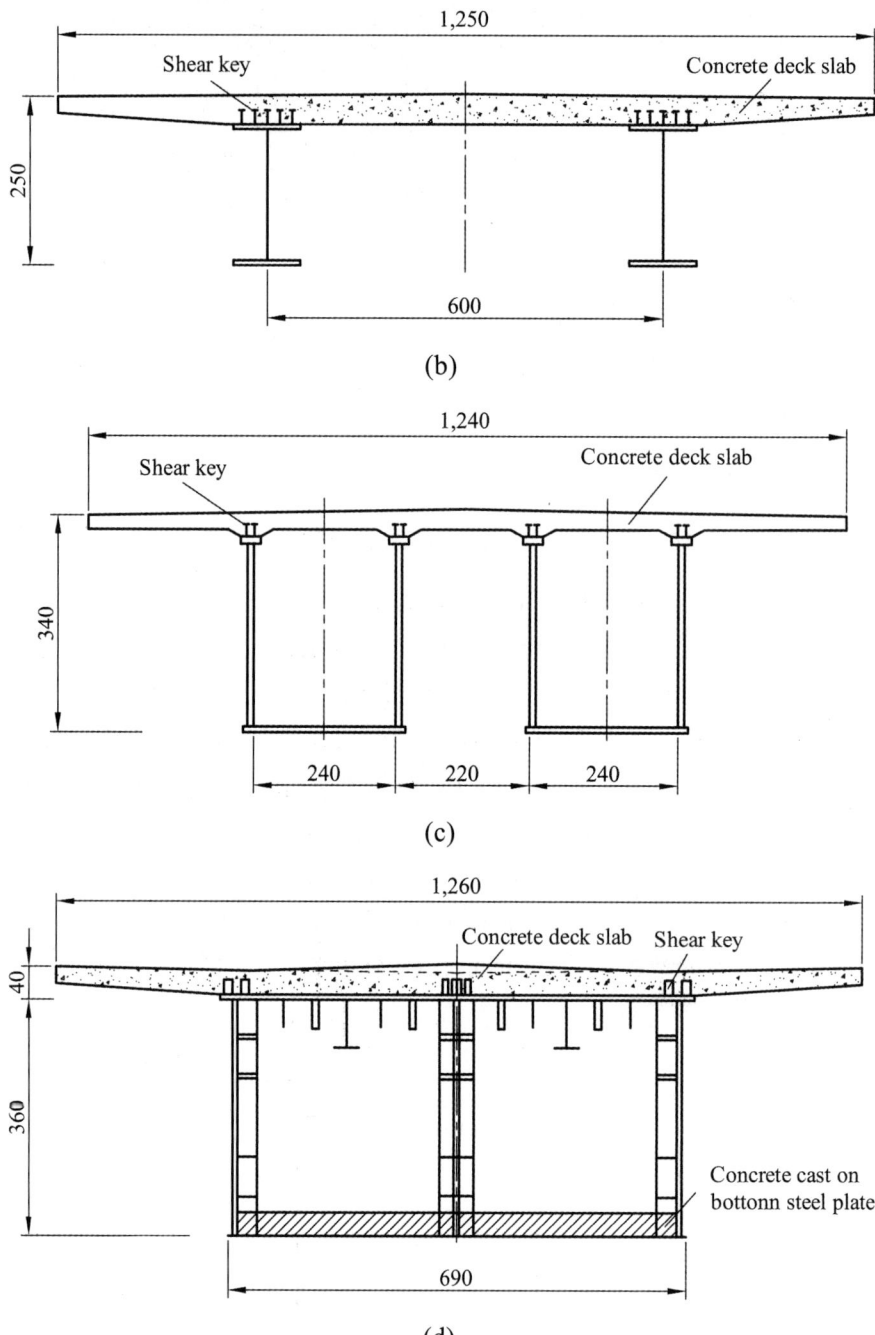

(b)

(c)

(d)

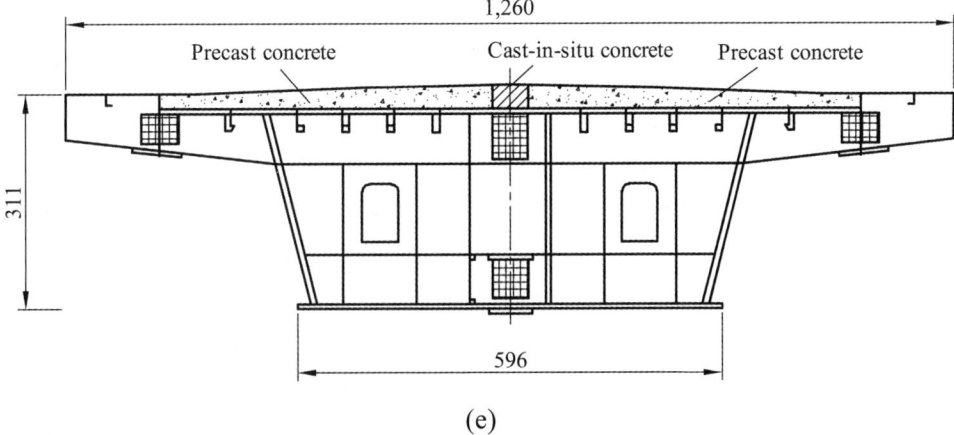

(e)

Figure 9.11 The composite steel-concrete deck girders for high-speed railways for span length of: (a) 45 m simple; (b) 32 m continuous; (d) 50 m continuous; (e) 50 m continuous; (f) 32 m simple (units in cm).

2. Highway bridges

Highway steel bridges have similar girder configurations to those of railway steel bridge but with different deck configurations. Due to wide deck, through girders are seldom used in highway bridges and most of highway girder bridges are built with deck girders. In general, there are two types of deck used in highway steel bridges: concrete deck and steel deck.

Steel highway bridges with concrete deck can be called non-composite or composite bridges, depending on whether the deck and the girders act in unison to resist loads. In a non-composite bridge structure, the steel girders act independently of the deck slab in resisting all loads. In composite construction, however, the self-weight of the steel girder is resisted by the steel girder alone, whereas the superimposed dead loads and the live loads are resisted by the composite action of the slab and the steel girder behaving as a unit. Figure 9.12 shows typical cross-sections of two non-composite steel-concrete highway bridges consisting of I-shape steel girders and concrete deck. Figure 9.13 shows a typical cross-section of a steel-concrete composite I-shape girder bridge with shear studs. Figure 9.14 shows the cross-sections of a two-span continuous steel-concrete composite box-girder highway bridges with shear studs. Some shear connectors often used in steel-concrete composite superstructures are shown in Figure 9.15.

Steel highway bridges with steel deck generally use the orthotropic steel deck consisting of a flat, thin steel plate which is usually 12 ~ 14 mm thick, stiffened in the longitudinal direction by a series of closely spaced and supported in the transverse direction by orthogonal floor-beams (Figure 9.16). The orthotropic steel deck has considerably different stiffnesses in the longitudinal and transverse directions. The main advantage of the orthotropic steel deck is that it is integral with the supporting superstructure framing as a top flange common to both the transverse floor-beams and longitudinal girders, which results in increased rigidity of the deck and savings of the construction material. The common types of the ribs for stiffening the deck plate are the U-type ribs and bulb ribs, as shown in Figure 9.16. Typical cross-sections of two steel highway bridges with orthotropic steel deck are shown Figure 9.17.

In the past decade, steel-concrete composite bridges found rapid applications in the construction of high-speed highway and railway-highway bi-purpose bridges. Usually, the highway composite bridges are built for the span length over 30 m.

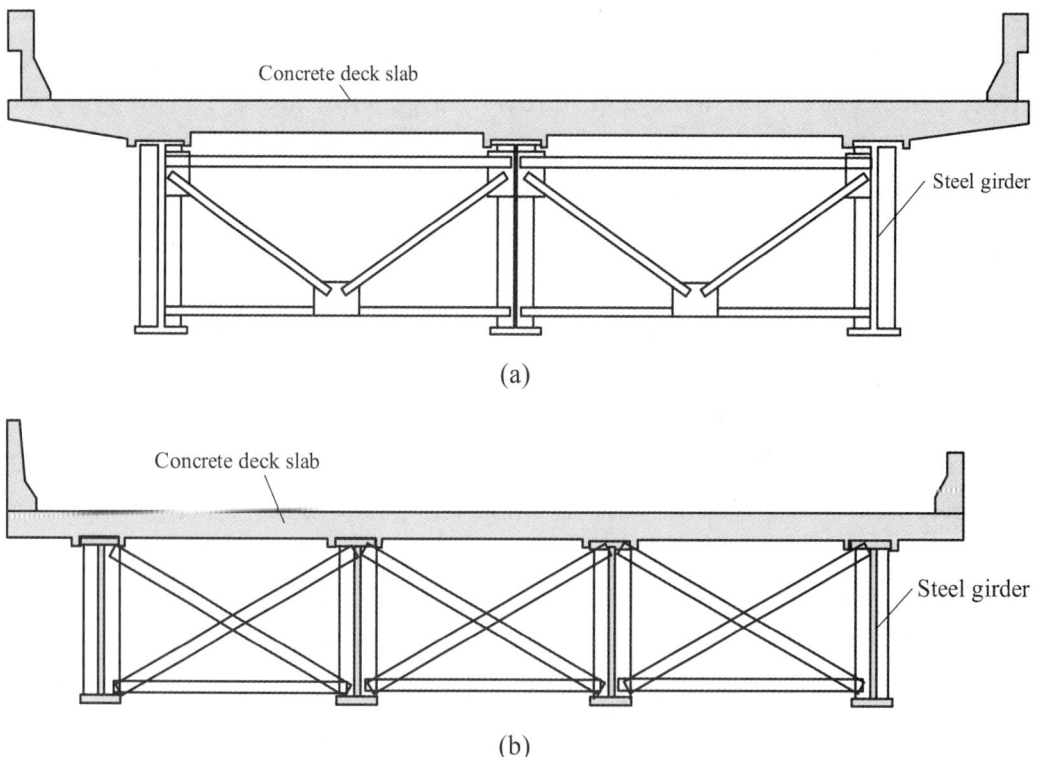

Figure 9.12　The non-composite steel-concrete highway bridges.

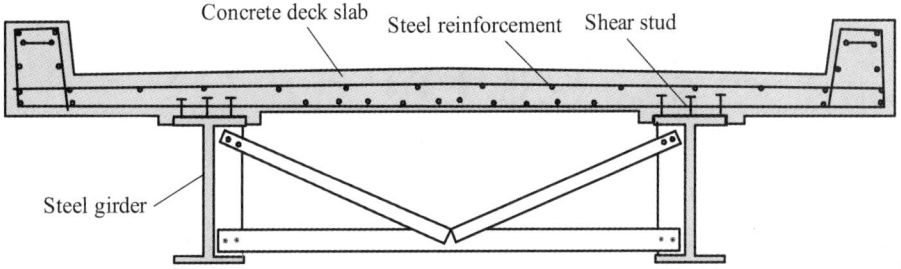

Figure 9.13 The cross-section of a typical steel-concrete composite I-shape girder highway bridge.

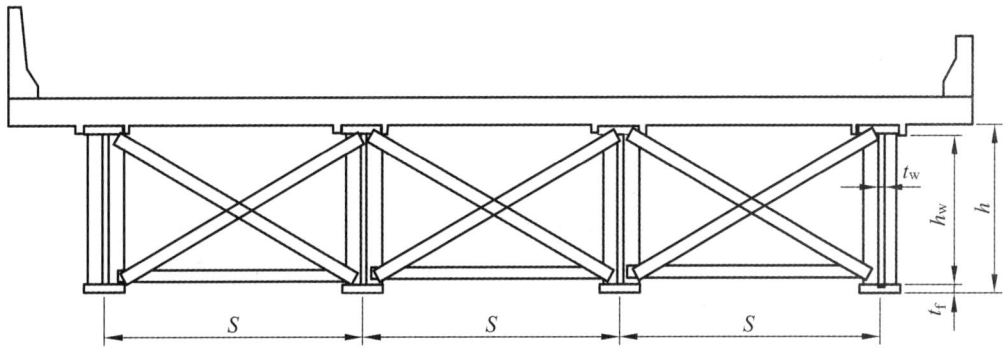

Figure 9.14 The cross-section of a two-span continuous steel-concrete composite highway bridges with span length of 40 m (unit: mm).

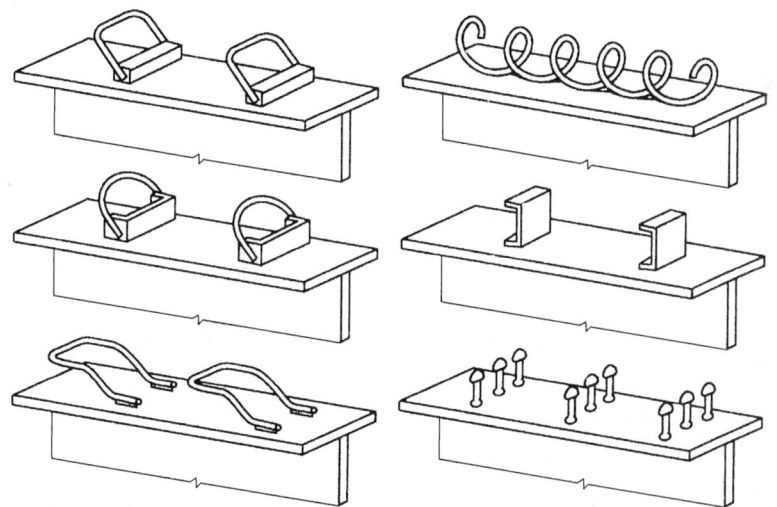

Figure 9.15 Shear keys for steel-concrete composite bridges.

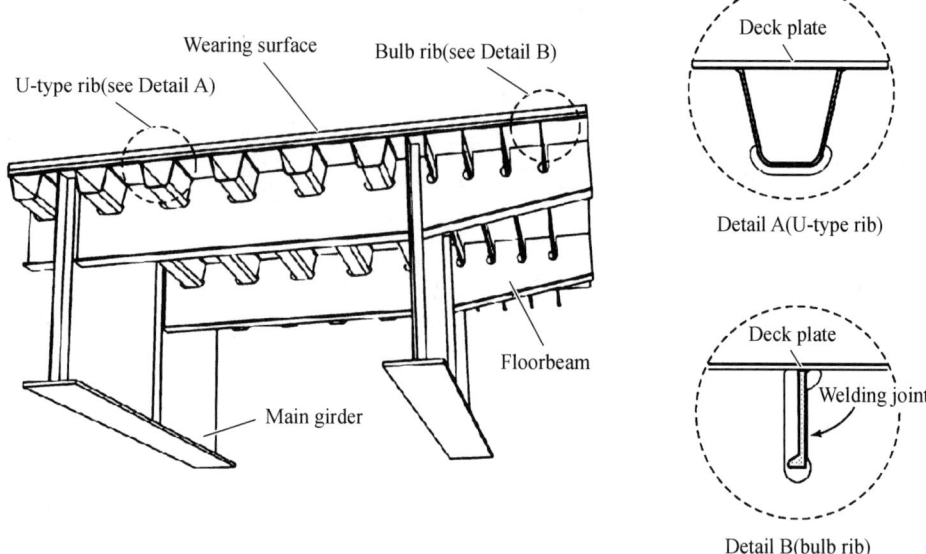

Figure 9.16　The orthotropic steel deck.

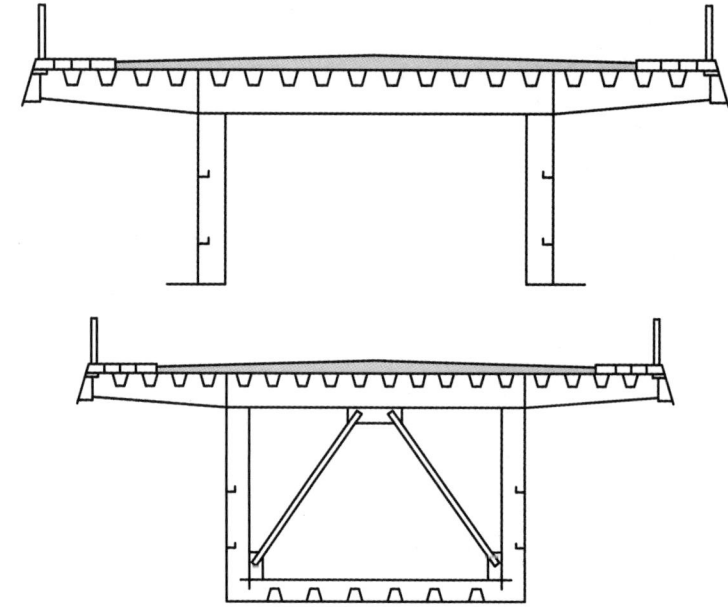

Figure 9.17　Cross-sections of steel bridges with orthotropic steel deck.

9.3.2　Design philosophies

Design of steel bridges can be based on the traditional Allowable Stress Design method (ASD) or the Limit State Design method (LSD) which is alternatively called the Load And Resistant Factor Design (LRFD) method in the United States. The LSD or LRFD method is based on the probabilistic analysis of the structure's condition reaching various limit states. Currently, the highway steel bridges in North America are designed by the AASHTO LRFD method, but the design of railway steel bridges is still based on the ASD, which is recommended by AREMA (American Railway Engineering and Maintenance- of-Way Association), since there is no clear and pressing need for the steel railway bridges to be designed by probabilistic methods. In UK, design of steel bridges is in accordance with BS 5400 or Eurocodes which is based on the principles of LSD method involving level-I probabilistic method for calibration of partial factors. In China, the Specifications For Design Of Highway Steel Bridges (JTG D64-2015) are based on the LSD method, while the Code For Design Of Railway Steel Bridges (TB 10091) is still based on the ASD method.

This chapter is focused on the design and analysis of railway steel bridges based on ASD method and in accordance with TB 10091. Some aspects related to the design of highway bridges based on LSD are also discussed briefly. Detailed design procedures for highway steel bridges can be found in other textbooks. Despite the difference in design philosophies, the principles of structural analysis are the same for both railway and highway steel bridges.

9.3.3　Dimensioning of the main girders

Main dimensions of a steel girder bridge include the span length, the depth of the girder, and the center-to-center spacing of the girders. In China, the traditional standard span lengths for simply supported railway steel bridges are 20 m, 24 m, 32 m, and 40 m, but the current railway design code TB 10091 does not require new bridges to have a standard span length. For highway bridges, the design code JTG D64 strongly recommend using the standard span lengths of　20 m, 25 m, 30 m, 35 m, 40 m, 45 m and 50 m for the span lengths less than 50 m. The depth of the girder is generally dependent on the span length, and the spacing of the girders is determined by the bridge deck configuration.

The preliminary dimensioning of plate girders is necessary before detailed design and analysis. Preliminary dimensions can be used for estimating dead loads, identifying splice requirements, assessing geometric constraints on fabrication and erection, and estimating cost.

1. Railway bridges

(1) The depth of the main girder, h.

The depth of the girder is determined by the following requirements:

(i) the amount of the steel should be minimized;

(ii) the deflection at the midspan of the girder shall satisfy the requirements put by the design code;

(iii) the depth of the web plate shall be less than the maximum available width of steel plate products;

(iv) the construction depth, which is defined as the vertical distance from the top of the rail and the bottom of the girder, should be as small as possible. In addition, the dimensions of the girder must satisfy the requirements for the railway clearances.

The main dimensions of a railway steel plate girder bridge are illustrated in Figure 9.18. Based on the past design experience, the economic depth of the plate girder can be estimated by

$$h = \sqrt{\frac{\alpha M}{[\sigma_w]t_w}} \qquad (9.1)$$

where, h is the vertical distance between the top surface and the bottom surface of the girder (Figure 9.18);

M is bending moment caused by total loads;

α is a coefficient, taken as 2.5 ~ 2.7;

t_w is the thickness of web;

$[\sigma_w]$ is the allowable bending stress.

It can be seen from Eq. (9.1) that the higher the steel strength, the smaller the depth of the girder.

If the girder depth is determined by the stiffness requirement that the maximum deflection at the midspan caused by the static live loads shall not be larger than 1/900 of the span length, the depth of the girder can be roughly estimated by

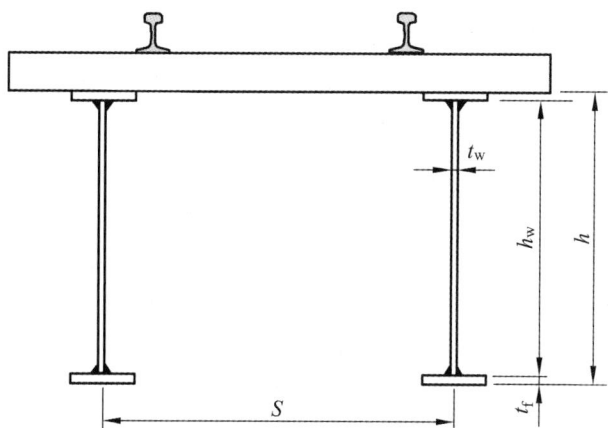

Figure 9.18 The main dimensions of a railway steel plate girder bridge.

$$h_{\min} = \frac{5}{24} \times \frac{[\sigma_w]}{E_s} \times \frac{L}{[\delta_{\max}/L][q_D/q_L + (1+\mu)]} \quad (9.2)$$

where, E_s is the elastic modulus of steel;

q_D is the dead load assumed uniformly acting on the girder;

q_L is the live load assumed uniformly acting on the girder;

$\delta_{\max}$ is the maximum deflection at the midspan;

$(1+\mu)$ is the dynamic factor.

It is shown in Eq. (9.2) that, for a given allowable stress, the depth of the girder increases with decrease of $\delta_{\max}$. In other words, the smaller deflection the girder is allowed, the larger depth the girder should have. In general, the minimum depth of the railway bridge girder is determined by the stiffness requirement. The maximum depth of the girder is determined by the allowable construction depth.

In North America, an economic, minimum depth-to-span ratio for steel freight railway bridges is about 1/15. Typically, the depth-to-span ratios in the range of 1/10 to 1/12 are appropriate for short- and medium-span steel girder freight railway bridges.

(2) The spacing of the main girders, s.

The spacing of the main girders should be determined by taking into consideration the following aspects:

(i) The span length of the sleeper can be neither too small nor too large. A large span length of the sleeper leads to large cross-section of the sleeper. However, if the span length of the sleeper is too small, the elastic flexural deformation of the sleeper is too small to be used for mitigating the dynamic effect of the railway traffic. A reasonable range of the girder spacing to balance these considerations is approximately between 2 m and 2.5 m.

(ii) The girder spacing shall be sufficient to prevent overturning by lateral loads.

(iii) The girder spacing should ensure sufficient transverse stiffness of the bridge. According to the railway design code TB 10091-2017, the girder spacing shall not be less than 1/15 of the span length of the girder to meet the requirement for the transverse stiffness.

Based on above considerations, the spacing of the railway steel plate girders in the current practice in China is $s = 2.2$ m.

2. Highway bridges

(1) The depth of the main girder.

For highway steel plate girder bridges, the depth of the girder can be estimated from the limit stress in the top and bottom flanges or from the maximum allowed deflection. However, the preliminary design based on the stiffness requirement usually overestimates the depth of the girder and in turn results in non-economic designs. In practical design, the girder depth is most often controlled by the strength requirement. The typical dimensions of a highway steel girder bridge are shown in Figure 9.19. Let's assume that the limit stresses in the top and bottom flanges are σ_c^{top} and σ_t^{top}, respectively, and that A_f^{top}, A_f^{bop} and A_w are the cross-sectional areas of the top flange, the bottom flange, and the web, respectively (see Figure 9.20). The depth of the web of the girder, h_w, that makes the cross-sectional area a minimum can be obtained as

$$h_w = \sqrt[3]{\left(\frac{h_w}{t_w}\right)\left(\frac{6M}{\sigma_c^{top} + \sigma_t^{bot}}\right)} \quad (9.3)$$

where, h_w / t_w is the depth-to-thickness ratio of the web, which dependent on the required shear capacity of the web and the arrangement of the stiffeners. The total cross-sectional area of the girder, A, corresponding to the h_w estimated by Eq. (9.3) is

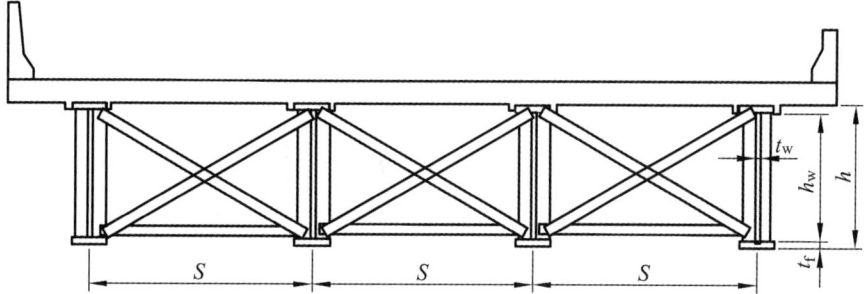

Figure 9.19 The typical dimensions of a highway steel girder bridge.

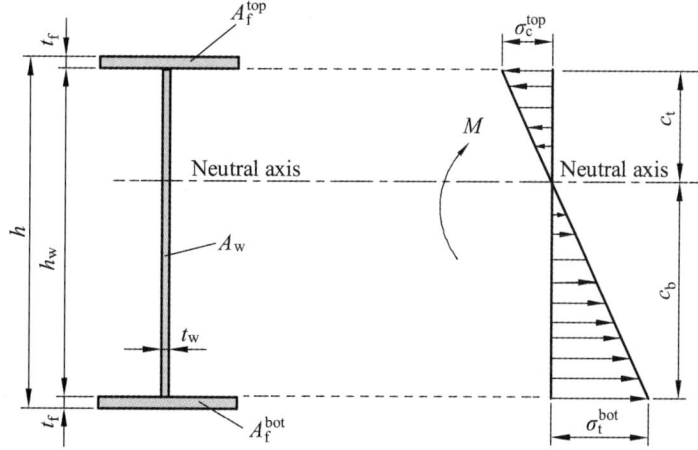

Figure 9.20 Stress distribution in a steel plate girder.

$$A = A_f^{top} + A_f^{bot} + A_w$$

$$= \left(\frac{M}{\sigma_c^{top} h} h_w - \frac{h_w t_w}{6} \frac{(2\sigma_c^{top} - \sigma_t^{bot})}{\sigma_c^{top}} \right) +$$

$$\left(\frac{M}{\sigma_t^{bot} t_w} - \frac{h_w t_w}{6} \frac{2\sigma_t^{bot} - \sigma_c^{top}}{\sigma_t^{bot}} \right) + h_w t_w \quad (9.4)$$

The total depth of the girder is

$$h = h_w + 2t_f \approx h_w \quad (9.5)$$

The h obtained by Eq. (9.4) may not satisfy the stiffness requirement. Adjustment of h is necessary if the deflection of the girder exceeds the allowable value specified by the design code. According to the Chinese highway design code JTG D64, the maximum deflection of the plate steel girder bridge under static live loads shall not be greater than 1/500 of the span length. Figure 9.21 shows the relation of the span-to-depth ration L/h with the span length L under different Chinese highway truck loads. It is seen that the ratio L/h increases with L nonlinearly, implying that h/L decreases with L. In other words, h increases with L, but a smaller h/L should be used for a longer span length. In Chinese practice, the ratio h/L is usually between 1/25 and 1/12. In North America, the ratio is about 1/25 for steel bridges under AASHTO highway loadings.

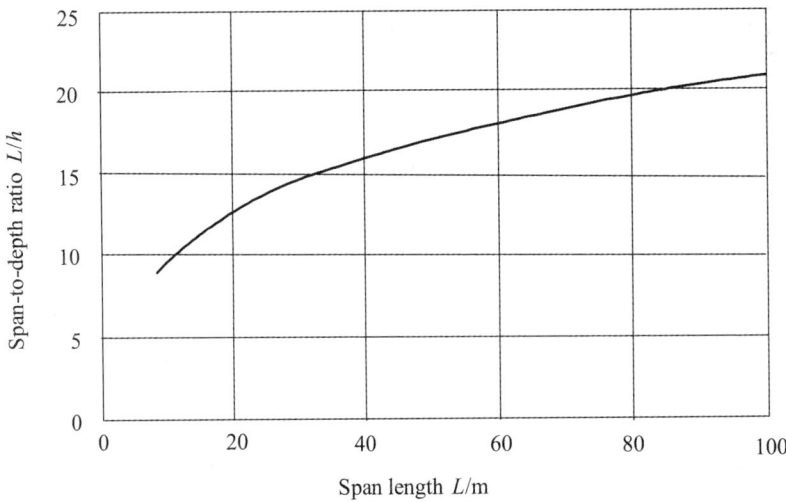

Figure 9.21 The relation of the depth-to-span ratio with the span length.

(2) The girder spacing.

The girder spacing of a highway steel plate bridge depends on many factors. An efficient steel plate bridge cross-section is generally influenced by girder spacing and overhang dimensions. The girder spacing and the number of girders directly affect the loads that each girder is subjected to. Wider girder spacing leads to deeper girders in order to carry more flexural loads. In addition, wider girder spacing also results in longer transverse span length of the deck slab and, in turn, results in thicker deck slab. However, wider girder spacing offers advantages of fewer bearings, lateral bracing members, and connection plates, etc., which can provide substantial savings. Some studies recommended a minimum girder spacing of 3 m. In Japan, the girder spacing is usually between 2.0 m and 3.5 m, and the length of deck overhang is within 1 m. Such a range of girder spacing leads to a maximum deck slab thickness of 260 mm at the deck midspan between girders and 36 mm at the deck support.

Using the prestressed concrete panels to form the deck can reduce the number of girders. For two-lane or three-lane girder bridges, two or three girders can be enough to carry the wide deck. Figure 9.22 shows a cross-section of a two-girder steel bridge with concrete deck of 11.2 m in width.

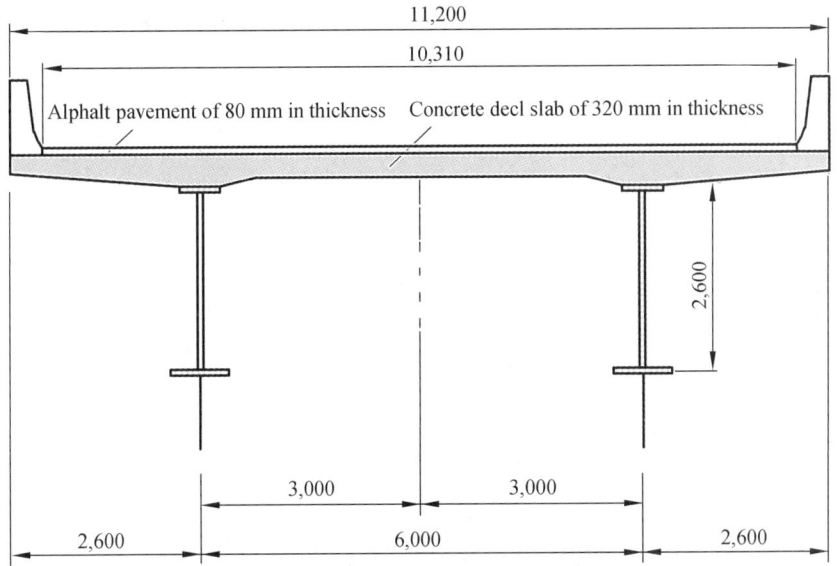

Figure 9.22 The cross-section of a two-girder steel bridge (lateral bracing frame is not shown) (units: mm).

From the fabricator's perspective, the use of fewer girders translates into less welding work, fewer cross-frames/diaphragms to fabricate, and a significant overall savings in fabrication cost. For the erector, fewer girders mean fewer pieces to erect, fewer field splices to be bolted, and fewer cross-frames to install. Overall, the use of fewer girders leads to shorter construction time.

For the bridges with orthotropic steel plate as deck, the girder spacing depends on the flexural capacity of the deck slab. In general, the girder spacing can reach between 4 m and 6 m. Figure 9.23 shows a 3.3 m girder spacing for a continuous bridge spanning 30.5 m+42.5 m+30.5 m. If properly braced in the longitudinal and transverse directions, the girder spacing of a plate bridge with orthotropic deck can reach more than 10 m. Figure 9.24 shows the cross-section for the Wiesbaden-Schierstein Bridge, Germany,

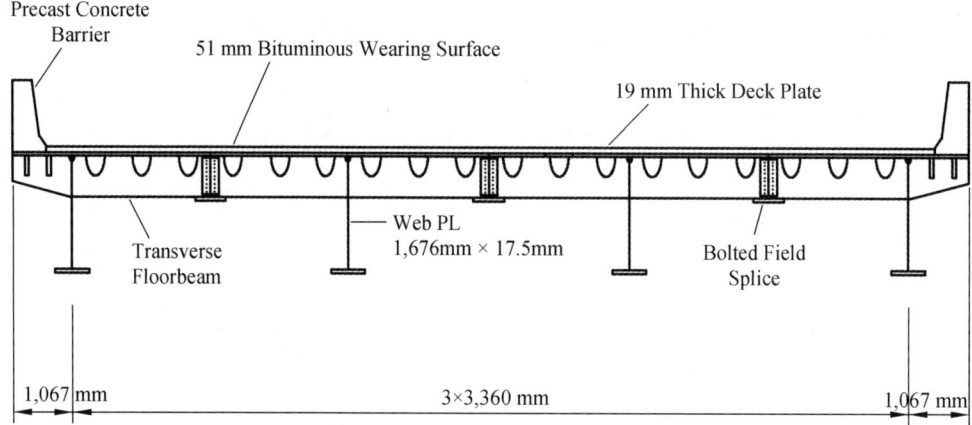

Figure 9.23 The cross-section of a three-span continuous bridge spanning 30.5 m + 42.5 m + 30.5 m (units: mm).

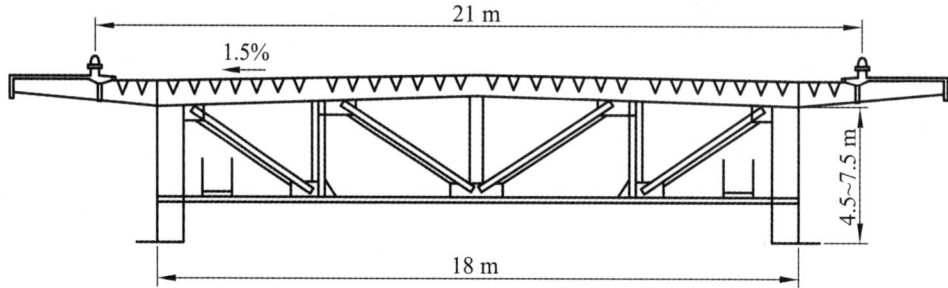

Figure 9.24 The cross-section of Wiesbaden-Schierstein Bridge, Germany.

which is a 14-span plate girder bridge with an orthotropic deck carrying a 20 m roadway and a sidewalk on each side of the roadway. The girder spacing is 18 m, and the girder depth varies from 4.5 m to 7.5 m, spanning from 46 m to 204 m. The 0.47-in. web has a maximum depth-to-thickness of 600.

9.4 Truss girder bridges

9.4.1 Structural configurations and nomenclature

A truss bridge is usually composed of main trusses, which are structures of connected elements forming triangular units for carrying vertical load, and a plethora of lateral bracings, which resist the wind and other lateral forces. Truss bridges can carry railway and highway traffic. Since railway truss bridges and highway truss bridges have similar configurations except for the deck configurations, only railway truss bridges are discussed in this section. The truss bridges can be classified into deck truss bridges and through truss bridges, depending on the location of the bridge deck. Typical configuration of a deck truss railway bridge for a simple span is shown in Figure 9.25. A typical through truss railway bridge is shown in Figure 9.26(a). To demonstrate the difference in the deck configuration between highway and railway truss bridges, a typical cross-section of a highway deck-truss bridge is shown in Figure 9.26(b).

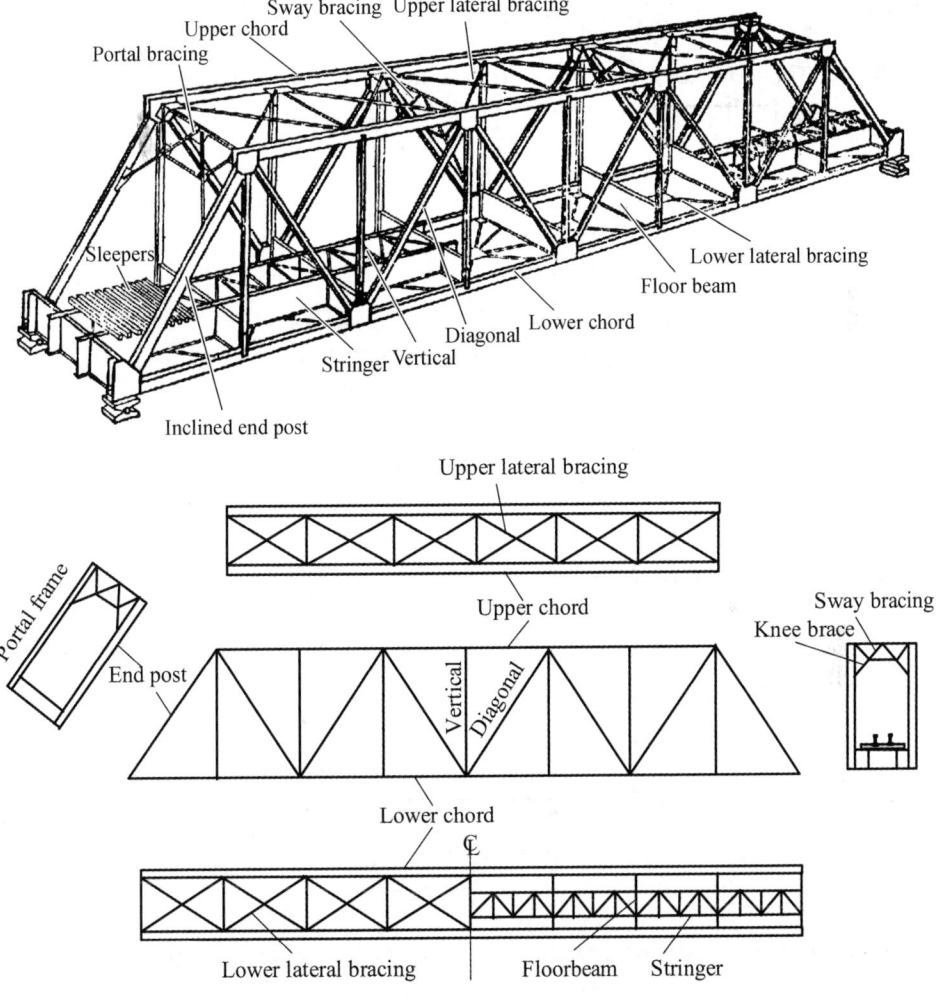

Figure 9.25 A through truss railway bridge with nomenclature.

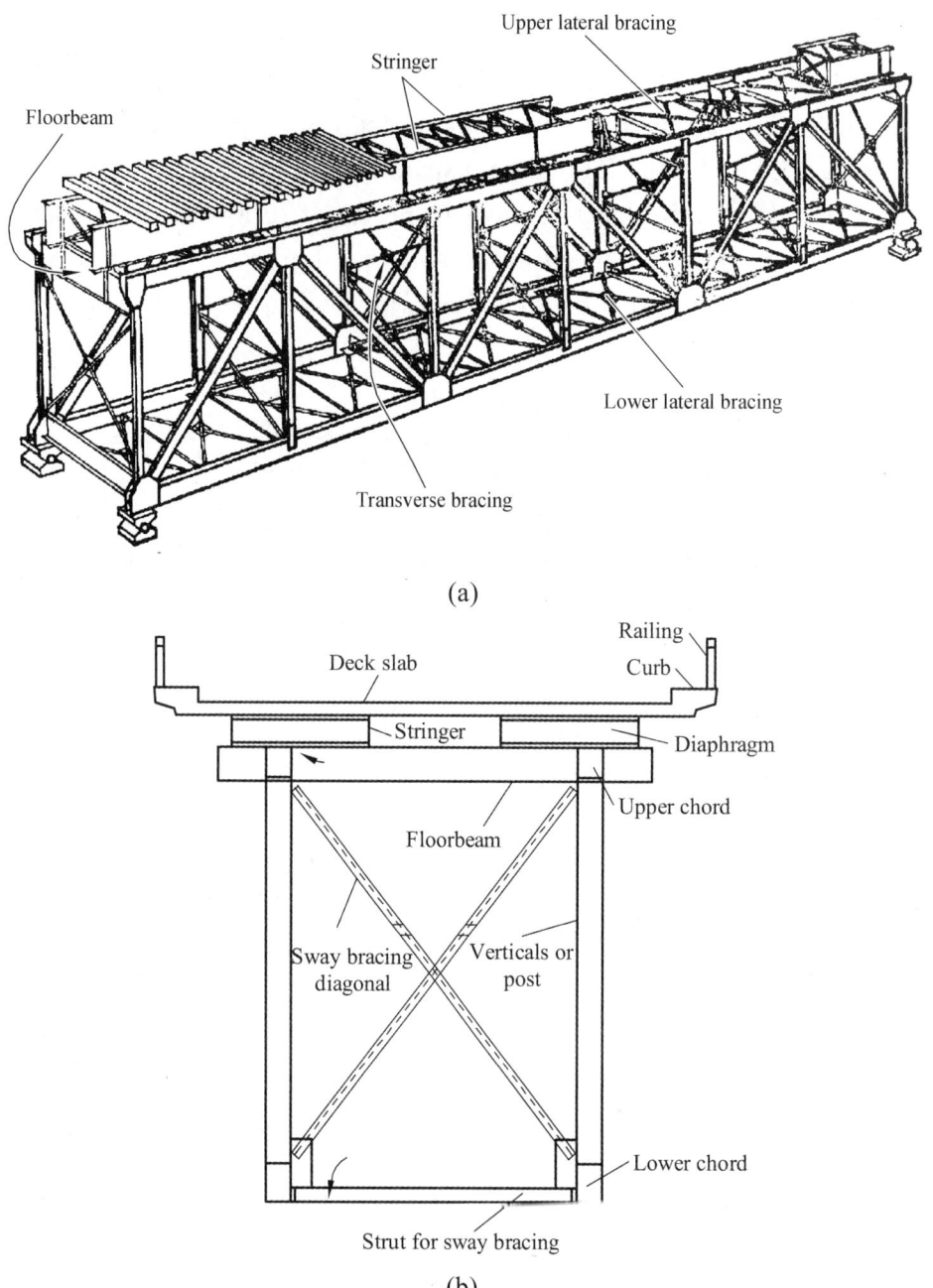

Figure 9.26 The deck truss railway bridge: (a) the perspective view; (b) the cross-section.

The lateral bracing members in the planes of the upper and lower chords resist wind loads and brace the compression chords. The function of the portal bracing is both to stiffen the end posts against vibrations and to assist them in transferring the wind pressure from the upper lateral system to the supports of the bridge. The sway bracings between truss verticals are to provide lateral resistance of the bridge in vertical planes and increase its torsional rigidity. The definitions and functions of typical members in a truss bridge are given below:

(1) Chords.

The upper and lower longitudinal members that extend the full length of a triangular section are called chords. For a simple span, the bottom chord will always be in tension, while the upper and lower chords will always be in compression. Chords are primary structural members.

(2) Diagonals.

The diagonal members connect successive upper and lower chords and resist either tension or compression depending on the truss configuration.

(3) Verticals.

Vertical web members connect the upper and lower chords and resist tension or compression depending on the truss configuration. Most vertical members are primary structural members.

(4) Floor-beams.

Floor-beams span between the trusses at panel points and carry loads from floor stringers and the deck system to the trusses.

(5) Stringers.

Stringers span between floor beams and provide primary support for the deck system. The dead and live loadings are transferred from the deck to stringers and then to the floor beams and finally to the trusses.

When the live loading is effectively applied at the nodes of the truss, the members in the truss will carry primarily only axial tension or axial compression forces. The bending moment in the girder is resisted by the couple formed by axial compression in the upper chord and axial tension in the lower chord. The shear force in the girder is carried by the diagonals, again either in axial tension or compression, depending on the truss configuration.

9.4.2 Structural types of truss

The pattern formed by the axially loaded members creates a specific truss type. There are numerous types of truss, but only a few of typical truss types and their variants are used in highway and railway bridges. Some popular truss types and their variants are shown in Figure 9.27. Historically, some of the truss types were patented, bearing the name of the people who developed the pattern, such as the Pratt truss that is named for Caleb and Thomas Pratt who patented it in 1844. Each type of truss in Figure 9.27 has different characteristic in carrying loads.

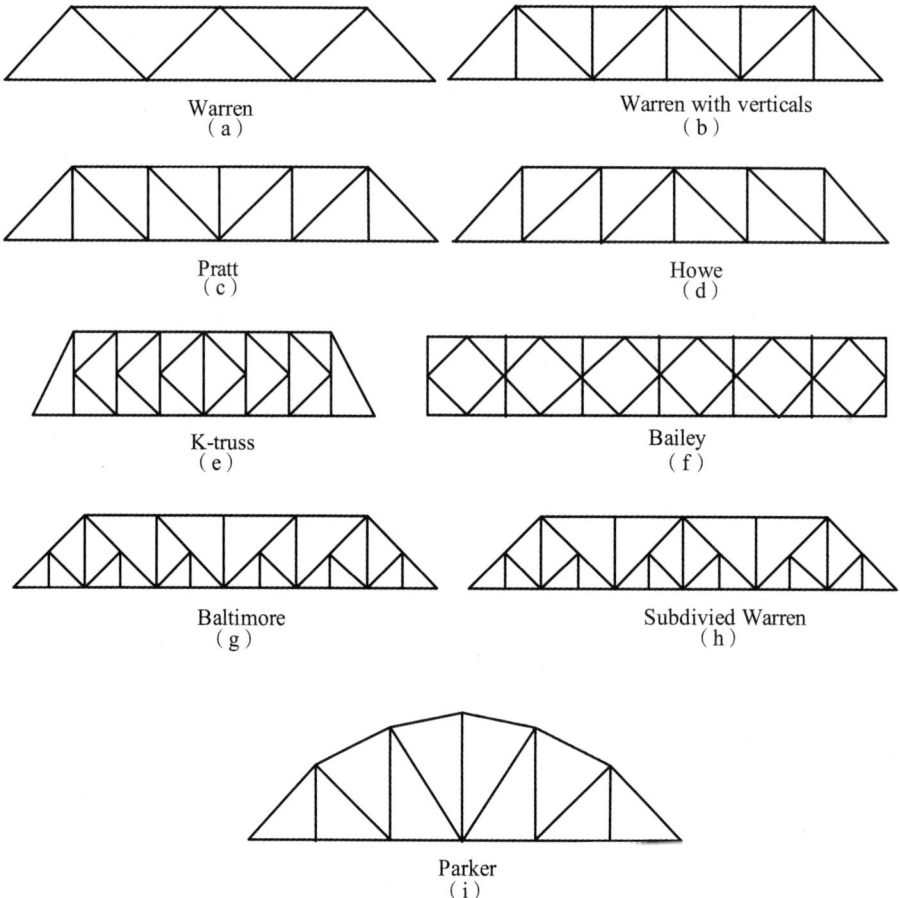

Figure 9.27　Typical types of trusses.

The Warren truss is distinguished by equal-sized members constituting a series of equilateral triangles, representing one of the earliest and simplest truss types. The diagonals act in both tension and compression. This type is generally characterized by thick, prominent, diagonal members. The modified Warren truss is the original Warren truss with added verticals, so as to increase stiffness. The Warren truss was developed and patented in 1848 by two British engineers, James Warren and Willoughby Monzoni, and has been used for a variety of highway and railway bridges since its development. The modified Warren truss has become the standard truss type for railway steel truss bridges.

The Pratt truss includes verticals and diagonals which are usually parallel and slope down towards the centre of the truss. This arrangement makes interior diagonals act in tension and verticals in compression when the truss is loaded. The Pratt truss was originally patented by Thomas and Caleb Pratt in 1844, and has been the most commonly used truss type for spans under 76 m.

The Howe truss slightly resembles a Pratt truss, but the diagonals in a Howe truss slope upward towards the center of the truss. In contrast to the Pratt truss, the diagonals are in compression and the verticals are in tension when the Howe truss is under loading. The Howe truss was patented in 1840 by William Howe and was common on early railways.

The K-truss is named after the K-shape formed in each panel by the vertical member and two oblique members. The idea of the K truss is to break up the diagonal members into smaller sections, in the hope of reducing their likelihood of buckling under compression. Due to its complexity and expensiveness, the K truss is not a popular truss type.

The Bailey truss was invented by a British engineer Sir Donald Bailey in 1940-1941 for military use during the World War II. The original design of the truss consists of prefabricated modular components, called rectangular panels, each comprising three verticals and squared bracings. These modular components can be easily and speedily assembled in various configurations without assistance of special tools or heavy equipment. The Bailey trusses are strong enough to carry heavy loads and cross long spans. After the World War II, the Bailey truss continues to be used extensively in civil engineering construction projects and to provide temporary crossings for pedestrian and vehicle traffic. Some long-span steel truss bridges built in China have the truss pattern of the Bailey type, such as the Wuhan Yangtze River Bridge (Figure 1.34) and Nanjing Yangtze River Bridge (Figure 1.35).

The Baltimore truss is a subclass of the Pratt truss. It has additional, auxiliary sub-struts or sub-ties in the lower section of the truss, linking the diagonals to the lower chords and verticals. The purpose of using additional sub-bracings in the lower section of the Pratt truss is to reduce the horizontal distance of the joints, so as to decrease the span length of the floor-beam supporting the bridge deck. It is mainly used for railway bridges. The Baltimore truss was developed in 1871 by engineers of the Baltimore and Ohio and Pennsylvania Railroad, and was popular into the early 20th century.

The subdivided Warren truss has additional bracings in the lower section of the modified Warren truss, serving the same purpose as those in the Baltimore truss. This type of truss is mainly used for long-spans.

The Parker truss is a Pratt truss with inclined top chords. The inclined top chords offer savings in material and place the greatest depth of the truss at the center of the span where it is most needed. The Parker truss was developed by C.H. Parker between 1868 and 1871. It was admirably suited for relatively long spans when it was developed and remained popular through the early decades of the 20th century.

9.4.3 Dimensioning of trusses

The main dimensions of a truss bridge that need to be determined before detailed design of the structural members are the truss depth H, the panel length L_p, spacing of truss girders s, and the inclination of the diagonal member θ (see Figure 9.28).

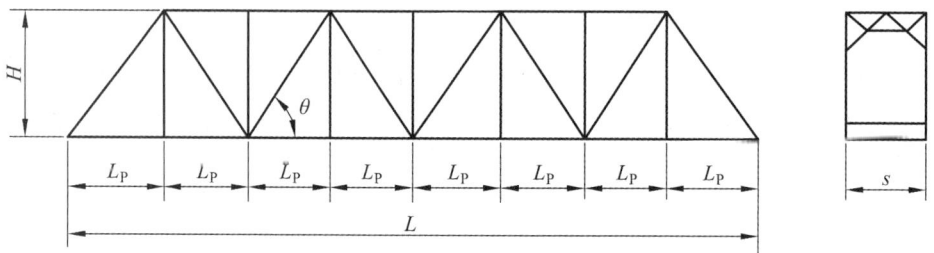

Figure 9.28　The main dimensions of truss bridges.

1. The depth of the truss

The depth of the truss is closely associated with the amount of steel used in the truss. For a given span length, a larger truss depth H will result in smaller axial forces in the upper and lower chords, which in turn lead to smaller amount of steel used. However, the length of diagonals increases with the truss depth, which results in increased amount of steel used. Based the many years of design practice, the depth-to-span length ratio H/L for railway through truss bridges has been found to be in the range of 1/10 to 1/5, and the economic depth-to-span length ratio is from 1/6 to 1/6.5. For highway steel truss bridges, a smaller depth-to-span ratio is used. AASHTO LRFD specifications set the minimum depth-to-span ratio of 1/10 for American highway truss bridges. An economical H/L ratio for American highway truss bridges ranges from 1/10 to 1/7, or even smaller provided deflections are within allowable limits. For the steel railway truss bridges, an economic depth-to-span ratio is usually in the range of 1/5 to 1/7. In general, deck trusses have a smaller depth than through trusses.

Table 9.1 summarizes the typical depth-to-span ratios that can be used in the design of modern Chinese railway and highway truss bridges.

Table 9.1 Typical depth-50-span ratios for simply supported truss bridges

Type of girders	Railway bridges		Highway bridges	
	With parallel chords	With inclined chords	With parallel chords	With inclined chords
Through-type	$\frac{1}{7}l$	$\left(\frac{1}{6.5} \text{ to } \frac{1}{5}\right)l$	$\left(\frac{1}{10} \text{ to } \frac{1}{7}\right)l$	$\left(\frac{1}{8} \text{ to } \frac{1}{5.5}\right)l$
Deck-type	$\left(\frac{1}{8} \text{ to } \frac{1}{7}\right)l$		$\left(\frac{1}{10} \text{ to } \frac{1}{8}\right)l$	

2. The length of the panel

The length of the panel is related to the number of floor beams, span length of the stringers, and the length of diagonals. Longer panel lengths reduce the number of joints, increase the span length of stringers and, in turn, results in larger cross-section of the stringer, which means the weight of the floor increases. These effects tend to offset each other within limits. In addition, longer panel lengths increase the length of the diagonals. An economic length of the panel ranges from $0.8H$ to $1.2H$. Generally, the length of the panel of a railway through truss bridge is in the range of 5.5 m to 12 m. For railway deck truss bridge, the panel length is usually in the range of 3 m to 6 m. Highway truss bridges can use longer panels than railway truss bridges. The standard panel length for railway truss bridges is 8 m, whereas the nonstandard panel lengths are 4 m, 6 m, 12 m, and 15 m.

3. The inclination of the diagonal

The inclination of the diagonals is dependent on the depth of the truss and the length of the panel, and has influence on the amount of steel used in the bridge. A small inclination angle of the diagonal not only increases the amount of steel used, but also make manufacturing and installation of gusset plate difficult. Usually, a reasonable inclination angle should be $30° \leqslant \theta \leqslant 50°$. For the truss without verticals, a properly larger inclination angle of the diagonals may be used.

4. The spacing of the truss girder

The spacing of the truss girder s should be sufficient to ensure that the bridge have required transverse stiffness and stability. If the spacing of truss girders is too small, the bridge can be subject to transverse vibrations under moving traffic. Furthermore, a small spacing of the trusses cannot prevent lateral overturning of the bridge. The ratio of the spacing of the truss to the span length is usually called width-to-span ratio, denoted by s/L. The ratio s/L ensuring sufficient transverse stiffnesses of simply supported railway truss bridges is usually around 1/20. For continuous bridges, this ratio can be reduced to 1/25. For deck truss bridge, the value of s is controlled by the resistance to the lateral overturning. For through truss bridges, the value of s must also meet the requirements for clearance. The Chinese single track through truss railway bridges with standard span lengths of 48 m, 64 m, and 80 m have the truss girder spacing of 5.75 in center-to-center distance. After the year of 2000, with increase of train speeds, the truss bridges with truss girder spacing of 5.75 underwent severe transverse vibrations. To address this issue, the typical truss girder spacing has been increased to 6.4 m for high-speed railway bridges.

For highway truss bridges, the width-to-span ratio, s/L, is generally in the range of 1/20 to 1/17. For deck truss highway bridges, the s/L ranges from 1/16 to 1/14.

5. The cross-sections of truss members

There are usually two types of cross-sections for truss members: H-shaped section [Figure 9.29(a)] and box section [Figure 9.29(b) ~ (d)]. Generally, truss members for roadway bridges are fabricated from steel plates by welding. Rolled sections are rarely used in building highway and railway bridges in China. The weld-fabricated H-shaped sections are widely used in Chinese truss bridges, since it is of simple construction, easy to fabricate with fillet welds, and convenient to install. The disadvantage of the H-shaped section is its small radius of gyration about the x-axis. Thus, the H-shaped section is mainly suitable for tension members or compression members with small slenderness ratios. The box section has large bending stiffness around the x- and y-axes, and is suited for long members subjected large tension or compression forces. However, fabrication of box-section costs much more labor work than that of the H-shaped section. Also, welding-induced distortion of plates during fabrication of the box section is not easy to correct.

If a truss member of box section is subjected to compression forces, diaphragms are usually provided along the member length so as to prevent buckling. For railway steel truss bridges, the spacing of the diaphragm is not greater than 3 m. To prevent corrosion of steel, the ends of the box section members are generally weld-sealed by end diaphragms.

The widths of the truss members, b, used in Chinese railway bridges are usually 460 mm, 600 mm, and 720 mm; the heights of the truss members, h, are usually 260 mm, 440 mm, 460 mm, 600 mm, 760 mm, 920 mm, and 1100 mm. The box sections in Figures 9.29(c) (d) are used for upper and lower chords, respectively. In the standard design of through truss railway bridges of 48 m, 64 m, and 80 m in span length, all the truss members have the same cross section width of 460 mm.

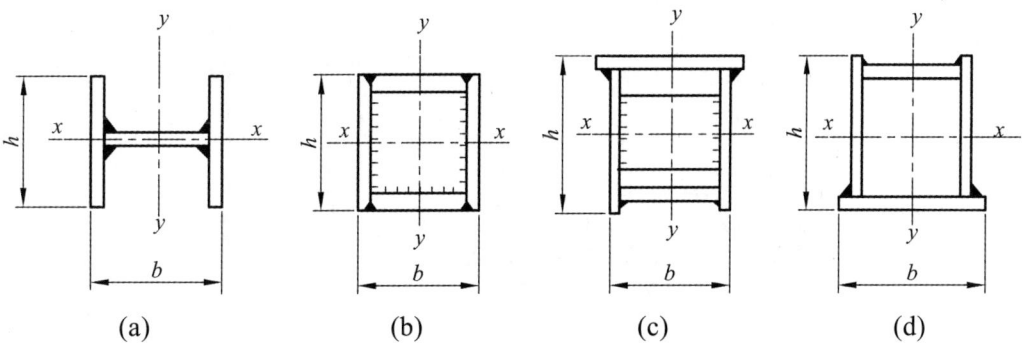

Figure 9.29 The cross-sections of truss members: (a) the H-shaped section; (b) the typical box-section; (c) the box section for upper chords; (d) the box-section for lower chords.

9.4.4 Configuration of truss joints and gusset plates

Truss members are typically connected at joints with gusset plates, as shown in Figure 9.30. The gusset plate is a steel plate used to interconnect vertical, diagonal, and horizontal truss members at a panel point [Figure 9.30(a) (b)]. Traditionally, the truss members are connected to the gusset plate by high-strength bolts or rivets. The floor beam at the panel joint is connected to the gusset plate by angles [Figure 9.30(c)]. To reinforce the connection between chords, splice plates are also added to the inside of the flange of the chord.

Truss connections are usually made by bolting or riveting truss members with gusset plates or splice plates. However, field bolting or riveting of connections costs long construction time and a great amount of field work. To speed up the construction of truss bridges and to save the field labor, a type of

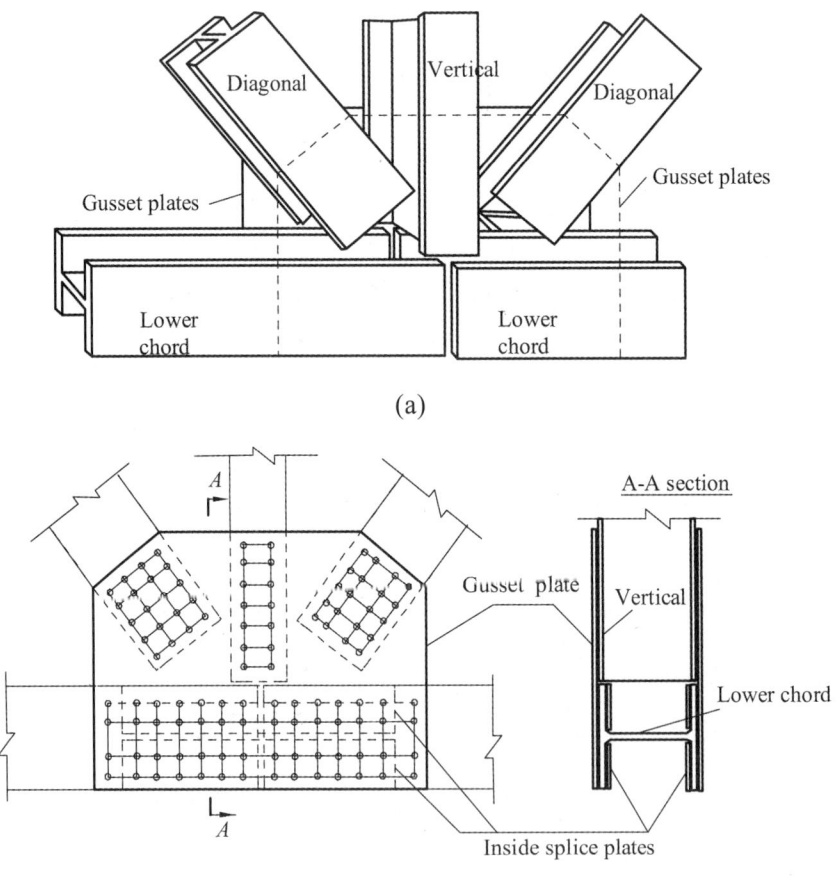

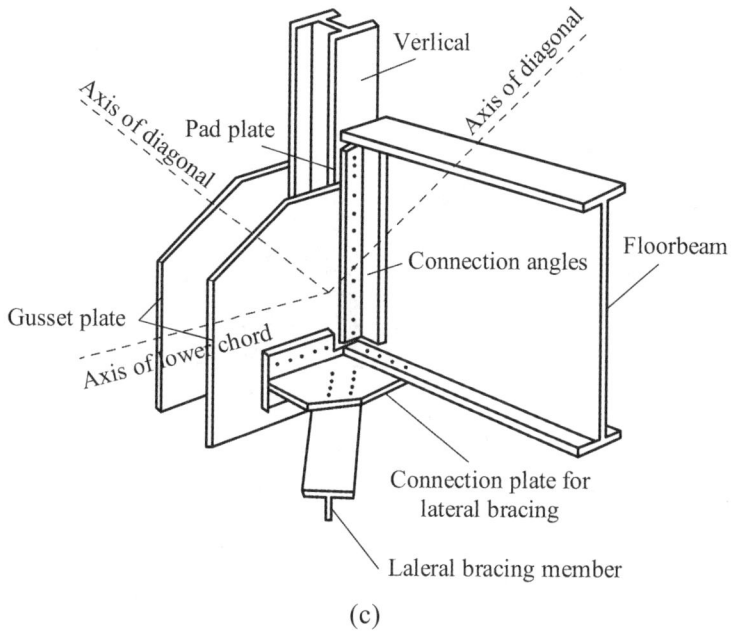

(c)

Figure 9.30 The configuration of gusset plate joint: (a) the isometric view of the truss members at a joint; (b) detail of the gusset plate connection; (c) detail of the connection with the floor beam.

truss joints, termed "the integral joint" has been developed since 1970s. Unlike the traditional joint, the integral joint is formed by first integrating the gusset plates, connection plates, and one section of a truss member in a connection block by shop-welding, and then field-bolting truss members with the integral unit (Figure 9.31). In the integral joint, some truss members are connected with their parts that have been welded in the connection block through splices at a distance from the gusset plate.

(a)   (b)

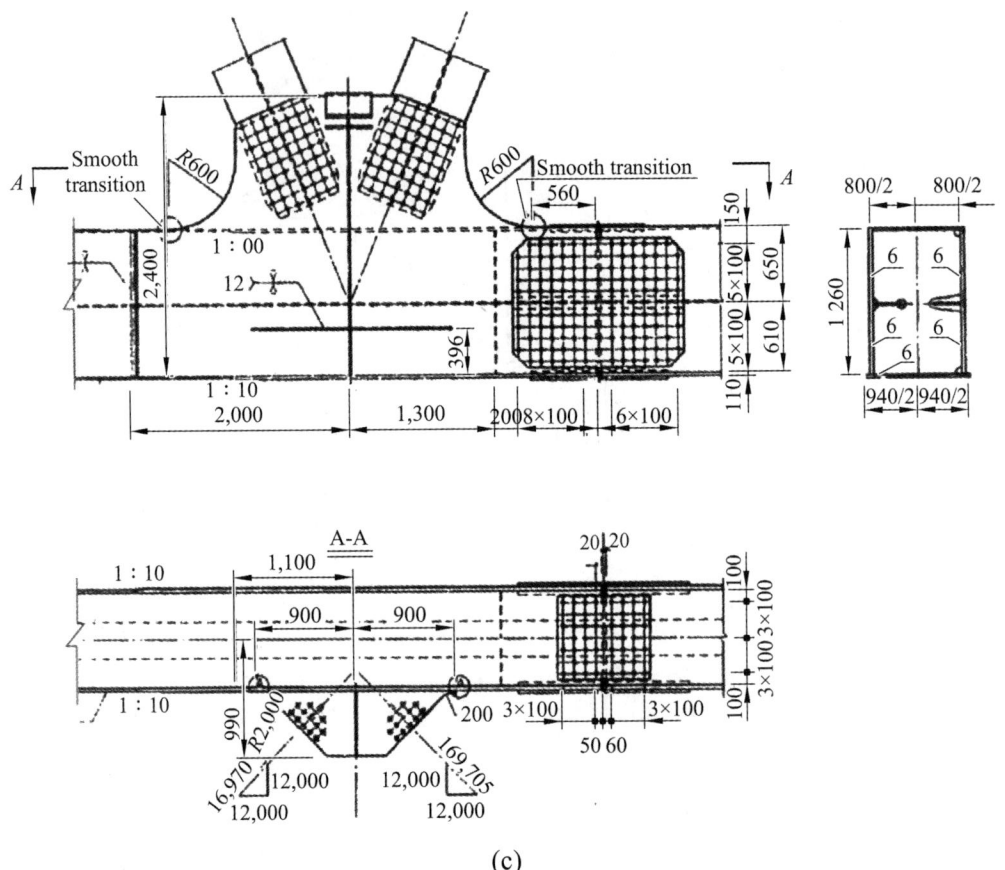

Figure 9.31 The welded integral joint: (a) photo of an integral joint for lower chords; (b) photo of an integral joint for upper chords; (c) details of an integral joint (units in mm).

The welded integral joints can facilitate assemblage of truss members and increase the speed of erection of truss bridges at fields, since much of the connection work can be completed in the fabrication shop. Although welded joints are efficient to fabricate and make the truss have high vertical stiffness, detrimental effects from welded fabrication, such as weld flaws, distortion, residual stresses, may occur that affect the performance of the integral joints.

9.5 Design calculations and analysis of steel components

9.5.1 Properties of steel

Structural steels used for bridges generally have more stringent performance requirements than the steels used for buildings and other structures. Bridge steels have to perform in an outdoor environment with large temperature changes, are subjected to cyclic live loading, and may be exposed to corrosive environments. Bridge steels are required not only to meet strength and ductility requirements, but also to provide atmospheric corrosion resistance without expensive protective coatings. For these reasons, the important material properties of modern structural bridge steels include strength, ductility, toughness, weldability, and corrosion resistance.

1. Strength

Strength of steel can be measured by the yield strength and tensile strength. The yield strength is the stress at which a further increase in strain occurs without an increase in stress. Tensile strength is the maximum stress reached in a tensile test of a steel specimen. In the Chinese railway steel bridge design code, the allowable stress of steel, $[\sigma_s]$ is specified as the yield strength divided by a safety factor of 1.7 or the tensile strength divided by a safety factor of 2.2. In the Chinese highway steel bridge design code, the design strength of steel, f_d, is the yield strength divided by a material partial factor 1.25.

2. Ductility

Ductility is the ability of steel to withstand inelastic deformation after yielding and prior to fracture. Ductility can be expressed as percentage elongation over a given gauge length or percentage reduction of the cross-sectional area of the specimen.

3. Toughness

Fracture toughness characterizes the ability of the steel to resist the propagation of cracks, and measures the energy that material can absorb without fracture. Fabrication-induced cracks, notches, discontinuities, or defects can cause stress concentrations that may initiate brittle fracture of components under the loads well below the level to cause yielding. The steel generally possesses a characteristic temperature property-the transition temperature, above which the steel is predominantly ductile and below which the steel is predominantly brittle (Figure 9.32). A steel with low fracture toughness is subject to brittle fracture if the service temperature of the steel is below its transition temperature. The Charpy V-Notch (CVN) test is commonly utilized to measure the fracture toughness for structural steel. A small 10 x 10 mm bending specimen with a machined notch is impacted by a hammer and the energy required to initiate fracture is measured.

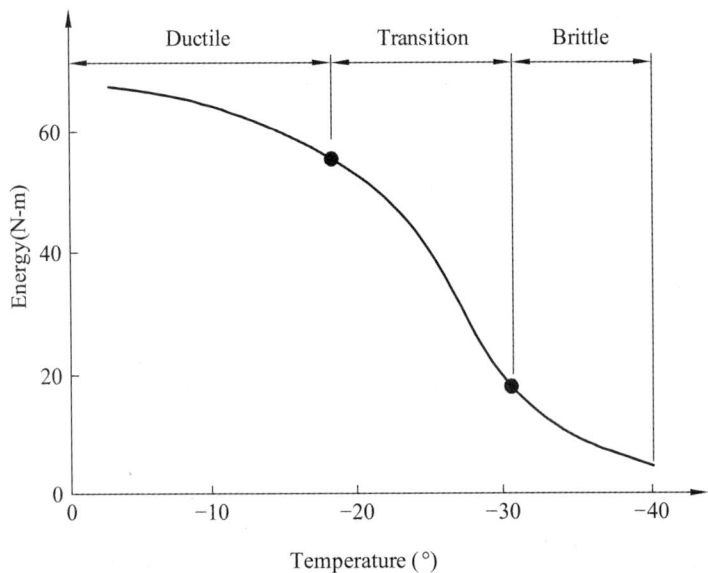

Figure 9.32   Transition of failure mode from ductile to brittle for low-carbon steel.

4. Weldability

The low-carbon steel is generally weldable when the carbon content is less than 0.30. The higher strength steels, where the increased strength is obtained by adding more carbon and manganese content, become hard and difficult to weld. The addition of other alloy elements, for increasing strength (by adding Cr, Mo, and V) and corrosion resistance (by adding Ni and Cu) will also reduce the weldability of steel. The weldability of steel can be evaluated by an empirical carbon equivalency equation (CE), defined by

$$CE = C + \frac{Mn + Si}{6} + \frac{Ni + Cu}{15} + \frac{Cr + Mo + V}{5} \qquad (9.6)$$

where C, Mn, Si, Ni, Cu, Cr, Mo, and V represent the contents of carbon, silicon, nickel, copper, chromium, molybdenum, and vanadium in the steel, respectively, in percentage. The American Welding Society (AWS) states that for a CE of 0.40% there is a potential for cracking in the heat-affected zone.

5. Corrosion resistance

As corrosion-resistance of steel can be increased by forming a thin iron oxide film on the surface of the steel, so comes the development of the weathering steel. This type of corrosion protection works well where there are alternate wetting and drying cycles. It may not be appropriate for steel bridges that are exposed to deicing chemicals and salts, located in a marine environment, and in locations with high sulphur content in the atmosphere. Weldability is slightly compromised because carbon equivalence, CE, is raised due to the addition of alloy elements such as chromium, copper and sometimes nickel for corrosion resistance. Thus the weathering steel requires special treatments in welding. Non-weathering steels can be protected with paint or sacrificial coatings, for example, hot-dip or spray-applied zinc or aluminum.

9.5.2 Structural analysis

For steel plate girder bridges, the classical beam analysis techniques can be used in the analysis of stresses and deformations. The influence line method and the load distribution method introduced in Chapter 5 can be used to obtain the maximum bending moments and shear forces at cross-section of the bridge girders and floor beams. The bridge deck slab can be simplified as one-way slabs or two-way slabs to obtain the critical bending moments and shear forces at the cross sections perpendicular to the transverse and longitudinal directions.

Box-shaped girders are generally considered more complicated structures than I-shaped girders. Box-shaped girders have more pieces and parts than I-shaped girders, and these parts work together as a structural system in more complicated ways than simple I-shaped girders. In practical design, the analysis of box-shaped girders is usually simplified by modeling them as line girders in the preliminary design and several additional calculations at the end of the analysis is required to determine the load effects on individual components, such as shear lag, torsional stress, and buckling strength. Rigorous three-dimensional analysis is usually necessary for long-span steel box-shaped girder bridges.

Structural analysis of steel truss bridges is based on two assumptions: (i) The truss members are joined together by frictionless pins. Although the actual bolted or welded connections do give some rigidity to the joint and this in turn introduces bending of the connected members when the truss is loaded, this assumption is generally satisfactory provided the center lines of the joining members are concurrent at a point. (ii) All loadings are applied at the joints. For truss bridges, this assumption is true. Because of these two assumptions, each truss member acts as an axial force member. To find the forces in truss members, two variations of the pin-connected truss model are commonly used: the method of joints, and the method of sections.

The method of joints is based on analysis of free-body diagrams of each of the truss joints [Figure 9.33(a)]. As long as the truss is determinate, there will be enough joints and equations of equilibrium to find the force in all the members.

The method of sections is based on the equilibrium of the free-body diagram of a section of truss. The equilibrium of the moment and the shear forces on the section of the truss can be sufficient to determine the two unknown truss forces. For example, the section of the truss shown in the Figure 9.32(b) is in equilibrium. The bending moment on the cross-section Q-Q is $M_{QQ} = R_G L_{GI}$ which is balanced by the force couple $F_{BC}H$ or $F_{IJ}H$. Thus the axial forces in the members BC and IJ are $F_{BC} = F_{IJ} = R_G L_{GI} / H$. The shear force at the section Q-Q is $(R_G - P)$, which is carried by the vertical component of the force F_{IC}. The equilibrium of the truss section in the vertical direction gives $F_{IC} = -(R_G - P)$.

In addition to vertical loads, a truss bridge is also subjected to lateral loads, such as the wind load, bogie hunting (nosing) force, and centrifugal force from live loads. The actual response of a truss bridge to the lateral forces is complicated and requires three-dimensional modeling and analysis. For design purposes, the lateral forces are resisted by the upper and lower lateral bracing systems. The upper and lower lateral bracing frame is assumed to be supported at the tops and bottoms of the end portal bracing, respectively (Figure 9.34). Then the upper and lower lateral bracing frame can be treated as horizontal trusses for analysis. One half of the wind load is assumed to act on the upper lateral bracing and the other half the lower lateral bracing. The load transfer path is as follows: the lateral force acting on the lower lateral bracing is directly transferred to the bearings at the ends of the bridge, while the lateral force acting on the upper lateral bracing is transferred to the portal bracing first and then to the bearings.

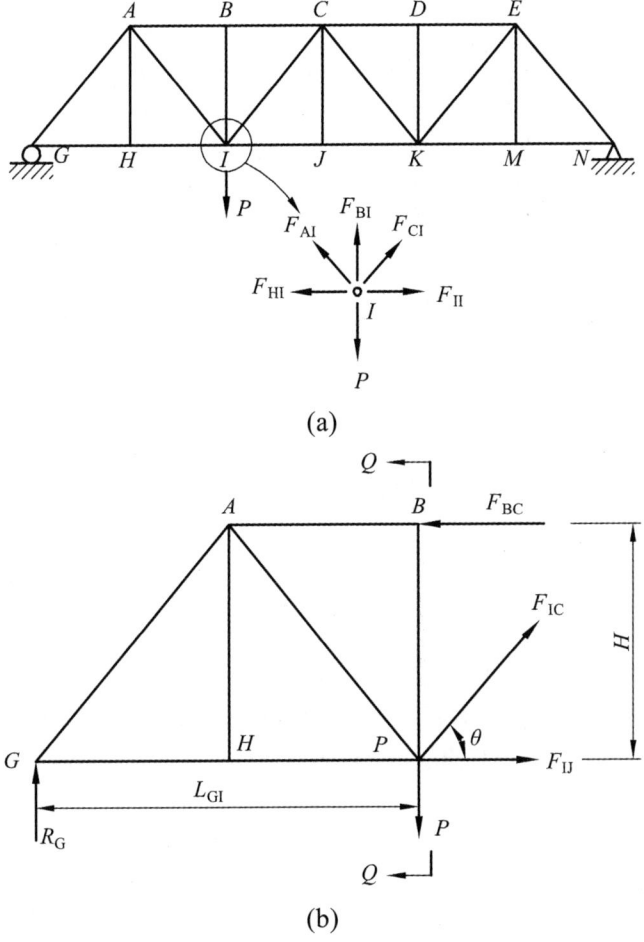

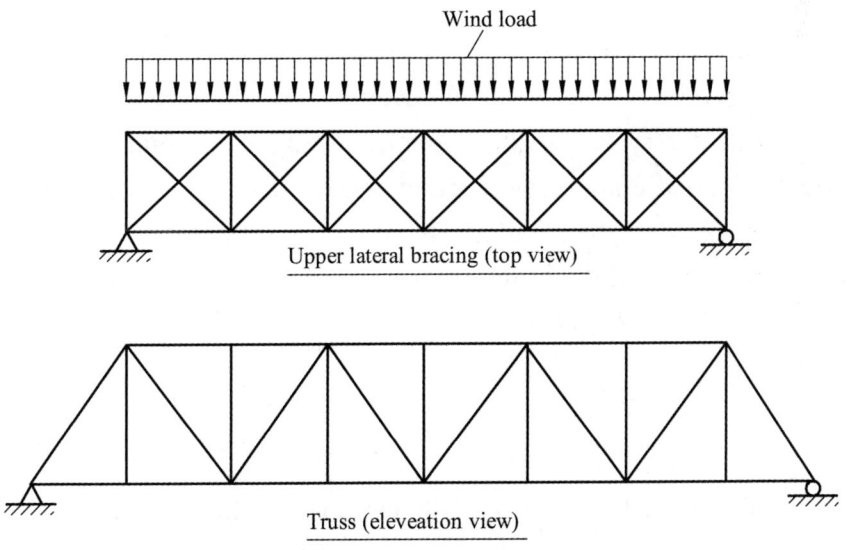

Figure 9.33 Methods for determining the forces in truss members: (a) the method of joints; (b) the method of sections.

281

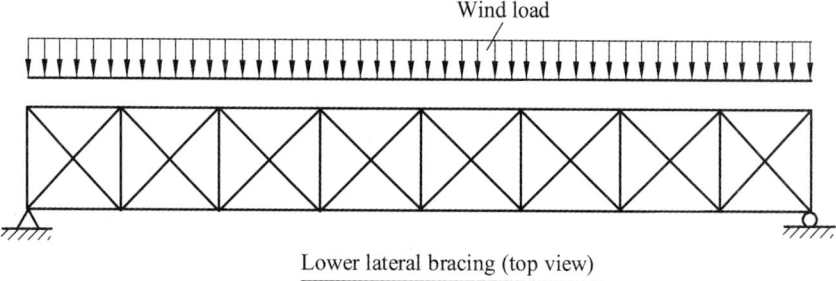

Figure 9.34 The analysis model for lateral bracings of truss bridges.

9.5.3 Axial force members

Truss and bracing members may be subjected to axial tension, compression, or both-due to stress reversal from moving loads. Axial members in tension must be designed considering the yield and fatigue criteria in the strength and fatigue limit states, respectively. The axial members in compression must also be designed considering the instability criteria in the strength limit state.

In the allowable stress design method, on which the Chinese railway steel bridge design code is based, the strength of axial force members are required to meet the following condition:

$$\frac{N}{A_{net}} \leqslant [\sigma_s] \quad \text{for tension} \tag{9.6a}$$

$$\frac{N}{A_g} \leqslant \phi_1 [\sigma_s] \quad \text{for compression} \tag{9.6b}$$

where N is the axial force; A_g is the gross cross-sectional area; A_{net} is the net cross-section area with connection holes removed; $[\sigma_s]$ is the allowable axial stress; ϕ_1 is the reduction factor considering buckling of concentrically loaded compression members, depending on the steel type, the cross-section shape, and the slenderness ratio.

Under the small deflection theory, the critical buckling load of a compression member N_{cr} is

$$N_{cr} = \frac{\pi^2 E_s A_g}{\lambda^2} \tag{9.7a}$$

where, λ is the slenderness ratio of the member, defined by

$$\lambda = \frac{KL}{r} \tag{9.7b}$$

in which, r is the radius of gyration of the section, defined by $r = \sqrt{I_g/A_g}$, L is the geometrical length of the member, and K is the effective length factor dependent on the end restraint of the member. KL is termed the effective length. The railway design code TB 10091 specifies the effective lengths for various truss members. The strength of a compression member is susceptible to instability or buckling. For short members with large cross-section, failure is governed by yielding; however, for members with large slenderness ratio, elastic or inelastic buckling controls the failure. The reduction factor ϕ_1 in Eq. (9.6b) reflects the decrease of the compressive strength of the member due to buckling.

9.5.4 Flexural members

Members designed to primarily carry flexural forces are typically girders, beams, floor beams, and stringers. These flexural members experience normal tensile, normal compressive, and shear stresses, and must be designed for strength, serviceability, and fatigue limit states. For the I-shaped girder with lateral supports, the flexural strengths requirements is expressed as

$$\sigma_{max} = \frac{M}{S} \leqslant [\sigma_w] \tag{9.8}$$

where, σ_{max} is the maximum normal stress, S is the section modulus, $[\sigma_w]$ is the allowable bending stress. The shear strength must satisfy the following condition:

$$\tau_{max} = \frac{VQ}{It_w} \leqslant C_\tau [\tau] \tag{9.9}$$

where, V is the shear force in the cross-section concerned, Q is the first moment of the area below or above the neutral axis, t_w is the thickness of the web (Figure 9.35), C_τ is a modification factor considering non-uniform distribution of the shear stress across the section, and $C_\tau \geqslant 1.0$.

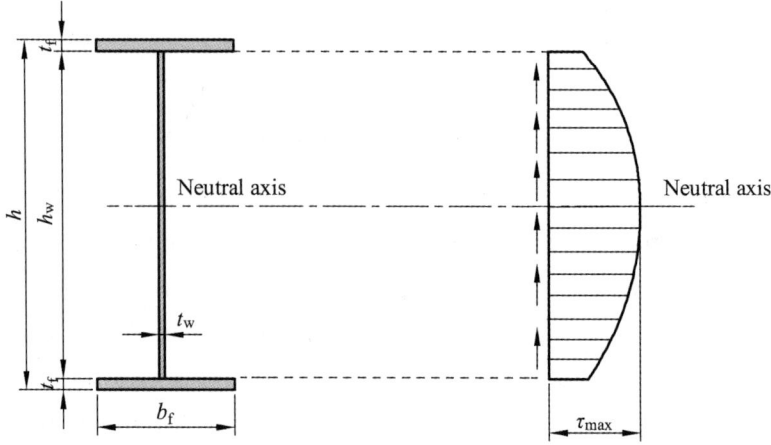

Figure 9.35 Distribution of the shear stress in a I-shaped girder.

If the compression flange of a girder is not laterally supported, global buckling can occur prior to yielding, and the girder may not be able to fully participate in resisting bending moment in the plane of the girder web. A laterally unsupported compression flange behaves similar to a column and tends to buckle out-of-plane between lateral supports. However, because the tension zone in the girder keeps the tension flange in line, the cross section twists when it moves laterally (Figure 9.36). The critical buckling moment is below the bending strength of a laterally supported girder. To prevent global buckling, the railway design code requires the bending stress satisfy the following condition:

$$\sigma_{max} = \frac{M}{S} \leqslant \varphi_2 [\sigma_w] \tag{9.10}$$

where, φ_2 is reduction factor considering global buckling of the girder, which dependent on the girder slenderness ratio, width-to-thickness ratio of the flange ($b_f / 2t_f$) and the web slenderness ratio h_w / t_w. The railway design code TB 10091 gives the method for determining φ_2.

Local buckling can occur if the width–thickness ratio of a component in compression becomes too large. The local buckling that occurs in the compression flange is called flange local buckling, and that occurs in the compression portion of the web is called web local buckling (Figure 9.37). To avoid flange local buckling, the Chinese railway design code TB 10091 requires the outstanding half flange width of a girder shall not be greater than 10 times the flange thickness. Vertical and longitudinal stiffeners are provided for the web to prevent web local buckling. In general, vertical stiffeners increase the resistance to shear buckling of the web while longitudinal stiffeners increase the resistance to the flexural buckling (Figure 9.38). The requirements for the sizes and spacing of these stiffeners are provided in the design specifications.

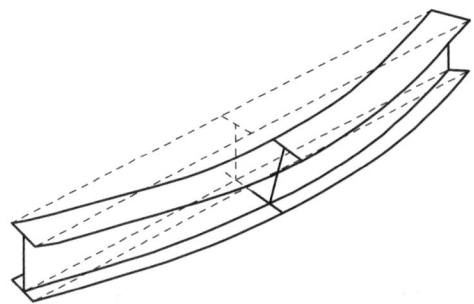

Figure 9.36 Global buckling of the plate girder.

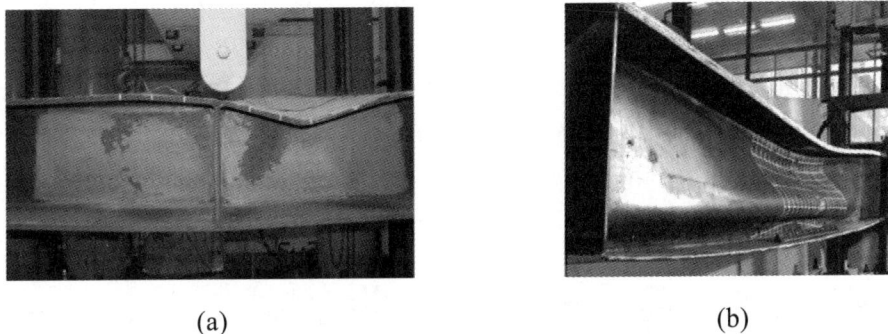

Figure 9.37 Local buckling of the plate girder: (a) local buckling of the flange; (b) local buckling of the web.

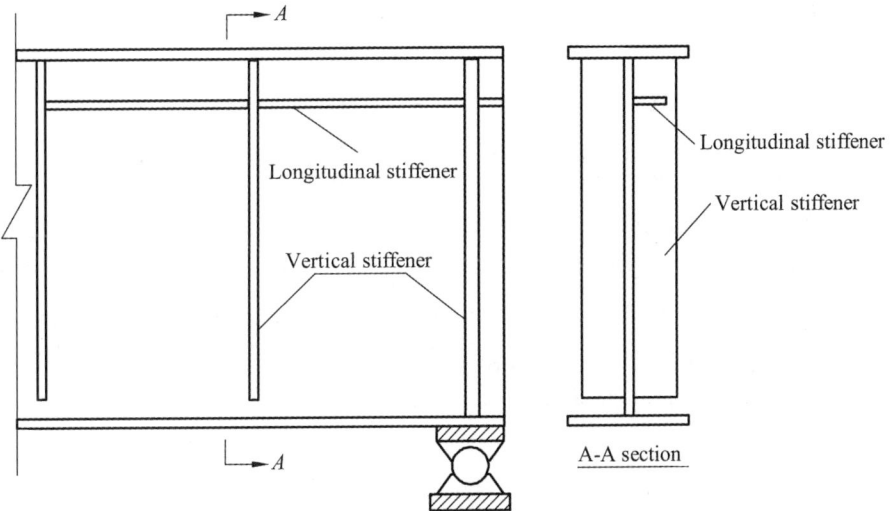

Figure 9.38 The vertical and longitudinal stiffeners in a plate girder.

9.5.5 Connections

The design of connections is as important to the strength and serviceability of steel bridges as the design of the members. Connections in modern steel bridges are made with welds and bolts. Typically, these connections transmit axial forces, shear forces, or combined axial and shear forces. Connection behavior is often complex but its design can be simplified by making some assumptions.

Design of welded connection must consider the force transfer path and strain compatibility between the weld and the base material. Fillet welds transfer forces by shear stress in the weld throat, and groove welds transfer forces in the same manner as the members being connected.

Bolted connections are a type of mechanically fastened joints. Bolting is relatively easy to conduct than welding. Fasteners used in modern steel bridges are either common steel bolts or high-strength bolts. The strength of the bolted connection is significantly affected by the bolt installation process. Forces in a bolted connection are transmitted through tension and shear in the bolts.

Design of connections is covered in the Chinese standard for design of steel structures GB 50017. In accordance with the railway steel bridge design code, the allowable stress of welds shall not be less than that of the base material. Detailed design calculations for welded and bolted connections are not discussed in this book. The reader is referred to textbooks or manuals on the design of steel structures and design manuals for further reading.

9.5.6 Fatigue strength

Fatigue is a phenomenon closely associated with material strength reduction due to stress fluctuations over time. The mechanism behind fatigue is progressive and localized structural damage, and the growth of cracks in the material. Fatigue strength is not a material constant like yield strength or modulus of elasticity. It is dependent on the number of stress cycles N and the stress range $\Delta\sigma_R$. Figure 9.39a shows the fluctuating stress with a constant stress range, and Figure 9.39b shows a typical $\Delta\sigma_R$-N curve for low carbon steel.

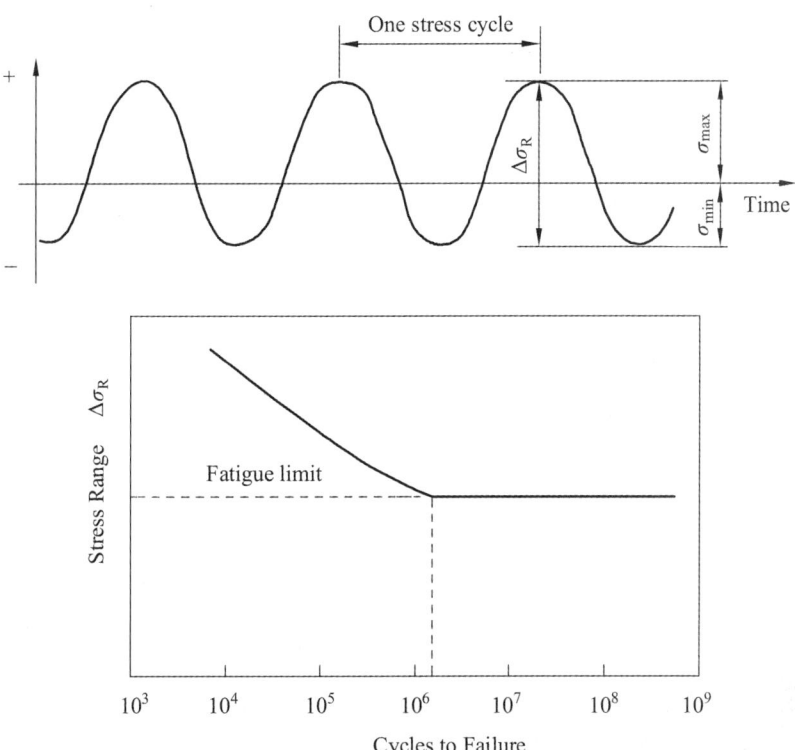

Figure 9.39 Fluctuating stresses and fatigue strength: (a) stress cycle; (b) typical S–N curve for low-carbon steel.

Steel components and connections in roadway bridges are susceptible to fatigue. Since welding process may create discontinuities within welds, distort the members, and cause residual stresses in the member, welded connections must be designed with careful consideration of fatigue. According to the railway and highway design codes, steel members and connections, welded or bolted, must be designed for the fatigue limit state or fatigue strength. The following requirements are specified the Chinese railway design code TB 10091.

1. The welded members and the welded connections

(1) For axial force members subjected to fluctuating tension or alternate tension and compression with $|\sigma_{max}| \geq |\sigma_{min}|$ or $\rho = \sigma_{min}/\sigma_{max} \geq -1$ (compressive stresses are designated as negative, tensile stresses as positive), the fatigue strength of the member shall meet the following condition:

$$\gamma_d \gamma_n (\sigma_{max} - \sigma_{min}) \leq \gamma_t [\sigma_0] \tag{9.11}$$

where, $[\sigma_0]$ is the allowable fatigue stress range; γ_d is a multi-track presence factor; γ_n is a modification factor considering the damage to intension-dominated members; γ_t is a modification factor considering different plate thickness, given by

$$\gamma_t = \begin{cases} 1 & \text{for } t \leqslant 25 \text{ mm} \\ \sqrt[4]{25/t} & \text{for } t > 25 \text{ mm} \end{cases} \quad (9.12)$$

(2) For axial force members subjected to alternate tension and compression with $|\sigma_{min}| \geqslant |\sigma_{max}|$ or $\rho = \sigma_{min}/\sigma_{max} < -1$, the fatigue strength shall meet the following condition:

$$\gamma_d \gamma_n'(\sigma_{max} - \sigma_{min}) \leqslant \gamma_t \gamma_\rho [\sigma_0] \quad (9.13)$$

where, γ_n' is a modification factor considering the damage to compression-dominated members; γ_ρ is a modification factor considering the stress ratio.

2. <u>The non-welded members and non-welded connections</u>

(1) For axial force members subjected to fluctuating tension, i.e., $\rho = \sigma_{min}/\sigma_{max} \geqslant 0$, the stress range shall meet the condition

$$\gamma_d \gamma_n(\sigma_{max} - \sigma_{min}) \leqslant \gamma_t [\sigma_0] \quad (9.14)$$

(2) For axial force members subjected to fluctuating tension and compression, i.e., $\rho = \sigma_{min}/\sigma_{max} < 0$, the stress range shall meet the condition

$$\gamma_d \gamma_n' \sigma_{max} \leqslant \gamma_t \gamma_\rho [\sigma_0] \quad (9.15)$$

The values of factors γ_d, γ_n (or γ_n'), and γ_ρ are given in the Chinese railway steel bridge design code TB 10091 Table 4.3.2, 4.3.6-1 to 4.3.6-4, and 4.3.6-5, respectively.

9.6 Construction of steel bridges

Construction is a key stage and the final step of building a steel bridge. It involves many challenging tasks. The aim of the construction is to produce the structural steel components to the proper unloaded shape, and have the members safely and efficiently fabricated in place, such that the completed structure satisfy the geometric and stress state requirements stipulated in the design drawings.

Construction of steel bridges includes two processes: fabrication and erection. Fabrication is the process used to manufacture steel bridge components that will, when assembled and connected, form a complete steel bridge. Erection is the process of erecting and connecting together the fabricated parts in the field at the project site.

9.6.1 Fabrication

The fabrication process involves many complex and interrelated activities in shops. The regular shop activities include material preparation, cutting, punching/drilling, fit-up assembly, bolting and/or welding, coatings and finishing, and quality control inspection.

1. Material preparation

Material preparation includes making of templates, marking of plates and shapes, cutting to shape, straightening, and edge preparation. The quality and dimensions of steel plates and shapes received from steel production mills must be in accordance with the requirements specified in the design drawings and other applicable specifications.

(1) Making of templates.

A template is a full-size model of a real steel component, and is used to mark the cut line and the positions of bolt holes in a steel plate. The templates are usually made up of thin steel sheet. A template used to drilling holes is shown in Figure 9.40.

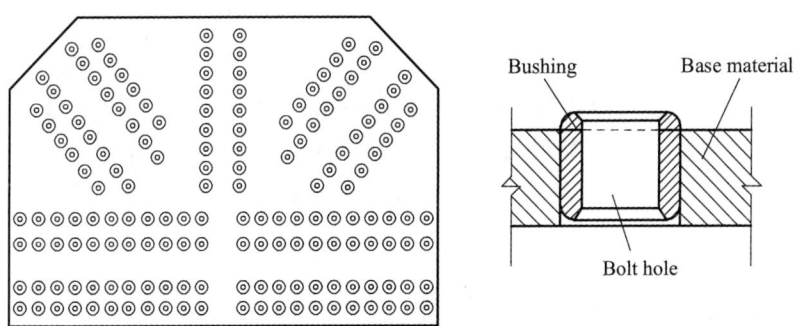

Figure 9.40 The template for bolt holes in gusset plate.

(2) Marking of plates and shapes.

The marking activity is to mark the cut lines and positions of holes in the surface of the raw steel plate using the templates, so that the steel plate can cut to size and shape according to the design requirements.

(3) Cutting to size and shape.

The cutting is an activity to cut the steel plates and shapes into designed sizes and shapes. The cutting methods depend on the thickness of plates, edge preparation specification, and dimensional tolerances. A common cutting method is the thermal flame cutting with oxy-acetylene or pure oxygen gases, which is used for cutting low-alloy steel plates. The metal powder cutting, the air carbon arc cutting, and the plasma cutting are usually used for cutting the high-alloy steel plates. Plasma cutting is fast and provides smooth and clean cut surfaces but is typically less effective than flame cutting for thick steel plates. The cutting of relatively thick plates is usually accomplished with mechanically guided thermal flame cutting equipment. Shearing and sawing are alternative cutting methods. Plates of moderate thickness can be sheared, while thinner plates may cut by laser and water cutting systems. Shapes may be cut by sawing or thermal cutting.

There are also many controlled automated cutting methods available to increase the cutting precision and shop productivity. Computer numerical control (CNC) laser cutting has proven to be one of the most efficient and cost-effective choices for precision metal cutting.

(4) Straightening.

Steel plates may be warped or deformed due to transportation or cutting. Thus, some plates and shapes may needs straightening to correct the distortion. Some plates need straightening before cutting, while others after cutting. The shot blasting or sandblasting technique is usually used to remove rust in the surface of the plates or shapes. Thin steel plates and shapes of small with camber or sweep can be straightened by cold bending. However, thick plates with distortion generally need heat or flame straightening.

(5) Finishing and edge preparation.

Finishing is generally required for the plates after being cut. Finishing by edge planing or end milling is often required for some members. Edge preparation is to bevel and groove the plate edges and prepare the edges for welding.

2. Hole drilling

Holes can be drilled or punched, or sub-drilled and reamed for mechanical connection bolts. The bolt holes in girders and trusses should be drilled to full size. Holes for bolts in bracing connections and diaphragms may be punched or drilled to full size. The drilling, punching, and reaming should be operated following the assembly requirements associated with different connection fasteners and satisfying the construction specifications.

3. Shop assembly for fit-up of steel components

Before formal welding and bolting, steel components and connections must be shop assembled to make sure that the fabricated members fit to within specified tolerances. The shop assembly involves bringing together the components using fit-up bolts, clamps, and tack welds according to the requirements in the design drawings. Full girder and truss may be required to be assembled in the shop to check the fit-up of the members and connections for accelerated field erection. Fit-up tolerances for welded and bolted connections are indicated in the construction specifications.

Short plate girders can be shipped completely assembled, including girders and transverse members. Longer plate girders and truss girders are usually first completely assembled in the shop, and then disassembled and shipped with girders, panels, connections, and deck system segments as separate subassemblies.

4. Welding

The welding process applies an electric current through an electrode to create an electric arc to the base metal, such that the welding rod and the base material at the ends of the arc are melted. Pieces are then joined by solidification of the molten metal pool. Shop welds can be made by the submerged arc welding, shielded metal arc welding, gas metal arc welding, electrogas welding, or other welding techniques. The types of weld, fillet or groove, are generally specified in the design and shop drawings.

5. Correction of welding-induced distortion

Welding-induced distortion is an intrinsic phenomenon occurring due to the thermally induced different strain distributions between the weld and surrounding material. The distortion can be minimized through control of weld size, edge preparation, heat input, sequencing, and joint restraint. If welding-induced distortion arises due to the inability to properly control weld shrinkage, post-welding straightening method can be adopted to correct the distortion. There are generally two methods for correcting the welding-induced distortion: cold mechanical straightening, hot mechanical straightening and flame straightening. The cold mechanical straightening is a process where the distorted member is straightened by applying force with a press or a hammer. The hot mechanical straightening is a process where heat is applied to all sides of the distorted member, and while the member is still hot it is straightened by applying force. The cold mechanical straightening may cause surface damage and work hardening of the steel, and may degrade the steel properties. Flame straightening is a process that eliminates deformation in welded structures quickly without impairing the material. In flame straightening, the deformed member is precisely and locally heated to a material-specific temperature at which plastic deformation occurs. Since the thermal expansion is restrained during heating, cooling of the member will result in shortening of the region around the deformed portion, leading to the desired change in length or shape.

6. Quality control inspection

After completion of fabrication, quality control inspection must be conducted ensure that the fabrication of plates and shapes into superstructure assemblies has been performed in accordance with the design requirements and specifications. The inspections include the following: examination of overall dimensions and geometry; nondestructive testing of fillet and groove welds in main members by magnetic particle testing (MPT), ultrasonic testing (UT), or radiographic testing (RT); checking of bolt hole locations, bolted connection clearances and fit-up accuracy; checking of splice plate orientation, fill plates, and all plies in contact when assembled; checking of member straightness and final sweep or camber.

7. Trial erection

Trial erection of bridge steelwork in the fabrication shop has been a traditional way of ensuring fit-up and geometry of steel members, so reducing the risk of delays in field erection. With the improved accuracy achieved by automated fabrication procedures, the need for trial erection for modern steel bridges has been reduced. Complete trial erection of a large structure may be impracticable. However, for some components with new structural configurations or manufactured with new materials or new techniques, partial trial erection is still necessary to avoid component misfit. Partial trial erection involves complex or close fitting connections, such as shear plate connections, gusset plate connections, girder splices.

After all the fabrication processes are completed, the steel bridge components are coated and marked, and then shipped with shop drawings to the project sit for erection.

9.6.2 Erection methods

There are many erection methods for steel bridges, which dependent on many factors, such as the site condition, the complexity of the structure, the availability of equipment, and the expertise of the erection organization. The erection methodology is closely associated with equipment. Erection of typical steel railway bridges involves the use of cranes, falsework, barges, and stationary and movable frames (gantries). The most commonly used erection methods for steel railway bridges are cantilever erection method, the incremental launching method, and the floating barge erection method. In selecting the erection method, consideration should also be taken into account regarding the access to and topography of the construction site, operating cost, and project schedule.

1. Cantilever erection method

The cantilever method is suitable for erection of steel truss bridges. The cantilever construction starts with assembling the steel truss sections over an interior pier using temporary bents or pier brackets to stabilize the truss panels. Once the panels at the top of the pier are erected, new panels are added to each end in an alternating fashion until mid-span or the abutment is reached (Figure 9.41). The same procedure is repeated again until the ends of the two cantilevers are ready for the installation of the closure pieces. Erection of truss bridges in this way involves the use of standard erection equipment and traveling derricks. Also, the cantilever erection can be conducted simultaneously from each interior pier, and geometry and deflection of trusses can be controlled by hydraulic jacks at the temporary supports. Cantilever construction precludes the need for falsework and has been used extensively for the erection of long-span steel truss bridges.

(a)

(b)

Figure 9.41 Cantilever erection of steel truss bridges: (a) Dashengguan Yangtze River Bridge; (b) Hutong Yangtze River Bridge.

2. The incremental launching method

This method of erection can be used for steel girder bridges and truss bridges. In this method of erection, the superstructure is first assembled on a roller system behind one of the abutments in segments of sufficient length to maintain stability during the launching. Then the structure is pulled or pushed over the abutment and across the opening until it reaches the first pier support (Figure 9.42). After the structure is properly aligned on the first pier, additional segments are assembled on the roller system behind the abutment and are advanced until the structure reaches the next pier. This launching process is continued until the entire superstructure rests on its permanent supports. Superstructures can be incrementally pulled with derricks or wire rope winches or pushed with hydraulic jacking systems.

This erection method requires minimal equipment to use, but the superstructure must be designed to resist the forces generated during launching. The erection forces in the girders can be minimized through the use of an erection nose attached to the leading end of the structure, which reduces the cantilever length of the structure.

The incremental launching method is usually used in the situation where the height of the bridge is excessive or the topography of the project site limit the access to erection cranes.

Figure 9.42　The incremental launching of the Shiji Yellow River Bridge.

3. The floating barge erection method

The basic idea of the floating barge erection is to use floating barges installed with lifting equipment to erect superstructure. In this method, barges are used to support stationary derrick cranes or mobile cranes, and the falsework on which the superstructure is supported. The erection operation involves assembly of steel members in the assembly yards on the shore, lift of the span onto the falsework, transportation of the assembly by barges to the erection site, and lowering the assembly into place by ballasting the barge or lowering the hydraulic jacks mounted on the tops of the falsework (Figure 9.43). In modern practices, floating cranes are usually used to transport the assembled bridge segment to the site and then directly lift the span in place (Figure 9.44). This erection method is suitable for the steel bridges crossing calm water with adequate depth. One of the advantages of this method is that the assembly of the steel members can be carried out concurrent with construction of substructures. Also, the docks and the barges can be used repeatedly.

(a)   (b)

Figure 9.43 The floating barge erection: (a) Qiangtan River Bridge (1943), Hangzhou, China; (b) George P. Coleman Bridge (1994), Yorktown, USA.

Figure 9.44 The floating barge erection of the Pingtan Strait Road-rail Bridge (2019), Fuzhou, China.

References

[9.1] Unsworth, J. F., *Design and Construction of Modern Steel Railway Bridges*, 2nd ed., CRC Press, London, 2018.

[9.2] Chatterjee, S., *The Design of Modern Steel Bridges*, 2nd ed., Blackwell Science, Oxford, 2003.

[9.3] Parke, G. and Hewson, N., eds., *ICE Manual of Bridge Engineering*, 2nd ed., Thomas Telford Ltd, London, 2008.

[9.4] Xanthakos, P. P., *Theory and Design of Bridges*, John Wiley & Sons, New York, 1994.

[9.5] Kulicki, J. M., "Highway Truss Bridges," in Chen W.-F., and Duan L., eds., *Bridge Engineering Handbook*, CRC Press, 2014.

[9.6] Taly, N., *Design of Modern Highway Bridges*, McGraw-Hill, New York, 1998.

[9.7] Barker, R. M. and Puckett, J. A., *Design of Highway Bridges: An*

LRFD Approach, 3rd ed., John Wiley & Sons, Hoboken, New Jersey, 2013.

[9.8] *Steel Bridge Design Handbook*, HWA-HIF-16-002, U.S. Department of Transportation, Federal Highway Administration, 2015.

[9.9] *Steel Construction Manual*, American Institute of Steel Construction (AISC), 14th ed., 2015

[9.10] Gorenc, B., Tinyou R., Syam, A. A., *Steel Designers' Handbook*, 7th ed., UNSW Press, Sydney, 2005.

[9.11] Fang, Q.-H., Gao, Z.-Y., and Li, J.-W., "Development course and prospect of steel railway bridges in China," *Journal of Architecture and Civil Engineering*, Vol. 25, No. 4, 2008, pp. 1-5.
方秦汉，高宗余，李加武. 中国铁路钢桥的发展历程及展望. 建筑科学与工程学报，2008，25（4）：1-5.

[9.12] Li, F.-W., Fu, K.-X., and Liu X.-X., eds., (Wang, H.-L., reviewer), *Steel Bridges*, China's Railway Press, Beijing, 1995.
李富文，伏魁先，刘学信. 钢桥. 王华廉，主审. 北京：中国铁道出版社，1995.

[9.13] Xu, J.-L., Sun, S.-H., eds., (Xiao, R.-C., Xu. G.-Y., reviewers), *Steel Bridges*, 2nd ed., China's Transportation Press, Beijing, 2011.
徐君兰，孙淑红. 钢桥. 2版. 肖汝成，徐恭义，主审. 北京：人民交通出版社，2011.

[9.14] Wu, C., ed., (Qiang, S.-Z., reviewer), *Modern Steel Bridges*, China's Transportation Press, Beijing, 2006.
吴冲. 现代钢桥. 强士中，主审. 北京：人民交通出版社，2006.

[9.15] *Railway* Bridges, Department of Engineering, Changsha Railway Institute, China's Railway Press, Beijing, 1984.
长沙铁道学院工程系主编. 铁路桥梁. 北京：中国铁道出版社，1984.

[9.16] Li, Y.-D., ed., Introduction *to Bridge Engineering* (in Chinese), 3rd ed., Southwest Jiaotong University Press, Chengdu, China, 2005.
李亚东. 桥梁工程概论. 3版. 成都：西南交通大学出版社，2014.

Chapter 10 Arch Bridges

10.1 Introduction

An arch is defined as a structural member that is shaped and supported in such a manner that the transverse loads are transferred to the supports primarily by axial compressive forces in the arch. For a specific loading pattern, the arch shape can be designed so as to avoid bending moments generated in the arch. Due to the curved design of the arch, an arch bridge usually exerts on the foundation both vertical and horizontal forces. Thus arch foundations must provide both vertical and horizontal resistance.

The arch bridge is one of the most popular bridge types, which came into use over 2000 years ago. The Anji Bridge in China is an ancient stone arch bridge built in Sui Dynasty (A. D. 581-618) and spans 37.02 m (Figure 1.6), which is the longest span length of stone arch bridge in the ancient world. The profile of the arch ribs of the Anji Bridge is a circular arc with a central angle of about 85° and the rise-to-span ratio of about 0.2. Its innovative design of the open spandrel with auxiliary arches reduces the self-weight of the main arch, which makes it span long distance. The Anji Bridge keeps standing firmly until today and was named an "International Historic Civil Engineering Landmark" by the American Society of Civil Engineers (ASCE) in 1991.

The analysis theory and construction technology of arch bridges were developed rapidly after the Industrial Revolution. As a result, arch bridges are widely employed in both the highway and railway transportation now. The longest railway arch bridge in the world is the Nujiang River Bridge on the Dali-Ruili Railway in China, whose main span length is 490 m. The longest span length of the highway arch bridge is 550 m, which is the span length of the Lupu Bridge in Shanghai, China. The Chaotianmen Yangtze River Bridge in Chongqing, China, has a span length of 552 m, which is the longest among those of the combined highway-railway arch bridges in the world.

10.2 Terminology of arch bridges

Terms used to describe various parts of an arch bridges are shown in Figure 10.1. The left half in the figure is a sketch of a solid spandrel arch bridge, while the right half is that of an open spandrel arch bridge.

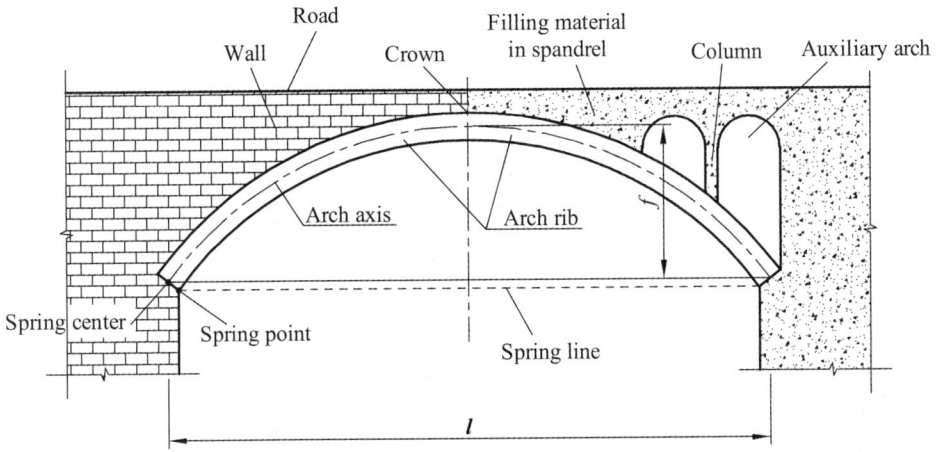

f – calculation rise, l – calculation span, f/l – calculation rise-span ratio

Figure 10.1 Arch bridge Terminology.

As shown in Figure 10.1, the spandrel of a solid spandrel arch is fully filled with the filling material, while there is some hollow space (sometimes divided by the columns) in the spandrel of an open spandrel arch. The calculation span length and calculation rise of an arch is defined with respect to the arch axis. The calculation span length is the horizontal distance between the two center of the springer, while the calculation rise is the vertical distance between the line connecting the centers of springers and the crown of the arch axis. The calculation rise-to-span ratio is the ratio of the calculation rise to the calculation span length. In the following discussion, unless otherwise specified, the term "rise", "span length", and and "rise-to-span ratio" stands for the calculation ones.

10.3 Materials for arch bridges

All kinds of known construction materials can be employed to build an arch rib. In fact, arch bridges can be classified into stone arch bridges, concrete arch bridges, steel arch bridges, and concrete-filled steel pipe (CFSP) arch bridges, depending on the materials used in constructing arch ribs.

10.3.1 Stone arch bridges

Stone arch bridges are usually the masonry bridges. The rib of a stone arch bridge is made from stone pieces, sometimes without any mortar or other adhesives. The compressive strength of a piece of stone is usually quite high while the tensile strength is very low. This means that an arch rib made from stone cannot afford bending moments.

The material properties limit the spans of stone arch bridges somewhat. However, they are still constructed in many places, especially in some areas of China, because the stone is usually cheap and convenient to be obtained. The span length of a carefully designed stone arch bridge can be longer than 100 m. The longest span length of stone arch bridges in the world is with the Danhe Bridge in Shanxi Province of China, which is 146 m in main span length.

In order to obtain a relatively large span, one must design the arch curve reasonably and reduce the spandrel weight as much as possible. The arch curve of the Danhe Bridge is a catenary, and this kind of arch curve will be discussed in Section 0. Also, the Danhe Bridge is an open spandrel arch bridge with a few auxiliary arches in the spandrel. The filling material in the spandrel is a specially chosen light-weight material.

Stone arch bridges are usually erected on the fully supporting scaffold. The scaffold should ensure the accuracy of arch profile. The disassembly process must be planned and monitored cautiously.

10.3.2 Concrete arch bridges

The tensile strength of concrete is quite low. Therefore it is usually reinforced by the steel, frames or fibers. Concrete is easy to be shaped into different rib sections and profiles and is cheaper than the steel. Therefore, the concrete arch bridges are widely used. Wanzhou Yangtze River Bridge in Chongqing, China, reinforced with stiffening CFST frame, possesses the longest span length (420 m) among the reinforced concrete arch bridges in the world.

The concrete arch bridges can be constructed by many methods. If the concrete is casted on site, the relatively light stiffening frame may be constructed first to support the concrete formworks. The concrete rib can be divided into many segments and casted one after another. Even one segment can be divided into a few sub-zones and casted in sequence.

10.3.3 Steel arch bridges

The material strength of steel is much higher than that of concrete. The self-weight of arch ribs made from steel is usually lighter than that made from concrete. Therefore, the horizontal thrust at the springing of a steel arch bridge is much smaller than that of a concrete one with the same span.

The ribs of steel arch bridges are usually made of steel boxes or steel truss. A rib with box-shaped section has high stiffness and bearing capacity, no matter it is bended or twisted. The connecting work of a box-shaped rib is relatively easier in comparison with that of a truss rib. However, the truss structures can usually obtain the large stiffness with less amount of steel. They consist of multiple smaller members which are easier to be delivered or erected. So the truss ribs are suitable to be constructed in mountainous areas where the large members may be difficult to be transported. The Lupu Bridge has the largest steel box section among all the steel arch bridges in the world, and the Chaotianmen Yangtze River Bridge has the longest span length among all the steel truss arch bridges.

With advent of high strength materials, the steel members are usually designed as the thin-walled members. Consequently, the stability problems of a whole structure, a steel member or a piece of steel plate become the major design issues. The stability problems may be even more dominant for a structure like arch bridges since the main internal forces in the arch rib are compressive forces.

10.3.4 Concrete-filled steel pipe (CFSP) arch bridge

When the CFSP arch rib is axially compressed, the concrete will expand transversely. However, the steel pipe will restrict the transverse expansion. Thus the concrete in the steel pipe will be compressed tri-axially. The concrete strength can be enhanced obviously when the concrete is tri-axially compressed. So the compressive bearing capacity and ductility of a CFSP arch rib are much larger than that of concrete one with the same section area. The material properties of CFSP rib make the CFSP arch bridge capable of spanning longer distances than concrete ones. The longest CFSP arch bridge is the Bosideng Bridge in Sichuan Province of China, with the main span length of 530 m.

The relatively lighter thin-walled pipes are easier to be transported and erected. Then the completed pipe rib can be used as the formwork to cast concrete. The concrete arch rib should be cast in a few batches. The amount of concrete casted in one batch should not be too large. Otherwise the weight of concrete may be too heavy for the pipe rib to afford. The concrete mixture must be designed very carefully to obtain the high workability. A key matter in the construction of a CFSP arch bridge is to ensure the concrete to fill the steel pipe thoroughly.

10.4 Structural classification of the arch

Depending on their structural forms, arches are classified into three types: three-hinged arch, two-hinged arch, and Hingeless arch.

10.4.1 Three-hinged arch

A three-hinged arch is an external statically determinate structure, as shown in Figure 10.2(a). The thermal deformations, concrete creep/shrinkage and uneven settlements do not cause any internal forces in the structure. This property makes the three-hinged arch bridges suitable to some relatively poor geological conditions. Nevertheless, it's quite hard to set a hinge in the concrete arch ribs. Even for the steel structures, the hinges are so complex that the construction and maintenance cost are high. Furthermore, the hinge on the arch crown may affect the evenness of the roadway. As a result, such type of arch bridges are rarely used nowadays.

10.4.2 Two-hinged arch

A two-hinged arch has one degree of external static indeterminacy, as shown in Figure 10.2(b). In comparison with a three-hinged arch bridge, a two-hinged arch bridge has no hinge at the arch crown. So the latter has higher stiffness and more even roadway, which enhances the serviceability of the bridge. Also, the internal forces in a two-hinged arch bridge is less influenced by the thermal deformations, concrete creep/shrinkage and uneven settlements than those in a hingeless arch bridge. The two-hinged arch bridges are still widely used in the world.

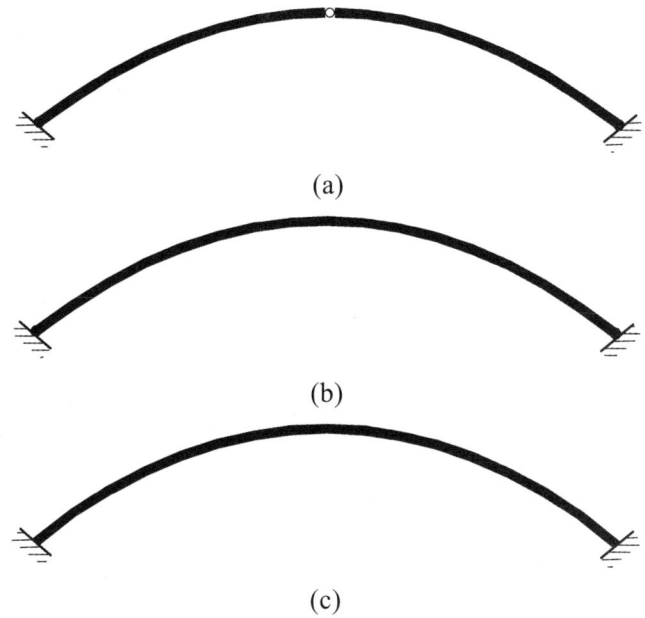

Figure 10.2 Three types of arches sorted according to their structural system: (a) Three-hinged arch; (b) Two-hinged arch; (c) Hingeless arch.

10.4.3 Hingeless arch

A hingeless arch has three degrees of external static indeterminacy, as shown in Figure 10.2(c). The absence of hinges make the hingeless arch bridges stiffer than the other two types. Besides, the construction of hingeless arch bridges is more convenient and the maintenance cost is lower. The bending moments and shear forces in the arch rib of the hingeless arch bridges are relatively uniform, which implies less material cost. Above all, the effects of additional internal forces resulted from the thermal deformations, concrete creep/shrinkage and uneven settlements will be less significant if the arch span is large enough. Consequently, the hingeless arches are the main option of the long-span arch bridges.

10.5 Structural characteristics of arch bridges

The arch bridges transfer the load downward to the foundation mainly through the internal compression in the ribs. The compression force at the arch springing therefore must cause a horizontal thrust to the substructure. On the one hand, if there's too large a bending moment in the arch rib, the tension failure may occur in some materials such as concrete and stone. Even if the steel rib is employed, there may be the problem of fatigue. On the other hand, the horizontal thrust may be a challenge to the foundation. If the arch springing is supported by a pier, the horizontal thrust may cause a large bending moment in the pier shaft. In summary, two of the most important aspects in the design of an arch bridge can be described as following:

(i) How can we keep the compressive force in the rib as dominant as possible?

(ii) How can we deal with the horizontal thrusts at the arch springing?

10.5.1 Shape of the arch axis and rise-to-span ratio

If we connect all the cross section centroids of an arch rib, the shape of the arch axis results. The points of application of the resultant compressive force on all cross sections form a line, which is termed line of pressure. If the arch rib axis coincide with the line of pressure at every cross section of the rib, the arch axis is called an "idealized arch axis". In this case, there is neither bending moments nor shear forces acting in the arch rib.

Let's consider a suspended wet soft cotton rope with two ends fixed, as shown in Figure 10.3. The rope droops because of its self-weight. A soft rope cannot resist any shear force, so there's only tensile force in the rope.

Figure 10.3 A suspended wet cotton rope.

If the wet rope is instantaneously frozen, the rope becomes a curved bar with a certain stiffness. The internal force in the bar is still tensile force only. Then we rotate the whole structure upside down and we get an arch rib, as shown in Figure 10.4. It's obvious that the profile of the arch rib is same as that of the original suspended wet cotton rope. The internal force in the rib is only compressive force, i.e. the axis of such a rib is an idealized axis. The axis of a suspended wet cotton rope is certainly a catenary, therefore the idealized shape of a homogeneous arch rib with a constant cross section is a catenary if it is loaded by the self-weight only.

It's evident that the idealized arch rib axis depends on the load pattern on the rib. Herein we can study a few load cases.

1. Load case I: self-weight of a vertically standing uniform arch rib

In fact, we can have a study on a symmetrical uniform plane arch rib shown in Figure 10.4. The arch is loaded only by the self-weight. The origin of a Cartesian coordinate system is fixed at the arch crown. The rise of the arch is f and the span length is l.

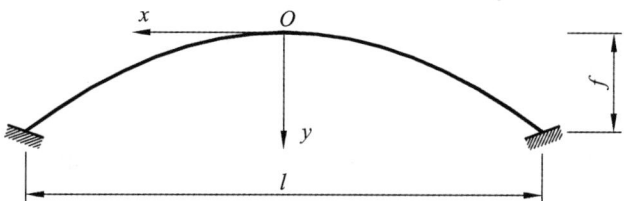

Figure 10.4 An arch rib with the same profile as a suspended wet cotton rope.

An arch rib segment of ds in length is considered, as shown in Figure 10.5. The self-weight of unit length of arch rib is q. If the centroidal axis of the arch rib is the line of pressure for the present load case, there are no bending moments and shear forces on the cross sections of the arch rib. The compressive axial force on the cross section corresponding to coordinate x is $N(x)$, while the axial force on the opposite cross section is $N(x) + dN$.

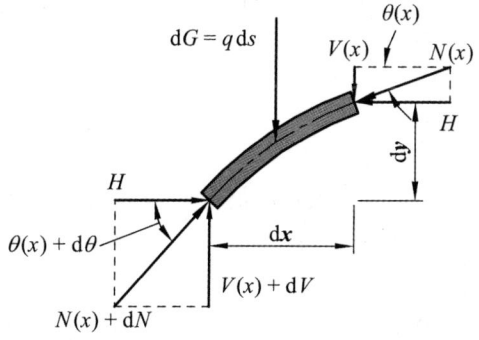

Figure 10.5 An arch segment whose length is ds.

The axial force N can be resolved into the horizontal component H and vertical component V. It can be concluded easily that the horizontal component of the axial force H is constant in the whole arch rib according to the horizontal equilibrium condition. If the angle between the tangent direction of the rib axis and the positive direction of x axis is θ, then the vertical component of the axial force is

$$V(x) = \begin{cases} H\tan\theta(x) = Hy' & (x \geqslant 0) \\ -H\tan\theta(x) = -Hy' & (x < 0) \end{cases} \quad (10.1)$$

The vertical equilibrium condition is written as

$$\begin{cases} V(x) + dV - V(x) - q\,ds = 0 & (x \geqslant 0) \\ -V(x) - dV + V(x) - q\,ds = 0 & (x < 0) \end{cases} \quad (10.2)$$

hence

$$dV = \begin{cases} q\,ds & (x \geqslant 0) \\ -q\,ds & (x < 0) \end{cases} \quad (10.3)$$

the length of the rib segment is nearly the distance between the two centroids of the two cross sections, i.e.

$$ds \approx \sqrt{(dx)^2 + (dy)^2} = \sqrt{1+y'^2}\,dx \quad (10.4)$$

substituting Eq. (10.1) and Eq. (10.4) into Eq. (10.3) results in

$$Hy'' = q\sqrt{1+y'^2} \quad (10.5)$$

this is an ordinary differential equation about the line of pressure of the arch rib $y(x)$. The boundary conditions for this equation are

$$y(0) = 0 \quad (10.6)$$
$$y'(0) = 0 \quad (10.7)$$
$$y(x) = y(-x) \quad (10.8)$$

The solution of Eq. (10.5) based on the boundary conditions Eq. (10.6) ~ Eq. (10.8) is a catenary function, i.e.

$$y = \frac{H}{q}\cosh\left(\frac{q}{H}x\right) - \frac{H}{q} \quad (10.9)$$

at the arch springing, $x = \pm l/2$, on can obtain the shear force by Eq. (10.1) as

$$V_s = H \sinh\left(\frac{ql}{2H}\right) \tag{10.10}$$

If the total length of the arch rib is L, it's obvious that

$$V_s = H \sinh\left(\frac{ql}{2H}\right) = \frac{qL}{2} \tag{10.11}$$

therefore

$$\frac{H}{q} = \frac{L}{2\sinh\left(\frac{ql}{2H}\right)} \tag{10.12}$$

the coordinate y at the arch springing is equal to f, i.e.

$$f = \frac{H}{q}\left[\cosh\left(\frac{ql}{2H}\right) - 1\right] \tag{10.13}$$

by substituting Eq. (10.12) into Eq. (10.13), we can obtain

$$f = \frac{L\left[\cosh\left(\frac{ql}{2H}\right) - 1\right]}{2\sinh\left(\frac{ql}{2H}\right)} \tag{10.14}$$

consequently, the horizontal thrust H can be obtained as

$$H = \frac{ql}{2\ln\frac{L+2f}{L-2f}} \tag{10.15}$$

on substituting Eq. (10.15) into Eq. (10.9), we can obtain

$$y = \frac{l}{2\beta}[\cosh(\beta\xi) - 1] \quad (-1 \leqslant \xi \leqslant 1) \tag{10.16}$$

where

$$\xi = \frac{2x}{l} \tag{10.17}$$

$$\beta = \ln\frac{L+2f}{L-2f} \tag{10.18}$$

Combination of Eq. (10.15) ~ Eq. (10.18) leads to the expression of the line of pressure for a vertically standing uniform arch rib loaded by its self-weight only.

The Taylor's expansion of the function in Eq. (10.16) at the point $\xi = 0$ is

$$y = \frac{\beta l}{4}\xi^2 + \frac{\beta^3 l}{48}\xi^4 + \frac{\beta^5 l}{1440}\xi^6 + \cdots \tag{10.19}$$

i.e., the first term of the Taylor's expansion is a parabolic function.

2. Load Case II : weight from the filling material of a solid spandrel arch

The material weight from the filling material of a solid spandrel arch is a distributed load shown in Figure 10.6 and q_0 and λ are two constant coefficients. The load density on the arch crown is q_0 and the arch rib axis is expressed as $y = y(x)$.

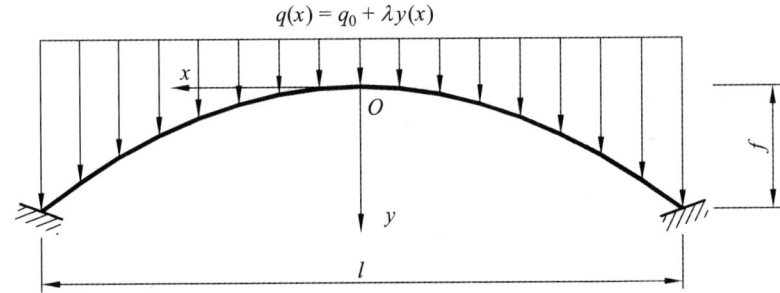

Fig 10.6   The spandrel material weight on an arch rib.

In a similar way with the first load case, the ordinary differential equation about the idealized arch rib axis $y(x)$ is

$$Hy'' = q_0 + \lambda y \tag{10.20}$$

the solution is also a catenary function, i.e.

$$y = \frac{q_0}{\lambda}\cosh\left(\sqrt{\frac{\lambda}{H}}x\right) - \frac{q_0}{\lambda} \tag{10.21}$$

at the arch spring, $x = \pm l/2$, we have

$$H = \frac{\lambda l^2}{4[\ln(m + \sqrt{m^2 - 1})]^2} \tag{10.22}$$

where

$$m = 1 + \frac{\lambda f}{q_0} \quad (10.23)$$

the load density at the arch springing is

$$q_s = q_0 + \lambda f \quad (10.24)$$

therefore

$$m = \frac{q_s}{q_0} \quad (10.25)$$

the coefficient m is usually called the arch axis coefficient. Then Eq. (10.21) can be rewritten as

$$y = \frac{f}{m-1}\cosh(k\xi) - \frac{f}{m-1} \quad (-1 \leqslant \xi \leqslant 1) \quad (10.26)$$

where

$$k = \ln(m + \sqrt{m^2 - 1}) \quad (10.27)$$

The Taylor's expansion of the function in Eq. (10.27) at the point $\xi = 0$ is

$$y = \frac{k^2 f}{2(m-1)}\xi^2 + \frac{k^4 f}{24(m-1)}\xi^4 + \frac{k^6 f}{720(m-1)}\xi^6 + \cdots \quad (10.28)$$

i.e., the first term of the Taylor's expansion is also a parabolic function.

3. Load Case III: uniformly distributed load

If a uniformly distributed load q_0 is acting on the arch rib, as shown in Figure 10.7, Eq. (10.5) is changed to

$$Hy'' = q_0 \quad (10.29)$$

The solution is a parabolic function, i.e.,

$$y = \frac{q_0}{2H}x^2 \quad (10.30)$$

at the arch spring, $x = \pm l/2$, there exists

$$H = \frac{q_0 l^2}{8f} \quad (10.31)$$

consequently

$$y = f\xi^2 \quad (-1 \leqslant \xi \leqslant 1) \tag{10.32}$$

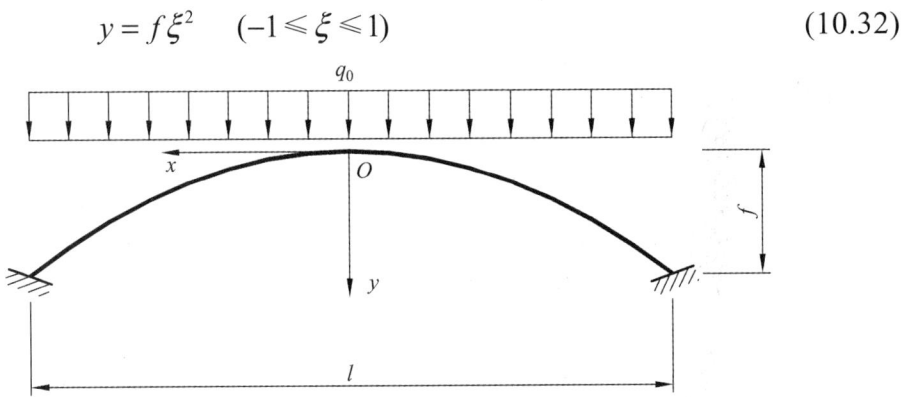

Figure 10.7 Horizontally distributed uniform load on an arch rib.

From the foregoing analysis of three different loading cases, we can draw the following conclusions:

(1) Since the dead load of a solid spandrel arch bridge consists usually of the self-weight of arch rib and the weight of spandrel material, its idealized axis shape should be a catenary.

(2) Since the first term in the Taylor's expansion of a catenary function is a parabolic term, a parabolic arch axis can be sometimes a good approximation to the idealized arch axis. With other parameters specified, the larger the arch rise is, the larger truncation error is obtained from such an approximation. Therefore, a parabolic arch axis should only be chosen when the rise-to-span ratio is small, or when an open spandrel arch bridge is used.

(3) A circular arc can only be the idealized arch axis when a circumferentially distributed uniform pressure is acting on the arch rib. However, most of the load patterns are quite different from such a case. Only when the rise-to-span ratio is fairly small or when the open spandrel is employed should a circular arc arch rib be chosen.

(4) If no bending moments and shear forces apear in the arch rib, a larger rise-to-span ratio can reduce the horizontal thrust at the arch springing. Since the span length of a bridge is usually determined by the site conditions, a reasonably larger arch rise may enhance the clearance under the bridge and may reduce the thrust.

In designing an arch bridge, the arch rib axis should be designed as close to the idealized one as possible. Nevertheless, the loads acting on the structure are so complex that it's hardly to find an idealized arch axis fitting for all the loading cases. As for the highway arch bridges, the dead loads are usually the dominant loads, so the arch rib can be designed according to the idealized axis for the dead loads. The railway arch bridges, however, are influenced by the live loads more obviously, so the arch axes are usually chosen as the line of pressure under the summation of the dead loads and one half of the live loads. The thus-designed arch rib axes are usually called "reasonable arch rib axes".

The loads acting on some kind of arch bridges, such as the open spandrel arch bridges, cannot be characterized by any of the aforementioned load cases. Hence it's very hard to find an idealized arch axis for any of these bridges. In these cases, a reasonable arch rib axis is usually determined in a way named "five-point method". In this method, we can choose such an arch axis that there are five points on the axis where the resultant axial compressive force acts at the centroid of the cross-section. The five points in this method are the arch crown, two arch springs, the one-fourth and the three-fourth of the span.

10.5.2 Structural measures to deal with the thrust

In most cases, an arch bridge should be constructed on a firm foundation to resist the horizontal thrust. The thrust need to be carefully handled in the design and construction process. First, the piers or foundations supporting the arch must have enough bearing capacity and stability. Pile foundations are widely employed for the arch bridges. Second, if the foundations are not strong enough to resist the thrust, a tie connecting the springers of the arch can be used to provide the reaction to the thrust. A tied arch bridge is similar to a bow, as shown in Figure 10.8.

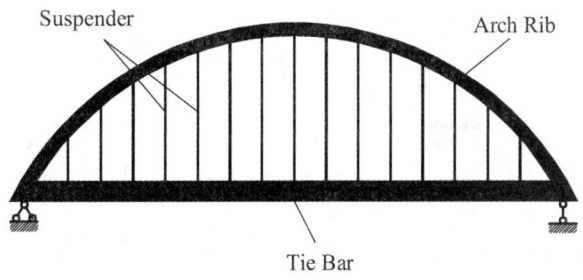

Figure 10.8 A tied arch bridge similar to a bow.

The two ends of bow limbs are tied by a bowstring. thus, the movements of the two ends of the bow are constrained by the bowstring. The thrusts in the bow limbs are counteracted by the tension in the bow string. At the two ends of the bow, there are no thrusts that need to be resisted by external structures

In a similar manner, if any loads are applied to the arch rib of a tied arch bridge, the opposite movements of two arch springing are constrained by the tie. Thus, the thrust at the arch springing are counteracted by the tension in the tie.

The tying element can be the roadway deck which made of steel girders, trusses, or cables. If a girder or a truss is employed as the tying element, the girder or truss may be erected on the scaffolds before the closure of the arch. A concrete tie should be prestressed because of the tension caused by the external loads. If the tie is made of the cables, the cable force may be exerted successively in different construction stages.

If two neighboring arches share the same pier, the thrusts transferred from the two arch springing must be balanced. Otherwise the pier may be pushed over. Thus, a multiple-span arch bridge should be designed with equal span lengths. If the span lengths of two neighboring arches are not equal, the following measures should be taken:

(1) The rise-to-span ratio of the arch with longer span length should be larger than that of the arch with small span length, as shown in Figure 10.9.

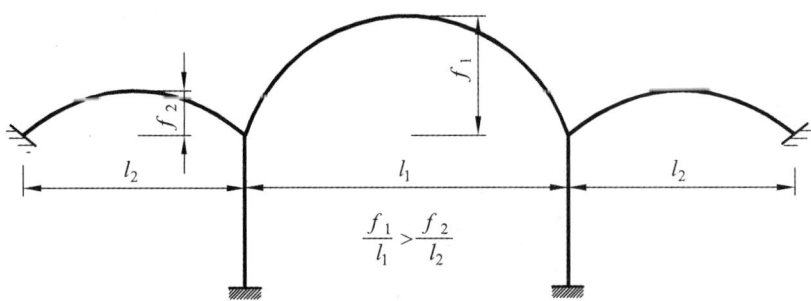

Figure 10.9 Multiple-span arches with unequal spans and unequal rise-to-span ratio.

(2) The arch with long span length should be designed with the open

spandrel, while the arch with short span length should be designed with solid spandrel arch, as shown in Figure 10.10.

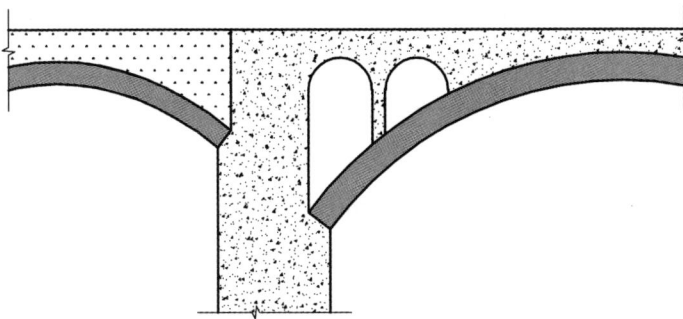

Figure 10.10 Multiple arches with different spandrel type, padding thickness and spring elevation.

(3) The depth of the filling material on the crown of the short-span arch should be larger than that of the long-span arch, as shown in Figure 10.10.

(4) The arch springings of the short-span arch should be located higher than that of the long-span arch, as shown in Figure 10.10, so that the bending moments generated by the thrusts in the adjacent archs can be balanced.

(5) The main span (i.e., the longest span) should be built with steel structure while the side span (usually the short span) should be built with concrete structure.

10.6 Construction methods for arch bridges

There are a lot of construction methods suitable for arch bridges, such as scaffold method, cantilever method, rotation method and lifting method.

10.6.1 Scaffold method

In this method, the arch bridge is constructed on a fully supporting scaffold. All of the self-weight of the arch bridge are supported by the scaffold before the arch ribs can afford them. The profile of the arch rib depends on the shape of the scaffold. During construction, the possible scaffold deformation must be taken into account.

The stress in the arch rib is very sensitive to the change of the arch axis.

The deviation of the rib profile from the reasonable arch axis may cause obvious bending moment which can reduce the compression resistance of arch rib. On the other hand, the compressive axial force in the arch ribs is usually very large, thus the buckling failure is one of the failure modes. The salient feature of the buckling failure is the sudden loss of stability without any obvious alert.. Therefore, monitoring the change of the arch axis during construction and during unloading of the scaffold is necessary.

The dismantling sequence of the scaffold is very important. Usually the scaffold should be symmetrically dismantled from the crown to the springing. For the multiple-span arch bridges, this should be done from the middle span to the side spans. The removal of supporters between the scaffold and the arch rib should be carried out in several steps. Only a small amount of supporters can be removed in a step.

The implementation of the scaffold method is complicated. The cost of scaffold may be high. The scaffold under the arch bridge may become an obstacle to the traffic under the bridge. Thus, this method is only suitable for the arch bridges with short span lengths.

10.6.2 Cantilever method

In the cantilever method, the arch rib is erected starting from the springing, and then the rib segments or members are added to the erected part, through the suspension cable and connected hangers. The erected part of arch rib looks like a cantilever, although it is usually supported by some stay cables anchored on the temporary pylons, as shown in Figure 10.11. At last, two cantilevers are closed with the closure segment and the whole arch rib is completed. Sometimes the stay cables may be replaced by a set of truss and cables for the erection of an arch bridge, such as the Krk Bridge in Croatia.

The cable system is somewhat vulnerable to strong wind. So the wind-resistance cables are necessary for the system. The structure stability under wind load and other loads before closure of the arch rib must be checked in the design process. The cable forces in the stay cables and backstays must be in equilibrium in order to ensure the stability of the temporary pylon.

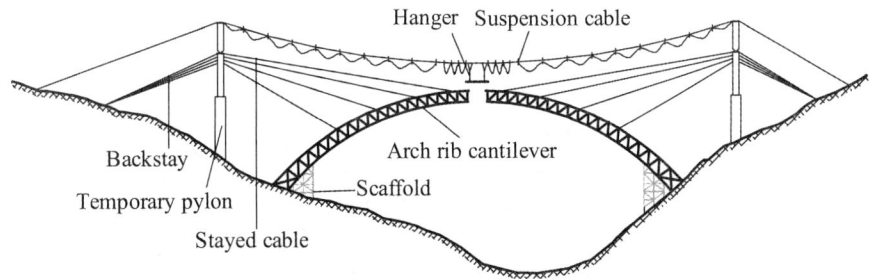

Figure 10.11 Sketch of cantilever method for arch rib erection.

The cantilever method doesn't require a lot of scaffolds under the arch rib and has little disturbance on the traffic under the bridge. This method is widely used for the construction of large-span arch bridges.

10.6.3 Rotation method

Sometimes the arch rib can be rotated in the vertical and horizontal planes. For example, the arch ribs can be erected at a lower position (Figure 10.12a) or at a higher position first so to save the scaffolding work (Figure 10.12b). Then the arch ribs are rotated vertically to the appropriate position before closure.

If the arch bridge is constructed over a deep canyon or a torrential river, it may be difficult to erect the arch ribs directly over the canyon or river. In this case, the arch rib can be erected and supported in the field parallel to the canyon or river and then rotated horizontally to the appropriate position before closure (Figure 10.13).

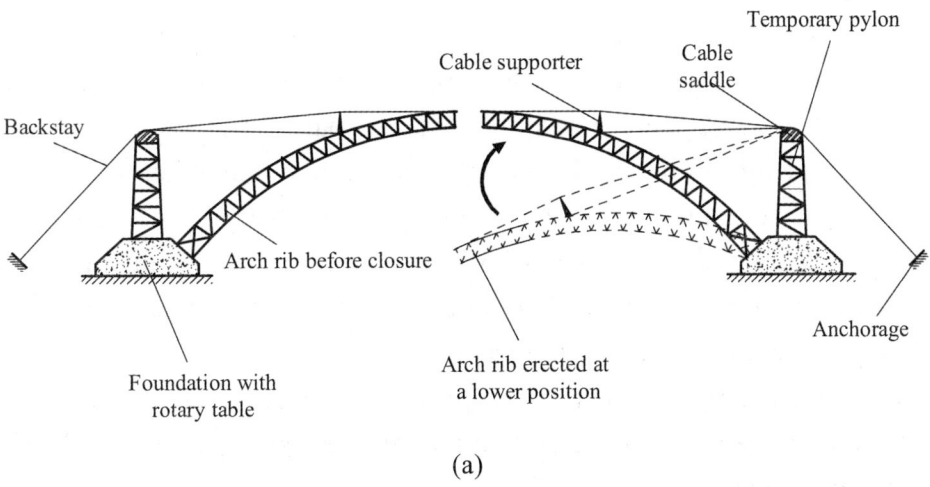

(a)

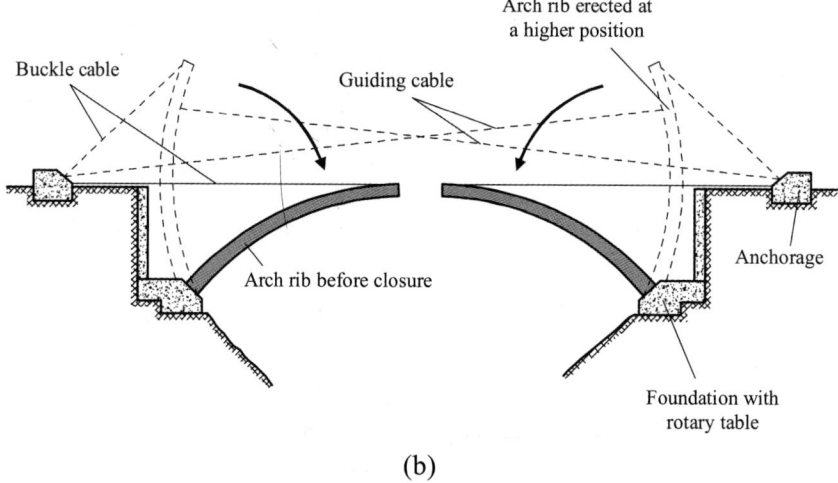

(b)

Figure 10.12 Vertical rotation of arch ribs.

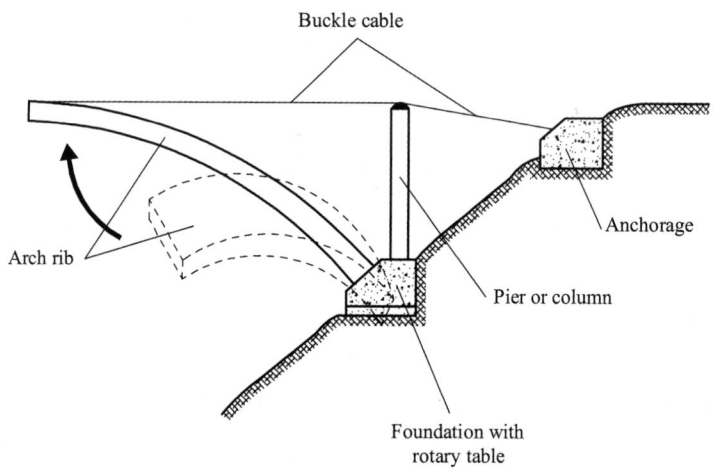

Figure 10.13 Horizontal rotation of arch ribs.

Sometimes, the erection process of an arch rib is the combination of both horizontal rotation and vertical rotation. For example, the Wenfeng Road Overpass in Anyang City, Henan Province, spans over 14 tracks of the Beijing-Guangzhou Railway. In order to minimize the obstruction to the railway traffic., the arch rib of the Wenfeng Road Overpass was constructed along the railway and then rotated horizontally to the design position before the closure. Before the horizontal rotating, the arch ribs were constructed at a lower position and then rotated vertically.

The horizontal rotation can be employed not only in the construction of arch bridges but also in the construction of continuous girder bridges and cable-stayed bridges.

References

[10.1] Parke, G. and Hewson, N., eds., *ICE Manual of Bridge Engineering*, 2nd ed., Thomas Telford Ltd, London, 2008.

[10.2] Xanthakos, P. P., *Theory and Design of Bridges*, John Wiley & Sons, New York, 1994.

[10.3] Karnovsky, I. A., *Theory of Arch Bridges—Strength, Stability, Vibration*, Springer Science+Business Media, 2012.

[10.4] Douglas, A. Nettleton, D. A., and John S. Torkelson, J. S., *Arch Bridges*, Federal Highway Administration, U.S. Department of Transportation, Washington, D.C., 1977.

[10.5] Hedgren, A. W., "Arch Bridges," in Brockenbrough, B. R., and Merritt, F. S., eds., *Structural Steel Designer's Handbook*, McGraw-Hill, New York, 2006.

[10.6] Li, Y.-D., ed., *Introduction to Bridge Engineering* (in Chinese), 3rd ed., Southwest Jiaotong University Press, Chengdu, China, 2005.

李亚东. 桥梁工程概论. 3 版. 成都：西南交通大学出版社，2014.

[10.7] Yao, L.-S, ed., (Xiang, H.-F., Gu, A.-B., reviewers), *Bridge Engineering*, 2nd ed., China Communications Press, Beijing, China, 2008.

姚玲森. 桥梁工程. 2 版. 项海帆，顾安邦，主审. 北京：人民交通出版社，2008.

[10.8] Fan, L.-C., ed., *Bridge Engineering*, 2nd ed., China Communications Press, Beijing, China, 1988.

范立础. 桥梁工程. 2 版. 北京：人民交通出版社，1988.

[10.9] Qiang, S.-Z., ed., Shao X.-D., assoc. ed., *Bridge Engineering*, 2nd ed., Higher Education Press, Beijing, 2011.

强士中. 桥梁工程. 2 版. 北京：高等教育出版社，2011.

[10.10] He, G.-H., Che H.-M., and Xie Y.-F., *Railway Reinforced Concrete Bridges*, China Railway Press, Beijing, 1986.

何广汉，车惠民，谢幼藩. 铁路钢筋混凝土桥. 北京：中国铁道出版社，1986.

[10.11] Shao, X.-D., ed., (Gu, A.-B., reviewer), *Bridge Engineering*, 4th ed., China Communications Press Co., Ltd., Beijing, China, 2018.

邵旭东. 桥梁工程. 4 版. 顾安邦，主审. 北京：人民交通出版社，2018.

Chapter 11 *Cable-Stayed Bridges*

11.1 Introduction

The cable-stayed bridges is a type of bridge in which the deck is supported by a number of diagonal cables running directly from the tower in a fan-like or parallel pattern. The towers transfer the cable forces to the foundations by vertical compression and tension forces in the cables also generate compression force in the deck.

The use of inclined stays as a tension support to a bridge deck has been evolving over a period of 400 years, and has become a well-known concept in bridge construction. The first "cable-stayed" bridge in Europe was built in 1784 at Freiburg. It was a timber bridge and the members suspending the girder are in fact wooden bars. An iron cable-stayed bridge was built in 1817 at Dryburgh Abbey, Scotland, as shown in Figure 11.1. The span was 261 ft., i.e., about 80 m. The girder of the bridge were supported by inclined chains consisting of iron rods.

This bridge collapsed in 1818 because of the failure of the connection between the rods. In fact, all of the early cable-stayed bridges suffered from large deflection or low strength of iron cables. The cables without pre-tension might relax and led to the failure of the whole structural system.

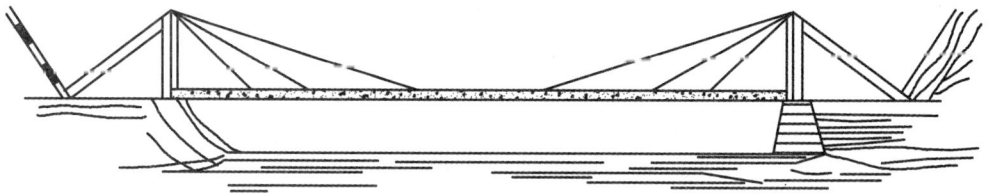

Figure 11.1   Iron cable-stayed bridge built in 1817 at Dryburgh Abbey.

The modern cable-stayed bridges use high-strength steel wires as the stay-cables which can be tensioned to a very high stress level. The pre-tensioned cables suspend the girder elastically. Such a supporting system can reduce substantially the bending moment in the girder., which is the reason that the span length of a cable-stayed bridge can be very long. The longest span length of cable-stayed bridges has reached 1,104 m, which is the span length of the Russky Island Bridge at Vladivostok, Russia.

However, the extra long span length increases the difficulties and risks of the construction work. For example, the construction control and monitoring become hard for long-span cable-stayed bridges, since the structure becomes a high-order static indeterminate due to a great number of stayed cables. Furthermore, the erection of each stay-cable changes the degree of determinacy of the bridge by one order. A lot of such changes make the structural analysis process more complicated. Fortunately, modern computer techniques made it possible to accomplish the complicated design calculation rapidly. The finite element analysis software makes the design calculation and analyses easier and convenient.

11.2 Structural characteristics of cable-stayed bridges

The load on a cable-stayed bridge is mainly supported by the girder, the cables, the pylons, and the piers. The dead load and some of the live loads, such as the vehicular loads and pedestrian loads, act on the girder. The girder is supported by the cables, the piers and, in some cases, the abutments and/or the pylons. Among these supporting elements, the cables support most (maybe about 90%) of the girder weight and live loads. The bending moments in the girder caused by the self-weight, secondary dead load, and live loads should be counteracted by the bending moments generated by the cable forces, as shown in Figure 11.2(a). Because all the cable forces have components parallel to the girder axis, the girder is compressed and the maximum axial compression usually occurs at the place intersecting with the pylons, as shown in Figure 11.2(b).

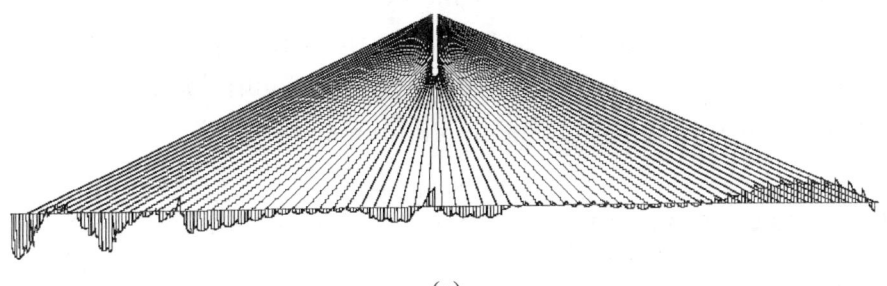

(a)

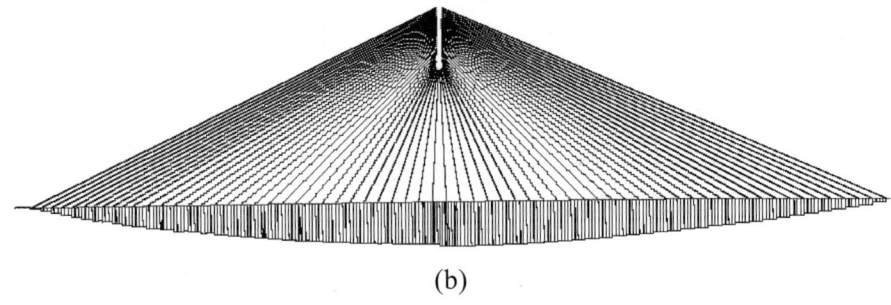
(b)

Fig 11.2 Typical internal forces diagram of the girder of a cable-stayed bridge: (a) Bending moment; (b) Axial force.

The upper ends of the cables are anchored on the pylons. The cable force can be resolved into two components: one parallel to the pylon axis and the other perpendicular to the pylon axis. The pylons are mainly subjected to the combined axial compression and bending moments. The bending moments in the pylons should be optimized through balancing the cable forces on the opposite two sides of the pylon. Since the pylons are usually slender, the unbalanced cable forces may lead to deformation of the pylon. Therefore the deflection of the pylon must be controlled carefully during the whole construction process and the service period.

Finally, all the dead loads and live loads are transferred to the foundation directly or indirectly through the pylons, pier and abutments. It can be seen that the load transfer path of a cable-stayed bridge is not as simple as that of other types of bridges. The girder, the cables, and the pylons act together to resist external loads, and at the same time, the behavior of the girder, pylons, and the cables are coupled together.

11.3 Configuration of cable-stayed bridges

The main concerns in the design and construction control of cable-stayed bridges are the deflections of and stresses in the girder and pylons, as well as the stresses in the cable Hence the structural configuration of a cable-stayed bridge should meet the relevant design requirements.

11.3.1 Span arrangement of girder

Usually a cable-stayed bridge has several spans. In most cases, the longest span is called the "main span". The main span is usually between two pylons and has longest span length Therefore the main span can be called "mid span". The other spans are usually at the two sides of the main span and are called "side spans". If the length of main span is L_m and the total length of the other spans on one side of the main span is L_s, as shown in Figure 11.3, the span ratio L_s/L_m is a key parameter in the cable-stayed bridge design.

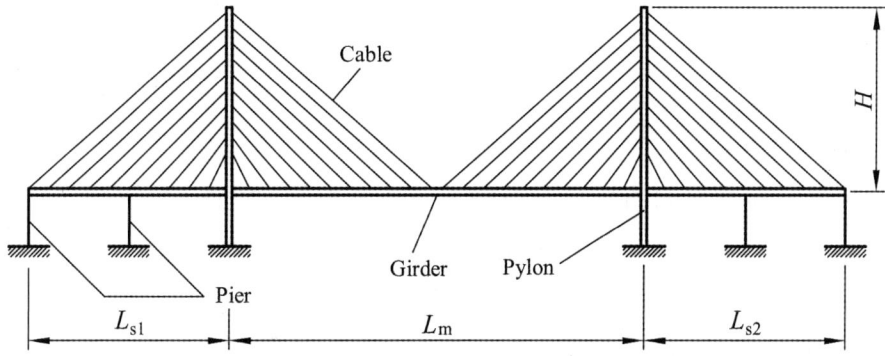

Figure 11.3 Typical components of a modern cable-stayed bridge.

Since the girders of cable-stayed bridges are continuous, the span ratio of a cable-stayed bridge has a similar sense as continuous girder bridges. If the span ratio is too large, the bending moment in the side span may be too large. On the contrary, if the span ratio is too small, the reactions at the side support may be a tensile force, which can result in increase of construction and maintenance cost. A problem existing for the high-speed railway cable-stayed bridge is that if the span ratio is too small, there can be a large rotation angle of the girder end at the transition pier (i.e. the pier located at the boundary of the main bridge and the approach bridge), which causes an uneven profile of track at that place. This is a potential threat to the riding quality of a high-speed railway bridge.

The main span is determined according to many factors, such as the function requirement, the structural feasibility, the geological conditions, the hydrological conditions, the navigation requirement, the construction convenience, the aesthetic consideration, etc. The largest ten cable-stayed bridges ranked by main span length are listed in Table 10.1. Once a length of main span is chosen, the length of side span can also be determined with a reasonable span ratio.

Table 10.1 Largest Ten Cable-Stayed Bridges Ranked by Main Span[a]

No.	Name of Bridge	Nation	L_m/m	L_s/m	H^b/m	Type of Girder	Year of Open
1	Changtai Yangtze River Bridge	China	1,176	632	289	Steel Truss	U.C.[c]
2	Russky Island Bridge	Russia	1,104	384	250.9	Hybrid	2012
3	Hutong Yangtze River Bridge	China	1,092	602	271	Steel Truss	U.C.
4	Sutong Yangtze River Bridge	China	1,088	500	236.3	Steel Box	2008
5	Stonecutters Bridge	China	1,018	289	222.5	Hybrid	2008
6	Qingshan Yangtze River Bridge	China	938	350	213.3	Hybrid	2019
7	Edong Yangtze River Bridge	China	926	275	218.5	Hybrid	2010
8	Jiayu Yangtze River Bridge	China	920	300/430[d]	213.2	Hybrid	2019
9	Tatara Bridge	Japan	890	270	194	Hybrid	1999
10	Pont de Normandie	France	856	451.75[e]	155.8	Hybrid	1995

Note: a. The data in table are updated by July 2019.
   b. The height of pylon is measured from the top of the lower cross beam of the pylon to the pylon top. If there's no a lower cross beam, it is measured from the top of the bridge deck.
   c. The abbreviation "U.C." means "Under Construction".
   d. The side span length on one side of the main span of Jiayu Yangtze River Bridge is 300 m while that on the other side is 430 m.
   e. The side span of Pont de Normandie is continuously connected with the approach bridge.

In fact, the span ratio L_s/L_m usually depends on the material of the girder. The girder can be made from steel and/or concrete. The steel girders are usually classified into steel truss girder, steel box girder, and steel plate girder. If all of the cross sections of a girder consist of different materials (e.g., as shown in Figure 11.4, the concrete deck slabs are supported and combined with the steel girders and steel cross beams), the girder is called as "composite girder". If the different region of the girder are made from different materials, the girder is called as "hybrid girder". The hybrid girders consist sometimes of the concrete segments and steel segments while in other cases the concrete or steel girder segments are connected with composite ones. As shown in Figure 11.5, different types of girder segments may form different combinations. The heavier part of a hybrid girder (e.g., the concrete segments) are mostly assigned on the side span while the lighter ones (e.g., the steel segments or composite segments) on the main span. In some cases, one of the side spans consists of concrete segments while the main span and the other side span include only steel segments or composite segments.

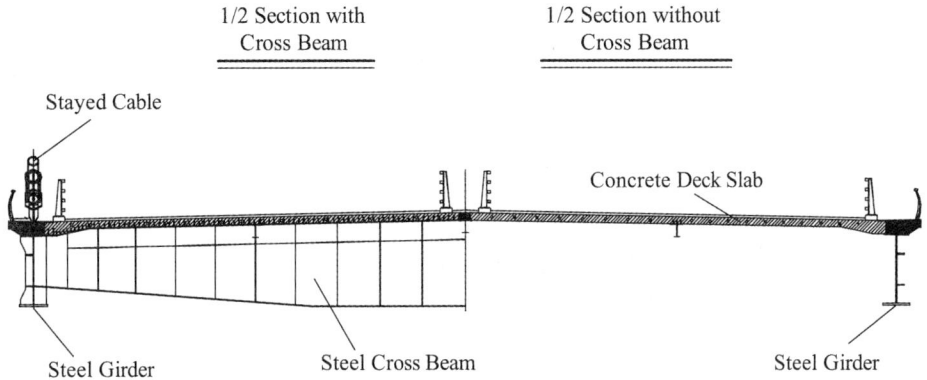

Figure 11.4   A typical cross-section of a composite girder.

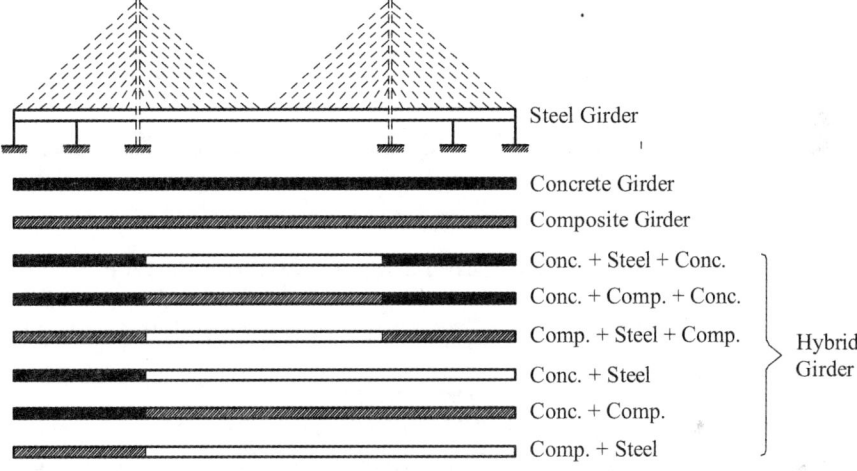

Figure 11.5   Different types of girders.

The span ratios of some cable-stayed bridges are shown in Figure 11.6. The main spans of these bridges are no less than 500 m. The different types of girders are marked by different symbols. In some cases, e. g. the Jiayu Yangtze River Bridge, one of its side spans is occupied by the concrete girder while the other comprises the steel box girder, which is the same as the main span. Therefore, there may be two different symbols assigned for the same cable-stayed bridge. The span ratio of the successful design can be considered as reasonable, so the varying range of the symbols in the figure has great significance as reference source. It should be noted that only the following cable-stayed bridges are included in Figure 11.6:

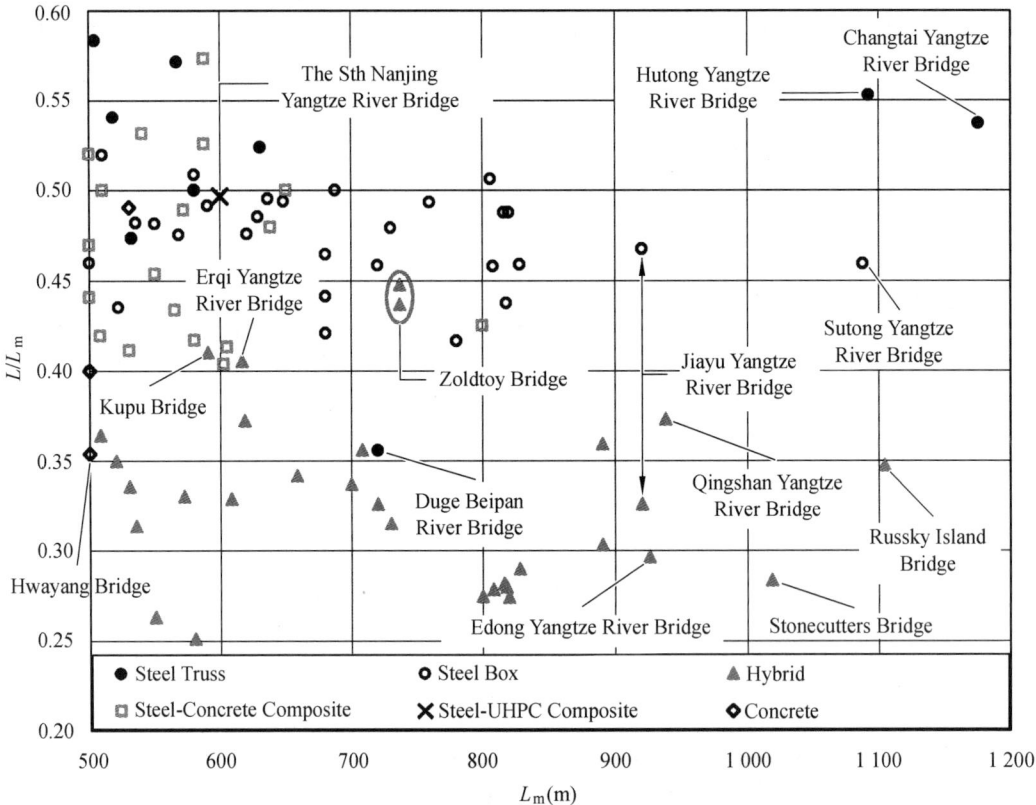

Figure 11.6 Span ratio of cable-stayed bridges with different types of girders.

(1) The girder of the cable-stayed bridge is not connected with the girder of other bridges continuously.

(2) The stay cables support almost all of the girder.

(3) The pylons of the cable-stayed bridge are of almost the same height same height.

(4) The transition zones between different regions on a hybrid girder are located close to the pylons.

The bending moment in pylons caused by the main span should be balanced to a certain degree by that caused by the side span. If the side span girder is made from concrete and the main span girder from steel, it's obvious that a smaller span ratio is preferred since the concrete girders are usually much heavier than steel ones on the same bridge. On the contrary, if the main span and side span are both made of the same material, the span ratio should be larger. That's why the triangle symbols in Figure 11.6 are mostly lower than the other ones. A suggestion can be provided to the designers of cable-stayed bridges on the basis of Figure 11.6 that the reasonable range of span ratio should be:

$$\frac{L_s}{L_m} = \begin{cases} 0.25 \sim 0.4 & \text{(side span is different from main span in material)} \\ 0.4 \sim 0.6 & \text{(side span and main span have the same material)} \end{cases} \quad (11.1)$$

It can be seen from Figure 11.6 that the span ratio of all hybrid girders ranges from 0.25 to 0.45. In fact, mostly the span ratio of hybrid girders is smaller than 0.40 except for a few cases. Two of the exceptional symbols belong to the Zolotoy Bridge in Vladivostok, Russia. The other two exceptional symbols stand for Xupu Bridge in Shanghai, China and Erqi Yangtze River Bridge in Wuhan, China. In fact, the main span girders of Xupu Bridge and Erqi Yangtze River Bridge are both the steel-concrete composite girders, which is heavier than the steel girders. Thus, the difference in weight between the main span and side span of composite-concrete hybrid girders is smaller than that of steel-concrete hybrid girders. As a results, it's reasonable for Xupu Bridge and Erqi Yangtze River Bridge to have the relatively larger span ratio.

As long as the type of the girder on side span is the same as that on the main span, the span ratio of most cable-stayed bridges ranges from 0.4 to 0.6, no matter whether the girder is made of steel, concrete, or composite materials. It is so even if the normal concrete is replaced by the ultra-high- performance concrete (UHPC), e.g. the 5th Nanjing Yangtze River Bridge.

11.3.2 Cables

The cables are the connections between the pylons and girder. Most of the loads acting on the girder is supported by the cables.

<u>1. Cable plane</u>

The cables are usually located in one or more planes. Such planes are called "cable planes". Some of the cable-stayed bridges have only one cable plane, as shown in Figure 11.7(a). The single cable plane may give the bridge a slim, light and concise look. However, the cables cannot resist torsion on the girder in the single plane. Accordingly, the torsion on girder in this case will be concentrated at the joints with the pylons, piers and abutments. The girder must have the ability to resist torsion. Thus box-type sections are usually used. Anyway, the deck supported by a single cable plane cannot be too wide.

Most of the cable-stayed bridges are supported by double cable planes, as shown in Figure 11.7(b). It's evident that the girders supported by double cable planes are more stable than those supported only by single cable plane. Most of the torsion acted on the girder can be balanced by the cable forces on the both side of the deck. Therefore, the deck can be wider than the deck with a single cable plane. In some cases, the girder can even be free from the vertical support of pylons. Besides, the transversely inclined cable planes can increase the wind resistance of the girder.

If the deck is too wide or the live load on it is too large, such as the train load, it may be necessary to provide additional supports on the central line of the girder, i.e. provide the third cable plane [Figure 11.7(c)]. Another possible solution is to divide the deck into two parallel ones and the girders are supported by four cable planes [Figure 11.7(d)].

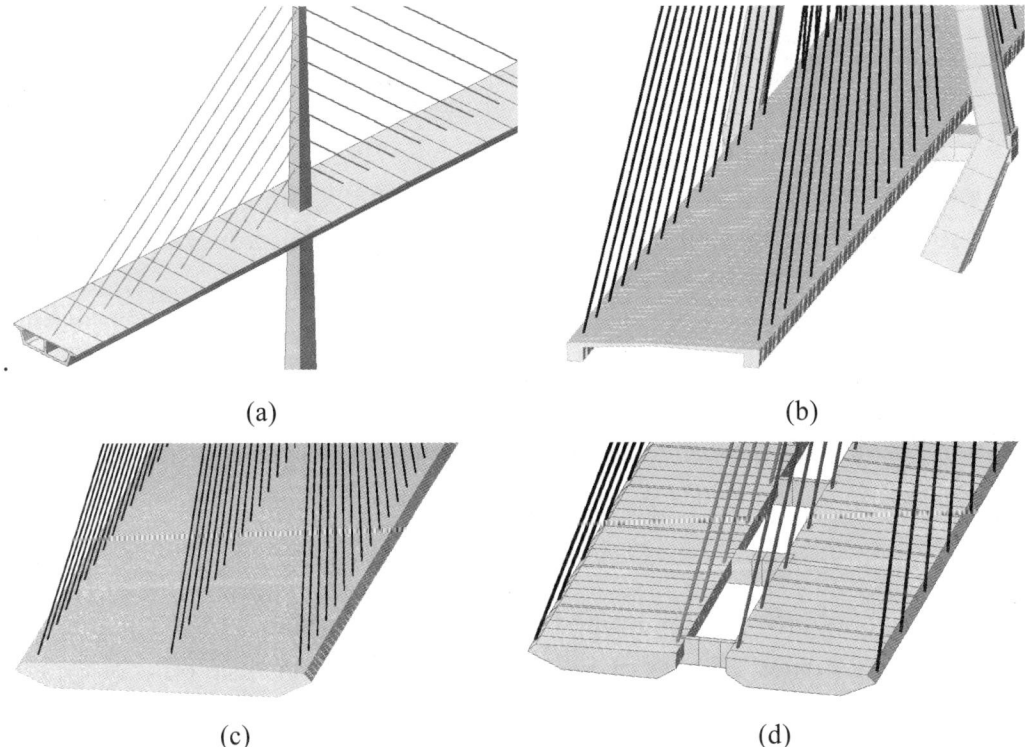

Figure 11.7 Single and multiple cable planes of cable-stayed bridges: (a) Single cable plane; (b) Double cable planes; (c) Three cable planes; (d) Four cable planes.

The cables in a cable plane can be arranged in many possible ways.

The upper cable anchoring points in Figure 11.8(a) are concentrated in a small zone. The shape of such a cable plane is called the "fan pattern". Since the fan-pattern cable plane has such a contracted anchorage zone, the pylon height of the cable-stayed bridge can be relatively small. This implies less cost of construction. Nevertheless, number of the cables in this case cannot be too many because of the structure complexity of the upper anchorage zone.

The cables in the cable planes in Figure 11.8(b) are parallel to each other and this arrangement is called the harp pattern. The parallel shape of cable planes makes it possible to assign enough cables and their anchorages on the pylon. Therefore, such a cable plane shape is more widely used in long-span cable-stayed bridges. However, a pylon with harp-pattern cable planes should be much higher than that with fan-pattern cable planes.

The modified fan-pattern cable planes in Figure 11.8(c) combine the advantages of the fan-pattern and the harp pattern. The anchorage zone on a pylon is neither too large nor too small. Since many cables can be anchored on the pylon by this pattern, the girders can be supported with sufficient cables. Furthermore, if the pylon height is the same, the span length of the girder supported by the modified fan-pattern cables will be longer than that supported by the harp-patterned cables.

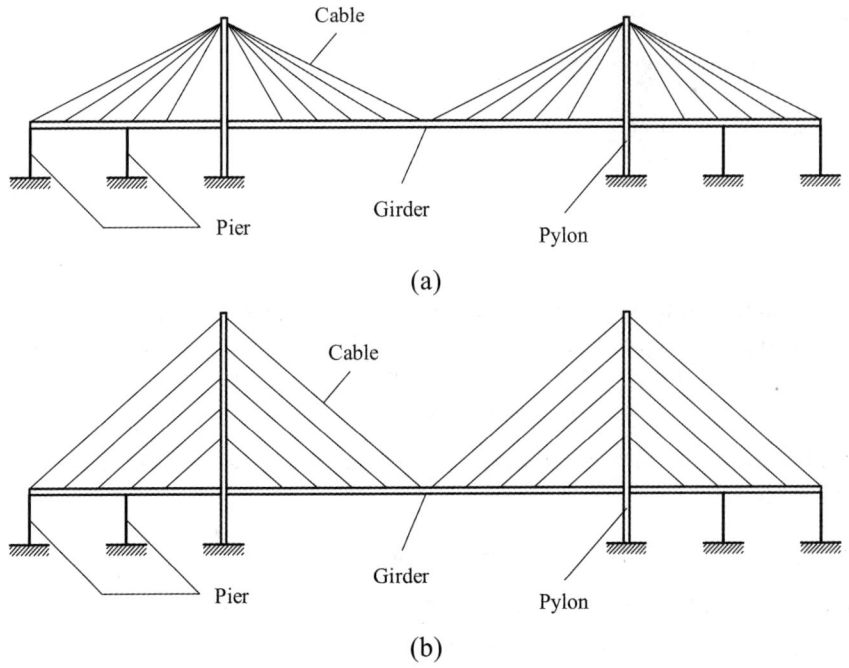

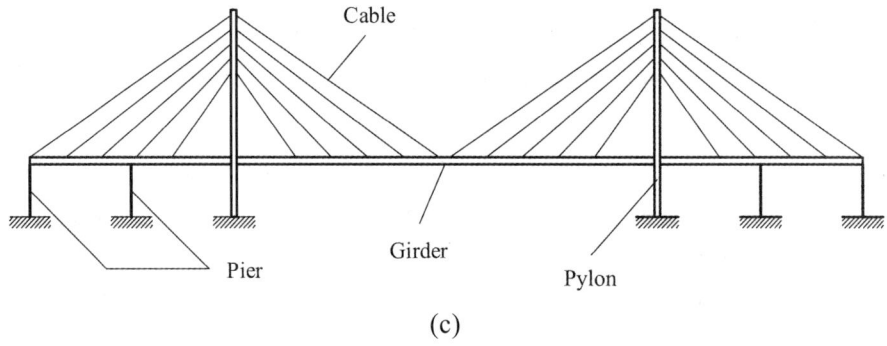

(c)

Figure 11.8 Typical shapes of the cable planes: (a) fan pattern; (b) Harp pattern; (c) Modified fan pattern.

2. Type of cables

There are two types of cables widely used in China: the steel strand cables (SSCs) and the parallel steel wire cables (PSWCs).

A SSC consists of multiple parallel steel strands. Each steel strand is enclosed by an independent high-density polyethylene (HDPE) pipe and the whole cable is also packed by a double-layered HDPE pipe. Figure 11.9 illustrates the cross section and ends of the SSCs.

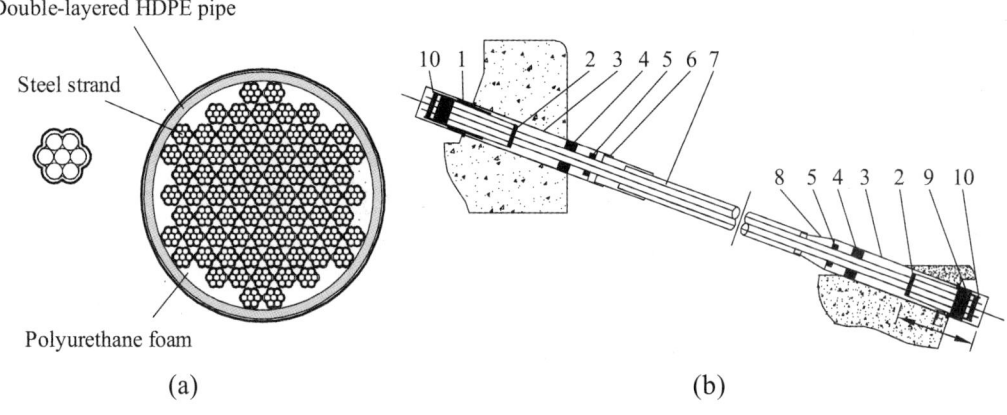

1–Tensioning anchorage device; 2–Sealing device; 3–Pre-embedded pipe;
4–Damping device; 5–Clamping hoop; 6–Water-proof transition device;
7–HDPE pipe; 8–Water-proof cover; 9–Fixed anchorage device;
10–Screw-loose-proof device.

Figure 11.9 Structure of a steel strand cable: (a) Cross section of cable and strand; (b)Ends of cable.

SSCs were developed in the 1980s. The stressed tendons consist mainly of galvanized steel strands with diameter of $\phi 15.2$ mm or epoxy coated steel strands. The strands can be tensioned one by one respectively. Then they are anchored with clamping piece jaw anchorages. The mortar, grease or oily wax can be injected into the pipes to prevent corrosion. In addition, the HDPE pipe of a steel strand itself gives more protection.

The SSCs can be transported to the construction site in the form of separate steel strands and then assembled at the site. So, this kind of cables are more suitable for the construction at some places which is difficult for transportation. Because the strands can be tensioned one by one, the tension devices may be smaller and simpler than those with which the whole cable are tensioned simultaneously. The strands in the cables are usually isolated from each other. Hence the contact and friction between them is prevented.

Another type of cable consists of parallel steel wires, as shown in Figure 11.10. A large amount of parallel steel wires is bound together into one strand. The whole strand is then enclosed by the polyester and a HDPE pipe. All the wires are anchored together at the both ends of the cable and are tensioned at the same time.

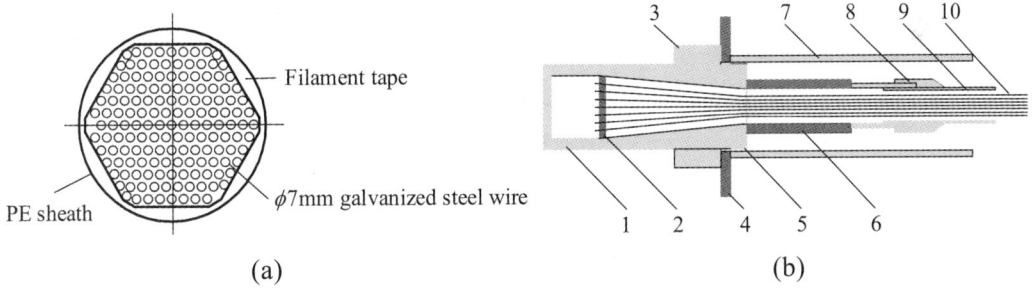

1–End cap; 2–Anchor plate; 3–Nut; 4–Bearing plate; 5–Socket;
6–Connection; 7–Guide pipe; 8–Head cap;
9–HDPE sheath; 10–Steel wires.

Figure 11.10 Structure of a parallel steel wire cable: (a) Cross section of cable; (b) End of cable.

All of the wires in a PSWC must be tensioned simultaneously. Therefore the tensile stress in the whole cable can be much evenly distributed than those in an SSC. It's easy to measure and control the cable force and the unstressed cable length. Since the whole cable is manufactured in the factory workshop, the quality can be assured. When the total number of wires is the same, the diameter of a PSWC is usually smaller than that of an SSC.

However, the simultaneous tension of a whole cable requires more capable and more complicated tension devices. The cable must be delivered as a whole, and as a result, the heavy-duty vehicles are needed.. The force in the wires can be transmitted to the packing layers of the cable, and may cause the fatigue failure of the layers. If some of the wires in the cable lost their bearing capacity, the whole cable must be replaced.

11.3.3 Pylons

1. <u>Form of pylons</u>

A typical pylon is shown in Figure 11.11. In most cases, there is a cross beam located at the lower part of the pylon (that's why it is called as the "lower cross beam") to support the main girder. The upper part of pylon is designed to anchor the stay cables. Hence the height of the pylon has great effect on the cable forces. For a pylon that doesn't support the main girder directly, there is no such a cross beam.

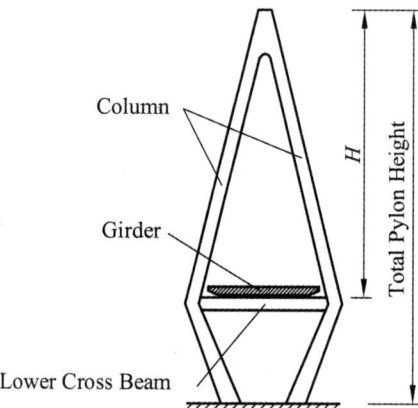

Figure 11.11 A pylon with the lower cross beam.

The pylon for cable-stayed bridges have many structural forms, as shown in Figure 11.12.

The pylon can be a single column [Figure 11.12(a)]. In this case, the traffic lanes should be arranged passing the both sides of the column. If the deck is narrow enough, a single cable plane is acceptable (e.g., Pont de Brotonne). If the deck is wide, the deck can be divided into separate parallel decks and the double cable planes (e.g., Stonecutter Bridge) or even four cable planes (e.g., Jiashao Bridge) can be used..

The stiffness of a single-column pylon is relatively small. The deflection of the pylon in the longitudinal direction of the bridge can be controlled with the adjustment of cable forces, but the deflection in the transversal direction can only be resisted by the stiffness of the pylon itself. If the large transversal stiffness is required, the size of column cross-section has to be increased.

A more effective way to get large transversal stiffness of the pylon is to use double columns. The double columns can be parallelly vertical [Figure 11.12(b)] or inclined [Figure 11.12(c)]. The two columns can be connected by one or more cross beams above the deck. If the double columns are both vertical, the deck should not be too wide to increase the length of the cross beam.

If much larger transversal stiffness is required, the two columns can be jointed at the tops, so comes the reversed V-shaped or Y-shaped pylon [Figure 11.12(d)]. In some cable-stayed bridges with an large span, four columns are used to form a frame-pylon [Figure 11.12(e)].

(a)

(b)

Figure 11.12 Some of the pylon forms of cable-stayed bridges.

2. Pylon height ratio

The height of the pylon is related to the inclination angle of stay cables. As shown in Figure 11.13, the higher the pylon is, the larger the inclination angles of stay cables are. A larger such angle can provide the girder with more efficient supporting effect. A cable force T can be decomposed into two components: the vertical component T_V and the horizontal component T_H, as shown in Figure 11.14. It's very evident that if the angle θ is enhanced, the vertical component T_V will take a more dominant proportion in the cable force. On the contrary, if the angle θ is too small, a large horizontal component T_H will be needed to provide the same supporting effect. A large horizontal component of cable force will lead to a large axial compressive force in the girder, which may cause instability of the girder or material failure.

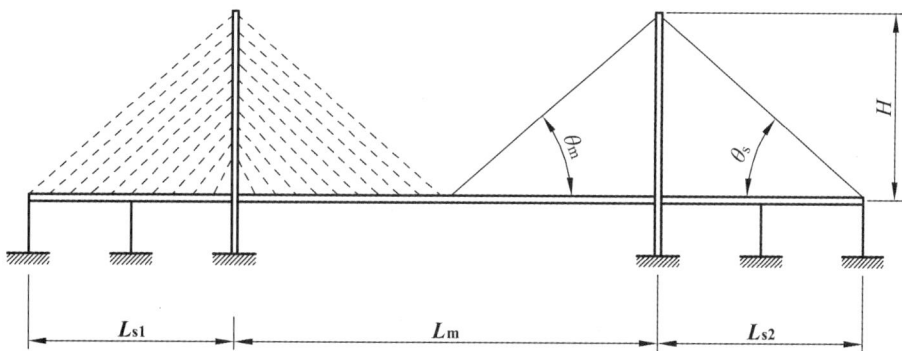

Figure 11.13 Relation between the inclination angle of stay cables and the pylon height.

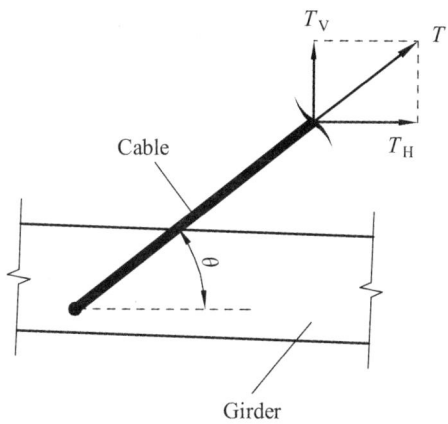

Figure 11.14 Decomposition of a cable force.

The pylon height ratio is defined as H / L_m. As the bridge site and main span length has been determined, the pylon height below the bridge deck can be obtained by comprehensive consideration about the terrain conditions, geological conditions, hydrological conditions, navigation requirements and foundation types. The pylon height ratios of some cable-stayed bridges are shown in Figure 11.15.

It can be seen from Figure 11.15 that almost all the pylon height ratios are in the range of 0.2 ~ 0.3, or only slightly go beyond this range. The only two exceptions are the New Millennium Bridge in Saecheonnyeon, Korea and the Liuguang River Bridge on Xifeng-Qianxi Expressway of Guizhou, China. Thus, we can conclude that a reasonable range of pylon height ratio is

$$\frac{H}{L_m} = 0.2 \sim 0.3 \tag{11.2}$$

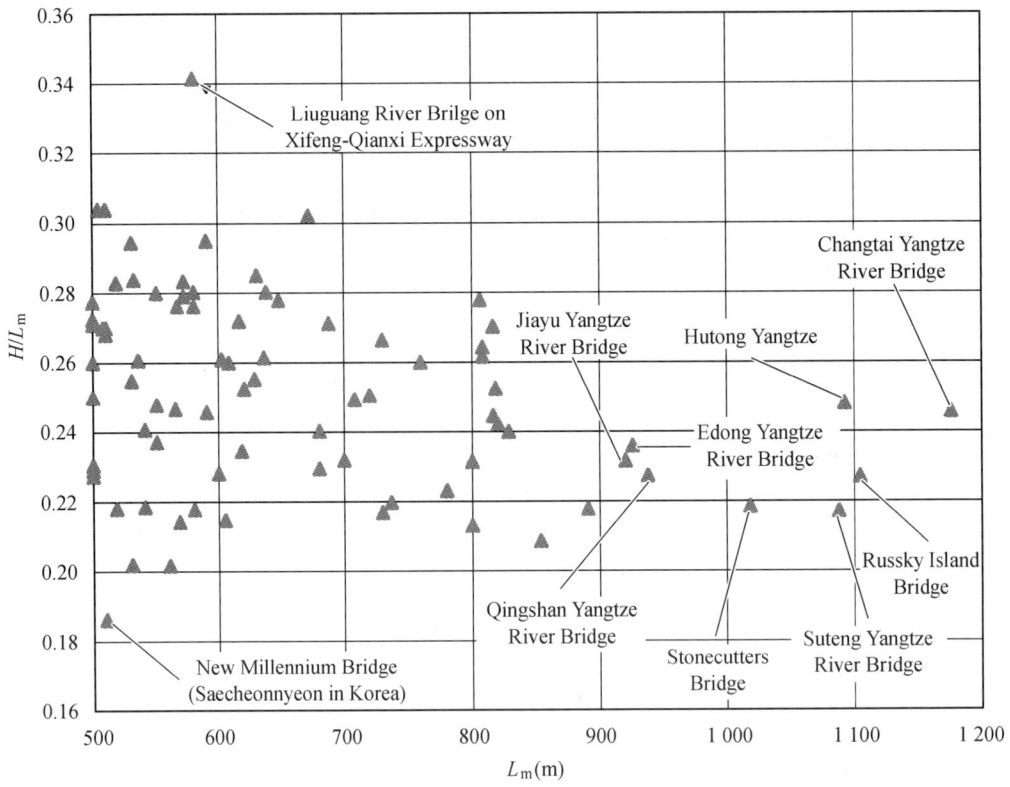

Figure 11.15 Pylon height ratio of some cable-stayed bridges.

11.3.4 Joint of the pylon and girder

There are four types of pylon-girder joints: the fully floating system, the semi-floating system, the rigid frame system, and the pylon-girder-fixed system, as shown in Figure 11.16.

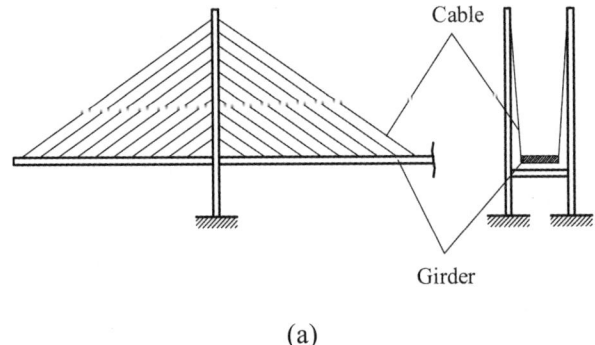

(a)

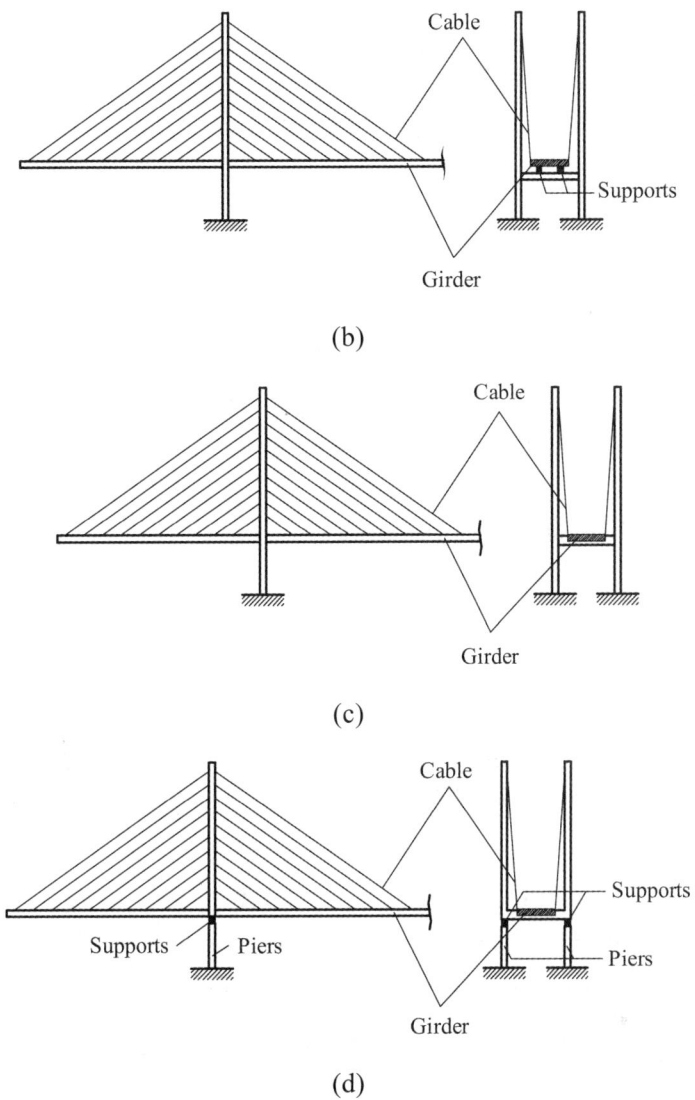

Figure 11.16 Four types of pylon-girder joint: (a) The fully floating system; (b) The semi-floating system; (c) The rigid frame system; (d) The fixed pylon-girder system.

In a fully floating system [Figure 11.16(a)], the girder is only supported by the cables. There are no vertical connections between the lower cross beam in the pylon and the girder. The pylon stand directly on the ground. In this case, the bending moment distribution in the girder may be relatively even, i.e. there should be no sharp change in the bending moment along the girder The stiffness of the system, however, is relatively small and the dynamic behaviors, wind resistance, seismic capacity and buckling problems should be taken into full consideration.

In a semi-floating system [Figure 11.16(b)], the girder is supported by not only the cables but the vertical supports on the lower cross beam of pylons. The stiffness of the system is larger than that of the fully floating system. But there may be very large negative bending moments in the girder at the pylon-girder joints.

In the rigid frame system, the girder is rigidly connected to the pylons [Figure 11.16(c)]. The stiffness of this system is very large and the flexural behaviors of the pylons may reduce the negative bending moments in the girder. The deflections of the pylons and girder are smaller than those in the other types of system. Such a system is especially suitable to the cantilever construction method because the girders are originally fixed with the pylons the temporary rigid connections at the pylon-girder joints are not necessary. Nevertheless, since the longitudinal deformation of the girder is restricted by the pylons, the system is very sensitive to the temperature change. There may be large bending moment at the pylon bottom. The rigid frame system is not employed in the cable-stayed bridges with very long span length.

In the fixed pylon-girder system, the girder is rigidly fixed with the pylons [Figure 11.16(d)] but the pylons are not supported directly on the ground. Instead, the pylons are supported on the separate piers. The bending moment at the pylon bottom is much smaller in this system than that in a rigid frame system. The temperature change has little effect on the internal forces. The stiffness of such a system is smaller than that of a rigid frame system. However, the girder rotations at the pylon-girder joints are relatively large, which cause the larger deflection of the pylon top and the mid-span of girder.

11.4 Construction method of cable-stayed bridges

Almost all the existing bridge construction methods can be used for cable-stayed bridges. It can be entirely or partly erected on falseworks, as indicated in Figure 11.17.

Some of the girder segments of cable-stayed bridges can be erected by the cranes or floating cranes. The crane operation requires the adequate lifting equipment and operating space. If the floating cranes are employed, the water level must be high enough, as shown in Figure 11.18.

Figure 11.17 A cable-stayed bridge partly erected on the falsework.

Figure 11.18 Floating crane lifting operation for Qingshan Yangtze River Bridge.

If the cable-stayed bridge is constructed over a busy transportation line, the horizontal rotation construction method is beneficial to reduce the interruption of the traffic, as shown in Figure 11.19.

Figure 11.19 Horizontal rotation of a cable-stayed bridge.

If the deck is too high from the ground, it's impossible to erect the superstructure on the falsework or by the cranes. Instead, the incrementally launching method is a possible solution, such as the method used in Millau Viaduct in France (Figure 11.20).

Figure 11.20 Incrementally launching construction of Millau Viaduct.

Most cable-stayed bridges with long spans are constructed with the cantilever method nowadays. This method requires little falsework and has almost no interference to the area below the girder (Figure 11.21). The stay cables can provide support to the cantilevering girder and adjust the elevation and internal forces of the girder.

Figure 11.21 Cantilever construction of a cable-stayed bridge with the steel truss girder

References

[11.1] Parke, G. and Hewson, N., eds., *ICE Manual of Bridge Engineering*, 2nd ed., Thomas Telford Ltd, London, 2008.

[11.2] Xanthakos, P. P., Theory and Design of Bridges, John Wiley & Sons, New York, 1994.

[11.3] Vejrum, T., Nielsen, L. L., "Cable-stayed Bridges," in Chen, W.-F., and Lian, D., eds., Bridge Engineering Handbook– Superstructure Design, CRC Press, Boca Raton, FL, 2014.

[11.4] Gimsing, N. J., Cable Supported Bridges, 2nd ed., John Wiley & Sons, New York, 1991.

[11.5] Walther, R., Houriet, B., Isler, W., Moïa, P., Klein, J.-F., Cable Stayed Bridges, 2nd ed., Thomas Telford, London, 1999.

[11.6] Li, Y.-D., ed., Introduction to Bridge Engineering (in Chinese), 3rd ed., Southwest Jiaotong University Press, Chengdu, China, 2005.

李亚东. 桥梁工程概论. 3版. 成都：西南交通大学出版社，2014.

[11.7] Yao, L.-S, ed., (Xiang, H.-F., Gu, A.-B., reviewers), Bridge Engineering, 2nd ed., China Communications Press, Beijing, China, 2008.

姚玲森. 桥梁工程. 2版. 项海帆，顾安邦，主审. 北京：人民交通出版社，2008.

[11.8] Fan, L.-C., ed., Bridge Engineering, 2nd ed., China Communications Press, Beijing, China, 1988.

范立础. 桥梁工程. 2版. 北京：人民交通出版社，1988.

[11.9] Shao, X.-D., ed., (Gu, A.-B., reviewer), Bridge Engineering, 4th ed., China Communications Press Co., Ltd., Beijing, China, 2018.

邵旭东. 桥梁工程. 4版. 顾安邦，主审. 北京：人民交通出版社，2018.

Appendix A: Distribution Factors for the Guyon-Massonnet Method

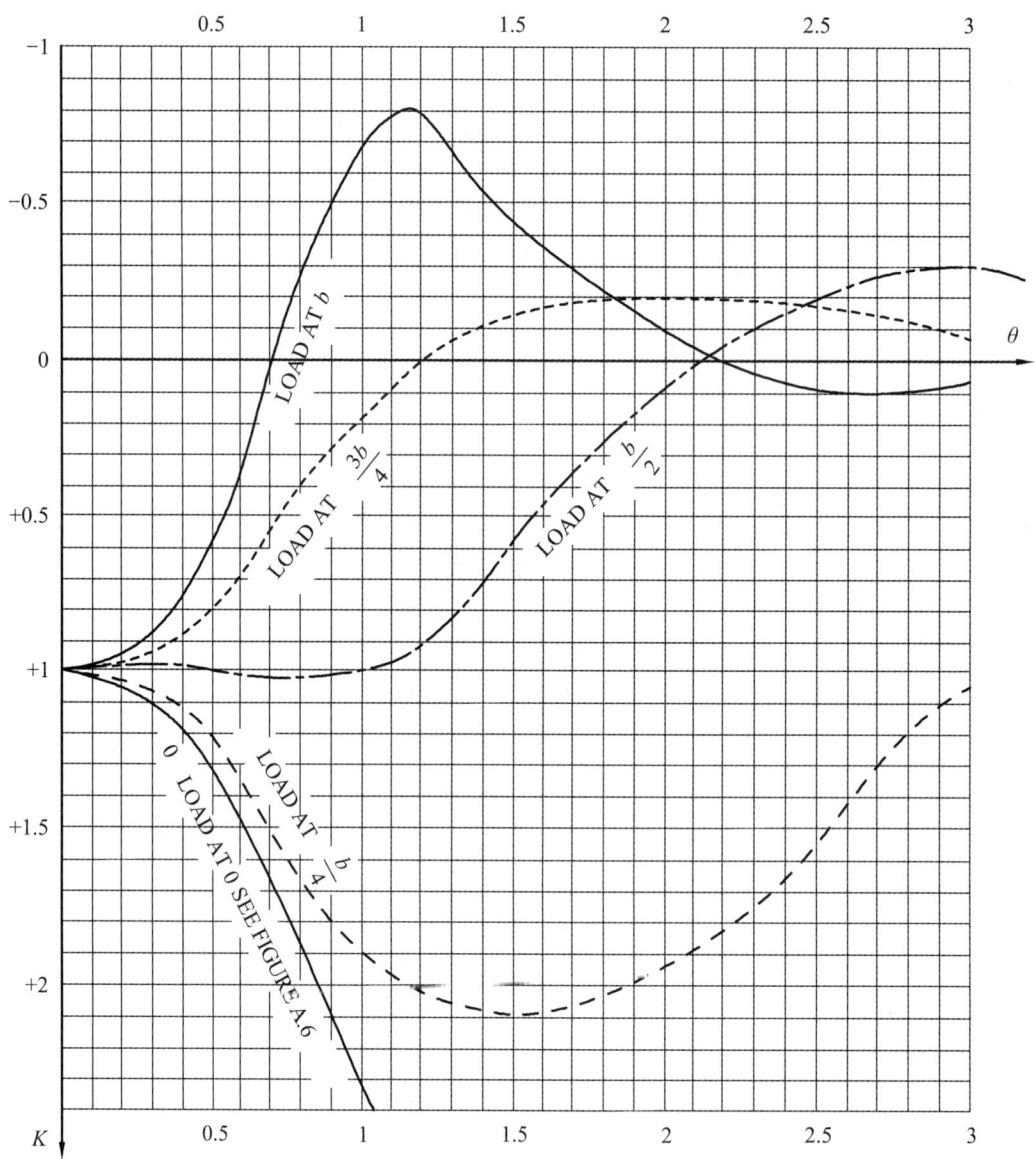

Figure A.1 Distribution coefficient K_0 for a beam at $f = 0$ (No torsion)

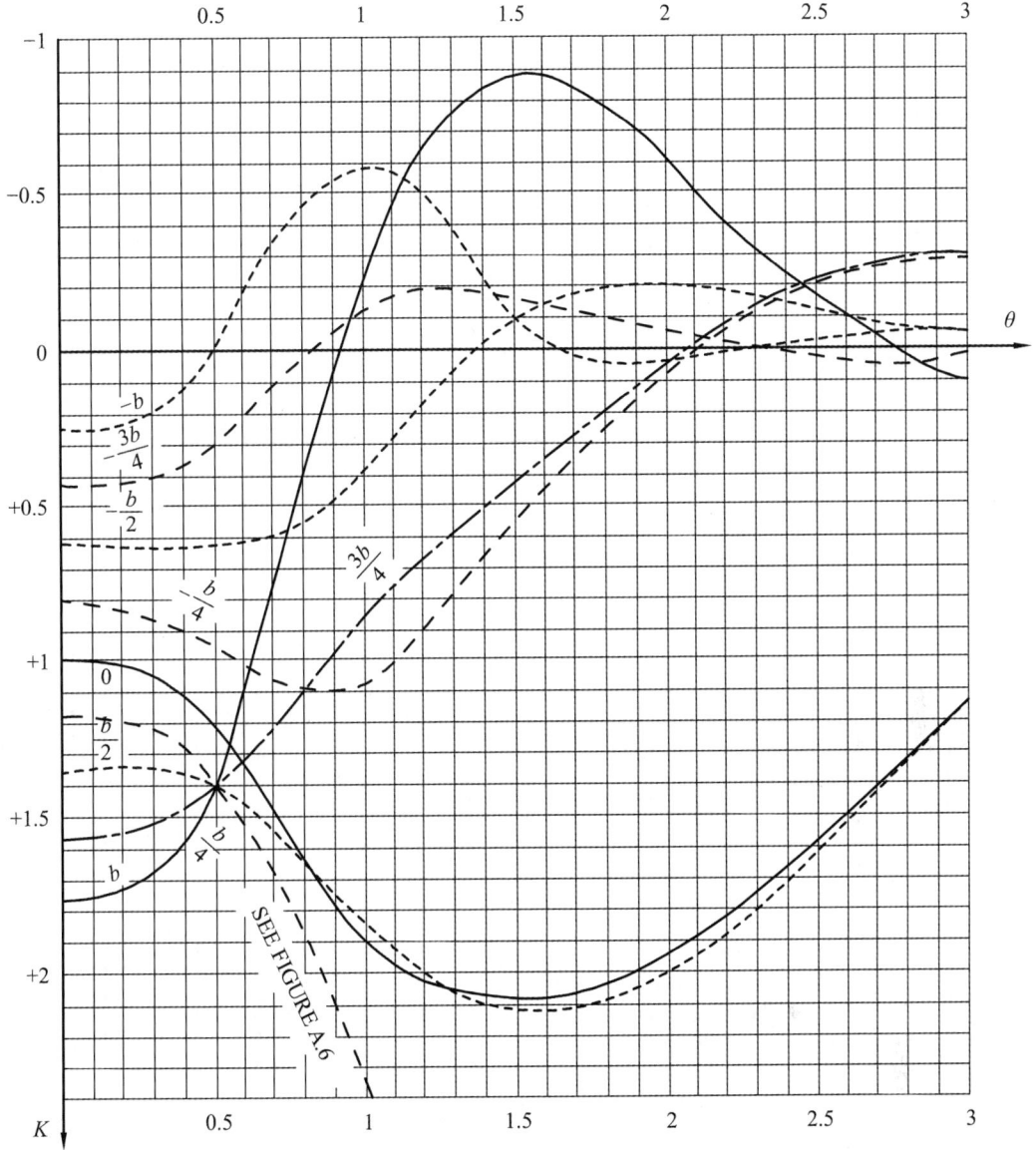

Figure A.2 Distribution coefficient K_0 for a beam at $f = b/4$ (No torsion)

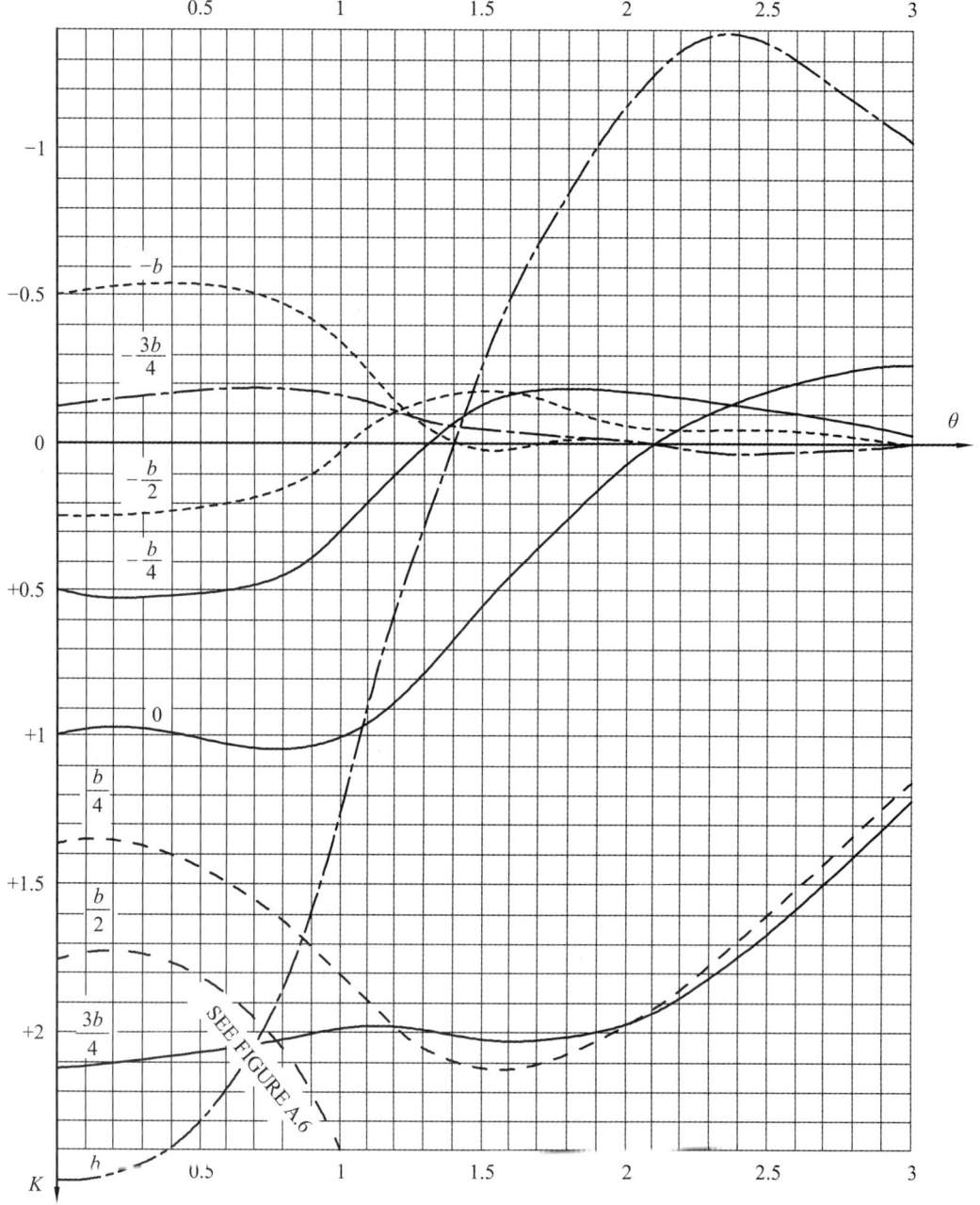

Figure A.3 Distribution coefficient K_0 for a beam at $f = b/2$ (No torsion)

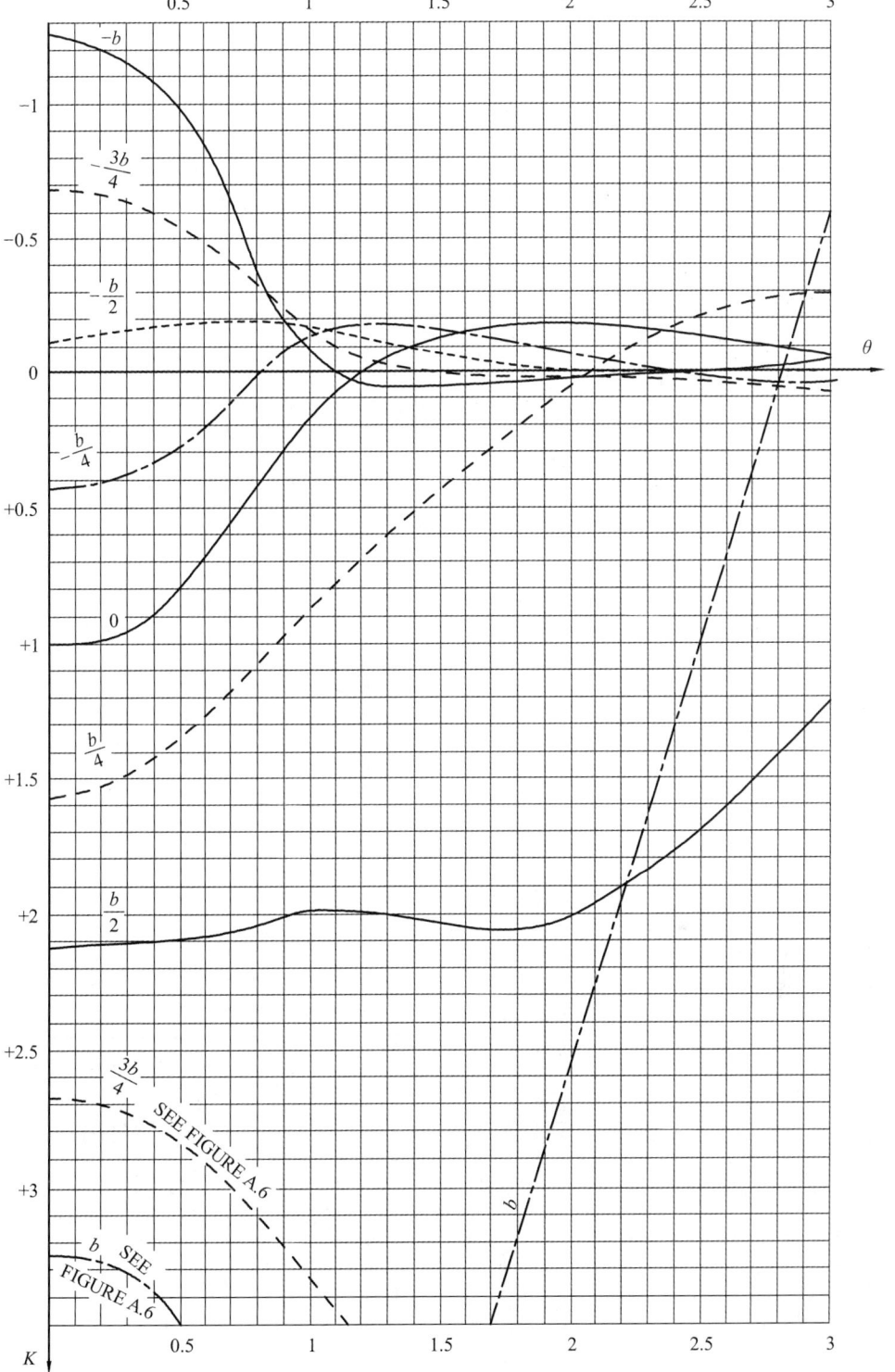

Figure A.4 Distribution coefficient K_0 for a beam at $f = 3b/4$ (No torsion)

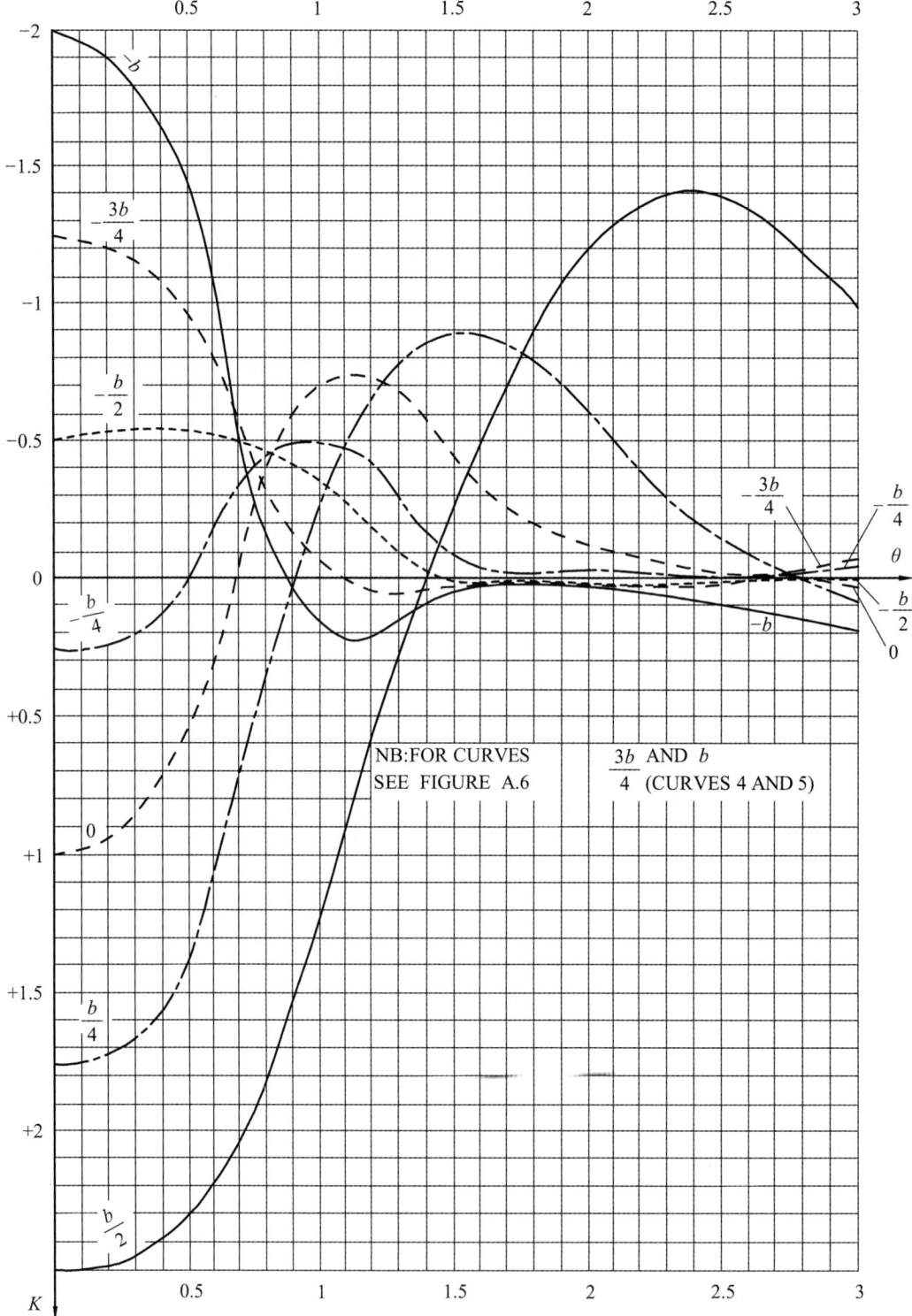

Figure A.5 Distribution coefficient K_0 for a beam at $f = b$ (No torsion)

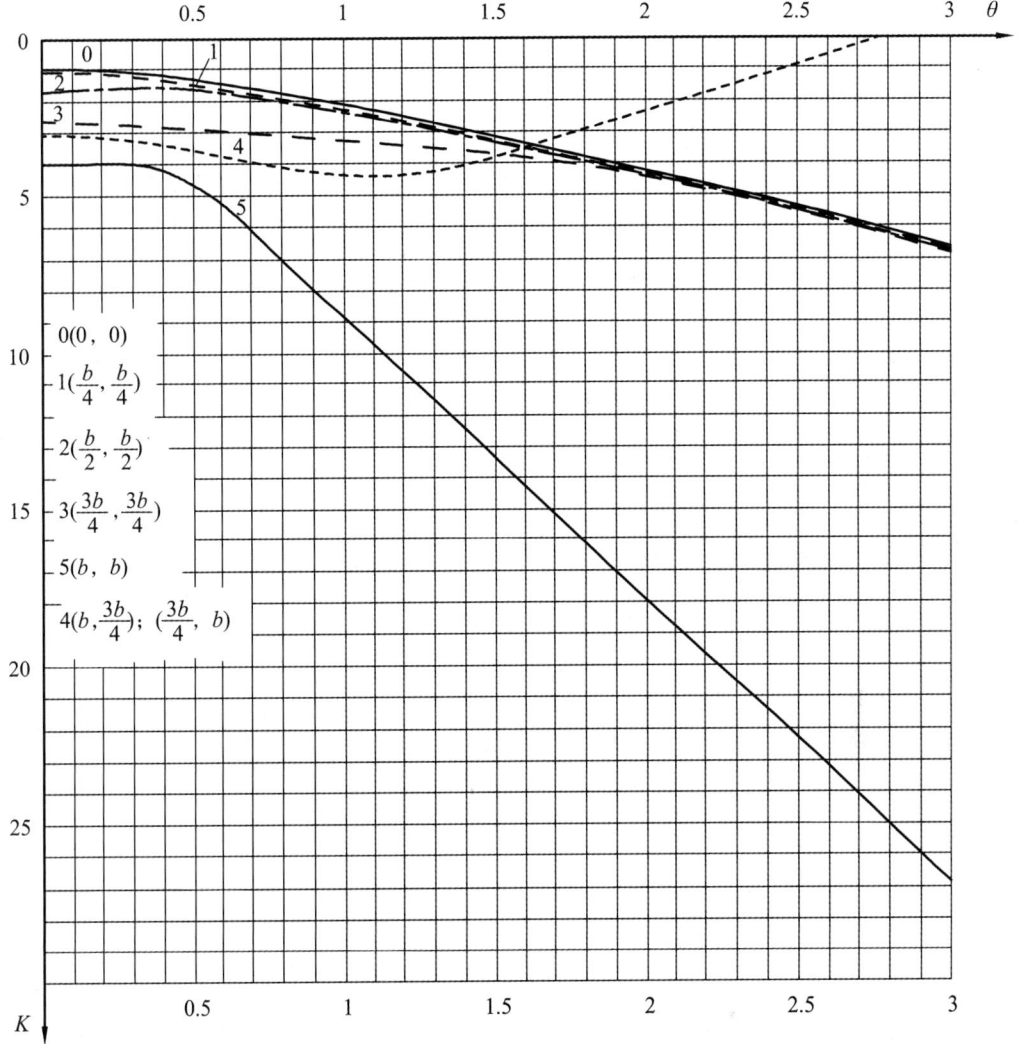

Figure A.6 Distribution coefficient K_0 with large range (No torsion)

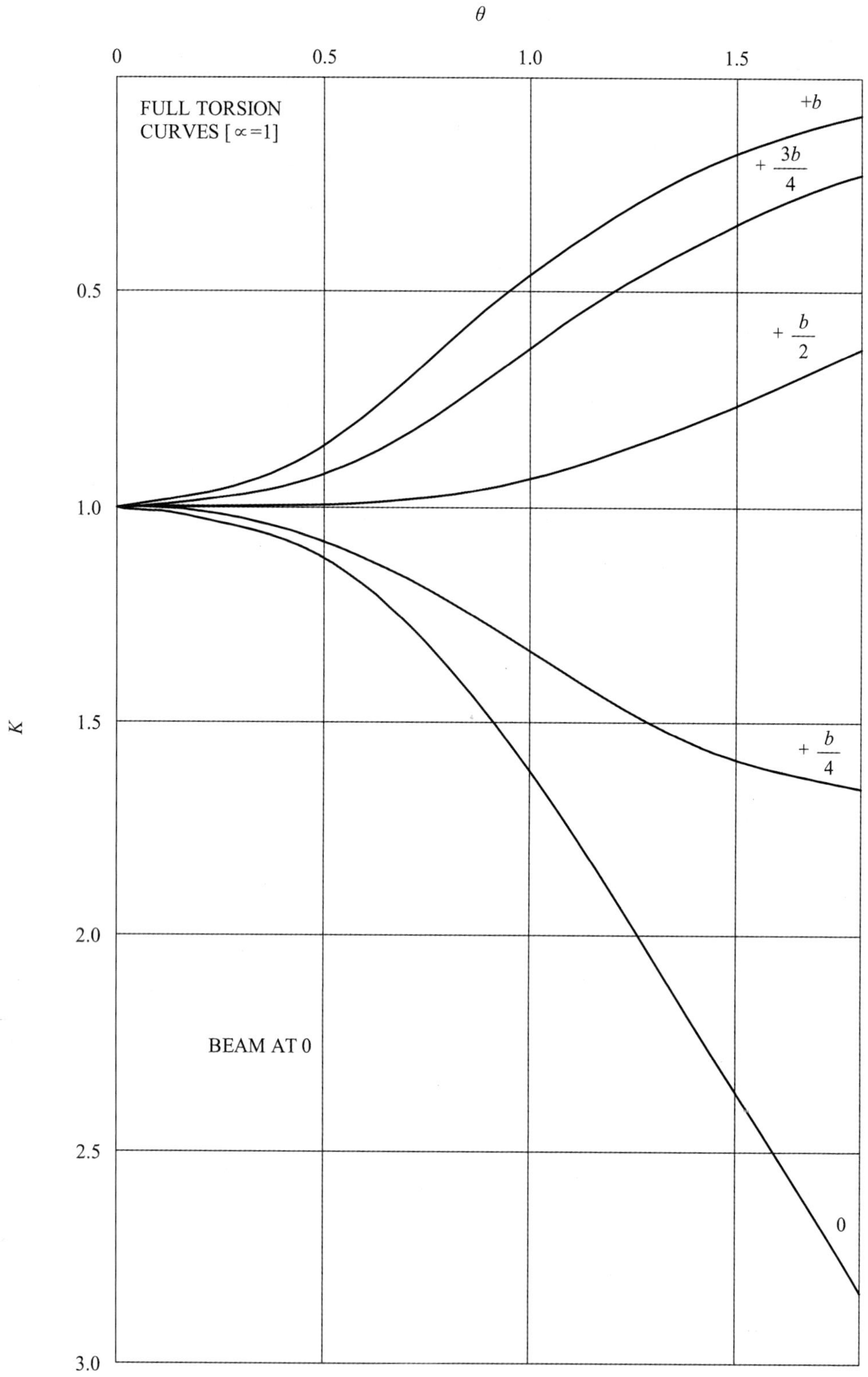

Figure A.7 Distribution coefficient K_1 for a beam at $f = 0$ (full torsion)

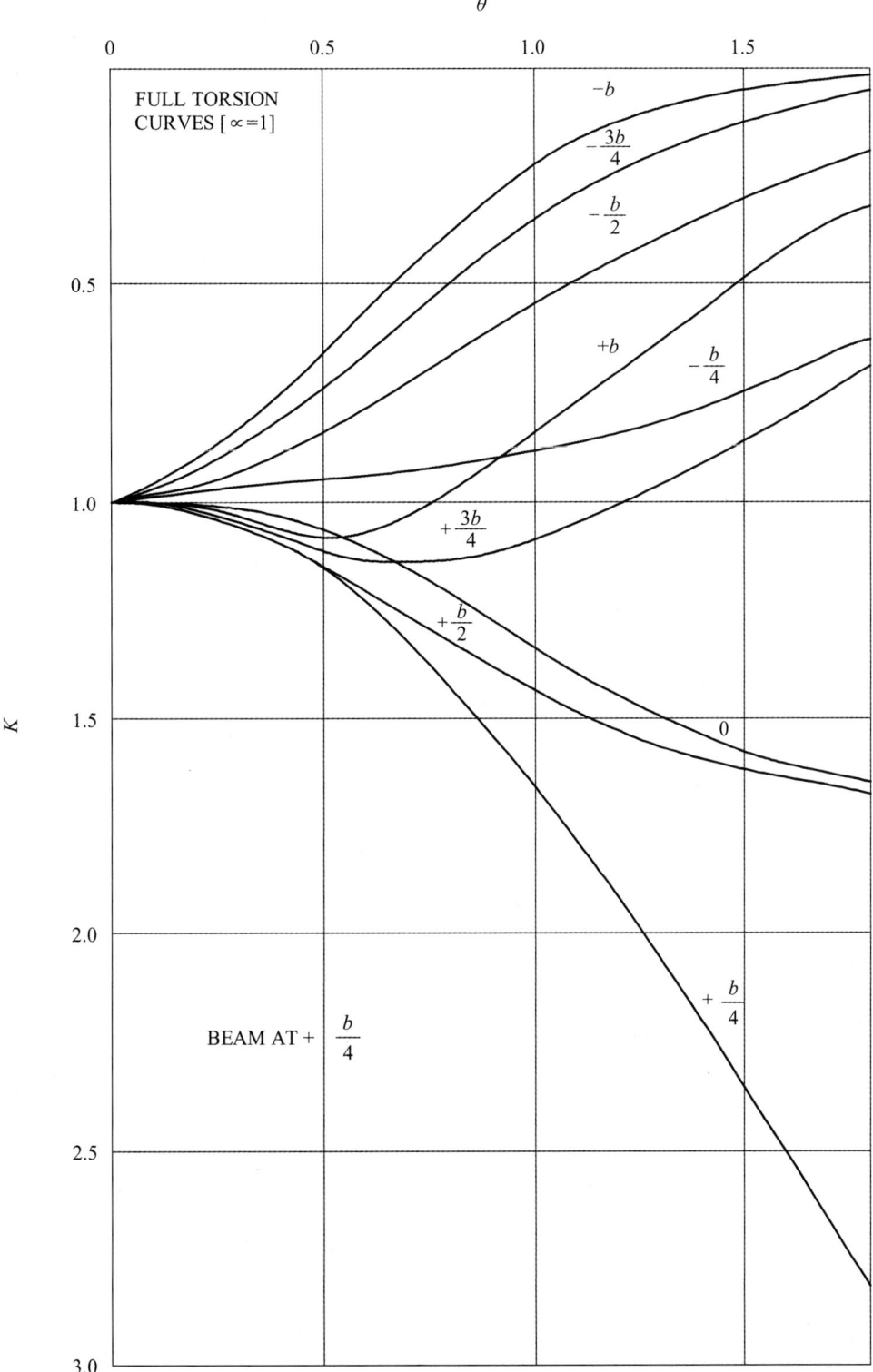

Figure A.8 Distribution coefficient K_1 for a beam at $f = b/4$ (full torsion)

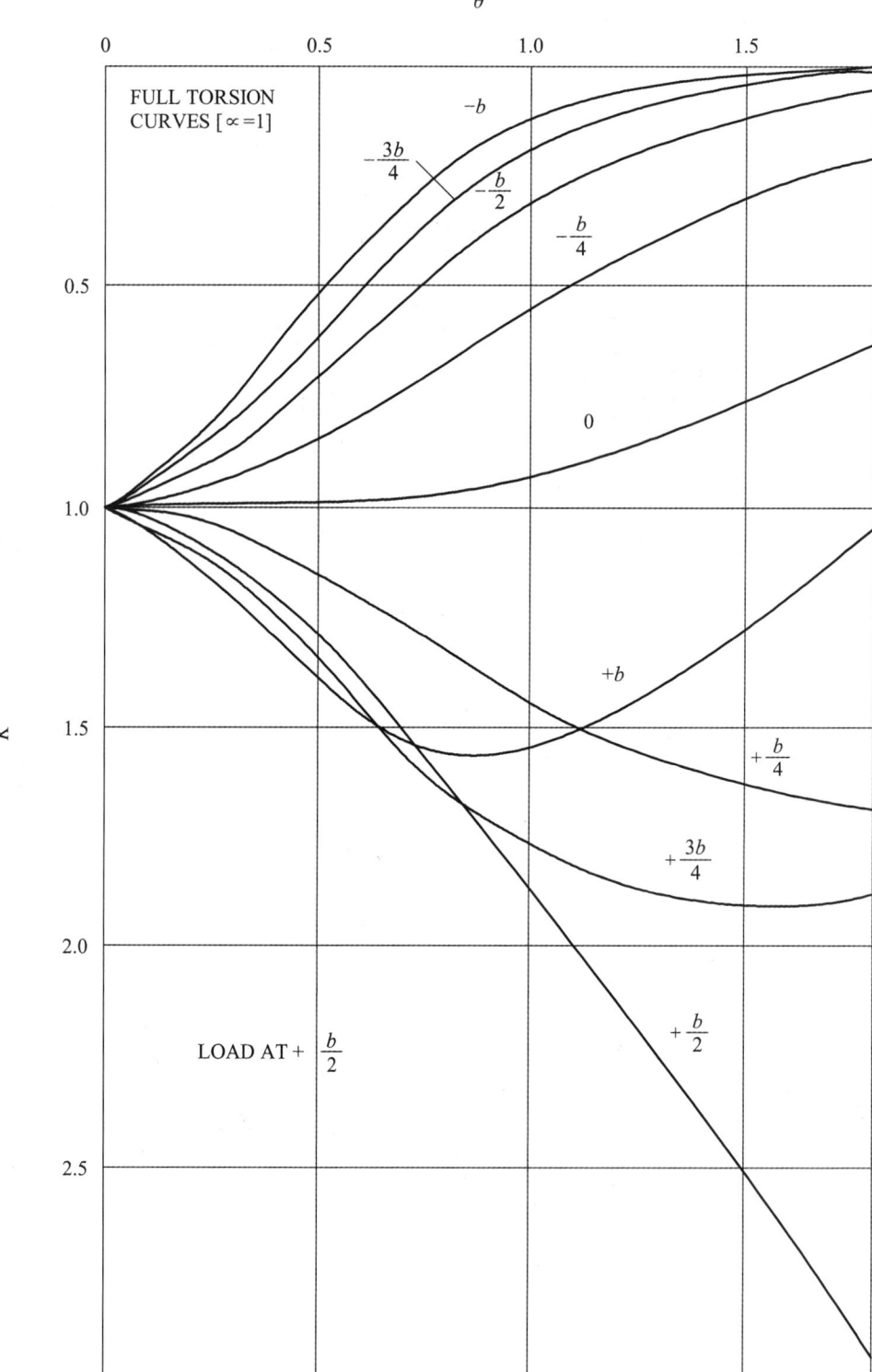

Figure A.9　Distribution coefficient K_1 for a beam at $f = b/2$ (full torsion)

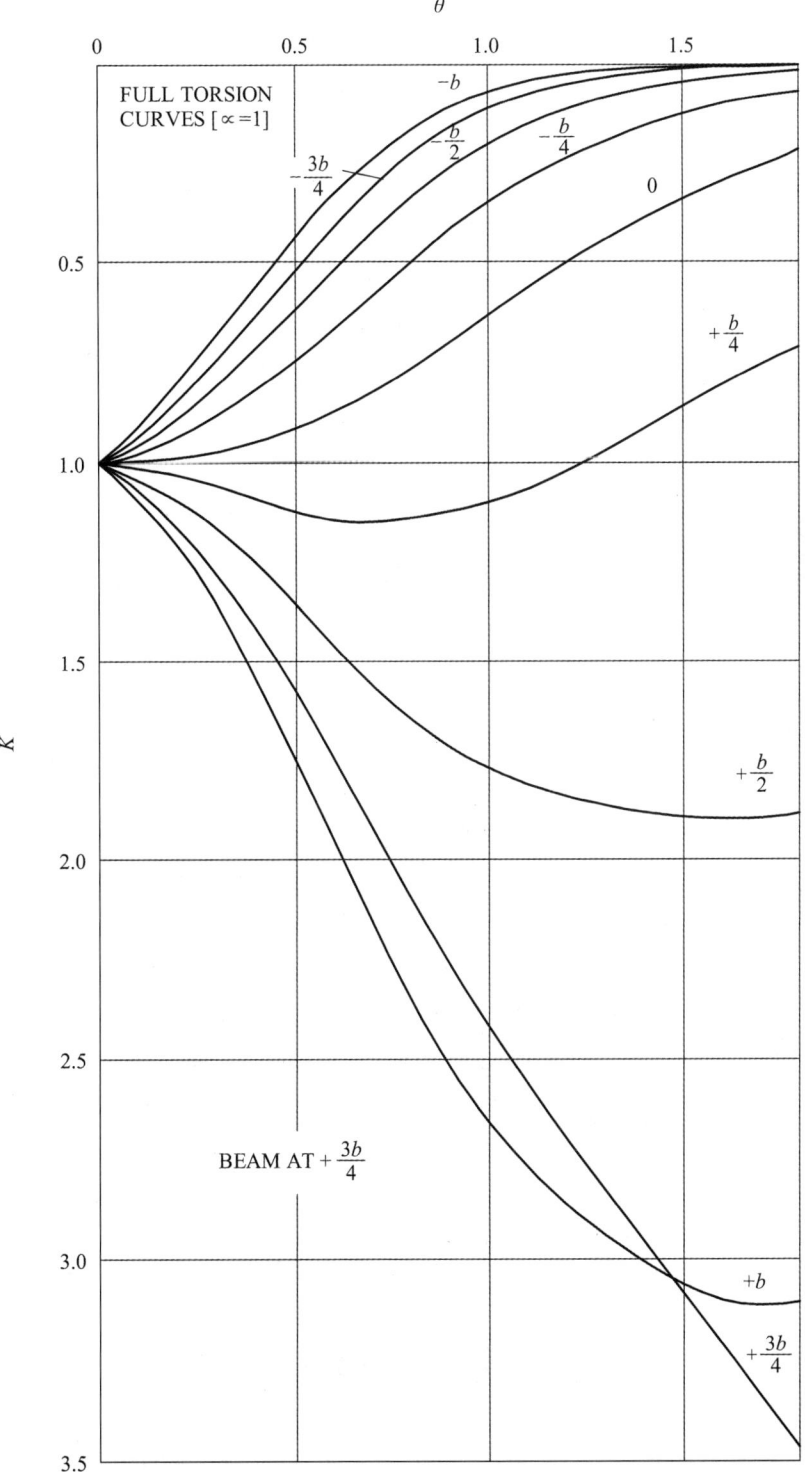

Figure A.10 Distribution coefficient K_1 for a beam at $f = 3b/4$ (full torsion).

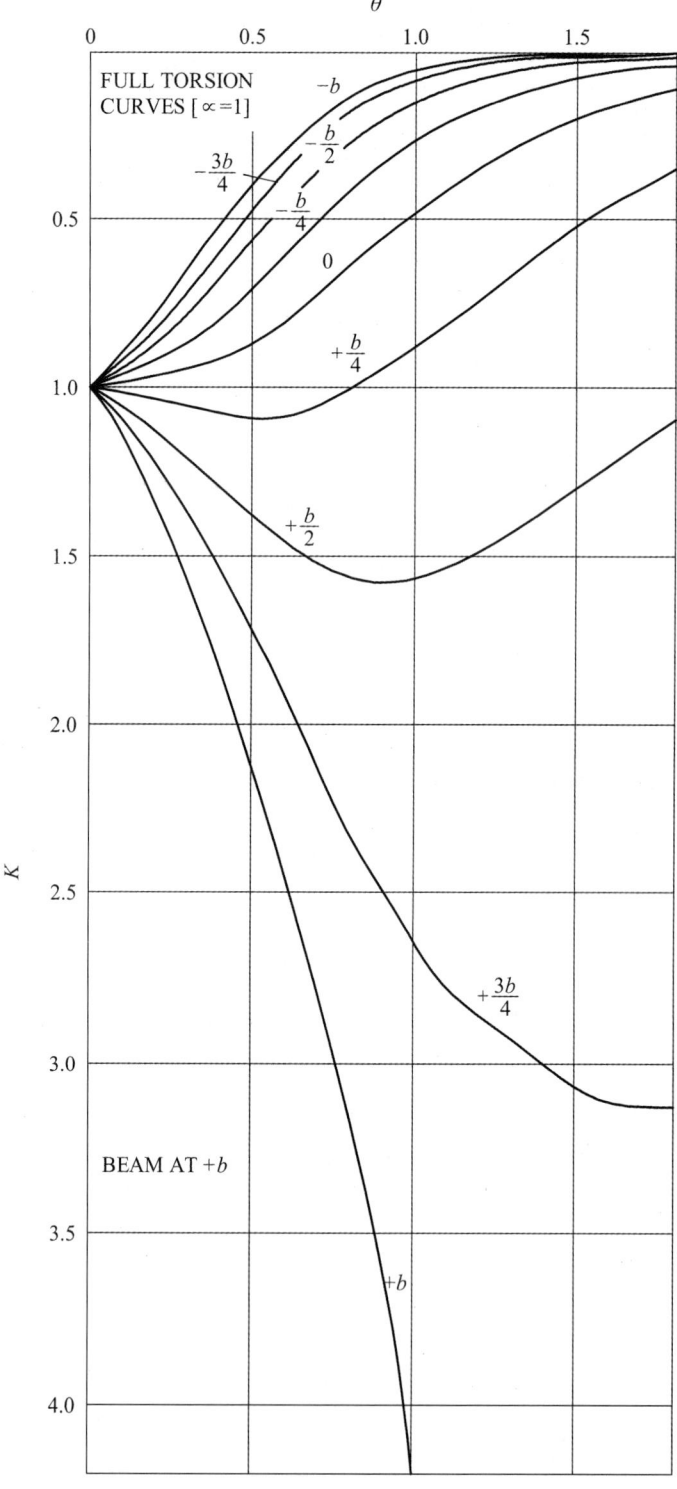

Figure A.11   Distribution coefficient K_1 for a beam at $f = b$ (full torsion).